The Mesoamerican Ballgame

The
Mesoamerican Ballgame

Edited by

Vernon L. Scarborough
and
David R. Wilcox

The University of Arizona Press   Tucson

Cover illustration: Rollout of a polychromed ceramic vessel from the Maya Area of the Central Lowlands. Date: A.D. 650 to 800. Dimensions: height, 8 1/16 in.; diameter, 6 1/4 in. Courtesy of the Dallas Museum of Art, gift of Mr. and Mrs. Raymond D. Nasher.

The University of Arizona Press
Copyright © 1991
The Arizona Board of Regents
All Rights Reserved

♾ This book is printed on acid-free, archival-quality paper.
Manufactured in the United States of America.
96 95 94 93 92   6 5 4 3 2
Library of Congress Cataloging-in-Publication Data
The Mesoamerican ballgame / edited by Vernon L. Scarborough and David
  R. Wilcox.
      p. cm.
  Includes bibliographical references and index.
  ISBN 0-8165-1180-2 (Cl : alk. paper); 0-8165-1360-0 (pb : alk. paper)
    1. Ulama (Game) 2. Indians of Mexico—Games.   3. Indians
of Central America—Games.   4. Indians of Mexico—Antiquities.
  5. Indians of Central America—Antiquities.   6. Mexico—Antiquities.
  7. Central America—Antiquities.   I. Scarborough, Vernon L., 1950– .
  II. Wilcox, David R., 1944– .   III. Title: Mesoamerican ballgame.
  F1219.3.G3M47   1991
  796.3'089'6872–dc20   90-21890
                                                                   CIP

British Library Cataloguing in Publication data are available.

Contents

Preface

The native American rubber-ball game played on a masonry court has in-trigued scholars of ancient history since the Spaniards redefined the societal underpinnings of the New World. In addition to evoking a natural curiosity, the game and its magnificent remains in the form of ballcourts and ballgame paraphernalia can provide a synthetic understanding of a key aspect of what was Mesoamerica. The game endured for 2000 years and extended over a million square miles. The Aztec nobility and warrior classes played a competi-tive version of the game that achieved pragmatic economic and political ends as well as revered prestige and respect (Stern 1949; Durán 1967; Santley et al. this volume). The importance and popularity of the game to the Aztecs is indicated by the approximately 16,000 rubber balls that were imported annu-ally into the Nahuatl capital of Tenochtitlán from the rubber tree-rich low-lands (*Codex Mendoza* 1938). In the Maya area, the game reached a zenith of elaboration as evidenced by both the varied paraphernalia and depictions on portable art (Hellmuth 1975a; Borhegyi 1980; Cohodas this volume; Ekholm this volume; Freidel and Schele this volume) as well as the more than 200 masonry courts identified (Taladoire 1981; Agrinier this volume; Scarborough this volume). Simpler versions of the game were played throughout Meso-america by people with simpler sociopolitical systems (Stern 1949; Wilcox and Sternberg 1983). Some groups in Sinaloa still play versions of the game (Leyenaar 1978).

The implications of this widespread tradition have only rarely been explored and its broader meaning to pre-Hispanic peoples remains unclear. In 1984, both of us had worked on case examples of the Mesoamerican ballgame, one in southern Mesoamerica (Scarborough et al. 1982) and the other on the northern frontier (Wilcox and Sternberg 1983). We each realized the need for a broader synthesis. Meeting at the Pecos Conference, we decided to co-organize an international invitational conference on the Mesoamerican ballgame. Dr. Raymond Thompson, director of the Arizona State Museum and professor of Anthropology, strongly encouraged the idea. Due to his efforts, the three-day conference was held in Tucson in 1985. It was generously sponsored by the University of Arizona Centennial Committee and the Arizona State Museum.

Representing a diversity of disciplines, 27 scholars from Europe, Latin America, Canada, and the United States participated in the conference. The regional coverage provided by the contributors brought together information on a great diversity of architectural detail and iconographic interpretation as well as ethnohistoric accounts. The conference was a significant undertaking because of the balanced pan-Mesoamerican coverage and the topical breadth of the participants. Participants were encouraged to grapple with the problems of synthesis on a continental or even hemispheric scale in a way previously impossible.

The vigorous exchange and associated intellectual results demonstrated the unique, unifying quality of the ballgame institution throughout Greater Mesoamerica. The ballcourt and associated paraphernalia provide a recurrent and quantifiable unit of analysis for pan-regional interpretation. These interpretations in part redefine the Mesoamerican "culture area" concept (see Blanton and Feinman 1984; Folan 1985). Although interregional studies examining Mesoamerica have been presented in textbooks, these studies have not focused on the inspection of an equivalent unit of analysis in comparing and contrasting Greater Middle America.

Two pioneer studies did have as their intent the interregional examination of the ballgame. Theodore Stern's invaluable study (1949) of rubber-ball games in the Americas provides sociopolitical insight from carefully examined ethnohistorical records, but could only draw from the very limited archaeological evidence of the time. Stephan Borhegyi's typological research (1980, but posthumous by a decade) into pre-Hispanic pan-Mesoamerican ballgames must also be considered pathbreaking. He recognized the potential of these data for a synthetic treatment of Greater Mesoamerica. Significant strides in the collection of new ballgame data as well as in the introduction of new models used by the humanities and social sciences for explaining sociopolitical institutions have been made since the completion of both examinations. Many such ideas are presented in the present volume.

The results obtained by an examination of the ballgame theme tied to the empirical base of the ballcourt and related paraphernalia can stimulate similar synthetic studies of other aspects of the cultural reality we call Greater Mesoamerica. Mesoamerican agricultural systems, household and suprahousehold organizations, regional systems, the boundedness of local settlement systems, and many other topical issues would be greatly elucidated by the controlled comparison of contiguous data sets on macroregional scales of analysis. The 1985 international ballgame symposium was an exploration of the possibility of synthesis on a scale that with rare exception has not been seriously contemplated for a long time. When the unity or diversity of the American Indian was the central focus of American anthropology, attention on this scale was commonplace (Putnam 1895; Hay et al. 1940). We believe that the last half century of more specialized research has produced the materials for a new effort of synthesis. The first step is to pool information of related value, and to facilitate dialogue among scholars in neighboring areas; the 1985 international symposium on the Mesoamerican ballgame has accomplished this.

The present collection of papers elucidates the temporal, spatial, functional, and symbolic aspects of the ballgame throughout Greater Mesoamerica (including the American Southwest). It represents 15 of the 24 original papers presented at the conference. Although the conference did not address or endorse one model or approach exclusively, the ballgame was studied as an evolving institution functioning, in part, to resolve conflict within and between groups. The role of mediation through the Mesoamerican ballgame emerges as a central theme in the present contributions.

Although many of the contributors to the volume have a strong archaeological orientation, there are numerous references to ethnohistoric and pre-Hispanic belief systems. Significant strides have been made in examining iconographic symbol systems with special reference to architecture and spatial frames (Cohodas 1980; Townsend 1979; Coggins 1980; Gillespie this volume). By incorporating these data under the thematic umbrella of the ballgame, new and creative interpretations are presented. A useful step toward overall synthesis has been taken through the symposium and the publication of these papers takes another.

Acknowledgments

Many people have helped shape the form and direction of this volume. Primary support has been provided by the University of Arizona. The generosity of the University's 1985 Centennial Committee and the Arizona State Museum in staging the ballgame conference, coupled with the intent of the University of Arizona Press to publish the book, represents a major commitment to

Mesoamerican studies and a thoughtful continuity to enterprise. Raymond H. Thompson, director of the Arizona State Museum, was instrumental in championing both the conference and the book. Dr. Thompson presented the ballgame conference idea to the University of Arizona as an important and legitimate event worthy of funding.

During the conference several individuals extended themselves far beyond the call of duty. Susan Brew is singled out for her attention to detail and her warm and patient demeanor when dealing with more than a hundred archaeologists during a four-day period.

The typing of the edited manuscripts was carried out through the Herculean efforts of Louella Holter at the Bilby Research Center of Northern Arizona University. She has worked closely with us in coordinating the needs of contributors with those of the press. Illustrations were provided by the individual contributors with the exception of Figures 4.1–5.6 and 10.1–11.2 for which Emilee Mead, Bilby Research Center, Northern Arizona University provided drafting support. We wish to thank the Department of Sociology and Anthropology at the University of Texas at El Paso and the Department of Anthropology at the University of Cincinnati for secretarial support. Partial subvention for the book was provided by the Charles Phelps Taft Memorial Fund at the University of Cincinnati. We would also like to thank our families who have been extremely supportive of the time and energy involved in the volume. Pat Mora has been a principal advisor for one of us (Scarborough) during the editing of the book.

Finally, mention must be made of those ballgame conference participants who were unable to contribute to the final volume. Mr. Nicholas Hellmuth, Dr. John Molloy, Prof. H.B. Nicholson, Mr. Pepe Ortiz Aguilu, and Prof. Jacinto Quirarte delivered stimulating presentations but elected against submitting to the final volume. Additionally, Dr. Ted Leyenaar, Deputy Director of the Rijksmuseum voor Volkenkunde in Leiden, did not contribute to the volume owing to a misunderstanding. We refer interested readers to his recent co-authored book *Ulama: The Ballgame of the Mayas and Aztecs* (with L.A. Parsons, 1988). If we have one regret, it is that no more of our Latin American colleagues were able to contribute to the success of the enterprise. We sincerely hope that this book will catalyze in some small way similar anthropological forums for addressing the complexity of ancient Mesoamerica.

Vernon L. Scarborough
David R. Wilcox

Contributors

Pierre Agrinier was born in Tunis, Tunisia, in 1924. He studied art in Paris at the Ecole de Louvre, then moved to the United States in 1952, where he received a B.A. from the University of Southern California-Berkeley in 1956 and an M.A. from Brigham Young University in 1978. He worked with the New World Archaeological Foundation from 1956 through 1989, when he retired.

Rani T. Alexander has worked on archaeological projects in Mexico, Honduras, and New Mexico. Her present interests involve the colonial period in northern Yucatán, Mexico, where she is conducting research. She is currently a doctoral candidate in the Department of Anthropology at the University of New Mexico.

Michael J. Berman is currently a Ph.D. candidate at the University of New Mexico. His interests include Plio-Pleistocene hominid subsistence, animal ecology, and the organization of state-level societies. His current research involves developing community profiles in Africa to describe the context of early hominid subsistence using modern studies of ecological relationships among animals.

Richard E. Blanton received his Ph.D. in anthropology from the University of Michigan in 1970. He is currently a professor of anthropology at Purdue University and is the author of *Monte Alban: Settlement Patterns at the Ancient Zapotec Capital* (Academic Press 1978). He is also a coauthor with

Stephen Kowalewski, Gary Feinman, and Jill Appel of *Ancient Mesoamerica: A Comparison of Change in Three Regions* (Cambridge University Press 1981).

Marvin Cohodas received his Ph.D. in Art History from Columbia University in 1974, with a dissertation on the Great Ball Court at Chichén Itzá. His subsequent analyses have emphasized the ritual structure and cosmological symbolism reflected in Maya architecture and sculpture, along with the evidence for individual creativity in relief sculpture and ceramic painting. He is the author of several journal articles and book chapters, including "The Epiclassic Problem: A Review and Alternative Model" (in *Mesoamerica after the Decline of Teotihuacan*, edited by R. Diehl and J. Berlo, Dumbarton Oaks 1989) and "Transformations in the Painting of Ceramic Texts by the Metropolitan Master" (in *Word and Image in Maya Culture*, edited by W.F. Hanks and D.S. Rice, University of Utah Press 1989). He is currently an associate professor in the Department of Fine Arts at the University of British Columbia.

Benoit Colsenet was born in 1966 and is currently a doctoral candidate at the Centre de Recherches en Archéologie Précolombienne, University of Paris I. With grant support he was able to spend two years in Mexico examining aspects of the Mesoamerican ballgame. His fieldwork bears on ballgame iconography and the relationship between ballcourts and ballgame-related monuments.

Susanna M. Ekholm received her M.A. in anthropology from Columbia University in 1966. She conducted extensive fieldwork and analyses in the state of Chiapas, Mexico, with the New World Archaeological Foundation. Her publications include *Mound 30A and the Early Preclassic Ceramic Sequence of Izapa, Chiapas, Mexico* (Papers of the New World Archaeological Foundation 25, 1969) and *The Olmec Rock Carving at Xoc, Chiapas, Mexico* (Papers of the New World Archaeological Foundation, 32, 1973).

Gary M. Feinman, associate professor of anthropology at the University of Wisconsin-Madison, received a Ph.D. in anthropology from the City University of New York Graduate Center in 1980. His dissertation research, which analyzed pottery collections made by the Valley of Oaxaca Settlement Pattern Project, discussed changes in the organization of ceramic production and distribution in pre-Hispanic Oaxaca. In 1984–1985 he directed an archaeological survey of the Ejutla Valley, which is adjacent to the southern edge of the Oaxaca settlement pattern survey region. In addition to ceramic analysis, regional-scale research, and Mesoamerica, Feinman's interests include the development of hierarchical social systems and long-term demographic change.

Laura Finsten was educated at the University of Western Ontario (B.A. 1976), the University of Calgary (M.A. 1980), and Purdue University (Ph.D.

1983). She has taught at McMaster University in Hamilton, Canada, since 1982, where she is presently associate professor of anthropology. Her major research interest is the political economy of pre-Hispanic complex societies. Since the completion of the Valley of Oaxaca Settlement Pattern Project, she has begun a study of changing household production and consumption at the major Classic/Early Postclassic center of Jalieza in the Valley of Oaxaca.

John W. Fox is a professor at Baylor University, where he has chaired the anthropology program for ten years. He received his Ph.D. from the State University of New York at Albany in 1975. Fox's research interests are in the Maya and the Pleistocene of North America, and he is the author of *Quiche Conquest* (University of New Mexico Press 1978), *Maya Postclassic State Formation* (Cambridge University Press 1987), "The Postclassic Eastern Frontier of Mesoamerica" (*Current Anthropology* 1981), and "On the Rise and Fall of Tulans and Maya Segmentary States" (*American Anthropologist* 1989).

David Freidel, associate professor of anthropology at Southern Methodist University in Dallas, Texas, received a Ph.D. from Harvard University in 1976. He is a specialist in the analysis of Maya architecture and has carried out research at Cerros, Belize, on Cozumel Island, and at Yaxuná, Mexico. He is coauthor with Jeremy Sabloff of *Cozumel: Late Maya Settlement Patterns* (Academic Press 1984) and with Linda Schele of *A Forest of Kings: Royal Histories of the Ancient Maya* (Morrow & Co. 1990). He has also published numerous book chapters examining aspects of the ancient Maya.

Susan D. Gillespie is research associate in the Department of Anthropology at the University of Illinois at Urbana-Champaign, where she received a Ph.D. in 1983. She participated in the Komchen Project in Yucatán, and she has directed archaeological excavations at Charco Redondo on the coast of Oaxaca and at Llano del Jícaro, an Olmec monument workshop in Veracruz. Her special interests are the role of ideology and the structure of native conceptions in the functioning of pre-Hispanic Mesoamerican society. She has given particular attention to mythological narratives and iconography of New World peoples in order to understand their cosmology. The ballgame, a pan–New World institution intimately related to these concerns, has proved a valuable focus for yielding insights into this topic. In addition to several articles on the role of ideology in Mesoamerican society, she is the author of *The Aztec Kings: The Construction of Rulership in Mexica History* (University of Arizona Press 1989).

J. Charles Kelley received his B.A. from the University of New Mexico in 1937 and his Ph.D. from Harvard University in 1948. He was director of the University Museum at Southern Illinois University for twenty years and inaugurated their Department of Anthropology. His early fieldwork was in Texas and the American Southwest, but since 1949 he has worked in Chihuahua, Durango, Jalisco, and Zacatecas, Mexico. He retired in 1976.

Stephen A. Kowalewski's anthropological interests are in prehistoric and historic regional social systems, political economy, and ecology. He was an anthropology major at DePauw University and received a Ph.D. from the University of Arizona in 1976. He has done research in Mexico and Georgia and has taught at the University of Georgia since 1978. He and the other members of the Valley of Oaxaca Settlement Pattern Project have written *Ancient Mesoamerica: A Comparison of Change in Three Regions* (Cambridge University Press 1981) and two monographs on the archaeology of Oaxaca. He and Suzanne K. Fish have edited a book on archaeological survey methods.

Edward B. Kurjack earned his Ph.D. in anthropology from Ohio State University in 1972. Since 1961 he has focused his research activity in the northern Maya lowlands, although he has also worked in the Philippines, Honduras, and the southeastern United States. His monographs and mapping contributions include *Prehistoric Lowland Maya Community and Social Organization* (Middle American Research Institute 1974), the *Map of the Ruins of Dzibilchaltún, Yucatán, Mexico* (with G.E. Stuart, J.C. Scheffer, and J.W. Cottier, Middle American Research Institute 1979), and the *Archaeological Atlas of the State of Yucatán* (with Silvia Garza, INAH 1980). Additional articles and book chapters include "Early Boundary Maintenance in Northwest Yucatán, Mexico" (with E.W. Andrews V, *American Antiquity* 1976), and "Contemporary Farming and Ancient Maya Settlement: Some Disconcerting Evidence" (with D.T. Vlcek and S. Garza, in *Pre-Hispanic Maya Agriculture*, University of New Mexico Press 1978). He is professor of anthropology at Western Illinois University.

Ruben Maldonado has worked in Highland Mexico and more extensively in the Yucatán. He was heavily involved in the restoration of the ballcourt at Uxmal in the late 1970s and was director of the Ake Project in northern Yucatán. As a senior member of the research staff for the National Institute of Anthropology and History, he served as coordinator of the Archaeology Section of the Yucatán Regional Center and subsequently as its director. Among his numerous publications are his article in *Maya Mural Painting in Quintana Roo* (INAH 1987) and his book *Offerings Associated with the Burials in the Balsas* (INAH 1989) (both in Spanish). Maldonado actively participates in the preservation of Mexican cultural heritage.

Lee A. Parsons received a Ph.D. in anthropology from Harvard University in 1964. He has held curatorial positions at the Milwaukee Public Museum; the Peabody Museum, Harvard; and the St. Louis Art Museum. He has conducted archaeological excavations on the Pacific coast of Guatemala and has published extensively in scholarly journals on pre-Columbian topics. Two of his more notable articles are "The Peripheral Coastal Lowlands and the Middle Classic Period" (in *Middle Classic Mesoamerica: A.D. 400–700*, edited by E. Pasztory, Columbia University Press 1978) and "Post-Olmec Stone Sculpture: The Olmec-Izapan Transition on the Pacific Coast and Highlands" (in *The Olmec and Their Neighbors*, edited by E.P. Benson, Dumbarton Oaks 1981).

Merle Greene Robertson is director of the Pre-Columbian Art Research Institute, San Francisco. She received an M.A. from the University of Guanajasto in 1963 and an honorary Ph.D. from Tulane University in 1987. For the past fourteen years she has been recording the art and sculpture of Palenque through black-and-white and color photographs and scale line drawings. Since 1973 she has organized the Palenque Round Table conferences and has edited the results. Her other publications include *Ancient Maya Relief Sculpture* (Museum of Primitive Art 1967), *Maya Sculpture of the Southern Lowlands, the Highlands and the Pacific Piedmont* (Lederer Street and Zeus 1972), and *The Sculpture of Palenque*, vols. I–IV (Princeton University Press 1983–1989).

Robert S. Santley received his Ph.D. in anthropology from Pennsylvania State University in 1977. He has conducted fieldwork in Pennsylvania, Guatemala, central Mexico, and most recently on the South Gulf Coast. Since 1982, he has acted as director of the Matacapan Project, which has been conducting a program of multidisciplinary fieldwork in the Tuxtlas Mountains of southern Veracruz, Mexico. His numerous articles and book chapters include "Obsidian Exchange, Economic Stratification, and the Evolution of Complex Society in the Basin of Mexico" (in *Trade and Exchange in Early Mesoamerica*, edited by K. Hirth, University of New Mexico Press 1984) and "Prehispanic Roadways, Transport Network Geometry, and Aztec Political-Economic Organization in the Basin of Mexico" (in *Economic Aspects of Prehispanic Highland Mexico*, edited by B.L. Isaac, J.A.I. Press 1986). He is also co-author with W.T. Sanders and J.R. Parsons of the book entitled *The Basin of Mexico: Ecological Processes in the Evolution of a Civilization* (Academic Press 1979). He is associate professor of anthropology at the University of New Mexico.

Vernon L. Scarborough received his Ph.D. in 1980 from the Department of Anthropology at Southern Methodist University where he spent two field years examining the water-control system and settlement adaptations made by Late Preclassic Maya of northern Belize. He has taught and carried out fieldwork at the University of Texas at El Paso, the University of Khartoum, Sudan, and the University of Peshawar, Pakistan. He is author of *The Settle-*

ment System in a Late Preclassic Maya Community (Southern Methodist University Press 1991) as well as several journal articles including "Water Storage Adaptations in the American Southwest" (*Journal of Anthropological Research* 1988), "Pakistani Water: 4500 Years of Manipulation" (*Focus* 1988), and "A Preclassic Water System" (*American Antiquity* 1983). His topical interests remain settlement patterns/architecture and water management. He is currently an associate professor in the Department of Anthropology at the University of Cincinnati.

Linda Schele first visited the Maya region in December 1970 as a studio teacher on Christmas vacation. The experience transformed her. Since then, the Maya and questions about their history, their art, and the way they understood reality have remained at the center of her world. After receiving a Ph.D. in Latin American Studies from the University of Texas in 1980, she joined the faculty of their art history department and has taught there ever since. The most influential of the papers and books she has had published is *The Blood of Kings: Ritual and Dynasty in Maya Art* (Kimbell Art Museum 1986). It was written with Mary Miller as the catalog to an exhibition of the same name, which was held in 1986, sponsored by the Kimbell Art Museum. Her latest work is *A Forest of Kings: Royal Histories of the Ancient Maya*, written with David Freidel (Morrow and Co. 1990).

Eric Taladoire was born in Toulon, France, in 1946. He specialized in history and archaeology at the Ecole Normale Supérieure, Paris; Agrégé d'Histoire. His doctoral dissertation in archaeology, Paris I University, 1977, is entitled "Les terrains de jeu de balle en Mésoamérique et dans le Sud-Ouest des Etats-Unis." His fieldwork experience includes the Classic Maya site of Tonina (Chiapas) and the Campeche Project, with the Centre d'Etudes Mexicaines et Centraméricaines (CEMCA) and the ER 312 (Dir. P. Becquelin) of the French Centre National de la Recherche Scientifique. He was acting director (1977–1978) then assistant director of CEMCA (1979–1981); assistant professor (1981–1986) then maître de conférences in Pre-Columbian Archaeology at the Paris I University, and director of the Centre de Recherches en Archéologie Précolombienne (1986–present).

Phil C. Weigand received his B.A., with honors, from Indiana University in 1962 with a major in history. His Ph.D. in anthropology was granted in 1970 at Southern Illinois University. He is currently Profesor de Investigaciones at the Colegio de Michoacan, Mexico, and a research associate at the Museum of Northern Arizona. His specialties are the archaeology and ethnography of Western Mesoamerica. Other interests include ancient mining and frontier dynamics along the northern margins of Mesoamerica and the southwestern U.S.A. His published works include "Turquoise Sources and Source Analysis:

Mesoamerica and the Southwestern U.S.A." (with G. Harbottle and E.V. Sayre, in *Exchange Systems in Prehistory*, edited by T.K. Earle and J.E. Ericson, Academic Press 1977) and a co-edited book with M.S. Foster entitled *The Archaeology of Western and Northwestern Mesoamerica* (Westview Press 1985).

David R. Wilcox is the curator of anthropology at the Museum of Northern Arizona, Flagstaff. He received his B.A. in anthropology and mathematics from Beloit College in 1966 and his Ph.D. in anthropology from the University of Arizona in 1977. Most of his research has been in southwestern anthropology, with interests ranging from Hohokam prehistory to the protohistoric period, the history of archaeology, and the reconstruction of social organization. His publications include *The Architecture of the Casa Grande and Its Interpretation, Snaketown Revisited, Hohokam Ballcourts and Their Interpretation* (Arizona State Museum 1977, 1981, 1983), "Multi-ethnic Division of Labor in the Protohistoric Southwest" (New Mexico Archaeological Society 1984), "An Historical Analysis of the Problem in Southwestern-Mesoamerican Connections" (Southern Illinois University Press 1986), and "The Changing Context of Support for Archaeology and the Work of Erich F. Schmidt" (Museum of Nothern Arizona 1988).

S. Jeffrey K. Wilkerson received his Ph.D. in anthropology in 1972 at Tulane University. He has conducted fieldwork in the state of Veracruz, Mexico, and the greater Maya Lowlands. Among his numerous publications are "The Northern Olmec and Pre-Olmec Frontier on the Gulf Coast" (in *The Olmec and Their Neighbors*, edited by E.P. Benson, Dumbarton Oaks 1981), "So Green and Like a Garden: Intensive Agriculture in Ancient Veracruz" (in *Drained Field Agriculture in Central and South America*, edited by J.P. Darch, BAR 1983), "In Search of the Mountain of Foam: Human Sacrifice in Eastern Mesoamerica" (in *Ritual Human Sacrifice in Eastern Mesoamerica*, edited by E.P. Benson, Dumbarton Oaks 1984), and "El Tajín: Great Center of the Northeast" (in *Mexico: Splendor of Thirty Centuries*, Metropolitan Museum of Art 1990). He is currently director of the Institute for Cultural Ecology of the Tropics in Veracruz.

PART I
Northern Mesoamerica

CHAPTER 1

The Politicization of the Mesoamerican Ballgame and Its Implications for the Interpretation of the Distribution of Ballcourts in Central Mexico

Robert S. Santley, Michael J. Berman, and Rani T. Alexander

At the time of the Spanish conquest the Aztecs played a game called *ulama-liztli*. This game greatly impressed the Spaniards because it was played with a solid ball that was heavy but bounced very well. The game was played in specially constructed courts which were widely distributed throughout pre-Columbian Mesoamerica (Clune 1963; Stern 1949; Taladoire 1981). One interesting property of the game was that the ball was struck mainly with the hip, buttocks, or knee: hence the term "hip-ball game" (Stern 1949). Another feature was that the scoring varied; placement of the ball through one of two rings set on tenons into the side of the central court won the game outright (Blom 1932). Various scholars have suggested that this element of play may have given Naismith the idea for scoring in modern-day basketball (Borhegyi 1960).

This chapter discusses the evidence for the hip-ball game in central Mexico. Our intent is to show how the game may be linked to certain attributes of political structure and how variation in those attributes may account for the distribution of ballcourts in time and space. Our presentation begins with a discussion of political centralization and competition, two variables that we feel had a great impact on the distribution of ballcourts in time and space. Second, we summarize the political history of central Mexico from the period when complex societies first developed until the Spanish conquest. We then briefly review extant archaeological and documentary evidence concerning the ballgame in central Mexico. Ballcourts, it appears, occurred considerably earlier in southern central Mexico, despite the fact that the inhabitants of the Basin of Mexico probably played the game. Next, we adopt a theoretical posture that suggests that court frequency and distribution is positively correlated with the incidence of intra- and inter-polity competition and negatively linked to degree of centralization of power. We conclude by illustrating how variability in ballcourt distribution may be profitably viewed as a function of differences in the structure of sociopolitical systems.

Political Centralization and Decentralization

Centralization refers to "the degree of linkage between the various subsystems and the highest-order controls in society" (Flannery 1972:409). Political centralization "occurs when one operating unit is in the position of having the power to make decisions for a large number of units" (R.N. Adams 1975:214). The amount of centralization manifested will vary relative to the specificity of the decisions being made, the kind of unit making the decisions, and the character and number of the linkages between the top-ranking authority and other units of political authority. State-level systems have political structures which are hierarchical in character. Hierarchical organization is necessary to insure the efficient processing of large amounts of information, a requirement that affects system behavior at several different scales.

Highly centralized states are characterized by a considerable amount of vertical connectivity, with general-purpose units making decisions that directly affect the behavior of lower order institutions, and there is little autonomy between the various operating units responsible for system stability on the local level. The degree of centralization represented, archaeologists claim, can be measured by the scale of the system, the proportion of its population that resides in the political capital, the size of the largest center relative to other central places, the relative amount of political architecture at the capital, and the extent of control over other elements of the system such as production and distribution (Blanton et al. 1982; Flannery 1972; Santley in press a; Turner et al. 1981). Centralized systems also cover comparatively large areas, have political capitals very much larger than any other central place which contain most of the system's "political" architecture, and exert controls over raw material extraction, craft specialization, and exchange. An outstanding example of a highly centralized political economy is the dendritic central-place system (C. Smith 1976).

In decentralized political systems, power and authority are diffused among elites who often reside in different central places (R. N. Adams 1975). Components of the system therefore retain considerable autonomy which is reflected by the redundant occurrence of similarly structured political units and few vertical linkages between them. Although the territory occupied may be quite large, generally no one center is predominant and political centers are comparatively small in size. Often the area occupied by the system is politically and economically Balkanized as well, with individual local units vying for regional control (Blanton 1975). In such politically competitive settings there is an emphasis on alliance building to enhance chances of acquiring tributary domains. Although craft specialization and trade exist, such activities are generally geared to the production and distribution of elite goods to reinforce alliances and insure the internal support of lesser elites and political clients (Adams and Smith 1981). Feudal society is an example of a system with a decentralized political structure (Coulborn 1956).

Political system organization is a consequence of participation in a stratified set of networks that impinge upon and condition political structure in specific situations. This variability in structure is primarily a function of the amount of centralization/competition exhibited at different system scales. Three scalar levels are important in this regard. The most fundamental is that of the local community or urban center. The political regime of local centers may be centralized or decentralized, depending on the degree to which power is shared by different groups. The city of Sparta is an example of the former (Kitto 1951), Republican Rome the latter (Bourne 1966).

Regional networks provide the matrix in which the political life of local towns is often embedded. The kind of political structure manifested regionally also varies from centralized on one end of the continuum to decentralized on the other. In fact, regional decentralization may partially account for why local political entities are frequently highly centralized, which is often the case in feudal regimes (Coulborn 1956). On the other hand, the regional system may be centralized, with top-ranking decision making taking place at a political capital, but with power at the capital shared by a consortium of elites who maintain constituencies in local towns. The disembedded capital is an example of this kind of political structure (Blanton 1976). Regional political structures in turn are a part of even more spatially extensive or macroregional networks. The degree of centralization and competition displayed macroregionally also varies considerably, depending on the scale, number, and internal organization of the polities that compose it and the structure of the linkages between them (Claessen and Skalnik 1978; Etzioni 1961; Krader 1968; Wolf 1966). In addition, larger systems tend to be more hierarchical, to have more levels of decision making superimposed one atop another, though they need not necessarily be more centralized (Johnson 1978).

Political centralization is therefore a characteristic of human organization which is variably manifested at different system scales. Some political systems are highly centralized locally but decentralized on the regional and macroregional levels. In contrast, other systems may be regionally centralized, with a number of groups sharing power on the local level, while still others may be centralized on all levels.

The Political Economy of Early States in Central Mexico

In 1519 the Aztecs were the dominant political and economic force in central Mexico. During the century before the conquest, the status of the Aztecs changed from one of a small client state to that of the head of an enormous empire which extracted large amounts of tribute from a substantial part of Mesoamerica (Bedoian 1973; Berdan 1982; Codex Mendoza 1938). The emergence of the Aztec empire was paralleled by the rapid growth of its capital, Tenochtitlán, which in the early sixteenth century had a population of at least 220,000 (Calnek 1972; Sanders and Santley 1983). Recent reconstructions of the internal organization of Tenochtitlán indicate that it was internally divided into different neighborhoods, many of which were occupied by craftsmen and other specialists who produced goods for sale (Berdan 1982; Calnek 1976; Hassig 1985). The urban center was dominated by two large complexes of public buildings: the great sacred enclosure in "downtown" Tenochtitlán, and the main marketplace in Tlatelolco (Davies 1973). Below Tenochtitlán-Tlatelolco were about 40 second-order centers which were the capitals of local territorial states; except for Texcoco and Tlacopan they paid some form of tribute to the Triple Alliance (Sanders et al. 1979). Tenochtitlán was connected to these centers by a series of earthen causeways and by canoe transport which allowed the efficient movement of goods to and from the city and its hinterland (Hassig 1985; Sanders and Santley 1983).

Although there is some disagreement as to how the Aztec political economy was organized (Evans 1980; M. Smith 1979, 1980), most authorities would agree that it was highly centralized by the early sixteenth century and that many aspects of production and exchange were dominated by the Aztec elite (Berdan 1982; Brumfiel 1980; Carrasco 1978; J. Parsons 1976). The Aztec political economy exhibits many of the features of a dendritic central-place system (Hassig 1985; Santley 1985). In dendritic central-place systems, large-scale bulking determines many aspects of system structure (English 1966; Kelley 1976; C. Smith 1976; Vance 1970). The central focus of that industry is bulking for export beyond local system boundaries; because urban industries must be supplied with raw materials, the direction of many raw material and commodity flows is up the settlement hierarchy. Lower order centers exist, but they function mainly as bulking places for resources extracted in their respective hinterlands and as markets for goods produced in the top-ranking urban center. According to Ross Hassig:

Until the greatly increased reliance on canoe transport and valley-wide economic integration [in the Basin of Mexico], the pattern of urban-rural interchange was based on the central location of the secondary-producing primary-consuming city within the primary-producing secondary-consuming hinterland. This changed with the shift in productive patterns. The cities were no longer major producers of secondary goods but rather producers of primary goods for Tenochtitlán, whose secondary goods they now consumed. . . . [As a result, under the Aztecs the Basin of Mexico] was converted from loosely linked disparate economic areas into a largely unified core-periphery system. Primary markets fed into their respective secondary markets, and each of these fed into Tenochtitlán to form a dendritic central-place system (1985:135, 144).

This structure was mirrored by the organization of the Aztec roadway system (Santley 1986, in press a).

Archaeological data indicate that the political economy of Teotihuacán may have been similarly structured in Middle Classic times (A.D. 300–750). Obsidian working was a dominant component of the economy of the ancient city (Spence 1981, 1984), and evidence from other sites in the Basin of Mexico and Mesoamerica at large suggests that much of the production of Teotihuacán's workshops was geared for export (Santley 1983a; Santley et al. 1986). Teotihuacán was at least 12.5 times the size of the next largest settlement in the Basin of Mexico, and the spatial distribution of dependent communities was size-sequential, not nested (Santley in press b, n.d.). Moreover, many second-order towns were located in positions to control the distribution of goods en masse to the urban center, in conformity with the dendritic model (Charlton 1978; Sanders et al. 1979; Santley 1979). Farther afield, heavy Teotihuacán influence is exhibited at centers dominating other exotic resource zones (Parsons and Price 1971; Sanders 1977; Santley et al. 1986). Sites such as Kaminaljuyú, Matacapan, and Tinganio appear to have supported enclaves of resident Teotihuacanos which, we suspect, were established to control the bulking of local resources as well as to act as bases for caravans hauling goods long distances (Santley et al. 1985; Santley et al. 1987).

The Middle Classic period was the only block of time before the rise of the Aztec state when central Mexico was unified under the aegis of a single authority and when regional political organization was apparently highly centralized. From about A.D. 750 to the middle of the fifteenth century, the area was split into a variable number of autonomous polities all vying for regional control (Davies 1977, 1980; Sanders et al. 1979). During the Early Toltec period (ca. A.D. 750–950) settlement patterns were highly aggregated, and many communities were situated in defensible locations, implying a very competitive and highly Balkanized political atmosphere (Blanton 1975). Al-

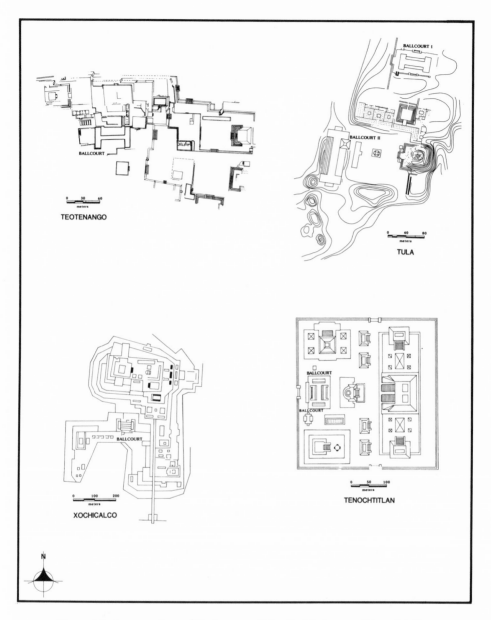

Figure 1.1. A comparison of Teotenango, Tula, Xochicalco, and Tenochtitlán.

though the Late Toltec period (ca. A.D. 950–1250) involved the rise of Tula as a principal power in central Mexico, the scale of its public architecture suggests that political authority was less centralized than its Middle Classic predecessor (Diehl 1983). In addition, Tula, with a maximum resident population of only about 37,000, was not a particularly large urban center (Diehl 1981). If any trust is placed in the native chronicles, the picture that emerges is one involving continual political strife and occasional open hostilities between factions of the city's elite, not effective centralization of authority (Davies 1977). Moreover, during the Toltec period central Mexico was split into at least five polities headed by Xochicalco, Cholula, Teotenango, and Teotihuacán, as well as Tula (Figure 1.1).

Political fragmentation and a lack of centralized authority also characterize the Early Aztec period (ca. A.D. 1250–1450). Before the conquests of Moctezuma Ilhuicamina, central Mexico was politically Balkanized, and internecine warfare between local states was endemic. In the words of Nigel Davies, each petty ruler:

> waged an endless struggle to impose tribute on his neighbors; and when successful he exacted a heavy levy. . . . The Aztecs repeated this pattern on a vaster scale, and the history of their empire is one long record of rebellions arising from attempts to avoid their tribute levy and of reconquest, often leading to the imposition of an even larger levy (1980:344).

The Ballgame in Central Mexico

Most of the information on the central Mexican ballgame comes from Conquest period documents (Cervantes Salazar 1936; Durán 1967; Gomara 1826; Hernandez 1946; Motolinia 1970; Muñoz Camargo 1892; Sahagún 1956; Tezozomoc 1980; Torquemada 1943–44). Although specific sources differ on particulars, they seem to be in agreement on the following points. The game was played by nearly all adolescent and adult males, noble and commoner alike. The game's widespread popularity is underscored by the fact that provinces on the gulf coast sent 16,000 rubber balls annually as royal tribute (Codex Mendoza 1938). Almost any level surface might be used as a playing field; masonry courts were built only in the principal towns or neighborhoods of the largest centers. Masonry courts were often located near the town's market or civic-ceremonial complex, and most were constructed by the ruler, other members of the upper class, or high-ranking civil servants for use first by the nobility and second by the public at large. Members of the nobility, including the monarchy, often prided themselves as players. Nobles are also said to have retained skilled "professional" players who were pitted against one another on major feast days. Some play involved pairs of individuals, whereas at other times teams of two, three, and occasionally as many as nine to eleven players were used. In addition, games between members of the nobility, their professionals, or groups of skilled amateurs were often accompanied by vigorous wagering, with the stakes varying according to the status and wealth of the gamblers.

The archaeological record on the ballgame is less adequate, due mainly to the kind of research conducted in central Mexico in recent years. For example, in the Basin of Mexico the ethnohistoric sources mention that most towns had courts, yet archaeological surveys found very few of them. This lack of "on-the-ground" confirmation is due to the fact that many sites which were Aztec towns are also modern communities and have been so since the time of the conquest, combined with the extensive rapid-coverage survey procedures employed (Sanders et al. 1979). On the other hand, there are large sites in the Tehuacán Valley not covered by dense modern occupation which do not have ballcourts (MacNeish et al. 1972). There are also other cases where the center contains several courts. Two, possibly three ballcourts are present near Tula Grande, the main zone of civic-ceremonial architecture in the Toltec capital, and the occurrence of pairs of low mounds in outlying barrios suggests that more probably await discovery (Yadeun 1974).

Ballcourt distribution varies by time period. During the Toltec and Aztec periods every major urban center had at least one, sometimes two ballcourts built either as a component of the site's civic-ceremonial complex or near the ruler's palace. Tula[1] and Tenochtitlán[2] each had two major courts (Diehl 1983; Stern 1949), whereas Xochicalco and Teotenango had only one (Kubler 1975; Piña Chan 1975) (Figure 1.1). All of these courts had enclosed I-shaped playing surfaces, with benches flanking the central alley and rings set in the upper part of the lateral wall. A small ballcourt also occurs at Tula Chico, the civic-ceremonial heart of the Early Toltec Tula (Diehl 1983), and there are two pairs of long platform mounds directly to the north, suggesting that several other courts may be present (Yadeun 1974). Ballcourts were also built at smaller centers such as El Tesoro (Mastache and Crespo 1974), Ixtapaluca Viejo (Blanton 1972; Grove and Nicholson 1965), Cerro Zapotecas near Cholula (Mountjoy and Peterson 1973), Ajacuba, Manzanilla, Tepoztlan, and Chimalacatlan (Taladoire 1981), as well as at six Postclassic sites in the Tehuacán Valley (MacNeish et al. 1972). Generally, the higher the rank of the center, the larger the size of the ballcourt and the greater the probability that several are present. No courts have been reported for sites that did not function in some fashion as a centralplace.

In the Middle Classic and Terminal Formative periods, by contrast, ballcourts are restricted to sites in Puebla-Tlaxcala and southern central Mexico. Ballcourts have been reported at Chalcatzingo (Grove 1984), at twelve Terminal Formative and six Classic sites in the Tehuacán Valley (MacNeish et al. 1972), at a number of civic centers in Puebla-Tlaxcala (Garcia Cook 1974, 1978), and at Capulac Concepción south of Cerro Malinche (Garcia Cook 1981). No ballcourts are known from Teotihuacán, from any of its large second-order centers such as Chingu, Azcapotzalco, Tepeapulco, and Portesuelo, or from any sites in the Teotihuacán corridor in Puebla-Tlaxcala (Diaz 1980; Garcia Cook and Trejo 1977; Millon 1973; J. Parsons 1971). Representations of people playing a ballgame are depicted on a mural painting from Tepantitla at Teotihuacán, but the game played involved the use of a bat to strike the ball and the players lack the usual costume of a heavy belt, knee pads, and bindings (Pasztory 1972, 1976). Hip-game players, however, in typical posture, are represented on another mural painting at Tepantitla, indicating that the game was played at Teotihuacán. A few ballgame yokes and *hachas* imported from Veracruz have also been found at Teotihuacán, as has a stone ring and a number of clay figurines portraying individuals dressed in ballgame costumes (Aveleyra 1963; Proskouriakoff 1954). Terracotta figurines depicting ball players from earlier periods are present at Tlatilco, Tlapacoya, and Loma Torremote (Bernal 1969; Coe 1965a; Pasztory 1972; Santley unpublished data). The occurrence of representations of ball players at Formative village sites in the Basin of Mexico is significant because they date to a time period some 1500–2000 years before ballcourts became widespread. Formative period courts, sculptures, or figurines of ball players have also been reported from the gulf coast, the Valley of Oaxaca, and the Maya Lowlands (Bernal 1968; Blanton 1978; Blanton et al. 1982; Coe and Diehl 1980; Flannery and Marcus 1976; Scarborough et al. 1982; Wyshak et al. 1971).

In the Tehuacán Valley the history of the ballgame can be defined in greater detail because most sites have not been obscured by modern occupation. The Tehuacán Valley has a long history of occupation (MacNeish 1964, 1972; Mac-Neish et al. 1972). The region was first occupied sometime during the Late Pleistocene. Small agricultural villages, several with mounded architecture, appeared around 1500 B.C., but a well-developed settlement hierarchy did not become firmly established until the Late Formative period. Except for a brief period in the Early Postclassic, the Tehuacán Valley was politically fragmented until the Spanish conquest. The Terminal Formative settlement pattern was aggregated, with sites clustering into three main groups: one in the north and two in the south. Each group was dominated by a single large town site. Most sites favored hilltop locations, suggesting that relationships between polities were frequently not peaceful. The Classic period settlement pattern was also more aggregated than before, with the valley apparently split into only two major political entities. The northern polity seemed to be the more powerful of the two, judging from the scale of its civic-ceremonial

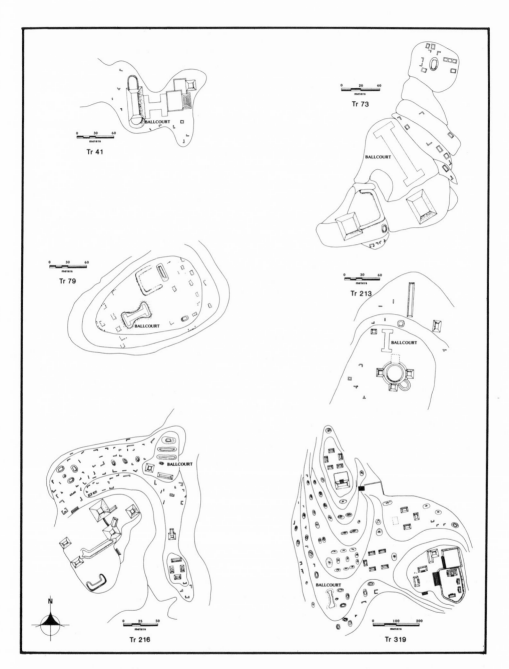

Figure 1.2. Ballcourts at TR41, 73, 79, 213, 216, and 319 (after MacNeish et al. 1972:Figs. 165–167, 185, 186, 195).

architecture, the size of the principal communities, and the total area occupied by settlements. There were also a number of outlying hilltop settlements, which may have maintained a degree of autonomy.

The valley may have been briefly unified in the Early Postclassic. Although sites still clustered in groups, the complex of public buildings at Tr 319 was by far the largest built in the Tehuacán Valley (Figure 1.2). Tr 319's hegemony over the region, however, was probably short-lived, for at least six centers were fortified and many others were situated in defensible hilltop locations. The valley was also split into a number of warring statelets at the time of the conquest. At least two Late Postclassic towns covered 200 hectares, and there were four others in the 80–100-hectare range. Two major settlement clusters are evident: one around Venta Salada, the other near Coxcatlán Viejo. Two other small clusters of sites, each with a small town, were located in the hills to the west of the valley. Except for the largest sites, which MacNeish classifies as cities, centers were again fortified or placed in readily defensible locations atop hills or on their flanks.

Ballcourts make their appearance very early in the Tehuacán Valley (MacNeish et al. 1972). Twelve Terminal Formative courts are known. The number of courts decreased to six in the Classic period, then two in the Early Postclassic and four in the Late Postclassic (Figure 1.2). Most of these ballcourts were I-shaped, though a few sites had open-ended courts. Ballcourts occurred at large towns as well as at small centers and, curiously, hilltop village sites. All of the latter had rather substantial civic-ceremonial complexes, including temples, platform residences, and other mounded architecture. At town sites ballcourt area correlates with size of settlement, implying that only labor from the center was involved in their construction. In contrast, ballcourt area at small hilltop sites does not covary with community size. In many cases court size is much larger than one would predict based on settlement area, suggesting that off-site labor was relied on to build them.

Each settlement cluster generally contained at least one court, which was typically located in the civic-ceremonial complex of the largest town. In the Terminal Formative period, large towns were surrounded by a number of small centers which also often had courts. Interestingly, courts first appeared at a time when subsistence strategies were shifting from dry-farming to hydraulic agriculture. Toward the end of the Formative period artificial water-control systems were developed on an increasingly larger scale throughout the valley (Spencer 1979; Woodbury and Neely 1972). Hydraulic agriculture in a semi-arid area like the Tehuacán Valley fosters high levels of competition and not uncommonly armed conflict because of the great potential for inequities in water distribution (Sanders 1968). Agricultural intensification may also be viewed as an aspect of the process of land disenfranchisement, since new land-use strategies are often developed in settings where the farmer is incapable of producing enough foodstuffs on what little land he has available (Cook 1982; Santley in press b). The same may be said of elites who derive material benefit from the surplus produce grown for their support. The reduction in court number in the Classic period associates with a drop in the number of competing polities and with the nucleation of the population in large towns, which occurred mainly at Tr 240 and Tr 366 in the north. As the process of urbanization continued and the valley was dominated by fewer and fewer political entities in the Postclassic, the number of ballcourts decreased even further.

Several conclusions may be drawn from the evidence just presented. First, the ballgame appears to have been played throughout central Mexico from at least the Early Classic period onward, and in the Basin of Mexico there is evidence that the game dates back to the Middle, perhaps the Early Formative period. Second, at the time of the conquest the ballgame had broad popular appeal; it was played by elites and peasants alike throughout central Mexico, and chances are that the game enjoyed widespread popularity during earlier time periods as well. Third, while masonry ballcourts appear in southern central Mexico in the Terminal Formative, they do not occur throughout central Mexico until the Late Classic or Early Toltec period, despite the fact that the inhabitants of Teotihuacán were aware of the ballgame and probably played it frequently. These ballcourts were generally located in public contexts in towns and urban centers, often in the main complex of civic-ceremonial architecture and sometimes adjacent to the ruler's palace. Finally, if the evidence from the Tehuacán Valley is representative of patterning elsewhere, there appears to be a negative association between ballcourt number and degree of political centralization. Ballcourts were widely distributed when the region contained a number of polities vying for control and less common when the area was split into fewer polities and most of the population lived in a few large centers. The fewest courts occurred at a time when the valley was apparently unified under a single political authority.

Competition Between Elites and the Ballgame

In addition to its role as sport, the ballgame was used as a vehicle to increase the power, prestige, and wealth of the elite who often bet vast sums on the outcome of contests. Torquemada (1943–44), for example, describes a game between the Aztec monarch, Axayacatl, and his ally, Xihuitlemoc, king of Xochimilco. Axayacatl, who lost the contest and eventually assassinated his colleague, wagered his annual income against several towns' tributary to Xochimilco. It may seem strange that monarchs who were presumably allies would bet sums of this magnitude on a game, but it must be remembered that, although Xochimilco had been conquered by the first Aztec king, Acamapichtli, the city still enjoyed a large measure of autonomy in the late fifteenth century and paid only nominal amounts of tribute to Tenochtitlán (Davies 1973). Another famous contest involved Nezahuapilli of Texcoco and Moctezuma Xocoyotzin (Blom 1932). In yet another story, Maxtla, ruler of Azcapotzalco, is credited with losing the Tepanec empire, due to his failure to win an all-important game (Chimalpahin 1965). The ballgame also looms large in the Quetzalcóatl-Tezcatlipoca myth of the Toltecs (Davies 1977), and Ixtlilxochitl (1952) recounts a story in which Topiltzin, the Toltec king, played the game against three rivals, the winner to rule the others. Another legend has the Toltec Empire dissolving because Huémac's behavior after a game so offended the gods that they laid waste to his realm (Leyenda de los Soles 1975). While the historical meaning assigned to these contests often varies from scholar to scholar, the objective of the game was always the same: personal political and/or economic gain.

Various arguments have been advanced to explain this politicization of the game. According to Theodore Stern, the game served as a substitute for direct military confrontation. In his words:

> It is no accident that strong parallels exist between warfare patterns and those of the competitive ball game. . . . The pitting of teams from two communities against each other in a game in which hard-driving, dexterous action wins high stakes, frequently though not everywhere, at the risk of injury or death, all lead to the occasional substitution of the game for overt warfare. . . . Not only may games of this type be consciously employed on occasion to secure ends usually attained by fighting, but it may also function as a safety valve to relieve suppressed intercommunity conflicts, thus operating to sublimate belligerent tendencies and directing them into harmless action (Stern 1949:96–97).

Clune (1963), in a later study, stands in agreement with Stern's interpretation but suggests that highly centralized political regimes tend not to encourage factional rivalries. Politicized competitive games, then, would not be expected in highly centralized oriental despotisms of the type proposed by Wittfogel (1957). We agree that competition and centralization can be conceived as opposing political variables; however, the mere presence of competing polities, in itself, is insufficient to account for either the appearance of ballcourts or the politicization of the game. Explanation here requires a closer look at the factors promoting political competition in central Mexico and the roles elites had in the process.

In Conquest period central Mexico, armed conflict generally stemmed from disputes over material resources, excessive tribute levies, or access to distribution networks (Davies 1973; Hassig 1985; Isaac 1983; Offner 1983). Monarchs carved out tributary domains to acquire goods for local distribution. The Aztec tribute system, which exacted staggering amounts of goods, simply duplicated the pattern practiced by the rulers of petty states. Although levies consisted of both luxury and subsistence goods, agricultural products were collected primarily from nearby provinces, whereas elite goods, both processed commodities and exotic raw materials, were obtained from the empire at large (Bedoian 1973; Berdan 1982; Hassig 1985). In reality, the tribute system was a mosaic. Some towns paid tribute to specific centers such as Texcoco and Cuautitlán; other centers, including the capitals of independent tributary domains, sent their goods to Tenochtitlán for distribution to members of the Triple Alliance; still others were obligated to pay tribute to both (Offner 1983). Subsistence goods were used for such purposes as the support of the royal palace, subsidy of building projects, emergency storage, and the maintenance of urban populations in Triple Alliance capitals (Berdan 1982). However, most of the sumptuary goods that entered Tenochtitlán, Texcoco, and to a lesser extent Tlacopan were given to the ruler's political clients, distinguished warriors, and dissident nobles, or passed on to the *pochteca* (professionally trained long-distance merchants) for long-distance trade in the emperor's name (Berdan 1982; Hassig 1985; Offner 1983). In general, the larger the tributary domain, the less bickering and factional rivalry were found among local elites. A successful monarch was one who brought in an adequate amount of tribute each year or had a sufficient store of goods on hand to squelch most sources of internal dissent.

Not uncommonly, the volume of incoming goods was inadequate for the ruler's needs, or the demands of the local elite and the populace at large exceeded the monarch's capacity to extract tribute. When faced with this situation, the ruler might simply increase the levy to be exacted, an action which often met with rebellion on the part of the tributary state. More often, favoritism was probably the rule of thumb, with certain nobles or factions receiving goods according to their needs and others virtually nothing at all. Monarchs attempting to placate clients and dissident nobles also tended to accumulate large numbers of wives, which led to a proliferation of elites, politico-economic disenfranchisement, and subsequently even more factional rivalry a generation down the line. One way around this problem was further conquest and the redistribution of conquered lands to disenfranchised nobles, a tactic often employed (Davies 1973; Offner 1983). The ability of a ruler to solidify his power base at home was therefore a function of the volume of incoming tribute, the size of the local elite stratum, and the productivity of the local agroecosystem, which had a dramatic impact not only on the amount of goods nobles had at their disposal but also on tribute production capabilities.

In consequence, competition would be retarded, if not suppressed altogether, in cases where there were adequate amounts of goods available for use by the ruler as a hedge against socio-environmental stress. Polities which had a high-surplus agrarian base and/or control over macroregional distribution networks would be the least likely to experience internal political strife. On the other hand, political systems whose agricultural support base had a comparatively low surplus-production capacity and/or which controlled relatively small-scale tributary domains or exchange networks would be much more prone to such political problems. Furthermore, in cases where no one polity enjoyed a demographic advantage and the region was split into a number of statelets, alliance building would be used as a basis for expansion against third parties, who would then tend to organize themselves similarly. Alliances were usually solidified by the exchange of females, a situation which also caused the nobility to swell in numbers. Because the number of new elite roles usually lagged behind the number of new persons claiming elite status, disenfranchisement occurred. The stage was thus set for a new round of conquest and land redistribution.

It is also in such decentralized contexts when alternative means of capital acquisition would be pursued by disenfranchised elites and when competitive games might be employed to meet that end. In our opinion, ballcourts were built by nobles for use by elites to acquire wealth and sometimes territory, though games were also played in connection with major ceremonials and by the populace at large. Axayacatl's contest with the king of Xochimilco makes considerable sense when viewed in this light. So does the politicization of such other games as tournaments in feudal Europe (Jewell 1977), circus races in the later Roman Empire (Auguet 1972), and the Olympiad of the modern era (Harris and Park 1983).

Political Centralization and the Distribution of Ballcourts

We believe that politicization of the ballgame largely accounts for the distribution of ballcourts in time and space and that information on the frequency and distribution of ballcourts may be used as a proxy measure of the degree of centralization in political structure. On the regional level, highly centralized political systems should lack ballcourts, whereas in decentralized settings courts should be present at most centers because the game was politicized as an alternative way of acquiring additional revenue or territory at minimum expense. The number of ballcourts at the capital in turn should be an ordered response to local political conditions, with more courts occurring at centers whose decision-making apparatus was more decentralized and competitive. This variability is closely related to the scale and diversity of resource base dominated by early states.

Broad-spectrum, high-volume production-distribution systems are capable of supporting more elites or a large proportion of their populations at a higher standard of living. The first such system to emerge in central Mexico was centered at Teotihuacán. Teotihuacán's political economy, archaeological evidence indicates, had control over more energy, more raw materials, more processed commodities, and more distribution networks than any of its political contemporaries or successors in central Mexico until the emergence of the Aztec empire in the late fifteenth century. The effect of this control is reflected at Teotihuacán by the presence of a substantial elite population resident in the city's center, the presence of apartment complexes which were decorated with elaborate mural paintings but apparently occupied by persons of intermediate status, the rebuilding of the city several times on a grid plan, and the occurrence of goods produced from all over Mesoamerica (Ester 1976; Millon 1973, 1976).

This higher standard of living was the outcome of three components of Teotihuacán's production-distribution system which served to differentiate it from political economies elsewhere. First, Teotihuacán's food production base involved a heavy focus on hydraulic agriculture (Sanders et al. 1979; Sanders et al. 1982). Hydraulic agriculture in an area like the Basin of Mexico is a very productive strategy of land use, often capable of producing a 100 percent surplus (Sanders and Santley 1983). Consequently, if the area devoted to canal irrigation was exploited to its fullest potential, persons in control of those lands would have had a substantial surplus at their disposal which could be distributed to lesser ranking elites. Second, a large part of all of the obsidian used in central Mexico during the Middle Classic came either from the complex of sources Teotihuacán dominated or from the city's workshops (Spence 1981; Santley 1983a, 1984). Teotihuacán, as a result, was in a position to extract resources from its neighbors and to control the distribution of its own resources because of its geographic location. Third, there is evidence that Teotihuacán set up enclaves at sites such as Kaminaljuyú and Matacapan which dominated other production-distribution networks (Kidder et al. 1946; Sanders and Michels 1977; Santley et al. 1984; Santley et al. 1987). Teotihuacán control over a wide range of goods in a number of areas is therefore implied.

The ways wealth may be accumulated are varied in the type of production-distribution systems just described (C. Smith 1976). Likewise, the larger the scale of the economy and the more goods that circulate in it, the greater will be the number of roles required for system maintenance. Our point is that at

Teotihuacán the economic bases for social stratification lay not only in control over critical capital resources such as land and water but also over other resources which probably provided as much "income" as irrigated land. This wide variety of alternative modes of capital acquisition may have had a very restraining effect on internal political strife and factional rivalry so long as the system operated smoothly and competing centers had little effect on Teotihuacán policies. Large-scale, broad-spectrum political economies also open new niches (or expanded niche breadth) which disenfranchised elites or their clients can fill. Under such conditions, there would be little need to employ competitive games as a means of resource acquisition, and ballcourts should not be built for that reason.

The economy of the Aztec capital, Tenochtitlán, also seems to have been heading in this same general direction. At the time of the conquest the pochteca were rapidly rising in economic (and presumably political) status, due to their domination of long-distance exchange networks, as were the lapidaries, featherworkers, and metalworkers who required exotic raw materials brought in by merchants or as tribute (Berdan 1982). The creation of new economic niches at the Aztec capital (Hassig 1985) of Tenochtitlán was a direct consequence of empire formation and the dominance of regional and extra-regional markets. Curiously, most references to specific Aztec monarchs using the ballgame as a means of acquiring resources came from early in the history of the empire. This is precisely what we would expect of a political system in transition: one that was becoming increasingly centralized but still not in firm control of a broad-spectrum economy.

Conditions in southern central Mexico during the Classic period and in the Basin of Mexico following the decline of Teotihuacán were very much different. In Puebla, Morelos, and the Tehuacán Valley ballcourts appeared much earlier than they did in the Basin of Mexico. Southern central Mexico, however, was never politically unified for long under the hegemony of a single authority, although Cholula may have exercised brief control over large portions of Puebla at several points in its history. Interestingly, when Cholula did increase dramatically in size, ballcourts are not reported at smaller centers (García Cook 1974, 1978). Moreover, in the Tehuacán Valley, which was split up into a number of warring statelets throughout most of its history, ballcourts occur even at small hilltop towns, several of which were fortified (MacNeish et al. 1972). Southern central Mexico also lacks critical resources like obsidian whose production-distribution could have been monopolized. Thus the political systems that emerged in this area were essentially simple agrarian states, with economic stratification based mainly on differential control of the means of production—land.

The political climate of the Basin of Mexico does not appear to have been all that different after Teotihuacán's power waned. Although it is still unclear why Teotihuacán declined, two facts are certain: The political systems that emerged in Teotihuacán's wake exercised very little control over the long-distance distribution of goods, and none, except for Tula briefly several centuries later and Tenochtitlán at the time of the conquest, dominated the Pachuca mines (Healan et al. 1983; Santley et al. 1986). The bases of economic power in the Postclassic Basin of Mexico were thus probably very much like those somewhat earlier in southern central Mexico. Conditions in both areas, then, probably directed political systems along a trajectory emphasizing the acquisition of tributary domains, and this set the stage for alliance building, disenfranchisement, and ultimately the politicization of the ballgame. The degree of political centralization at major centers also varied at this time. Ballcourts were built at many of these centers, but Tula contained the most, implying that its political authority was decentralized and its political climate was competitive. Recent interpretations of native chronicles describing the same time period point to the same conclusion (Davies 1977, 1980).

Expanding the Scope of the Model

Basically we have argued that under conditions of political Balkanization, competition, and elite disenfranchisement, the ballgame was used as an alternative means to acquire wealth and territory. Conversely, when polities were centralized and the economic bases of stratification were varied, the ballgame was not politicized to the degree that it was in areas characterized by political fragmentation. With reference to central Mexico, we suggest that the number of ballcourts at specific sites may monitor the degree to which competition characterized the political economy of local centers. Further examples of the applicability of this model for which adequate independent data are available can be drawn from the Valley of Oaxaca and the Maya Lowlands.

The archaeological evidence of the development of complex political and economic systems in the Valley of Oaxaca has been extensively documented (Blanton 1978; Blanton et al. 1982; Drennan 1976; Flannery 1976; Flannery and Marcus 1983; Pires-Ferreira 1975; Whalen 1981). One interpretation suggests that the urban center of Monte Albán was founded as a disembedded capital during the Late Formative (Blanton 1978). Although the degree of centralization exhibited at Monte Albán varied from one time period to another, the capital probably continued to dominate valley politics until the end of the Classic period. Balkanization emerged in the wake of Monte Albán's collapse, a political climate that persisted until the Spanish conquest (Flannery and Marcus 1983).

Blanton's version of Oaxaca prehistory would imply that competition and warfare were primarily between the Zapotecs of the disembedded political authority at Monte Albán and polities outside the Valley of Oaxaca (Blanton 1978). An alternative interpretation offered by Sanders, Santley, and others contends that Monte Albán did not necessarily function as a disembedded capital and that the claim that it functioned as the valley's top-ranking central place from the Late Formative through the Classic can be questioned (Sanders and Santley 1978; Santley 1980, 1983b, c; Santley and Arnold 1984; Willey 1979). Instead, they suggest that a considerable amount of fighting among different polities within the valley continued following the Late Formative and that Monte Albán did not emerge as the eventual victor until relatively late in its history.

According to Kowalewski et al. (this volume), ballcourts first appeared in the Valley of Oaxaca in the Late Formative. Other lines of evidence, such as the building of monuments commemorating conquests at Monte Albán and San José Mogote (Flannery et al. 1981; Marcus 1980) and the construction of defensive walls at Monte Albán (Blanton 1978), indicate that the political climate during the Late Formative was characterized by fierce competition among centers. It appears that ballcourts were first built as a part of civic-ceremonial complexes in the Valley of Oaxaca at a time when fighting among polities had reached endemic proportions. The data also indicate that a number of major sites in the valley never had ballcourts, and except for the peak during the Terminal Formative, the number of courts in simultaneous use during different time periods was more or less the same. During most periods ballcourts were present at centers in the valley's three arms, a distribution which also characterized the Late Postclassic when the region was split into a number of warring statelets. Monte Albán, however, always had more courts than other sites (during the Late Classic eight of the fourteen courts in use were at Monte Albán), and within the site itself the largest ballcourt is found on the Main Plaza with smaller courts in outlying barrios.

In terms of the model of ballgame politicization presented earlier, the distribution of ballcourts suggests that the Late Classic political and economic system was highly centered on the capital of Monte Albán. The tiering in ballcourt sizes also implies that the elite at the Main Plaza were the top-ranking decision-making authority, a view also advanced by Blanton (1978). The proliferation of ballcourts in outlying barrios, on the other hand, would suggest that local elites still had a fair amount of economic (and perhaps political) power. The elite of district capitals may also have physically resided at Monte Albán, which would account for the lack of ballcourts at important secondary and tertiary centers. The model would therefore suggest that the

Late Classic Zapotec polity was centralized at the regional level, but that the political climate of the capital was characterized by greater competition or was more decentralized than the regional system as a whole. This interpretation is in keeping with the hypothesis that Monte Albán acted as a disembedded capital, in the sense that disembeddedness of political authority implies the existence of a number of allied political entities and associated elites of more or less equal rank. In the Early Classic, in contrast, more ballcourts occur at other valley centers than at Monte Albán (Kowalewski et al. this volume), and the region contains more large centers than it did in the Late Classic (Blanton et al. 1982), implying greater regional decentralization.

The political organization of the Late Classic Lowland Maya has been reconstructed from various bodies of epigraphic, iconographic, and settlement pattern data (Marcus 1976; Bullard 1960; Turner et al. 1981; R.E.W. Adams 1981). Most interpretations indicate that Maya political organization was decentralized and acephalous, predicated upon intensive agricultural production and control of redistribution (Adams and Smith 1981; Sanders 1981; Freidel 1981a). During the Late Classic, conditions of rapid population growth and the ultimate failure of the subsistence system imply that access to land and adequate agricultural produce was severely constrained and that a major portion of the population, including elites, may have been disenfranchised from the agricultural power base (Culbert 1988; Lowe 1985; Santley et al. 1986). Evidence that the Maya social structure was becoming more rigid, with less mobility and fewer opportunities for individuals to gain wealth and status, is reflected in mortuary patterning and skeletal evidence, which indicate marked differences in status, paleonutrition, and paleopathology (Haviland 1967; Rathje 1970; Saul 1973). Moreover, the epigraphic and iconographic evidence shows that the Late Classic Maya were continually involved in warfare and alliance formation and dissolution, which points to a high degree of local and regional competition among polities (Marcus 1976; Morley and Brainerd 1983).

This is a context in which we would expect the ballgame to be politicized. The number and distribution of ballcourts in the Maya Lowlands mirror the decentralized and highly competitive nature of the political system. Ballcourts in Belize, the Petén, and northern Yucatán are found at both major and minor centers, suggesting competition on the local, regional, and macroregional levels. Only the smallest, hamlet-sized communities lacked ballcourts. They are almost always located in or near the center's major civic-ceremonial complex. Exceptions to this pattern occur at Tikal and Chichén Itzá, which have at least five and nine courts, respectively (Carr and Hazard 1961; Ruppert 1952) (cf. Kurjack et al. this volume), and at Dzibilchaltún which lacks ballcourts (Kurjack 1974). Generally, late Postclassic sites in northern Yucatán also did not have ballcourts.

Epigraphic and material evidence from Tikal (W. Coe 1962) and Chichén Itzá (Ruppert 1952; Andrews and Robles 1985) indicate that they headed political systems that were probably more highly centralized and participated in a wider, more competitive macroregional system than neighboring centers. The greater frequency of ballcourts may reflect a greater degree of political centralization, with the elites of conquered lesser polities relocated at the major center, a pattern not unlike that for Monte Albán. Interpretations of the political climate of the northern Yucatán polities during the Late Postclassic do not suggest any decrease in competition. Arguments for increased mercantilism and coastal trade, however, imply that a switch to a broader-spectrum economic system may have provided increased opportunities for individual acquisition of wealth and status, thus reducing the need for politicized ballgames (Sabloff and Rathje 1975; M. Miller 1986). The absence of ballcourts at Dzibilchaltún can be interpreted in a similar manner. The site may have controlled the salt trade around the Yucatán Peninsula, and the ceramics show connections to Tabasco, Campeche, and Chiapas (E. Andrews 1981; A. Andrews 1983), indicating the Dzibilchaltún may have participated in a wider economic sphere than other Late Classic Lowland Maya centers.

Conclusions

The position advanced in this paper is that ballcourts functioned as facilities built for use by elites as an alternative means to acquire wealth and territory. Ballcourts occur in the archaeological record from several areas of Mesoamerica at times when regions were fragmented into competing political units, when local polities were apparently attempting to carve out tributary domains, and when access to agricultural production became more differential, implying disenfranchisement of segments of the population from the agrarian resource base. In each case, there is evidence as well that significant amounts of wealth and political power of the elite were not derived from the control of specialized production systems such as obsidian working or long-distance distribution networks. On the other hand, in the three cases where ballcourts are lacking (i.e., Middle Classic Teotihuacán, Classic period Dzibilchaltún, and Late Postclassic northern Yucatán), archaeological evidence suggests the presence of broader-spectrum political economies in which power was derived from control over both the agrarian base and alternative production-distribution systems.

Notes

1. A third pair of mounds occurs immediately to the east of the Tula Grande, the main acropolis, which may also be a ballcourt (Yadeun 1974).

2. Sahagún (1950–82) reports that the central enclosure at Tenochtitlán had two courts, called *tezcatlachco* (mirror ballcourt) and *teotlachco* (divine ballcourt) respectively. Both courts were situated in the large plaza directly west of the Temple of Ehécatl (Marquina 1951).

CHAPTER 2

Pre-Hispanic Ballcourts from the Valley of Oaxaca, Mexico

Stephen A. Kowalewski, Gary M. Feinman, Laura Finsten, and Richard E. Blanton

Introduction

Ballcourts are familiar features at the better-known archaeological sites in Oaxaca. They are easily recognized, at least the formal, I-shaped ones. Ballcourts have been reconstructed for the public at Monte Albán, Dainzú, and Yagul, and archaeologists have excavated four others at San Luis Beltrán, San José Mogote, and two more at Monte Albán.

Despite their ease of recognition and familiarity, the ballcourt's place in past cultural systems remains enigmatic. While I-shaped ballcourts are depicted frequently in the Mixtec codices, the Zapotec historical sources are almost silent on the subject; we must go farther afield, to the Aztecs, for accounts of how the game was played and what it meant. We cannot be sure that the game had the same meaning for people in Oaxaca in quite different cultural systems of earlier times.

The full-coverage regional survey we have recently completed found 32 more ballcourts in addition to the previously known corpus (Figure 2.1). The aims of this paper are to present basic data on all the ballcourts in the Valley of Oaxaca, to report on patterning in these data, and to draw connections between these patterns and variation in the regional cultural system. The study is limited to aspects of the general problem that are within the reach of our archaeological methods.

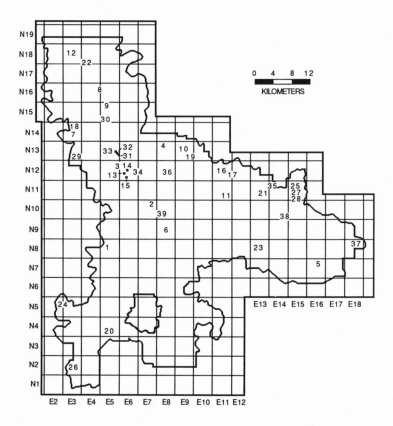

Figure 2.1. Distribution of all known Valley of Oaxaca ballcourts. Grid squares measure 4 km on a side. The numbers 1–39 show the locations of ballcourts and correspond to the case numbers in Tables 2.1 and 2.2.

Ballcourt Data

Full reports on the methods and results of our settlement survey are available elsewhere (Blanton 1978; Blanton et al. 1982; Kowalewski et al. 1989). Tables 2.1 and 2.2 present basic ballcourt data. A ballgame can be played on a flat surface without any standing architecture, as is the current game (Leyenaar 1978). Between these featureless plains and the variable I-shaped court are other possibilities, which we also include with notations.

The period of ballcourt use was determined from associated ceramics. We looked for sherds in mound fill wherever possible; then sherds on the structure; and, failing that, dates for adjacent areas or features. The dates listed are only those for which the associations are strong and positive. Approximate orientations are expressed in degrees east of true north. The regional boundary column describes whether the site is at the region's boundary during the time of its occupation (+), or not (−).

Dimensions of the ballcourt field or alleyway (in meters) are given in the next five columns of Table 2.1. The terminology is that of Satterthwaite (1944). The field length is the maximum length of the flat playing surface. The central field length lies between the two bars of the I. The field width is the distance between the two side mounds or walls at the center of the field. The end-field length is measured perpendicular to the long axis of the field, while the end-field width is perpendicular to that. Table 2.2 documents the available measurements (in meters) for the mounds that define the ballcourt features.

The notes that follow contain information that does not fit into Table 2.1. An important item discussed in the notes is the position of the ballcourt in its site and in relation to other mounds and plazas.

Monte Albán Late I and II (Formative Period) Courts

1. This is not an I-shaped ballcourt; it is defined only by two parallel side mounds that have similar dimensions. The greater site is a single component, Late Formative occupation, so this ballcourt would be an early one. The site is an isolated outlier of a cluster of Late I settlement. The main administrative center is in the middle of the settlement cluster, 400 m away. In form, dating, and relationship to the rest of the site this is an anomalous case.

2. The ballcourt at CE-AT-AT-1 is not quite I-shaped, but closer to that type than just two parallel mounds. It is attached to the southwest corner of a four-mound group near the center of the site. It might have been a subregional boundary site during the Late Formative.

3. The El Gallo site subdivision of Monte Albán has a single ballcourt attached to the west mound of its principle four-mound group.

4. San Luis Beltrán was investigated by Ignacio Bernal (1965:804). We assigned the ballcourt to Monte Albán IV on the strength of his conclusions. The major phases of occupation for the site and most of the mounds are Late I and V. The ballcourt is 50 m west of the main four-mound group, and adjacent to several plazas in the center of a considerably landscaped sector of the Late I and V sites.

5. Matatlán's ballcourt is in the low piedmont, within the modern town. This is noteworthy because the largest community ever in the Matatlán area, El Palmillo, was a Classic and Early Postclassic hilltop site that had no ballcourt. But in the Late and Terminal Formative, and in the Late Postclassic, this lower site was the area's main center. The ballcourt is 50 m south of a double quadrangular complex, and has the same orientation as that group. We found Early Monte Albán I, Late I, II, and V ceramics around the double

Table 2.1. Valley of Oaxaca Ballcourt Characteristics*

No.	Site	Structure No.	Age and Rank						Approx. Orientation (E of N)	Regional Boundary	Field Length (m)	Central Field Length (m)	Field Width (m)	End Field Length (m)	End Field Width (m)
			LI	II	IIIA	IIIB	IV	V							
1	ZI-CIE-CIE-15	2A,3A	III						0	+	x	31	14	m	m
2	CE-AT-AT-1	1,4,5	UN						10	−	m	21	m	x	x
3	Monte Albán (El Gallo)	EGT2	I			I			8	+	33	15	6	m	m
4	San Luis Beltrán	1	III				UN	III	93	+	43	23	8	24	10
5	Matatlán	4,5	V	UN					123	+	m	24	3	m	m
6	CE-SBC-SBC-9	7,8,13	IV	IV					105	−	36	26	10	m	3
7	ET-SFT-SFT-19	3	UN	V					90	+	36	29	5	19	4
8	Reyes Etla	10	IV	III		III		IV	9	−	43	36	8	24	4
9	San José Mogote	7S	II	II				V	0	−	42	27	6	24	9
10	Tlalixtac	5	UN	UN				II	100	+	40	40	3	25	m
11	Dainzú	BC	UN	II	II		II	I	111	−	m	m	m	m	m
12	Suchilquitongo	BC	II	II	III	II			87	+	30	m	4	10	m
13	Monte Albán (Main Plaza)	T1447	I	I	I	I	II		10	−	37	21	9	21	9
14	Monte Albán	T1456	I	I	I	I	II		101	−	37	20	7	27	8
15	Monte Albán (Siete Venado)	T1458	I	I	I	I	II	I	7	−	42	18	1	12	11
16	TL-TEO-TEO-25	1-3	UN	UN					110	+	m	26	9	x	x
17	TL-TEO-TEO-26	BC	UN	UN					113	+	m	m	11	m	m
18	ET-SFT-SFT-48	6	II	II		III			96	+	39	30	3	22	4

No.	Site	Units	LI	II	IIIA	IIIB	IV	V	±	LI est.	II est.	IIIA est.	IIIB est.	IV est.	V est.
19	CE-TLX-TLX-30	4			III		II		+	107	40	28	6	17	6
20	ZI-VDF-LB-3	BC		IV	VI				+	44	29	m	m	15	m
21	TL-SAV-SAV-2	5,6		IV	V				+	115	38	22	m	20	6
22	Tlaltinango	9		III	V	IV			+	3	m	44	8	m	m
23	San Bartolomé Quialana	1,2		IV	III				+	105	47	m	6	x	x
24	Santa Cruz Mixtepec	14		III	IV		IV		+	140	35	25	m	15	5
25	TL-VDO-SMV-3	1,2		VI	V	V	V		+	m	44	29	11	29	6
26	El Choco	8		IV			III		+	120	36	28	7	15	4
27	TL-VDO-VDO-12	8,9		UN			IV		+	101	42	34	7	22	3
28	TL-VDO-VDO-12	3-5		UN			IV		+	33	45	28	3	m	3
29	El Mirador	4	III						+	132	50	26	8	20	12
30	Loma Trapiche	6	II						−	175	34	26	5	30	4
31	Monte Albán (Azompa)	AZT3	I						−	5	27	9	3	9	5
32	Monte Albán (Azompa)	AZT448	I						−	8	44	26	5	22	8
33	Monte Albán (Azompa)	AZT449	I						−	97	28	x	8	x	x
34	Monte Albán	T1177	I				I		−	86	87	70	24	36	18
35	TL-SAV-SAV-9	4				V			+	14	m	35	5	m	m
36	Loma Montura	6,8				III			−	14	m	30	6	x	x
37	Cerro Guirún	7				V	VII		+	22	31	21	8	18	5
38	Yagul	25					II		−	112	47	30	6	27	8
39	CE-SMC-SMC-20	2					II		−	106	36	30	10	37	3

*LI—Monte Albán Late I, Late Formative, 300–100 B.C.; II—Monte Albán II, Terminal Formative, 100 B.C.–A.D. 250; IIIA—Monte Albán IIIA, Early Classic, 250–500; IIIB—Monte Albán IIIB, Late Classic, 500–650; IV—Monte Albán IV, Epiclassic or Early Postclassic, 650–850; V—Monte Albán V, Late Postclassic, 850–1520. The Roman numerals in these six columns give the position of the site in the regional population hierarchy during that phase. Population estimates depend on site area or such features as countable household clusters. Each phase is ranked independently, Rank I sites being the largest of the phase. UN—'unranked', a site with fewer than 100 inhabitants; X—absence of a feature; m—missing data.

Table 2.2. Mound Measurements (in Meters) of Valley of Oaxaca Ballcourts*

No.	Site	Structure No.	North Mound Base l*	w	Top l	w	Hgt
1	ZI-CIE-CIE-15	2A,3A	x	x	x	x	x
2	CE-AT-AT-1	1,4,5	x	x	x	x	x
3	Monte Albán (El Gallo)	EGT2	m	m	m	m	m
4	San Luis Beltrán	1	25	15	20	11	4
5	Matatlán	4,5	24	7	14	1	4
6	CE-SBC-SBC-9	7,8,13	27	15	14	3	1
7	ET-SFT-SFT-19	3	29	10	23	5	1
8	Reyes Etla	10	42	9	m	m	3
9	San José Mogote	7S	m	m	m	m	m
10	Tlalixtac	5	40	20	23	3	4
11	Dainzú	BC	m	m	m	m	m
12	Suchilquitongo	BC	x	x	x	x	x
13	Monte Albán (Main Plaza)	T1447	x	x	x	x	4
14	Monte Albán	T1456	x	x	x	x	m
15	Monte Albán (Siete Venado)	T1458	m	m	m	m	m
16	TL-TEO-TEO-25	1-3	26	13	16	2	2
17	TL-TEO-TEO-26	BC	42	16	36	3	1
18	ET-SFT-SFT-48	6	30	13	16	3	2
19	CE-TLX-TLX-30	4	28	5	20	2	3
20	ZI-VDF-LB-3	BC	m	m	m	m	2
21	TL-SAV-SAV-2	5,6	24	8	20	2	2
22	Tlaltinango	9	m	m	m	m	m
23	San Bartolomé Quialana	1,2	36	12	18	1	4
24	Santa Cruz Mixtepec	14	18	15	12	9	4
25	TL-VDO-SMV-3	1,2	29	11	20	4	2
26	El Choco	8	x	x	x	x	x
27	TL-VDO-VDO-12	8,9	35	20	20	2	3
28	TL-VDO-VDO-12	3-5	36	7	15	2	1
29	El Mirador	4	28	5	m	m	1
30	Loma Trapiche	6	45	9	36	5	6
31	Monte Albán	AZT3	x	x	x	x	2
32	Monte Albán (Azompa)	AZT448	23	7	16	2	5
33	Monte Albán	AZT449	29	8	19	5	5
34	Monte Albán	T1177	x	x	x	x	1
35	TL-SAV-SAV-9	4	m	m	m	m	m
36	Loma Montura	6,8	x	x	x	x	x
37	Cerro Guirún	7	x	x	x	x	x
38	Yagul	25	30	14	26	4	4
39	CE-SMC-SMC-20	2	30	17	18	2	5

*l = length; w = width; x = feature absent; m = missing data.

| East Mound | | | | | South Mound | | | | | West Mound | | | | |
| Base | | Top | | | Base | | Top | | | Base | | Top | | |
l	w	l	w	Hgt	l	w	l	w	Hgt	l	w	l	w	Hgt
31	11	21	4	2	x	x	x	x	x	31	11	21	4	2
25	12	m	m	3	x	x	x	x	x	21	17	19	5	3
33	12	17	3	3	m	m	m	m	m	25	12	9	3	5
35	11	23	1	2	23	15	9	3	4	32	10	27	2	2
21	6	14	3	1	24	7	14	3	3	26	8	18	1	1
30	m	m	m	1	25	18	13	3	1	37	7	16	2	1
30	10	19	2	1	30	10	24	5	1	30	10	20	2	1
36	17	21	3	3	42	9	20	2	3	36	17	21	3	3
m	m	m	m	m	m	m	m	m	m	m	m	m	m	m
20	10	15	1	2	36	25	24	10	2	20	10	15	1	2
m	m	m	m	m	m	m	m	m	m	m	m	m	m	m
x	x	x	x	x	x	x	x	x	x	x	x	x	x	x
21	m	18	m	10	x	x	x	x	4	21	m	21	m	9
x	x	x	x	m	x	x	x	x	m	x	x	x	x	m
m	m	21	5	2	m	m	m	m	m	m	m	16	7	4
18	10	12	2	1	26	13	16	2	2	x	x	x	x	x
x	x	x	x	x	42	16	36	3	1	x	x	x	x	x
15	8	11	5	2	27	13	16	2	2	13	5	11	2	1
17	4	9	2	2	28	5	20	2	3	17	4	9	2	2
15	m	m	m	2	m	m	m	m	2	15	m	m	m	m
20	4	20	2	1	22	10	18	2	2	20	1	20	1	1
44	m	40	15	4	m	m	20	5	m	44	m	40	7	2
x	x	x	x	x	43	12	17	2	2	x	x	x	x	x
25	m	m	m	2	18	15	12	9	4	25	m	m	m	2
x	x	x	x	x	29	12	20	4	2	x	x	x	x	x
28	15	23	4	3	x	x	x	x	x	28	15	23	4	3
x	x	x	x	x	34	20	16	2	3	x	x	x	x	x
28	8	16	2	3	x	x	x	x	x	28	17	16	2	3
35	10	20	2	3	28	5	m	m	1	35	10	18	2	3
26	15	15	5	6	45	9	36	5	6	26	15	15	5	6
19	6	14	2	3	x	x	x	x	m	x	x	x	x	m
25	8	17	2	5	x	x	x	x	2	27	15	20	11	7
x	x	x	x	x	m	m	24	m	8	m	m	m	m	m
x	x	x	x	x	34	7	15	1	2	x	x	x	x	x
35	3	m	m	2	m	m	m	m	m	35	3	m	m	2
30	17	28	4	4	x	x	x	x	x	38	15	30	12	4
21	10	20	2	4	21	9	18	2	2	21	10	20	2	4
m	2	m	1	2	30	14	26	4	5	x	x	x	x	7
37	10	30	4	1	29	15	18	2	5	m	m	m	m	m

quadrangle, which has the form of a Period V palace. Period V is well represented in this locale. We found only one Period V sherd at the ballcourt, but it may have been used at that time.

6. CE-SBC-SBC-9 was a low-order civic/ceremonial center from the Middle to Terminal Formative. The ballcourt is in the center of the site, attached to the south mound of a four-mound group. While not on the regional boundary, prior to the Early Classic this might have been a boundary site for the Valle Grande subregion, as it faces the passes into the Tlacolula subregion.

7. The ballcourt at ET-SFT-SFT-19 is midway between and adjacent to two plazas and three platforms with the same orientation. Late I and II sherds were found on the ballcourt and other structures. Period V sherds occur on the site but not on the structures. The site is on the top of a ridge in the rugged piedmont, about 2 km south of a much larger hilltop site, case 18.

8. At Reyes Etla the ballcourt is roughly in the center of some thirty mounds, adjacent to the southwest corner of a four-mound group. The structure is between several plazas. We observed a 4.0- × 0.75- × 0.5-m stone on the eastern edge of the field.

9. The ballcourt at San José Mogote was excavated by Moser. Flannery and Marcus (1983:113) published a drawing and comments. The ballcourt was built into a massive platform defining the west side of the main plaza. The structure has the same orientation as other Period II temples and palaces on the plaza.

10. The ballcourt at Tlalixtac is the principal of several scattered mound groups. It shares the north mound of a four-mound group and has the same orientation as this and most of the rest of the structures at the site. It was near the west side of the settlement in Period V and rather isolated in the earlier periods.

11. The ballcourt at Dainzú has been excavated, and half of it reconstructed. Unfortunately we did not take measurements, and there are no published sources. Aveni (1980:313) measured an orientation for the ballcourt 'axis' of 196°22'. But the long axis of the field is in the opposite quadrant, east–west. Bernal's excavations in the archaeological zone found Late I, II, and IIIA materials. We mapped substantial settlement outside the archaeological zone and near the ballcourt from Late I, II, IIIA, IV, and V. Around the ballcourt are Monte Albán II and IIIA mounds, with about the same orientation. In these periods the ballcourt was at the center of the site in the main cluster of public architecture. The mounds to the west and south were unusually broad and flat-topped, and there is an elaborate residence adjacent to the west end of the ballcourt. In the Postclassic the ballcourt was toward the southern end of the town. In Monte Albán IV times the major construction was to the north near the International Highway, including two market and

administrative mound and plaza groups, but no new ballcourt construction.

12. The northernmost ballcourt in the survey area is at Suchilquitongo, a major boundary site from the Late Formative through the Late Classic. Suchilquitongo has two major and several minor mound groups. The ballcourt is within one of the major groups incorporated into a set of massive platforms. These buildings include a three-mound and a four-mound group. The field is sunken into the platform construction. The complex has a long history of rebuilding. A Period V reuse is possible, since there are materals from that phase at other structures of the same complex.

13. The Main Plaza ballcourt at Monte Albán had a long history of rebuilding, from as early as Late I through IIIB. Monte Albán Periods IV and V use is possible. This is a "sunken" ballcourt, with no end mounds (see Blanton 1978 for Main Plaza architectural and traffic flow patterns).

14. The excavated Terrace 1456 ballcourt at Monte Albán is adjacent to the house of Tomb 105. It has occupation from Late I to IIIB, and possibly IV and V. This is a sunken, I-shaped ballcourt.

15. This is the "Siete Venado" ballcourt at Monte Albán. It is within the Monte Albán Period IV portion of the city and is associated with pottery from Late I through IIIB and V. The ballcourt is attached to the east mound of a four-mound group.

16. This is an unusually isolated ballcourt from Period II. There is a Period II three-mound and plaza group with the same orientation on the hill 300 m to the west. Across the arroyo about 70 m away is a small Period V occupation. If the ballcourt were reused in Period V, it would have been at the western end of the Rank I Macuilxochitl site. The ballcourt's western end is open and the field may be slightly sunken.

17. TL-TEO-TEO-26 is about 2200 m east of the previous case. The ballcourt is at the north end of a small Period II site. The two green obsidian blades found and the substantial Period V settlement, beginning 100 m away, make a Period V use possible. If so, this ballcourt would have been near the western end of the Macuilxochitl Rank I site. There are no other mounds on the site, but a Period II four-mound group with a different orientation lies 750 m upslope.

18. At ET-SFT-SFT-48 the ballcourt is adjacent to a four-mound group with three plazas, within a string of mound and plaza groups along a narrow ridge line. The ballcourt's north mound is the south mound of the four-mound group. Structures, including the ballcourt, are perpendicular to the ridge line.

19. Another ballcourt in the Period V Tlalixtac sprawl is at CE-TLX-TLX-30. It was at the center of a Terminal Formative site and in the south-central part of the Period V town. On the west end of the ballcourt is a four-mound

group and on the other three sides are three plazas. The south plaza has two obsidian work areas.

20. ZI-VDF-LB-3 is a probable garrison in Period II that continues into the Early Classic. It is on a high mountain ridge separating the southern Valle Grande from the Ejutla Valley. The court's orientation is transverse to the narrow ridge like the other mounds at the site.

21. Late Postclassic settlement is extensive between Teotitlán and Santa Ana del Valle. There is also a Terminal Formative and Early Classic mound center with a ballcourt at TL-SAV-SAV-2. The ballcourt is attached to the south end of a four-mound group. The complex includes at least three other plazas, with the ballcourt's west mound acting as a retaining wall for one of them. Other mounds in this complex have Period V ceramics. If the ballcourt were reused in that phase, it would have been at the east end of the Macuil-xochitl Rank I center.

22. The main site at Tlaltinango runs from the edge of the modern town up into the hills to the north. The ballcourt is located in the northern part of the site. The southern sector also has mound groups, but no ballcourt. Structure 9 is flanked on the east by a plaza, which in turn is bordered by a three-mound group. On the opposite side of the ballcourt, 100 m to the west, is another large platform and mound group, so the ballcourt is between two major architectural foci.

Monte Albán IIIA and IIIB (Classic Period) Courts

23. San Bartolemé Quialana is mainly a Period IIIA site. The ballcourt, terraces, and other structures are oriented transversely to the axis of a broad ridge. The ballcourt is between two mound and plaza groups, closer to the larger one, roughly in the center of the site. It is probably not I-shaped; the central field is closed at the east and west ends by low walls connecting the corners of the side mounds.

24. Santa Cruz Mixtepec, another hilltop site, has a ballcourt within a linear arrangement of mounds and plazas on the narrow, principal ridge. As at El Choco, the ballcourt is "downtown," where downtown is actually up, and most of the site's inhabitants lived on residential terraces on the lower slopes. Access to the ballcourt would have been difficult.

25. TL-VDO-SMV-3 in Monte Albán V was part of a sprawling, discontinuous settlement along the Díaz Ordaz tributary stream. In this period there were three other mounded structures within 150 m of the ballcourt. The situation was different in Monte Albán IV, when the site was at the southern end of a smaller cluster, and in IIIA when it was a single small settlement. The ballcourt is an I-shaped structure, but the ends are terrace retaining walls,

not mounds. The western end is completely open, dropping to the terrace below. We do not have a measured orientation, but it is approximately east–west.

26. El Choco's ballcourt is I shaped but without end mounds, either because they were plowed down or because the field was sunken into a platform. It is oriented along a narrow ridge, in the built-up area on the highest part of this hilltop site. In the Early Classic and Late Postclassic it was located between two administrative/ceremonial mound and plaza complexes. While we did not find Monte Albán IV pottery at the structure, it occurs in other mounds. This phase had a substantial occupation, so a Monte Albán IV use of the ballcourt seems likely.

27. The ballcourt at TL-VDO-VDO-12 is 350 m south of the previous case. In IIIA the site was a single isolate, and in the Late Postclassic it was part of the same large sprawl as above. No other mounds are nearby. The ends have retaining walls, not mounds, and the west end is open.

28. TL-VDO-VDO-12 Structures 3–5 are 1 km south of the previous case, toward the south end of the Period V sprawl. The ballcourt is adjacent to a two-mound and plaza group with the same orientation. The ballcourt has three mounds; the south end is open and overlooks an arroyo.

29. El Mirador is a Late Classic site in the mountains west of Monte Albán. The ballcourt is midway along a string of one- and two-mound and plaza groups on the ridge line. Its long axis parallels the ridge line.

30. Loma del Trapiche is a major Late Classic center on a low hill just above the valley floor. The site has several scattered mound groups in addition to major northern and southern groups. The ballcourt is between two plazas in the middle of the southern string of mounds. The northern string has a four-mound group.

31. This is a ballcourt on the same terrace as an unexcavated single mound and an excavated elaborate residence. It is almost adjacent to the main Azompa ballcourt (case 32), off the southeast corner of the huge platform on which the most important buildings were constructed. The surfaces above the ballcourt, except for the east mound, are slopes rather than mounds.

32. The main Azompa ballcourt has been excavated, exposing niches in the northeast and southwest corners and plaster surfaces on all four mounds and the floor.

33. The Azompa Terrace 449 ballcourt is another structure with a less than full I shape. The structure is built across a steep slope and its ends are open. It was built next to a terrace that has an elaborate residence. This terrace in turn is just below Terrace 8, part of the main mound complex on the top of the hill.

34. This is the most dubious ballcourt in the sample: extremely long, unusually wide, and not entirely I shaped. It is the only ballcourt at Monte Albán not near an elaborate residence, adjoining instead an open plaza.

Monte Albán IV and V (Postclassic) Courts

35. TL-SAV-SAV-9 is on top of the mountain above the case 21 site. We found IIIA sherds on the site, but they were not apparent on the mounded structures. The major occupation was in Period IV. Period V, when this was a Rank III center, saw the reuse of several mounds and possibly the ballcourt. The mounds and plazas are along the flattened ridge top, oriented transversely to the ridge line. The ballcourt is midway between an area of more open public plazas, terraces, and mounds to the east, and a secluded four-mound group to the west.

36. Loma de la Montura is an Early Postclassic hilltop site. Structures 6 and 8 form a possible ballcourt, but it is not I shaped and not precisely symmetrical. It shares the west mound of a four-mound group in the main civic/ceremonial part of the site. Its position is between a temple plaza group atop a hill to the west and the administrative area around the four-mound group.

37. The Cerro Guirún is east of Mitla. Its ballcourt adjoins the south side of a four-mound group, so there is no north mound and the end-field is limited by a stone wall. This complex was probably the largest of several mound groups at the site. It is located roughly in the middle of the site.

38. Yagul's ballcourt was excavated in the 1950s (Wicke 1957; Bernal and Gamio 1974). Wicke states that few sherds were found in the excavations and argued for a Late Postclassic date. This is how we coded the structure in Table 2.1. There is Late I, II, IIIA, and IV occupation around and within the huge platform on which the Late Postclassic structures are built, so an earlier use is not precluded. In these earlier phases Yagul was an administrative center. The Period V complex is the best understood. In that phase the ballcourt was at the center of the congested, acropolis-like complex. On its southeast is a four-mound group, and to the west is a closed temple plaza. To the north, across a small plaza, rises the Palace of the Six Patios.

39. CE-SMC-SMC-20 is a small site with three structures and virtually no surface sherds. We consider it "undated." The ballcourt and the two other structures all have the same orientation and form a long string. The other sites in the vicinity date primarily to Period V and to a lesser extent to Late I and IIIA. The orientation and dimensions are similar to the Late I ballcourt at CE-SBC-SBC-9 (case 6), about 4 km to the south, but these attributes are not reliably time dependent. If this were a Late I structure, it could have been on a subregional boundary, but as a Monte Albán V occupation it would not have been on a boundary.

Analysis

The earliest ballcourts in the valley could date to Late Formative, Monte Albán Late I times. There are 15 with Late I dates, though in some cases the chronological placement could be questioned. Eight cases away from Monte Albán have both Monte Albán Late I and II dates, and perhaps Late I materials were incorporated in some of these Period II constructions. Two sites (Animas Trujano and La Ciénega) have only Late I materials, but their ballcourts do not have the classic I shape.

By Monte Albán II there is no doubt. There are 15 sites with ballcourts, not counting those at Monte Albán. Two of the excavated examples have stages dating to Monte Albán II. Period II is a high point for ballcourts in the Valley (there are 18); the frequency drops in the Classic (14) and Postclassic (10 Early and 14 Late).

No criteria of form separate the earlier ballcourts from the later ones. Between the Formative and later periods, orientations and field dimension are not statistically separable and we see no qualitative changes in form.

In Period V fields tend to be slightly longer. We thought this might be due to rebuilding of older courts, but field widths are no different in Period V, and there are no statistical differences in field dimensions between long-occupied and briefly occupied ballcourts.

Long axis orientations are plotted in Figure 2.2. Most ballcourts were aligned a few degrees east of north or at right angles to that. There is no east–west or north–south preference and orientation tendencies do not vary by time period. For the two quadrants independently the mean azimuths are 11° and 107° (S.D. 12.5° and 13.7°). If the east–west orientations are converted to north–south, the average is 15° east of north. The ballcourts are aligned no differently than most other structures. They are aligned around a general Mesoamerican north, or at right angles to it. Figure 2.2 is little different from Aveni's data (1980:235) showing the main axes of Mesoamerican ceremonial centers. The wide spread of orientations about the mean is greater than expected, even given our measurement error, if precise orientation were important for those who laid out the structures.

More than half the ballcourts are located on the regional boundary. A few others are at possible subregional boundaries in certain periods. Twenty-two of the 31 non-Monte Albán ballcourt sites are on the edge of the region. In Late I and IIIB there are more ballcourts in the interior, while Monte Albán II and IIIA have high frequencies of ballcourts on the regional boundary.

Most ballcourts, in all phases except IIIB, are found in lower ranking centers. About 60–70 percent of the ballcourt sites are Rank III and lower. Most of these lower ranking sites are situated on the edge of the region. Yagul,

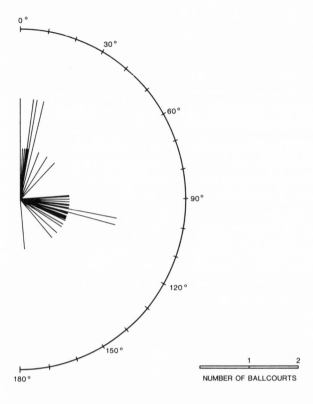

Figure 2.2. Plot of long axis orientations (from true north) for Valley of Oaxaca ballcourts.

Dainzú, Loma del Trapiche, San José Mogote, and Reyes Etla are nonboundary ballcourt sites that were major subregional capitals. Thus almost all Valley of Oaxaca ballcourts are at regional boundary sites or are at regional or subregional capitals.

While boundary, regional, or subregional capital locations are favored for ballcourts, not all boundary sites or capitals have ballcourts. The list of important sites with no apparent ballcourts includes Magdalena Apasco, Cacaotepec, Noriega, Xoxocotlán, Cuilapan, Zaachila, Trinidad, San Martín Tilcajete, Jalieza, Santa Inés Yatzeche, Tejas de Morelos, Tlapacoyan, San Pedro Mártir, Abasolo, Tlacochahuaya, the Teitipacs, Lambityeco, Tlacolula, and Mitla, to mention a few. All were administrative and demographic centers as large or larger than most of the sites with ballcourts.

Field lengths vary from a low of 27 m at Azompa to a high of 87 m at Terrace 1177 at Monte Albán. The mean, excluding T1177, is 38 m, and 20 of 29 cases fall between 36 and 47 m. Of those with field lengths less than 36 m, most were constructed in complexes where the available space was constrained by other structures, as at Azompa, El Gallo, Suchilquitongo, and Loma del Trapiche, or where narrow ridges made a longer court difficult to build, as at Santa Cruz Mixtepec or ZI-VDF-LB-3. Four of the cases with the shortest field lengths also have orientations more than one standard deviation away from the mean for either north or east. Thus it was possible to alter not only the length but the orientation if the overall architectural design so dictated.

Center field length averages 26.8 m (S.D. 6.9 m). Fifteen cases have center field lengths between 26 and 30 m, a frequent mode. Five of the six shortest center fields are at Monte Albán.

Center field width varies from 1 to 14 m, not including Terrace 1177. The distribution is flat, with five cases at 3 m and six at 8 m. Width is thus more variable than field length or central field length. It is probably more susceptible to error caused by erosion (cf. Drennan 1979:189), but the flat distribution still suggests variability rather than conformance.

End fields are present in two-thirds of the sample, and again their dimensions vary considerably. Lengths range from 9 to 37 m, with a mean of 21.6 m; widths range from 3 to 12 m, with a mean of 6.1 m. Quite legitimate ballcourts are found at both ends of these ranges.

The side and end mounds are more difficult to study statistically. However, a good indicator of the massiveness of ballcourt construction is the mound height above the playing surface. The average height is between 2 and 3 m, with a few as low as 1 m and one, the Main Plaza ballcourt at Monte Albán, at 7 m. At the low end of the range are ballcourts at small and administratively low-ranking sites (CE-SBC-SBC-9, TL-TEO-TEO-26, and ET-SFT-SFT-19). The most massive examples come from Rank I and II sites (Monte Albán, Azompa, El Gallo, Loma del Trapiche). Scale of construction thus varied with position in the regional hierarchy.

All ballcourts, except the dubious structure at ZI-CIE-CIE-15, are in one of three specific contexts. More than half the ballcourts are adjacent to complexes in which three or four mounds more or less tightly enclose a small courtyard. Public plazas are sometimes still visible next to these closed groups. Other ballcourts that were not adjacent to three- or four-mound groups were nonetheless components of complex architectural groupings: San José Mogote, Loma del Trapiche, ET-SFT-SFT-19, and perhaps Dainzú. Complex architectural groupings, especially the enclosed mound and plaza features, seem to be material remains of state administrations. The evidence for this inference is based on their prominent placement in known political centers such as Monte Albán and Mitla, sixteenth-century descriptions of still-functioning palaces at Mitla, central location within settlements, enclosure, public character, architectural standardization, high-status tombs, stone sculpture, costly ceramics, urns, and obsidian. A majority of Oaxacan ballcourts are adjacent to these state administrative buildings. The rest are in more ambiguous contexts, some of which might be part of the state apparatus.

Some cases, including El Choco, Santa Cruz Mixtepec, El Mirador, ZI-VDF-LB-3, and perhaps San Bartolomé Quialana, are on narrow ridges where the architecture consists of single- or double-mound and plaza groups strung out along the ridge line. The ballcourt is usually midway along this linear arrangement. Conceivably this is an adaptation of the more complex architectural grouping to mountainous terrain.

Five more sites without the three- or four-mound groups are low-ranking or unranked villages with small ballcourts (cases 16, 17, 25, 27, and 39). There might be a Period V tendency among them, in which the ballcourt sites would be constituents of the large dispersed settlements characteristic of the phase. However, two of these sites also have IIIA sherds and two have some from Period II. The Period II courts could be associated with three- and four-mound groups 300 and 750 m away.

Discussion

Oaxaca and adjoining Tehuacán, and to a lesser extent Chiapas, Puebla, and Morelos, have the earliest good evidence for ballcourts in Mesoamerica (Taladoire 1981:335, 338; Agrinier this volume). Indeed the time when the regional context of ballcourts seems clearest in Oaxaca is the Terminal Formative, after a possible but poorly known Late Formative origin.

The Terminal Formative peak in ballcourt construction occurs at a significant moment in political evolution. Marcus, Spencer, Redmond, and Drennan have contributed to what is now known about the Terminal Formative Zapotec "empire," its margins, and its extent (summarized in Flannery and Marcus 1983); our project has described the empire in its core in the Valley of Oaxaca. Earlier, in the Middle Formative, political units in Oaxaca were small regional chiefdoms. In Monte Albán I times some regions, including the valley, underwent considerable hierarchical growth. There was an increase in the public display of individual, named war captives. Around the end of this period political units had become large enough and sufficiently centralized so that not only conquest, but subjugation and transformation of conquered regions became feasible. This was marked by more fortification and the display of stone monuments on which named places, not just individuals, are shown as conquered. One of several extra-valley regions conquered by the valley state was the Cuicatlán Cañada, but the Zapotecs did not extend militarily into Tehuacán.

Within the valley, our studies show that the Terminal Formative had a small percentage of its rural population living near the edge of the region, com-

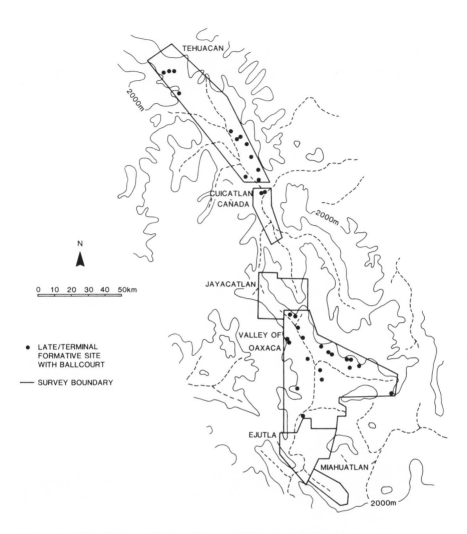

Figure 2.3. Distribution of Late and Terminal Formative ballcourts from Tehuacán, Puebla, to Miahuatlán, Oaxaca.

pared to other periods. But the sites that were on the boundary were relatively large compared to other periods. Period II had a higher percentage of its "formal" architecture (the closed, three- or four-mound groups) on the edge of the region than in other phases. Thus boundary activities were carried out from a small number of central places with administrative architecture.

The ballcourt sites on Figure 2.3 are all those dating to the Late and Terminal Formative, based on surveys of an almost continuous strip 270 km long (MacNeish et al. 1972; Drennan 1979; Drennan and Nowack 1984; Redmond 1981; Spencer 1982; Drennan and Vásquez Cruz 1975; our project; Feinman

1985; Markman 1981). The map shows a cluster in the northern Tehuacán Valley, separated by about 40 km from a second group at the southern narrow end of the valley. Included in this cluster are two ballcourt sites in the northern Cuicatlán area. To the south there is another 70-km area with no ballcourts. The Valley of Oaxaca ballcourt sites are strung along the northern valley margin, a pattern even more pronounced if the Monte Albán Late I cases are removed. There is only one Period II ballcourt in the southern valley; none occur in Ejutla or Miahuatlán.

The ballcourt clusters are not simply coterminous with settlement. Towns and villages are in general spread evenly over the area, usually along the major and tributary streams. The ballcourt sites tend to be situated differently, on higher, potentially defendable ground. Many ballcourt sites have the remains of fortification walls.

The northernmost ballcourt sites in the Cuicatlán Cañada are the fortified communities above Quiotepec and the canyon of the Río Santo Domingo, the traditional route to Tuxtepec and Veracruz. Quiotepec was the frontier of the Monte Albán empire. To the north, the next ballcourt site is at Tecomovaca, the southern frontier of the Tehuacán region, never conquered by the Zapotecs.

We conclude that the peak of ballcourt building in the Terminal Formative was part of the growth of specialized military institutions formed in the context of expanding regional states. Redmond already has made a similar point relating ballplaying to soldiery (1981:183–186), citing Borhegyi to the same effect.

Interregional military conflict was present earlier, but by the Terminal Formative its organization had increased in scale and complexity. Emergent states were able to perpetuate profound changes in regional settlement patterns and redirect regional economies. Military conquest and defense against other similarly organized polities required permanent, specialized institutions. The form of fortifications points to mass participation in war.

Staging points and outposts were necessary in this system, both on the frontiers and in the important towns at home. Ballcourts were probably a frequent feature at such places. Ballplaying perhaps occupied idle time, helped maintain readiness, reinforced state and elite ideology among key cadres, trained people to take punishment, and provided a ritually appropriate setting for torture and execution.

Subjugation of conquered peoples and administration of territory by the state required an administrative apparatus, which was reflected in special architectural complexes since the Middle Formative. These complexes proliferated and some became much more elaborate during the period of hierarchical growth in the Late Formative. By the Terminal Formative the administrative architecture of the state is also associated with ballcourts, at the regional and subregional capitals, and on the frontier, but rarely if ever in the nonmilitarized interior.

We have focused on the Terminal Formative peak in ballcourt construction because it offers the best interpretive possibilities. After this time ballplaying continued, undergoing changes and revivals in different circumstances. One is reminded of gladiatorial contests, jousting, the Olympics, and Oriental martial arts for cross-cultural parallels of games with similar origins and subsequent redefinitions (Weigand this volume).

After the Terminal Formative, the strong frontier pattern diffused in all of the areas in Figure 2.3. In the Early Classic the valley state no longer controlled the Cañada. Within the valley, the most active boundary switched from the north to the south. All the southern ballcourts were in use at this time. After the Early Classic the ballcourts were less likely to occur in frontier settlements; they were often found in larger towns in the interior. Regional boundaries tended to be more permeable (Kowalewski et al. 1983). Throughout the Classic and Postclassic ballcourts maintained their associations with state and military administrations, whether at regional or subregional boundaries or important centers in the interior.

A major theme of the 1985 ballcourt conference was the role of the game in the symbolic expression and resolution of conflict; that is, as a boundary mechanism (e.g., Fox this volume; Gillespie this volume). Ballcourts as geographical boundary phenomena are clear for the Terminal Formative, less so for later. But another sense of "boundary" emphasized at the conference is the contact between the usually hierarchically organized segments of complex societies, or internal boundaries (see also Trinkhaus 1987). Perhaps the larger and more complex states of the Classic and Postclassic required institutions such as ballplaying to mediate between their internal constituents. We suggest that the ballgame on formal courts functioned mainly for external boundary maintenance in the early periods, but later its role was enlarged to include mediation of competition between internal segments.

Why was the ballgame so widespread (yet variable) and perdurable, to the extent that it helps define a culture area (Kirchhoff 1943)? The answer lies in a nascent theory of macroregions or world systems (e.g., Blanton et al. 1981; Blanton and Feinman 1984; Mathien and McGuire 1986; Renfrew and Cherry 1986). What makes a macroregion is the interdependence among its smaller scale parts: states, cities, trade organizations, etc. In early village life in the Americas, culture areas were formed through the interaction spheres that drew emerging elite of ranked societies into a common competitive arena. In a broad Mesoamerica, partly defined by the occurrence of ballcourts, the ballcourts are significant in the transmittal of information that crosses frontiers, even of regions with vastly different scales of organization, because the institutions involved are specifically designed for interregional and intersegmental communication. Their history transcends local perturbations, yet they are modified to serve the needs of particular regions: Witness the variation in both ballcourt form and social context from Snaketown to Chichén Itzá.

Note

We are grateful for the support given to the Valley of Oaxaca Settlement Pattern Project by the National Science Foundation, the Social Science Research Council, the City University of New York, Purdue University, the University of Arizona, the University of Georgia, and Arizona State University. Authority to carry out fieldwork, and valuable assistance, was granted by the Instituto Nacional de Antropología e Historia and the Centro Regional de Oaxaca, first directed by Manuel Esparza and then by Rogelio Gonzalez. We thank the many members of our field and lab crews, and the Oaxacans whose land we walked over. We thank Gisela Weis, who drafted the figures.

CHAPTER 3

And Then They Were Sacrificed: The Ritual Ballgame of Northeastern Mesoamerica Through Time and Space

S. Jeffrey K. Wilkerson

A few years before the arrival of the Spaniards, the Aztec Emperor, Moctezuma II, and Nezahualpili, the experienced ruler of Texcoco, played the ballgame to test a grim prophecy. As a famous sage, Nezahualpili had interpreted
the startling appearance of a comet in the east as a harbinger of destruction
for the Triple Alliance. Moctezuma declined to accept the explanation and
the ballgame was played to decide the validity of the revelation (Torquemada
1943 [I]:212–213).

As predicted, Moctezuma lost the game, and eventually his empire. It is
interesting to note, however, that two of the most powerful personages in
pre-Columbian Mexico sought knowledge of an uncertain future in one of the
most ancient and widespread rituals of the Mesoamerican world.

In general, playing *tlachtli* was a prerogative of the elite. Although played
by mortals, the outcome was thought to be controlled by the gods alone. By
virtue of imitation it was a mode of communication with the supernatural
originators of the "game." In most respects, it was considered a ritual reenactment first and a game of divine chance second. Sacred for millenia, its
roots can be sought eastward on the gulf coast, in the direction of Moctezuma's
perplexing comet, were the metropolitan center of Classic civilization was El
Tajín.

A Chronological Summary

A series of subculture areas characterized the lowland portions of eastern Mesoamerica (Wilkerson 1974). These areas changed with time as the result of cultural processes that led ultimately to the florescence of successive regions. It is interesting to note that the four major areas north of the Isthmus of Tehuantepec attained their point of florescence in sequential order. Running from south to north, and extending from the end of the Early Formative period through the Late Postclassic, each subarea achieved a cultural apogee.

The southern gulf area (Figure 3.1) appears to have obtained its greatest expression, dynamism, and impact during the latter portion of the Early Formative period and the beginning of the Middle Formative. At this time the major Olmec centers of San Lorenzo, La Venta, Laguna de Los Cerros, and Tres Zapotes flourished primarily in the southern portion of the area. The influence of these centers extended, seemingly, in all directions. Along the

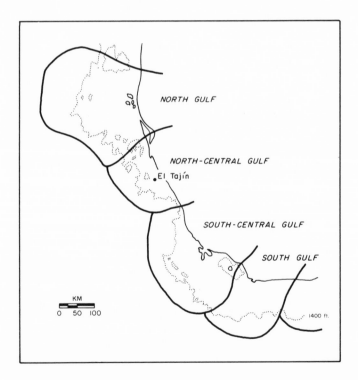

Figure 3.1. Cultural subareas of the Mesoamerican gulf coast, Late Formative–Postclassic Periods (after Wilkerson 1974).

Figure 3.2. Stela from Tepatlaxco, Veracruz.

gulf coast the Olmec presence and influence began to affect the direction of culture change, as throughout much of Mesoamerica. None of these sites, however, has positively identified ballcourts or ballgame depictions.

With the demise of Olmec culture sometime during the Middle Formative, the adjoining area immediately to the north, south-central Veracruz, reveals a period of intense activity, population concentration, and site construction. During this period of florescence small centers, such as Cerro de las Mesas and Lerdo de Tejada, largely north of Tres Zapotes begin an intensification that culminates at the sprawling site of Cerro de las Mesas. There, stone and ceramic sculpture and long count dates indicate a new peak of cultural complexity. Following an apparent fragmentation of larger, centralized social units during the Early Classic period, social diversification is manifested by a proliferation of cults as represented by the abundance of ceramic sculpture (Wilkerson 1968).

The earliest known stone yokes have been encountered throughout this subarea. Numerous fragments have been found in undated deposits or in surface finds at sites up to 1000-m elevation; for instance, at "Coatepec Viejo." At Buena Vista, 400 m in elevation, fragments were found in a clear Middle

Formative context (Berta Cuevas pers. comm.). Far southward at nearly sea level and dating to a comparable time, depictions on a stela near Lerdo de Tejada (Figure 3.2) show a yoke-like object being tied on the waist of a ball player. It seems virtually certain that the ritual ballgame was widely practiced throughout this subarea. It also appears that the paraphernalia necessary for participation was already sufficiently important to be depicted on sculpture and to accompany burials.

By the Late Classic, the region of north-central Veracruz begins its period of florescence. There, the great site of El Tajín becomes the center of a state that extended its influence throughout that area and into adjoining regions of both the highlands and the lowlands (Wilkerson 1972). In several respects, the florescence in north-central Veracruz exceeds in intensity and in social centralization the earlier apogees in the areas to the south.

The ballgame ritual greatly intensifies during this period, reaching a peak that may not have been equaled anywhere else in Mesoamerica. Ballcourts are ubiquitous at centers throughout the north-central gulf area. Vertical-wall courts come into being and are particularly popular in the immediate region of El Tajín. Yokes, *palmas*, and *hachas* greatly proliferate and become common offerings in elite burials throughout the subculture area. In general, the ballgame and everything associated with it assume central roles at Tajín culture sites (Wilkerson 1971).

Sometime following what can be described as a brief Epiclassic period, perhaps extending from A.D. 900 to nearly 1100, there is an eclipse of the Tajín culture brought about by intrusive migration and conflict. The north gulf area, which had earlier felt the influence of El Tajín, began its expansion and florescence. This was a period of extensive trade along the gulf coast and of culture contact between the Lowlands and the Highlands. The Huastec inhabitants of the region became very influential in the events of northern Mesoamerica and along the gulf coast, like their Tajín predecessors. This florescence was in the process of further intensification when suppressed by the Aztec conquest in the fifteenth century and the slightly later Spanish conquest of the early sixteenth century.

The Ballcourts at El Tajín

Scores of sites throughout the north-central subculture area built ballcourts during the Classic period, but only at El Tajín are there *at least* 11 ballcourts. Three were vertical-wall courts located on the valley floor of the site (Figure 3.3); two of these have sculptured panels at the ends and centers. The other courts have sloping walls and at least one of this variety had sculptures located at the same end and center points. All courts had "endzones" giving them a

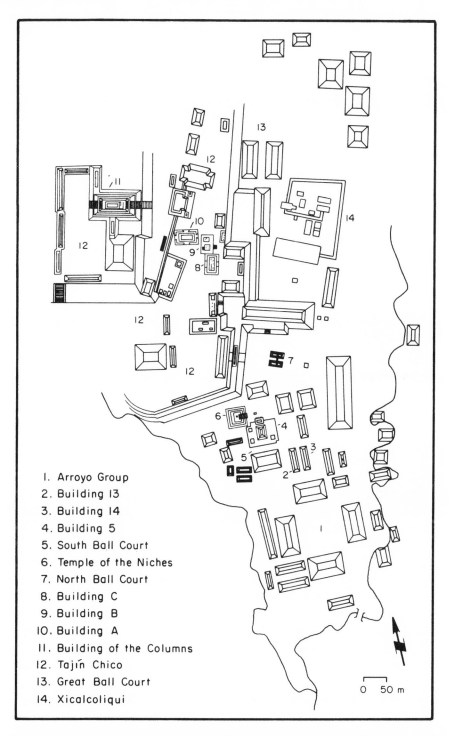

1. Arroyo Group
2. Building 13
3. Building 14
4. Building 5
5. South Ball Court
6. Temple of the Niches
7. North Ball Court
8. Building C
9. Building B
10. Building A
11. Building of the Columns
12. Tajín Chico
13. Great Ball Court
14. Xicalcoliqui

0   50 m

Figure 3.3. The central portion of El Tajín (after Wilkerson 1976).

"capital I" form in plan view. In one instance overlapping endzones may have existed; that is, two courts were established at right angles to each other. In this configuration the South Ballcourt runs east–west and Court 13/14 north–south. The former is vertical walled and the latter sloping. The deliberate proximity clearly suggests linked ritual functions.

While excavation of the courts has focused primarily on two of the vertical-walled examples (the South and North Ballcourts), there is sufficient evidence to suggest that most of the courts were refurnished repeatedly and continued in use until the site ceased to function as a metropolitan center at the end of the Epiclassic.[1]

The original construction dates for the courts have yet to be determined with certainty, but architectural and sculptural contexts suggest the following rough breakdown: (1) four Early Classic courts (three sloping and one vertical walled); (2) five Late Classic courts (three sloping and two vertical walled); and (3) two Epiclassic courts (both sloping walled). There is little doubt that further exploration at the site will produce still more courts of both varieties and alter this very tentative listing.

Considerable care and effort were taken in the construction of the courts, particularly the vertical-walled variety. These courts were formed from huge sandstone flags quarried among the few outcroppings in the Oligocene Meson Formation of the region. One of these shaped flags is 11 m long and weighs upward of 10 metric tons (José García Payón, pers. comm. 1963). Their transport, placement in courses, and *in situ* carving at the site were major feats of pre-Columbian engineering. It is not by coincidence that these vertical-walled courts were situated in the center of the site, roughly along its main north–south axis, and in proximity to most major temple and palace complexes. As we will examine shortly, major rituals that go far beyond the ballgame are associated with these courts.

Ballcourt sizes vary greatly. Exclusive of endzones, vertical-walled courts range from 25 to 63 m in length. Sloping-walled courts also vary from 15 to 67 m in their central portions. Ground-level widths of the "playing area" of either variety vary from 6 to 12 m. Vertical-walled courts have less height than most of the sloping-walled courts, rising from 1 to 1.8 m above the "playing area." In general, the probable earlier courts (the North Ballcourt and those associated with the Xicalcoliqui complex) are smaller in all dimensions.[2]

Some courts, such as the North Ballcourt, were constructed and maintained as independent architectural units; others were built to share walls with major temples that faced other complexes (SB, 34/35, Great Ballcourt). Still others, such as those in Xicalcoliqui and 7/8, may have been originally independent units before being incorporated into a larger complex of buildings and walls.

At other north-central gulf area sites both forms of ballcourts occur, but never in numbers remotely comparable to the extraordinary concentrations found at El Tajín. Vertical-walled courts have been found at Yohualinchan and Vista Hermosa. Sparse archaeological evidence or historical documentation suggests such were also present at Santa Luisa, Mapilca, Cinco de Mayo, and Francisco Madero. Certainly, further excavation at the many unexplored sites of the region will result in verification of a wider pattern for this court form. Nevertheless, sloping courts are likely to be far more common.

No census of courts exists, but given the ubiquitous presence of such structures at even small sites, it would seem likely that there are more courts in the north-central gulf area than in any other subculture area of the gulf coast. Regardless of size, however, most sites have only one court. Even Aparicio, a major Late Classic and Epiclassic center south of El Tajín (and Tajín's possible political rival), appears to have only one principal court (sloping). In general, most courts in the region are small to medium sized by El Tajín standards. Only Aparicio and Yohualinchan have similar large courts.

The implication is that for the subculture area as a whole, the ballgame was extremely important; consequently considerable labor was expended in the construction of courts in the central portions of Classic sites. The presence of yokes and palmas as elite burial offerings throughout the area underscores the core importance of the ballgame ritual for those that governed.

Clearly, El Tajín was the regional focal point for the various cults associated with ballgame ritual, particularly those activities that took place in the vertical courts. It is reasonable to interpret that the successful growth of broad political and resource control emanating from El Tajín led to an increased number of elite satellite centers. These in turn expanded the practice of the ritual, so important at the metropolitan center itself.

Status and Rulership in the Rituals of El Tajín

Rituals involving sacrifice in the pre-Columbian world, including human sacrifice in the ballgame, are not purely religious in nature. They also function to allow public reaffirmation of power and to demonstrate the prerogatives of status. This is amply confirmed during the Postclassic period by the numerous descriptions of Aztec rulers beginning major sacrificial ceremonies, especially those that commemorated construction or warfare carried out at their request.

These actions are not simply the results of the dual civic and religious duties of pre-Columbian rulers. Sacrificial ballgame ritual serves a secular purpose in making the ruler visible doing what only he, or only he and a few

Figure 3.4. Roll-out depiction of one of Thirteen Rabbit's column scenes. Drawing by Richard Schlecht (Wilkerson 1980). Copyright National Geographic Society.

others, are permitted to do. Late Classic El Tajín provides a very specific example for the gulf coast.

The palace known as the Building of the Columns at the site has a series of carved pillars which commemorates an important ruler named Thirteen Rabbit. Dating is not precise, but on architectural and stylistic grounds they must be very late in the history of El Tajín—approximately tenth century. Each of the five columns has a series of three registers depicting distinct rituals, most of which are shown as exterior scenes. Several show human sacrifice but only one of these highly fragmented registers can be adequately reconstructed at this time.

The ceremony shown in that scene (Figure 3.4) is divided into three units: a central portion showing Thirteen Rabbit overseeing a sacrifice, and two flanking processions leading to the central activity. There are 16 participants in the ritual, all with name glyphs appearing above them. In the center, prominently seated on a lashed pole throne with his hands ritually crossed on his chest, is Thirteen Rabbit (11). He overlooks a recently completed sacrifice by decapitation and disembowelment (12). The headless torso lies supine on a low bench with its bowels spread upward over a wooden rack decorated with tassled maize plants. Two assistants flank the scene. One (13) steps on the lifeless body while the other (10), named Four Axe, speaks and holds ritual accoutrements associated with the ballgame. The depiction of the latter, including a specter, sash, and ball, suggests his role as Thirteen Rabbit's steward or noble attendant. The position of Thirteen Rabbit as the controller of

the ritual is further underscored by his feet placed directly on top of the victim's severed head. The dominance of Thirteen Rabbit over the sacrificed individual and the ritual itself is thus explicitly presented and is the major theme of the register. The presence of the ballgame paraphernalia may suggest that the locale depicted is a ballcourt; in fact, the scene may be immediately following the completion of the ballgame ritual.

The bifurcated procession around the core scene of sacrifice is secondary and supportive. Prisoners and their captors are shown in the lines of participants. The prisoners are mostly nude with little ornamentation. Their hands point upward to their name glyphs and sometimes those of their captors. Frequently, their hair is held by the captors in the traditional Mesoamerican symbol of conquest. These latter figures, clearly socially more important, are dressed in warrior attire and are often shown in larger proportions than their captives. Lest anyone overlook Thirteen Rabbit's personal involvement in the conquests, he is shown once more (6), this time holding the hair of a submissive prisoner. As the names of the captives, now largely eroded, are sufficiently significant to be shown along with Thirteen Rabbit and his major nobles, it is not unreasonable to assume that they are rulers of subjugated towns or provinces.

Although human sacrifice has definite religious overtones, this scene at El Tajín functions to enhance the power of Thirteen Rabbit. It commemorates secular conquest, hereditary prerogatives, and a social position in a ritual context. The multiple sacrifice of captives, probably following the ballgame

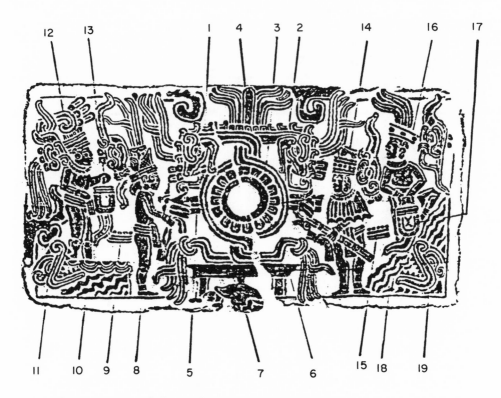

Figure 3.5. Carved altar or throne from Building 4, El Tajín.

ritual, symbolically reaffirms the two highly structured and essential institutions of rulership and religion. In format and purpose this ritual constitutes a harbinger of more grandiose ceremonies reported for the fifteenth century Aztecs.[3] Its occurrence, in so parallel a form, at the end of the Classic period suggests greater time depth for many rituals described for the last century of the Postclassic period in the Valley of Mexico. It also demonstrates the early participation of the cultures of the Veracruz coast in the broader institutionalization of multiple sacrifice.

There is still another remarkably explicit sculptural depiction that portrays the prerogatives of rulership within the ritual ballgame format of El Tajín (Figure 3.5). Found associated with Building 4, it is really stylistically and conceptually linked with the North Ballcourt. (The sculptural sequence of this earlier court is similar to the South Ballcourt, but focuses upon pulque and the rain god without the Venus cult.)

Seemingly an altar, it shows two serpents (1,2) intertwined to form a *tlax-*

malacatl, or ballgame marker (3). The marker is further modified by a spear bundle (5), a symbol of warfare in late Mesoamerican times. The tlaxmalacatl encircles a perforation that traverses the stone slab. The composite representation has a headdress duplicating the one always shown on the death deity rising from the *olla* in the South Ballcourt panels. The entire composition sits upon a throne (6) with a turtle (7) in the foreground.

To the left stands a figure (8) holding in his right hand the sash frequently associated with ballgame scenes at El Tajín. In his left hand is the same form of sacrificial knife seen brandished in two of the South Ballcourt scenes. The composite headdress contains a curled hand and the same cap shown in the sacrifice scene of the South Ballcourt. About the knees are the "protective bands" that form part of the prescribed gear for the ballgame. At the back of the figure is the number 19 in bars and dots. Presumably this is his name glyph from the calendar, or his ceremonial rank in the ritual portrayed.[4]

Behind this figure is a vat of ritual drink (10) with a reptilian guardian (11). Beyond the vat is a secondary personage (12) holding a feathered incense bag with no identifying glyph (13).

On the opposite side of the intertwined serpents is the most important individual present (14). Dressed in a cape, often associated with rulership in the lowlands, he also holds the sash in his right hand. In his left, he holds a lashed bundle which is almost certainly a torch. The central element of his headdress is the same cap form worn by the other major personage. The figure stands in a full-front position with his arms and head turned toward the serpents and tlaxmalacatl on the throne. At his side is the number 20 (15) in the form of three bars and five dots.

Behind the caped individual is another secondary figure (16) which is lifting an ollin glyph-marked bag (17) from a liquid (18) guarded by a reptile (19) identical to that in the vat.

Here is a scene charged with symbolism of the ritual ballgame and rulership. Although the two principal figures and their retainers are arrayed with the accoutrements of the ballgame and positioned in front of the altar (connoting both warfare and the ballgame), the format of the scene is basically of ritual recognition. That is, the figure of authority, named Twenty ————?, is receiving the submission, or the offering of the ballgame paraphernalia from Nineteen ————? The positions, headdresses, and the names suggest a relationship between the two; a lineage situation may exist, not unlike that of the Temple of the Foliated Cross at Palenque, where a ruler confronts his father across the form of a foliated cross. At El Tajín the elite prerogatives of warfare, pulque, and the ballgame are merged in the constant necessity to affirm rulership and lineage.

Decapitation and the Ballgame

Thirteen Rabbit's ritual sacrifice shows death by decapitation and disembowelment. Based on all sculptural portrayals, this was the standard methodology employed at El Tajín. Bowels, at least in some rituals, were extracted and spread on racks above the sacrifice. This was probably not a common procedure elsewhere in Mesoamerica at the time. Severed heads were not displayed on a *tzompantli*, but not necessarily discarded either. Throughout north-central and south-central Veracruz skulls are found as burial offerings or buried singly during the Late Classic period. The practice of obtaining trophy heads, especially in warfare, continued until European contact among the Huastecs. Heads also came to figure prominently in the ballgame.

The significance of the game was such that the accoutrements of the ceremony were reproduced in stone and acquired ritual importance in their own right. During the Late Classic, heads were depicted on the ends of yokes, hachas, and some palmas in north-central Veracruz. Further south they were more common as motifs in small tenoned stone sculptures fastened to buildings or associated with ceramic sculpture. So sacred were the portable ballgame sculptures that small fragments were preserved and appear as offerings in non-elite burials in Late Classic domestic interments.

The skull as a symbol of death is not a common theme on the gulf coast until this time period. Representations of the gods of death also become frequent. They occur in the same figurine styles as the death heads, on portable sculpture such as hachas, and on panels at El Tajín.

Plain yokes, representing the waist protectors used on the court, were first fabricated in south-central Veracruz, possibly as early as the Middle Formative period (as mentioned above). The first carved yokes followed in the Late Formative and spread along the coast. These yokes are associated with the earth monster motif. This motif became increasingly more elaborate with time and continued until the end of the yoke tradition at the beginning of the Postclassic. The significance of the earth monster is that it places the wearer symbolically in the "underworld" or its entrance and, therefore, in a symbolic closeness to death.

The earth monster had a major role in the Mesoamerican world view. In Aztec times the monster whose back was the earth, Tlaltecuhtli, was thought to be female. Her head was in the east, and the entrance to the Underworld was through her jaws (Klein 1975:70–71). In terms of such cosmology, wearing a yoke carved in the form of the monster symbolically located the participant within a sacred and mythical framework. Participating in the ballgame meant not only a ritual awareness of death and afterlife but the actual possibility of death through sacrifice.

Figure 3.6. Ballcourt panel from Aparicio, Veracruz.

As indicated earlier, sacrificial death in the ballgame at El Tajín was accomplished by decapitation. That this pattern may have been widespread is
suggested by other ballcourt sculptures at Aparicio, in Veracruz, and Chichén
Itzá, Yucatán (Figure 3.6; Cohodas 1978a, b, this volume Figure 14.2). Severing of the head is also recounted in the *Popol Vuh* where the Lords of Death
address One Hunter and Seven Hunter:

> You shall be sacrificed,
>   said One Death
>   and Seven Death
> And then they were sacrificed
>   and they were buried
> At Dusty Court, as it is called,—
>   They were buried then.
> One Hunter's head was cut off
>   Only his body was buried with
>   his younger brother's.
>
>   *(Edmonson 1971:2156–2161)*

The same Lords later play ball with Hunter (Hun Hunahpu) and Jaguar Deer (Xbalanke), the descendants of the earlier sacrificed nobles, and use a skull as a ball (Edmonson 1971:3693). It is thus not surprising to find death heads and skulls as a major theme of hachas.

Palmas can be viewed as a similar variety of portable sculpture that evolved from hachas. They vary from hachas in showing ritual scenes, some of explicit sacrifice, ritual accoutrements, or secondary deities. One of the latter was excavated at Santa Luisa. It is from a large group of "bird" motif palmas which date to the end of the Classic and have attributes similar to Harpy eagles[5] and vultures. Not precisely the Coxcualcuathli of later times, this mythical bird is shown at El Tajín devouring the bowels of the recently sacrificed, and dancing in panels of both sculptured ballcourts. Sometimes it wears the mirror and chest band associated with the rain god at El Tajín.

The position of this carrion bird, with its implications for death and sacrifice, is sufficiently important to be a major theme of ballgame sculpture. It parallels the death motifs of the hachas and suggests an increased focus on sacrifice in the ballcourt ritual during the Late Classic period. The extension of yokes, hachas, and palmas southward through the Isthmus to Guatemala and El Salvador almost certainly corresponds to the diffusion of an intensified, sacrificial version of the ballgame.[6]

Cult Convergence and the Ballgame Ritual at the End of the Classic Period

The sculptures of the South Ballcourt at El Tajín constitute a succinct example of the syncretistic evolution of Mesoamerican religion as well as the convergence of sacrificial rituals. This court has an east–west axis and is located between two temples just south of the Temple of the Niches at the ceremonial focus of the city. It is half of a "double ballcourt," the other half of which has the same end zone but extends north–south between two low platforms to the east. Contrasting with its companion court with its sloping walls, the South Ballcourt has vertical sides. These walls of immense sandstone flags were carved *in situ* to form six panels which have survived mostly intact. Located at the ends and center of each parallel wall, the panels provide a graphic portrayal of the ballgame ritual and its cosmology. Given the explicitness of the scenes, and their value for reconstructing a rite of central importance to eastern Mesoamerica, they warrant consideration here.

Preparation

These sculptures essentially depict the ritual in a "stop-frame" manner from initiation to completion. They begin with the ceremonies of mortals and end

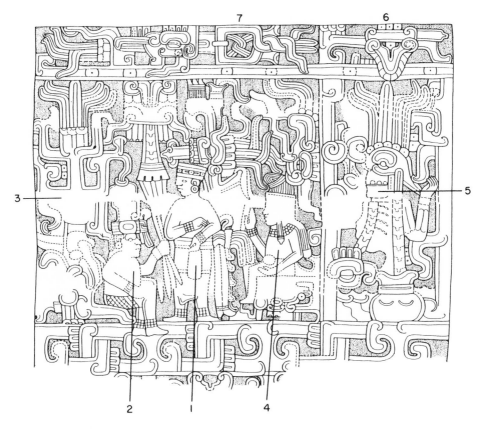

Figure 3.7. Southeast panel of the South Ballcourt, El Tajín (after Kampen 1972).

with the successful intervention of the appropriate gods. The start of the sequence is the southeast panel which shows the ritual dressing of the protagonist as a warrior (Figure 3.7). He stands in the center (1) and is being handed a bundle of spears by an attendant (2) seated at the base of a plant (3), perhaps maize. The central figure holds an incense bag and stands in front of an individual (4) seated on a throne and wearing his hair in the style of the "old hunchback" or rain god at El Tajín. The scene is of ritual preparation and is conceptually parallel to the upper east register of Room 1 at Bonampak. The entire scenario is viewed by a death deity (5) arising from a pot or olla, floating on a vat of liquid. Over the panel are a series of interlocked glyphs, including a Venus form at the far right (6) and an ollin sign (7) within a cartouche in the form of a stylized incense bag. If El Tajín has an emblem glyph, it is likely to be this.

Figure 3.8. Southwest panel of the South Ballcourt, El Tajín (after Kampen 1972).

Contemplation

The second panel in the sequence is in the southwest corner of the ballcourt
(Figure 3.8). The ritual at this point has progressed to another preparatory
phase which involves music and perhaps contemplation. The protagonist (1)
reclines in the center of the composition on a sofa-like item of furniture. His
arms and legs are in ritual position which imitates one of the pulque gods. He
is flanked by two musicians, one playing a turtle carapace drum or a *teponaztli*
(2), and the other using two clay rattles, or *sonajas* (3). The gods themselves
are also present. In front dances the eagle shown so frequently on palmas and
associated with sacrifice (4). The defleshed figure of Venus (5) floats above.
The death god (6) arising from an olla placed in a vat of ritual drink again looks
on variations (7) of the same earlier glyphs aligned across the top of the entire
panel.

Figure 3.9. Northwest panel of the South Ballcourt, El Tajín (after Kampen 1972).

Beginning the Ballgame

The sculpture in the northwest corner of the court (Figure 3.9) shows that events have now moved into the ballcourt itself. The scene is immediately prior to the ballgame. Two individuals, identifiable as players by their waist protectors, speak and confront each other with the ball and intertwined sashes between them. The protagonist, presumably on the left (1), looks across at a priest-player holding a flint knife (2). These central characters are flanked by two figures which may be god imitators. The figure on the left (3) uses the cap and baton of the Tajín rain god and the one on the right (4) may be dressed as a dog or jaguar, one of the representations of Venus (Thompson 1966a:22, 218). Both figures are atop buildings (5, 6) approximating the actual ones that flank the ballcourt today. The death god (7) continues to view the ritual from the side.

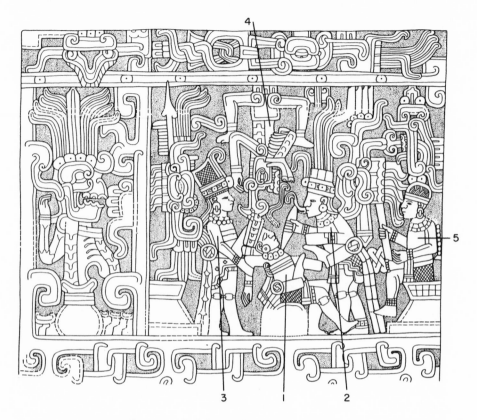

Figure 3.10. Northeast panel of the South Ballcourt, El Tajín (after Kampen 1972).

Ending the Ballgame

The fourth sculpture in the series is in the northeast of the ballcourt and depicts the termination of the game (Figure 3.10). The protagonist is center front
in the composition, seated on a rounded object with his arms held back (1).
The priest-player of the previous panel is wielding a knife in the act of decapitation (2). His helper (3), also dressed as a player with knee protectors, wears
a peculiar form of cap. This type of headgear, similar to a "Huastec hat," is
associated with the wind god at El Tajín and may indicate another impersona-
tion in the ceremony. Directly above the individual being sacrificed, the
Venus figure descends with a speech scroll coming from his mouth (4). Behind
the sacrificer sits the impersonator of the rain god (5). It seems quite probable
that all of the players in this particular game are impersonating various deities.

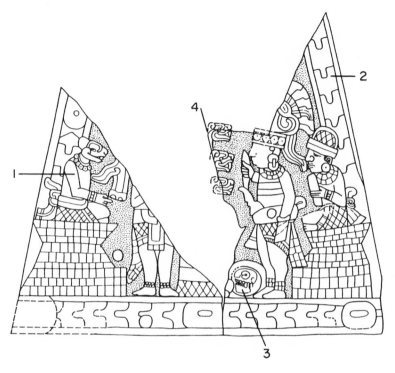

Figure 3.11. Ballgame sculpture from the Temple of the Niches, El Tajín (after Kampen 1972).

Sacrifice

There is a fifth scene which takes the end of the game somewhat further in the direction of the Underworld. Interestingly, it is not in the ballcourt but rather on a tablet placed in the corbeled arch at the entranceway to the sanctuary of the Temple of the Niches (Figure 3.11).[7] Carved in a stiff, somewhat later style, the partially recovered sculpture shows the same figures as in the northeast panel. Once again we have the zoomorphic impersonator (1) shown at the beginning of the game. The entire scene is surrounded by a design (2) used to represent the vertebrae of a skeleton and death. Significantly, the ball is now shown as a skull (3) and the blood issuing from the body appears as snakes (4). Although this particular sculpture is fragmentary, another ballcourt in the El Tajín region at Aparicio also shows a decapitated player with seven snakes surging from the torso (Figure 3.6). A similar scene is found at Chichén Itzá (Cohodas 1978a, this volume Figure 14.2).

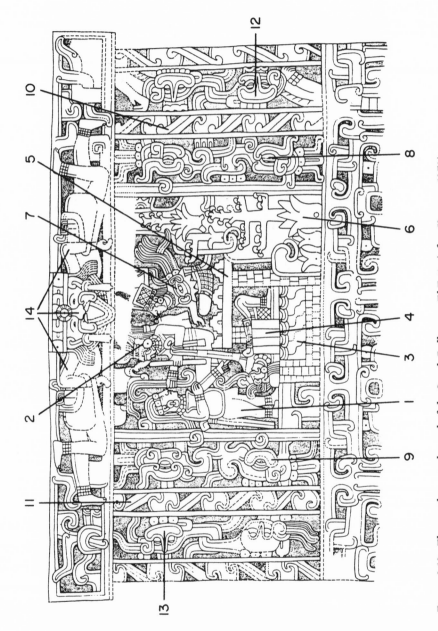

Figure 3.12. The north-central panel of the South Ballcourt, El Tajín (after Kampen 1972).

Supplication of the Gods

The scene located in the center of the north wall of the court (Figure 3.12) takes place in the Underworld and, in ritual terms, is the climax of the entire ceremony. The protagonist (1), now with his head back on his body, literally stands before the gods. He holds an olla in his right arm and looks up at the rain god (2) who presides over the event. His left hand points at the *ometecomatl*, or pulque vat (3), with its guardian, a *chac-mool* positioned deity (4). The location is a temple with merlons situated against a large place glyph showing maguey plants (6) in flower. Above the temple are seated the wind god (7) wearing the *ehecatlcoxcatl* or wind jewel, and the rain god (2) with his sash, baton, and snake-like scepter. To further emphasize that the ritual is in the Underworld, the panel is flanked by vertical rows of lunar glyphs (8, 9), femurs (10, 11), and Venus glyphs (12, 13). Above all is a bifurcated version of the pulque god (14) in a compositional format similar to the earth-monster motifs on yokes.

The scene shows the reason for the entire ritual and sacrifice. The supplicant is requesting the ritual drink, pulque, from the gods, and the rain god in particular. The pulque gods at El Tajín appear to be alternate forms of the rain god or controlled by him. This deity, thought to reside in Tlalocan, his realm in the Underworld, could only be approached through death. The ballgame was the vehicle for this necessary step in the ceremony.

The location of the temple within the domain of the rain god is extremely important as nearly one-third of the depiction is devoted to the place sign (6). The elements of the glyph are a mountain and flowering maguey.[8] This is the Tajín version of Popzonaltepetl, or the "Mountain of Foam," the mythical place recorded by Sahagún (1956 [III]:211) as the origin of pulque.[9] The ritual in the South Ballcourt at El Tajín is thus directed toward the continued propitiation of maguey and pulque by the gods and access to it by mortals through the proper use of ceremony.

Response of the Gods

That the ceremony and request in the Underworld were successful is shown by the last panel, in the center of the south wall (Figure 3.13). There the same temple (1) by the Mountain of Foam is illustrated. The god of wind (3) remains above the temple and the moon (4) in the form of a rabbit floats above. By the vat, now lowered in level, the rain god (5) fills the container, guarded by a deity with a fish helmet, by running a perforator through his penis. The act of self-sacrifice by the god, also a symbol of rulership throughout Mesoamerican Lowland cultures, provides pulque for the reverent people of El Tajín. Blood becomes pulque and the stage is set for the cycle to begin again.

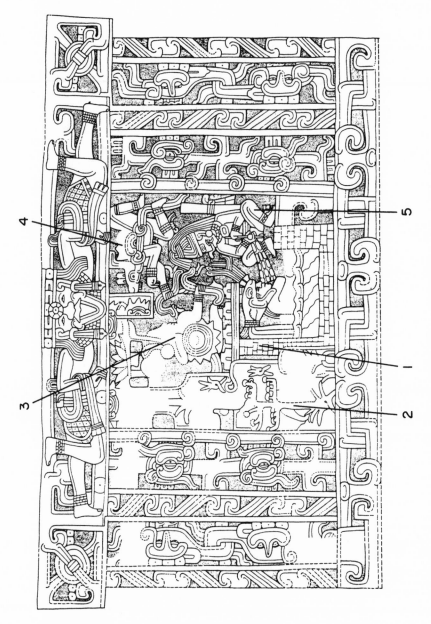

Figure 3.13. The south-central panel of the South Ballcourt, El Tajín (after Kampen 1972).

Cult Convergence

Various rituals embodying concepts of sacrifice converge in this Late Classic ceremony. The core is the old ballgame with its critical relationship to the Underworld. Grafted to it are cult aspects of Venus, perhaps equally old, and the newer rites of the pulque gods. The presence throughout of Venus figures and glyphs suggests the ritual is associated with the 584-day Venus cycle.

Especially appropriate is the nine-day period in which Venus disappears as an evening star and is thought to remain in the Underworld until it rises as a morning star. This period of disappearance and the subsequent rising was considered particularly dangerous and was a major focus of the Venus cult (M. Coe 1973:120). In the context of the Tajín ritual, the descent into the Underworld by the sacrificed participant was probably enhanced by his association with the deity. The game itself may have been in the context of a game between the gods, impersonated by the players. Venus inevitably loses and goes to the Underworld. There, during his nine-day stay, proper entreaties are made to the deities that control and make pulque.

By the end of the Classic period in north-central Veracruz, the ballgame ritual had become a core rite associated with various cults as well as the affirmation of rulership and status. The ballgame, with its great antiquity on the gulf coast, came to be a logical focus for cult convergence. As religion became more complex and independent cults began to overlap, the ballgame became the common denominator in the ritual process with its central theme of imitating the gods. It is certainly clear that at El Tajín the ballgame was associated with various cults and resulted in multiple ballcourt construction.

Since rulership and status are constantly re-affirmed in all societies, it is natural that those governing the Tajín state would seek to do so through visible cult participation; what better way than in the ballgame? Thirteen Rabbit's conquests appear to have been celebrated in a ballcourt and the vanquished rulers sent to the Underworld by decapitation.

It is significant that the merging of sacrificial rituals and the depiction of long, cyclic impersonations of the gods existed at least 600 years before the well-described Aztec rites. The degree of similarity between the ritual practices of El Tajín and those of the fifteenth century inhabitants of the Valley of Mexico is vividly shown by the recently excavated Temple of Tlaloc. There in the first Great Temple of the Aztecs is the sanctuary of Tlaloc with its Chac-Mool statue, as found at El Tajín. The similarity is striking and the implications for coastal influence strong.

The Postclassic Huastec Preservation of Tajín Ritual

The ritualism of El Tajín, and especially that associated with the ballcourt and sacrifice, continued among the Huastecs in the north gulf area after the fall of El Tajín. Although relatively little excavation has focused on Postclassic sites in this region (therefore we know little of the ballcourt distribution), the widespread nature of the ritual is indicated by the shell artwork of the Huasteca.[10] An excellent example is in the collections of the Middle American Research Institute. A shell pendant from the region of Panuco, Veracruz, depicts nothing less than one of the major scenes found in the South Ballcourt of El Tajín. The pendant (Figure 3.14) is carved in a style typical of the Postclassic period in the north gulf area. At the top are two figures (1, 2) dressed as deities. They stand and sit on the open mouths of two intertwined serpents (3, 4) that rise from a large vat of liquid at the base.

The figure in the upper right, the female (2), is dressed with a fish headdress and is handing a bundle of arrows or atlatl darts to the male figure on the left. This latter figure (1) is dressed as a warrior and is running a spike through his penis. The figures may represent the wind/rain god and the deity, Tlazolteotl. Between the serpents is a bowl (5) inscribed with the incised motifs typical of the Postclassic period in the region which holds a foaming substance. The bowl is supported by the serpents, which are plumed and intertwined to form the ollin symbol and perhaps the Tlaxmalacatl, or ballgame marker. The vat (6) itself is filled by a liquid with shells and in its center floats a temple (7), the latter having a sharp "flying" cornice not unlike that of El Tajín. Above is a feathered ornament (8) very close in style and identical in form to the feathered headdress of the death deities that rise from the floating olla in four scenes from the South Ballcourt at El Tajín. Beneath is a zoomorphic figure (9), perhaps that of a jaguar or coyote, holding up the vat.

The entire scene is derived essentially from the same mythological base as that of the south-central panel of the South Ballcourt of El Tajín. In both, the gods produce pulque through the ritual of self-sacrifice.[11] The iconography of the ballgame, the Underworld, and death is associated with both scenes. In fact, the shell gorgets which were found with the pendant show death heads with speech scrolls emerging from their mouths, and a glyph, not dissimilar to that associated with the sacrificer in the South Ballcourt scene. The significance of the pendant is that the ballgame ritual and its relationship both to the Underworld and the pulque ritual survive after El Tajín in essentially the same format, yet further north. The ritual itself may even begin to take on greater solar overtones.

Returning to our earlier observations on cultural florescence in north-central Veracruz and the centralized nature of El Tajín, we should consider the possible impact of such developments on areas beyond the Mesoamerican frontier. El Tajín is situated in the northeastern quadrant of Mesoamerica, about equidistant from the central Valley of Mexico and the upper limit of the north gulf area. Waterborne trade certainly occurred and could easily have linked the center with distant areas.[12]

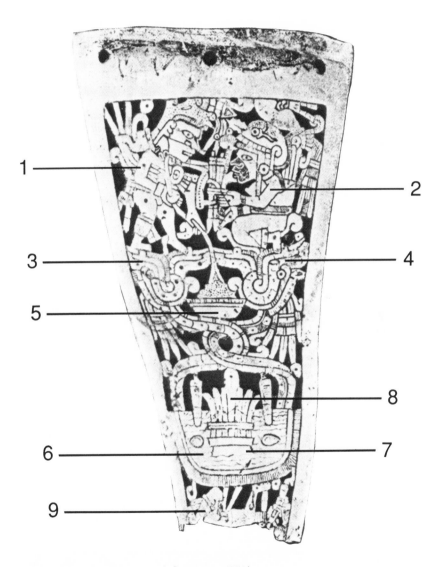

Figure 3.14. Huastec gorget (after Beyer 1933).

Another factor is chronology. El Tajín experienced a brief Epiclassic period that left it functioning dynamically when other regions had already entered the Postclassic. With the demise of this large site and its centralized control over a broad region, the north gulf area experienced its own cultural florescence. But with disruptive migrations, the lack of large, centralized political units, and the Aztec conquests of the fifteenth century, the level of florescence was not as great and generally more diffuse than elsewhere in Mesoamerica. Nevertheless, the region became a filter for Mesoamerican cultural complexes traveling via trade or migration out of Mesoamerica.

In terms of the ballgame and the associated cults examined, it is expected that the Huastec version, albeit with its earlier Tajín influence, was the model carried elsewhere. Trade moves both necessary and luxury goods from point to point. Luxury items are essentially exchanged by the elite and incorporated into their own systems. Concepts of the ballgame and associated cults, central to northeastern Mesoamerican religion and rulership, would certainly have been carried too. As they did in successive areas along the gulf coast, these concepts proved useful to the elite at centers, even in distant regions, in stimulating their own florescence.

Notes

This chapter is an excerpt of the Gulf Coast data in "Sacrifice at Dusty Court: Evolution and Diffusion of the Ritual Ballgame of Northeastern Mesoamerica." Portions of this study of the relationships in terms of ritual between Mesoamerica and the American Sòutheast were presented at the Tucson conference in 1985. The analysis of a number of the El Tajín sculptures was also presented at the Dumbarton Oaks conference on ritual human sacrifice (Wilkerson 1984).

1. Modern reconstruction of the South Ballcourt was undertaken in the 1950s by Arq. José García Payón. With a small budget and little mechanical aid, the north wall and all the panels were carefully replaced in position. In 1984–85 the south wall was reconstructed using mechanical means but, alas, considerable chipping of stone blocks took place.

2. These dimensional ranges are approximate and are included here to give a sense of proportion. Many of the courts have not yet been totally cleared or precisely measured. Nevertheless, these rough figures provide us with some reference points for considering the shape of ballcourt construction at El Tajín.

3. The sacrifices at the dedication of the Great Temple in Tenochtitlan are extreme examples of this practice. The sacrifice of captured Huastecs by Moctezuma at the fixed feast of Tlacaxipehualiztli (Durán 1967 [I]:174) is more typical.

4. The figure in the northwest panel of the South Ballcourt (Figure 3.8, No. 1) may also have this number shown.

5. The raised crest feathers of the Harpy eagle, common until the twentieth century deforestation in Veracruz, is a distinctive element which appears on a number of sculptural depictions.

6. The southward migration of Late Classic peoples, such as the cotogue (Chicamulteltec) speakers (a branch of the Huastecs), may be involved in the spread of these sculptures. Present dating, however, suggests that the spread had begun before the massive migrations toward the end of the occupation at El Tajín. It is interesting to note that many major Maya sites have only one ballcourt, many of Late Classic date, placed in a prominent central position in the site.

7. The Temple of the Niches apparently became a summary shrine during the end of the Classic period. Its sculptures focus primarily on the cult of the rain god but also relate to distinct cults associated with other buildings around it.

8. The region of El Tajín is too low in elevation for maguey to flower in the current environment.

9. García Payón (1973) also considers the South Ballcourt and its relationship to pulque and particularly the identification of the Mountain of Foam.

10. There is also carved shellwork from the north-central gulf area which has received little attention as a result of the emphasis on stone sculpture. Most finds, however, have been fragmentary and from nonsecure contexts. In terms of technique and motifs they are very similar to the north gulf examples and are likely to date to the same time frame.

11. In the southwest panel of the North Ballcourt at El Tajín, another court depicting scenes of the pulque ritual, a female death deity stands in a pulque vat and helps feed bowels (of the recently sacrificed?) to the same winged figure seen in the South Ballcourt.

12. Willett E. White (1975) has begun to explore this aspect from a technological perspective. Waterborne trade beyond areas of high culture was the norm in the Old World and should not be ignored in studies of pre-Columbian America.

CHAPTER 4

The Western Mesoamerican Tlachco: A Two-Thousand-Year Perspective

Phil C. Weigand

This presentation will focus on the ballcourts found by the Teuchitlán Mapping Project in the highland lake zones of Jalisco. Using the fine examples of group figurine art from Late Formative tombs (Figure 4.1) in conjunction with well-preserved architecture, it has been possible to suggest an evolution of ballcourt form and function through two millenia: ca. 600 B.C. to the Late Postclassic. The study area is the core of the Teuchitlán Tradition, which is marked by a signal type of circular architecture, and, from the Late Formative through the Classic, a distinctive series of ballcourt forms (see Weigand 1979b, 1985 for general discussions of chronology and phase characteristics). The zone is a resource-rich area which saw an early development of complex society first marked around 1500 B.C. with a series of elaborate burials (Oliveros 1974; Kelly 1980b; Weigand 1985).

Formative Period Ballcourts

The first possible evidence for ballcourts is considerably later than the beginnings of complex society, ca. 600 B.C. at Campanillo (Figure 4.2). This court is poorly preserved and is not a good example of Type II-A or Type III ballcourts (Figure 4.3), which are the more usual forms of the Formative period. The court is attached to a San Felipe phase (Middle Formative) burial mound, though it may well be a later addition.

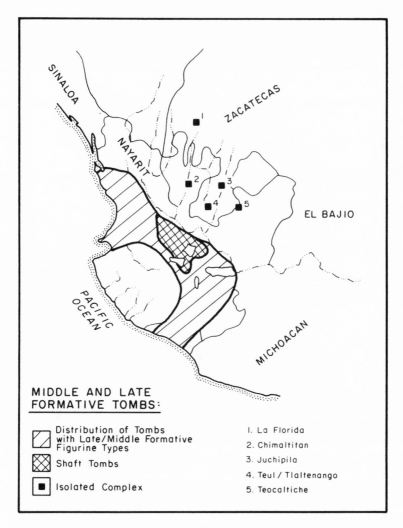

Figure 4.1. Distribution of the Teuchitlán Tradition, western Mexico, relative to Middle and Late Formative tombs.

Certainly the evidence is clearer by the El Arenal phase (Late Formative, ca. 300 B.C. to A.D. 200). Ballcourts are free-standing and can be studied from ceramic group figurines recovered in status burials as well as through the architecture itself (mostly Type III varieties with some Type II-A examples). The ceramic figurines depicting ballgames and courts are rare. Von Winning estimates that only five or six verified examples exist (von Winning and Ham-

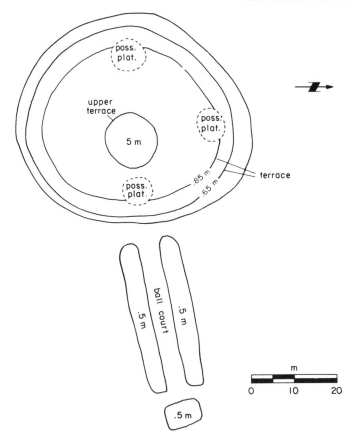

poss.
plat.

upper
terrace

poss.
plat.

5 m

poss.
plat.

.85 m

.65 m

terrace

ball court

.5 m

.5 m

.5 m

.5 m

m

0   10   20

Figure 4.2. Site map of Campanillo Circle B.

mer 1972). Architectural examples are equally scarce with only seven definite
and two possible additional courts dating to the Late Formative. Type III
courts are shown in figurine art in three basic forms with the Colima example
(von Winning and Hammer 1972:Pl. 76) unique in every regard. This latter
form is made from stone and portrays a static scene on an almost square court.
There are no known architectural parallels.

The other two forms of the Type III court have architectural parallels (von
Winning and Hammer 1972:Pl. 73, 74, 75). Both of these variants are characterized by parallel ridges that mark the lateral confines of the court. One
variety has ridges with terraced end sections (Pl. 75) and the other does not.
Otherwise, they are virtually identical. Architecturally these courts are small,
about 30–40 m long and 10 m wide, with the ridges seldom more than 0.5 m
high and 1.5–2 m wide. The ridges are made of undressed field cobbles of all
sizes, stacked carefully, and according to the figurines, covered with painted

plaster. The ridges are straight and exhibit no associated platforms. While free-standing, they are often found in association with residential compounds.

Type III courts, as represented by the ceramic figurines, have between four and six players accompanied by many spectators along the ridges and at the court ends. Conch trumpets appear to be part of the game equipment. The ball is depicted as being large, and could have easily weighed as much as the 4 kg mandated by later custom elsewhere in Mesoamerica. One figurine shows what appears to be the hip shot in progress, also mandated as the only legal manner by which to touch the ball while the game was under way. The *Tlachtlemalacatl*, or serpent hoops, of ballcourts elsewhere in Mesoamerica are never depicted in the figurines, nor do they appear architecturally in courts of any period in the west. Obviously the game is played by two sides, but how the spectators are divided in their support is not indicated by the figurines except in the most simple sense of two groupings along each ridge.

Late Formative Elaboration

As the Late Formative period evolved, and as the circular, ceremonial five-element architectural pattern became formalized (Weigand 1985), the ballcourt became more complicated. These Late Formative Type II-A courts are often indistinguishable from courts associated with minor Classic period cen-

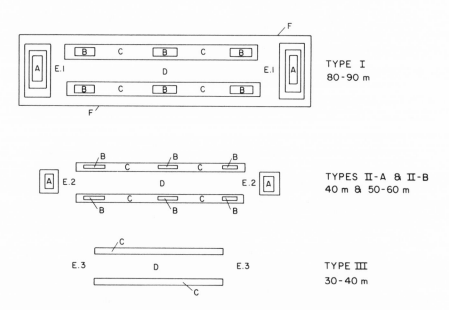

Figure 4.3. Comparison of three types of ballcourts in the Teuchitlán area, Jalisco.

ters. In general, Type II courts come in two sizes: those 40 m long and those 50–60 m long. The longer Type II-B courts are late and definitely associated with the Classic period. The shorter Type II-A courts are probably Late Formative or Proto-Classic, although some seem to have been built and maintained during the later Classic period.

Type II-A courts are depicted as free-standing architectural units in both group ceramic figurine art and in site architecture. The figurines are rare, with only two verified examples: one in the Diego Rivera collection in Mexico City and the other in the Indianapolis Museum of Art. These figurines show social differences in costume as well as seating arrangements. Especially notable are the dignitaries stationed atop the platform/house structures at the courts' ends. These individuals appear to be attended. The other spectators are along the ridges, which provide a gallery atmosphere (as was the case with the Type III figurines). The ridges are complex and elaborate; they are particularized into sectors by platform dividers which in themselves form part of a gallery. These same ridge and end platforms are prominently visible in the architecture examined during field survey.

Type II-A and Type II-B courts display all but one of the fundamental characteristics associated with Classic period ballcourts of the Teuchitlán Tradition (see Figure 4.3). These characteristics are:

1. two parallel ridges marking the sides of the playing field;
2. playing fields with prepared floors, which at times have dividers and are elevated as floor platforms;
3. end platforms which are terraced and serve as foundations for simple wattle and daub structures;
4. ridge platforms which apparently serve as particularizing gallery areas;
5. an open-I arena between the end platforms and the playing field and lateral ridges (E-1, the open I is set off with F, a whole court platform; E-2, the open I is basically at the same level as the ground surrounding the court; E-3, no end platforms, hence no actual open I); and,
6. a whole court platform, including the end platforms, lateral ridges, and playing fields. This form occurs infrequently or only partially on Type II courts.

Type II-A courts are 4–6 m wide. Ridges can be as high as 1 m, with ridge platforms seldom more than 1.5 m high. The end platforms are usually rectangular, but are often of different sizes and numbers of terraces within the same court. These platforms seldom measure more than 8 × 12 × 1.5 m, though end platforms as high as 3 m have been surveyed.

The end platforms, and possibly the ridge platforms, are clearly marked as the places of honor within a ballcourt. Culhua Mexica sources mention places

of honor for the *hueytlatoani* (sovereign) and the priests of Quetzalcoatl, Tezcatlipoca, and Tlaloc. The figurines of western Mesoamerica, however, are
not so specific as to identify special social categories.

Since some of the free-standing Type II courts do have playing field dividers, as well as symmetrically opposed ridges and end platforms, it is reasonable to suggest that the same principles of religious duality so prominent in
late ballgame accounts are represented in the west by Late Formative or
Early Classic times. Nevertheless, there exist no iconographic, epigraphic,
or direct historical materials describing a western Mesoamerican ballgame
played on the variety of courts associated with the Teuchitlán Tradition, aside
from the highly ethnographic character of the Type II and Type III figurines.

*Figure 4.4. Core area of the Teuchitlán Tradition, western Mexico, in the Classic
period.*

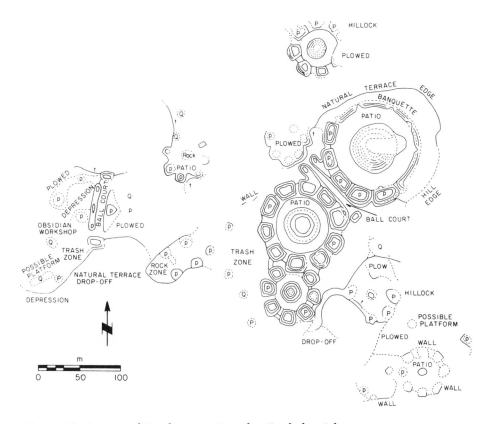

Figure 4.5. Site map of Guachimonton Complex, Teuchitlán, Jalisco.

Classic Period Ballcourts

From the Ahualulco phase through Teuchitlán I and II phases (ca. A.D. 200–400, A.D. 400–750, and A.D. 759–900/1000, respectively; see Figure 4.4), we have the ability to stratify the survey samples of ballcourts. Architecture dating to these periods permits the examination of internal data from the courts themselves, and also the association of the different types of courts (Types I, II-A, and II-B; see Figure 4.3) with adjacent site structures (e.g., circular compounds, rectangular courtyards, workshop areas, terrace systems, stairways, and other ballcourts).

At the outset, a description of Type I or monumental ballcourts is needed. The playing fields of these courts are 80–90 m long, but seldom more than 6–8 m wide. These data indicate a rather balanced progression of playing field sizes from Type III through Type I courts. The playing fields were made from layered, tamped earth. Ridges serve as gallery particularizers, with

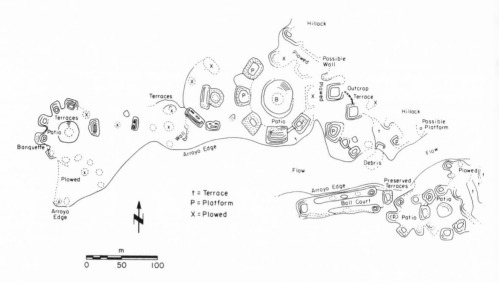

Figure 4.6. Site map of the Santa Quiteria Rancho Nuevo Complex.

three ridge platforms each. These ridges are higher, more terraced, and wider than Type II ridges, ranging from 8 to 12 m wide, 2 to 4 m high, and with a ridge platform about 1 m higher. The end platforms are complexly terraced and always adjoin a circular ceremonial structure.

At Guachimonton (Figure 4.5), the great ballcourt lies between two circles; at Santa Quiteria (Figure 4.6) and Ahualulco the great courts abut the circle platforms in a perpendicular fashion. Ridges and platforms were constructed from rock and earthen fill, faced with undressed cobbles placed in well-built terraces, and covered with daub plaster. Since there are only three of these monumental ballcourts, it is interesting to note that each is directly associated with one of the three most grand monumental building complexes of the Classic period in the western highland lake zone.

The Guachimonton, Ahualulco, and Santa Quiteria complexes are impressive even if viewed as isolates, but all three complexes are parts of still larger habitation zones and settlement systems. The Teuchitlán habitation zone, containing the Guachimonton complex, is by far the largest. The Guachimonton complex is the most important precinct within the greater habitation zone. The settlement hierarchy for this zone has been detailed elsewhere (Weigand 1979b, 1985). Classic period ballcourts, by type, formally fit into the hierarchy. Nevertheless, some inconsistencies exist, especially with regard to the very limited distribution of Type I courts.

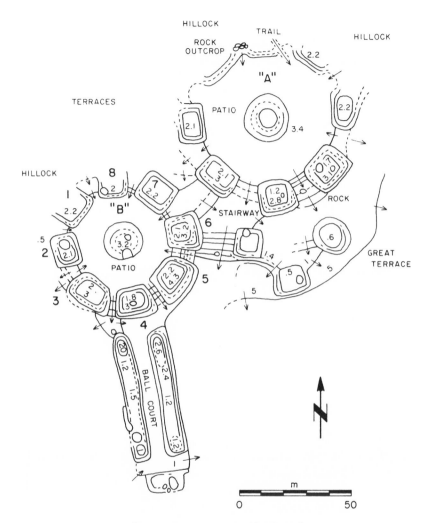

Figure 4.7. Site map of Santa Quiteria, Mesa Alta Complex.

If the ballcourt served politically centralizing functions through formalized social opposition in public ritual, then the size and complexity of Type I courts should reflect a comparable distribution to that of the most important political and economic centers of the region. In the settlement hierarchy, six Tier 1 habitation zones have been defined, but only three Type I ballcourts have been found in association. Huitzilapa, Las Pilas, and Tala have no Type I courts, though the major monumental complex at Tala is so damaged by plowing, fill removal, and looting that very few details remain. Perhaps additional survey will elucidate this apparent inconsistency.

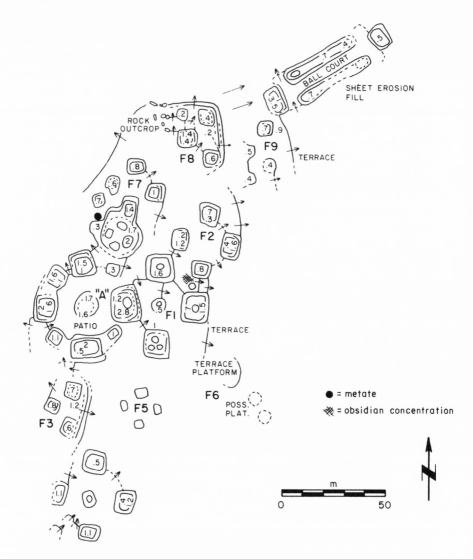

Figure 4.8. Site map of Huitzilapa, Cerro de las Navajas.

Five of the habitation zones of the Tier 1 variety contain 3,000–5,000 ha. Teuchitlán is in a class by itself with over 30,000 ha. Its habitation zone displays many urban characteristics (e.g., elaborate internal community settlement patterns, highly specialized economic activity areas, complex in-field horticultural systems; see Weigand 1985). There are 14 circular complexes within the community settlement pattern at Teuchitlán: one Tier 1 precinct and four Tier 2 complexes, comprising five districts or wards within the zone. Only one of these districts lacks a Type II-B ballcourt. Ahualulco has at least two and possibly three districts, but only one of them has a Type II-B court. Santa Quiteria has three districts, but only one of them manifests a Type II-B court (Figure 4.7). Huitzilapa and Las Pilas have only Type II-B courts. At Huitzilapa the court is freestanding, though much of the associated compound architecture dates to the Late Classic period (Figure 4.8). One structure is very similar to an Ixtlá del Río–type circular platform.

Tier 2 settlements in the zonal pattern of the regional hierarchy are characterized by sub-monumental circles and are often associated with one or two Type II-B ballcourts. Like those in the large habitation zones, these courts are seldom free standing but rather are attached in a perpendicular manner to the outside edge of a ceremonial circle.

In general, when ballcourts are attached to a circle, the end platform is differentially developed and becomes a shared platform within the ceremonial circle. With the exception of the Guachimonton complex, the perpendicular ballcourt-circle platform format, which looks like an old-fashioned keyhole from above, is the distinctive architectural characteristic of the Teuchitlán Tradition. The orientation of the ballcourts was examined by Anthony Aveni for possible astronomical significance. Aside from noting the unique elongated format, he could find no regularities to suggest astronomical orientation (pers. comm. 1979).

Classic Period Integration

Based on the overlapping distributions of circular ceremonial complexes and types of ballcourts, the postulated settlement hierarchy is suggested to include a hierarchy of politically integrative ballgames. The monumental Type I courts may have been used to represent the interests of political elites within the entire region and their dealings among themselves. Type II courts may have been more compatible with interdistrict concerns, either within a common habitation zone or between a political center and its hinterland. Centers without ballcourts presumably used the courts at the centers that controlled them, if indeed separate teams were generated at Tier 3 or Tier 4 settlements.

The distribution of different types of ballcourts during the Classic period suggests a well-integrated social hierarchy. This hierarchy used the ceremonialism invested in the format of circular architecture with that of the ballgame to obtain the dispositional commonality needed for its political and economic maintenance. By drawing oppositions into formalized ritual both between and within communities, the ballgame offered the overall polity a discipline and self-restraint that might parry intraregional competition for resources, both strategic and rare. A hierarchy of ballgames meant that parrying economic and political competition could be carried out at multiple social levels.

The figurines from the earlier periods of the Teuchitlán Tradition clearly show the shared costume and attitudes of ball players and warriors. It is suggested that these two latter categories were actually one; i.e., the ball players and the gladiator/warriors were a single social category from which two functions were determined that fitted political needs: (1) gladiatorial in terms of intra-community or intra-polity ceremonialism and integration; and (2) warrior in terms of extra-community or extra-polity political competition for hegemony and resources.

The ballcourt functioned in the integrative realm at all levels, expressing dualistic, ritualized oppositions. As previously mentioned, the Type I ballcourt may have served the larger arena of extra-polity competition, though more evidence is required to support the hypothesis. Nevertheless, ballcourt Types I and II during the Classic period are not found outside the area of the Teuchitlán Tradition. While survey for Classic settlements in western Mesoamerica is incomplete outside these adjoining lake basins and canyons, no architectural examples of ballcourts have yet been reported.

Postclassic Ballcourts

Given the quantity of Formative and Classic period ballcourt data, the lack of pertinent materials from the Postclassic period is surprising. Joseph Mountjoy (pers. comm. 1985), among others, regards this informational hiatus as puzzling. Postclassic ballcourts are reported from Amapa (Clune 1976) and Chacalilla (Guevara López 1981), both of which are located in the coastal areas of Nayarit. While abundant archaeological remains from the Postclassic exist in the highland lake zones abutting the Nayarit coastal plain, only one possible ballcourt has been identified.

The transition from Classic to Early Postclassic cultures was accomplished only after massive displacements and relocations. The great habitation zones declined rapidly, and the distinctive five-element circular architectural format was abandoned and replaced by central Mexican–like rectangular pyramids and plazas. The reorganization of the area was complete and far-reaching (Weigand 1979b, 1985). While the ballgame must have persevered, the open-I court that characterized the Teuchitlán Tradition disappeared. Impressive architectural complexes of the Postclassic exist at Tala, Santa Crúz de Barcenas, Tabacal, Xochitepec, Etzatlán, Oconahua, and Las Cuevas, to name but a few from the immediate area.

Despite relatively good preservation, none of these complexes, with the possible exception of Las Cuevas, shows clear-cut examples of ballcourts. Upon the citadel at Las Cuevas, there exists an elongated, patio-like feature which may be a closed-I ballcourt. It is about 125 m long and 20 m wide, with the western edge dug into the citadel hill, and the eastern edge terraced over the natural slope. In contrast to the much smaller residential terraces, this feature has very little ceramic or lithic debris. Also, looters have found walls of stone veneer on the feature, another indication of its special architectural nature. The stelae left at the citadel, or found as building stone embedded in the modern structures of San Juanito, do not provide a pictorial representation of the ballcourt or the ballgame.

Simply stated, from A.D. 900 to 1000 to the time of conquest, there are only three known ballcourts, including the Las Cuevas possibility, from the vast area inclusive of the Nayarit lowlands and the adjoining highland lake zone.[1] In contrast, in just the Teuchitlán–Tequila–Etzatlán region during the Classic period (ca. A.D. 200 to 900–1000), there are over 50 clear examples and many others that are possible. Perhaps during the Postclassic in the lake zone the ballgame became a field rather than a formal court event. A field ballgame would leave far fewer archaeological vestiges. In either case, the social centrality figured by the ballgame/ballcourt seems to have undergone de-emphasis during the transition from the Teuchitlán Tradition into the Postclassic period.

Notes

This project owes its existence to the field and laboratory aid of Celia García de Weigand, Francisco Ron Siordia, Dolores Soto de Arechavaleta, Luís Figaroa, Pedro Figaroa, Joseph Mountjoy, Emil Veakis, Michael Cinquino, Douglas Holmes, Robert Shadow, Robert Koll, Michael Spence, James Schoenwetter, and many others. Otto Schöndube and Javier Galván, both of the Centro Regional de Occidente of the INAH, greatly facilitated the work by way of permits and constructive critique. Javier Galván also aided in several aspects of the fieldwork. Funding and support came from the Mesoamerican Co-operative Research Program of Southern Illinois University, the State University of New York Research Foundation, the Secretaría de Recursos Hidraulicos, the Instituto de Investigaciones Antropológicas of the Universidad Nacional Autónoma de México, and the S.U.N.Y. at Stony Brook Graduate School.

1. Kelly (1980b) reports a possible court from the Chanal Phase, ca. A.D. 1100, from El Barrigón, Colima. Her description of the feature follows: "At the south end of the mound area there is a marked 'trough', which workmen call a *canoa* (canoe) or a *calle*

(street); it is 80 or 90 m long and about 20 m wide, and has a tallish mound at the western termination. The proportions suggest a ball court" (p. 48). Also, a walk-over survey of the palace complex at Tonalá, Jalisco, has produced a feature which might be a closed-I ballcourt on the lower citadel. All structures in this area appear to be Late Postclassic. The feature is ca. 45–50 m long and 17 m wide, with one end platform larger than the other. Looters exposed an interior corner of the possible "I" and the feature had a fine veneer finish.

CHAPTER 5

The Known Archaeological Ballcourts of Durango and Zacatecas, Mexico

J. Charles Kelley

The known archaeological ballcourts of the Durango–Zacatecas area fall easily into two categories: I-shaped and open-ended. At the major site of La Quemada there is a very long court, shaped roughly like a capital I, with some aberrant features. There is problematical evidence that a similar but smaller court was once present at the Chalchihuites ceremonial center of Alta Vista. A large I-shaped ballcourt has been reported by some observers from the Cazcan site of Teul de Gonzales Ortega in southern Zacatecas but others deny its existence. It is quite possible, however, that such courts exist not only at Teul, but also at Las Ventanas, located near Juchipila. In the second category, there are several very small, open-ended ballcourts, found in the state of Durango with one Zacatecas exception. Two of these courts have been partially excavated and five additional unexcavated examples are known.

The I-Shaped Courts

La Quemada

Batres (1903) identified a large rectangular room at La Quemada as a "Juego de Pelota" (G, Central, plano número 1). This identification has led to some confusion because this room is a rectangular masonry-walled structure measuring about 22 × 30 m, located on the third terrace of La Quemada. It seems obvious that Batres was referring to a Mexican handball court, not the

Mesoamerican ballgame court. But there was a Mesoamerican ballcourt at La Quemada. On the lower level of the ruin, extending northeast from the great court termed "La Catedral" with its attached Hall of Columns, there is a gently inclined open area ending at the *"piramide votiva."* Batres (1903, "plano general, e") identifies this area as a *"calzada."* In an early paper, I referred to it as "a sort of sacred way, possibly a ballcourt, partially paved and walled" (Kelley 1956:128). Later excavation makes it clear that this was indeed a large roughly I-shaped ballcourt. This structure has now been mapped by Ben Nelson and Peter Jimenez but the plan is not yet available. The ballcourt's situation emphasizes its importance in the ceremonial precinct of La Quemada. There is still uncertainty about the age of La Quemada and the ballcourt. Earlier structures there may date at least as early as the Middle Classic but available data suggest that site florescence occurred in the Early Postclassic.

Alta Vista (?)

Under my direction, the University Museum of the Southern Illinois University, Carbondale, excavated in 1971, 1974, and 1975–76[1] at the ceremonial center of Alta Vista, Chalchihuites,[2] located in western Zacatecas. Aerial photographs of the site and its environs were made by archaeologist Morrison Limon B. of CETENAL[3] in 1974. In one photo the vague outlines of an apparent large I-shaped ballcourt were visible; subsequently, however, it could not be located on the ground, but another area at Alta Vista may represent an unexcavated ballcourt.

Discussion

It is somewhat surprising that only one definite I-shaped ballcourt (the La Quemada court) is known from the Durango–Zacatecas area. Major sites such as Las Ventanas and Teul de Gonzales Ortega to the south may have such ballcourts but these sites are poorly known. Weigand (1979a [II]:111) described a possible ballcourt at Rancho la Florida, near Valparaiso, Zacatecas, in association with Chalchihuites-like architecture and ceramics. Apparently, the nearest excavated I-shaped ballcourt to the south was excavated by Román Piña Chan (1982) at the site of Tinganio, located near Uruapan in the highlands of Michoacan. This is a classic I-shaped court, built in Teotihuacan style *(talud y tablero)*. Piña Chan refers it to the second building period there, with a suggested date of A.D. 600–900. It seems probable that sites such as Ixtepete, near Guadalajara, should have I-shaped ballcourts, but they have not been reported. At Amapa in Nayarit a transitional-style ballcourt (open-ended, but with end platforms) was excavated (Cline in Meighan 1976). Weigand (1985) has illustrated several long and narrow ballcourts, possibly transitional in type, associated with the Teuchitlán/Shaft Tomb Tradition in the Jalisco highlands (Figs. 2.11 and 2.12).

If Weigand (1978 [I]:79) is correct in associating La Quemada with the Tula–Toltec expansion, the remote source for the La Quemada I-shaped court might be Tula. The La Quemada court would then be Postclassic in age. Notably, the two "public" ballcourts at Casas Grandes in northwestern Chihuahua are modified I-shaped structures (Di Peso 1974 [2]:410–413). The source of the Mesoamerican influences on Casas Grandes has not been definitely determined; probably, imported traits have an indirect origin in the Valley of Mexico via the Greater Aztatlan–Mixteca Puebla trade system (Kelley 1983).

The Small Open-Ended Courts

Schroeder Site

In 1956, the Southern Illinois University, Carbondale, excavated a small, open-ended ballcourt, Structure 6 (Figure 5.1), at the Schroeder site,[4] located some 8 km south of Durango, in the Guadiana Valley. Excavations at this

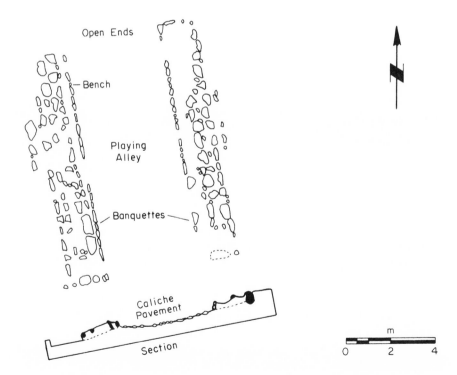

Figure 5.1. Plan of the Schroeder site court (Structure 6).

structure, supervised by Frank Eddy, involved partial clearing of the lateral mounds as well as exploratory trenches within the court. This feature consisted of two parallel mounds of slabs, field stone, and rubble bordering a longitudinal open area paved with caliche. The ends of the playing alley were open; its floor was continuous on the same level with the surrounding natural surface (Figure 5.1). No zone markers were found.

The Schroeder site, type site for the Guadiana Branch of the Chalchihuites Culture, was occupied throughout the Guadiana sequence, Ayala through Calera phases. In terms of a revised and somewhat problematic dating, this occupation extended from ca. A.D. 875–1350+ (Kelley 1985:286). The Ayala phase of the Guadiana Branch is correlated with the Calichal phase of the Suchil Branch which developed just before the abandonment of the ceremo-

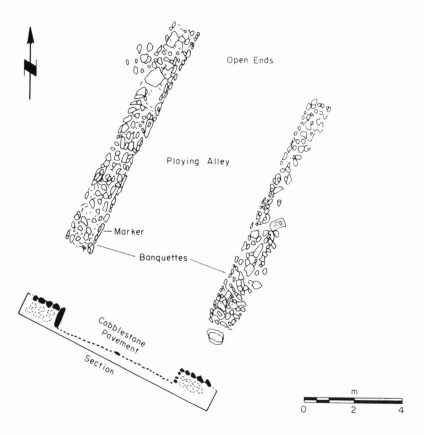

Figure 5.2. Plan of the Gualterio Abajo court (Structure 4).

nial center of Alta Vista at ca. A.D. 850–900. No sherds were found in the ballcourt construction; sherds in the fill belonged to the Ayala and Las Joyas phases. Its situation near the pyramid suggests that it was part of the ceremonial precinct of the site and associated with the Ayala phase. However, the area also was occupied by the sub-Mesoamerican Loma San Gabriel culture,[5] which here apparently was largely contemporaneous with the Chalchihuites occupation (with the exception of one early structure). It is conceivable that the ballcourt belongs with this earlier Loma San Gabriel component.

Gualterio Abajo

In 1972 and 1973, together with Ellen A. Kelley, I carried out minor excavations for the Southern Illinois University at the Chalchihuites Culture (Suchil Branch) site of Gualterio Abajo. This site is situated on a natural terrace on the side of a high hill overlooking tepid water springs near the Ejido Gualterio on the Río San Antonio branch of the Río Suchil. On top of the high hill is the fortified Chalchihuites Culture site of Gualterio Arriba. Gualterio Abajo was occupied only during the earliest Canutillo phase of the Suchil Branch and apparently early in that phase. The site consists of a long, double row of Canutillo phase house platforms and courts conforming to the semicircular area of the natural terrace. The platform structures were crudely made, resembling the stone slab architecture of the Loma San Gabriel Culture. Near the center of the village, on the uphill side, there was a rectangular cobblestone-paved plaza approximately 35 m east–west and 70 m north–south. In this plaza we excavated a small, open-ended ballcourt, clearing its banquettes and trenching the plaza and the playing alley (Figure 5.2).

This ballcourt was quite similar, even in its dimensions, to the Schroeder Site court, but much better preserved (E. Kelley 1976:45, 48). It was composed of two long, parallel banquettes, outlined by vertical stone slabs and filled with rubble. The slightly depressed playing alley between the two banquettes was paved with cobblestones set in black earth, like the plaza area of which it is a continuation; it was open at both ends. No zone markers were found.

Although the site is in other ways a pure Canutillo phase component, we did recover a number of sherds characteristic of the Loma San Gabriel Culture ceramic complex, specifically of types Loma Plain, Loma Textured, and Chico Red-on-brown. These sherds were found almost entirely among the cobblestones used in paving the plaza and the alley of the ballcourt, whereas sherds diagnostic of the Canutillo phase were found almost exclusively in platform structures and associated refuse deposits. As in the case of the Schroeder site ballcourt, there is a very real question as to whether the court is to be associated with the Chalchihuites Culture (Canutillo phase) village in whose plaza it was situated or with an earlier Loma San Gabriel phase occupation.[6] Nearby Loma San Gabriel components appear to be contemporaneous with the Canutillo phase site. One radiocarbon date of A.D. 575 (455–695) [GX-3882] was obtained from late refuse at Gualterio Abajo; other Canutillo phase components have been dated to the first centuries A.D.

Unexcavated Sites

Los Castillo Site

Approximately 31 km southeast of the city of Durango is a site called Los Castillo, situated on La Mesa de Los Tapias[7] near the village of Nicholas Romero in the southeastern section of the Guadiana Valley. Architectural features here include two small, open-ended ballcourts (A and B), both heavily overgrown with prickly pear and other vegetation. These courts are located some distance apart, one higher up the slope than the other; both lack other closely associated structures. Both ballcourts conform to the pattern of those at Schroeder and Gualterio Abajo (Figure 5.3).

Zone markers were not visible in either court. The same problem regarding cultural affiliation exists at Los Castillo as previously discussed for the Schroeder site and Gualterio Abajo ballcourts. Sherds collected from the surface of Los Castillo include diagnostic types of both Chalchihuites (Guadiana Branch) and Loma San Gabriel cultures. No special association of sherd types with the ballcourts was seen. Among the various structures visible at the site were architectural forms characteristic of both Loma and Chalchihuites cultures. Accordingly the age and cultural affiliations of the ballcourts cannot be well determined.

Cacaria Ballcourt

The Cacaria site, discovered by Drs. Jaime Ganot and Alejandro Peschard of Durango, is located some 42 km north-northwest of the city of Durango, southwest of the town of Nicolas Bravo. It is situated on a relatively low hill at the edge of the village of Cacaria. For the most part the hill is exposed bedrock covered with prickly pear trees; on the side opposite the village there is a lower, more-or-less level area of grass-covered alluvium. At one end of this rectangular, plaza-like area is a small, open-ended ballcourt. Nearby are various rectangular or circular structures of vertical slab or boulder construction, suggesting Loma San Gabriel architecture; no sherds, other artifacts, or debitage were found in the entire "plaza" area, apparently because the original living surface is now covered by alluvium (dimensions from notes of Michael Foster 1987).

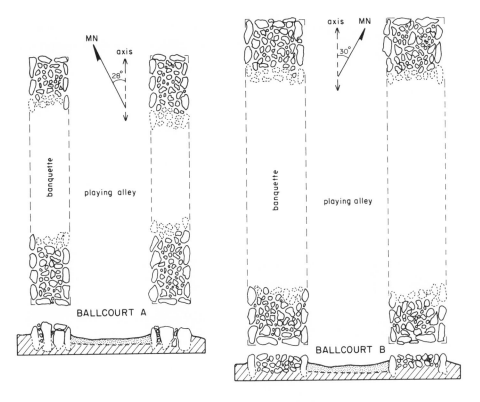

Figure 5.3. Two unexcavated, open-ended courts at the Los Castillo site.

Paralleling the plaza-like area on the far side is a long rocky ridge. Scattered along this ridge were constructions in Chalchihuites-style architecture and considerable occupational debris, including potsherds of Chalchihuites types. The ridge occupation may or may not have been coeval with that of the ballcourt and associated structures situated below it. Again, there is some evidence of both Loma San Gabriel and Chalchihuites occupation, but direct evidence is present only for the latter.

Sotolitos Sites

In 1936, the late J. Alden Mason carried out an archaeological reconnaissance of much of the state of Durango (Mason 1937). Although much of his fieldwork was concerned with the Chalchihuites Culture (and incidentally with Loma San Gabriel sites in the Zape region), he also recorded other sites (Mason 1937:142–143). In the Sotolitos region of the Sierra Madre Occidental, about 120 km northwest of Durango, he found small sites resembling those found near Zape, where they are identified with the Loma San Gabriel Culture. Near Los Fresnos he found two sites where small, open-ended courts[8] were identified, conforming to the type already described (Figure 5.4). Sherds were rare in these sites; those found are clearly Loma San Gabriel in affiliation.

The location of the Los Fresnos/Sotolitos sites is of interest. They are situated in a mountain valley on the Los Fresnos branch of the Río San Lorenzo. This river enters the Pacific lowlands below Culiacan and was one of the passable routes across the Sierra Madre Occidental from the west coast to the highlands of Durango. According to Sauer (1932:9–10), one of the explorations made by the Nuno de Guzman party of 1531–32 successfully followed the Río San Lorenzo across the sierra to the plains of Durango. Previously,

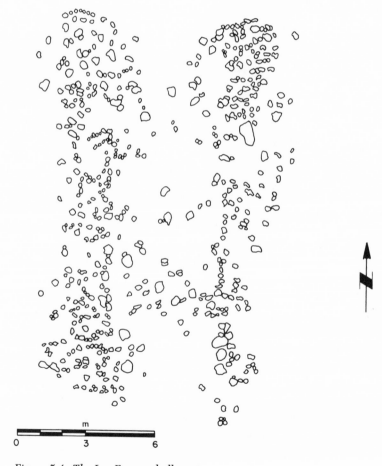

Figure 5.4. The Los Fresnos ballcourt.

Table 5.1. Rough Dimensions and Orientations of Small, Open-Ended Courts (in meters)

Site	Length	Width/Alley	Banquettes	Height	Orient.*
Schro.	10.0	4.0+	W 1.75; E. 1.6	0.50	10° W/N
Gualt.	9.5	5.0	W 1.25; E. 1.0	1.0	35° E/N
Cas. A	12.7	4.5	W 1.93; E. 2.0	1.46	65° E/N
Cas. B	16.8	4.57	W 3.00; E. ???	???	40° E/N
Cacar.	15.0	5.25	W 2.10; E. 2.30	3.5/4.5	30° E/N
Fres.	15.5	4.0+	W 2.00; E. 2.00	???	???
Soto. 2	no data on dimensions or orientation				

*Based on 10° east of north declination; pocket compass observations are not precise.

they had failed in this effort while following successively the two main branches of the Río Culiacán through the Topia region, the better-known route across the sierra. The Los Fresnos/Sotolitos sites were located in southern Tepehuan country near the Xixime–Acaxee border. The Tepehuan are believed to be the cultural descendants of the Loma San Gabriel Culture (Riley and Winters 1963).

Discussion

Two excavated and five known but unexcavated ballcourts of the small, open-ended type provide a fairly consistent pattern for this form and establish it as the popular Durango–Zacatecas type. Common to all the courts is the open-ended playing alley with lateral banquettes made of vertical stone walls with rubble fill. Playing alleys are paved in some way in the excavated examples but zone markers have not been found. Regardless of minor differences, the known small, open-ended courts constitute an easily recognized cultural pattern. Dimensions and rough orientations of the small, open-ended courts are given in Table 5.1.

Notably, all of the small, open-ended courts occur in rocky locations where stones abound. Banquettes were easily constructed with stones obtained largely by clearing the court area and the open ends. If the Hohokam ballcourts were derived from the small, open-ended courts of Zacatecas–Durango, as may well have been the case, obvious differences between the two sets may be explained by the difference in site situations. Most of the Hohokam ballcourts are built on alluvial terraces; the playing floor is either the basal caliche or other alluvium; the banquettes were earthen mounds, presumably made by scraping up earth to form the playing alley and court ends or by obtaining it from a nearby barrow pit. Rarely, stones were used in construction of the banquettes (Wilcox and Sternberg 1983:175–177). It seems probable that the banquettes were plastered with caliche, just as platform mounds were plastered at Snaketown (Haury 1976:82–94) and at the Gatlin site (Wasley 1960). In both instances earthen construction has produced rounded structures, inasmuch as vertical-sided banquettes and mounds cannot be maintained with earthen fill alone, in contrast to the slab and rubble constructions of the Zacatecas–Durango courts (and platforms).

Identification of the small, open-ended ballcourts as true ballcourts is verified by fortunate finds of pottery models in collections from shaft tombs, primarily in the region of Ixtlan del Rio in the state of Nayarit. Three such models of open-ended courts complete with ball players and spectators have been illustrated by von Winning and Hammer (1972:68, Figs. 73–75). One of these courts (shown in their Fig. 73) is also illustrated by Meighan and Nicholson (1970:47, Fig. 34). A court of the intermediate type (open ends but with temples at each end) is represented in a model illustrated by Paul Gendrop (1970:19,h). In order to compare the illustrated shaft tomb models of open-

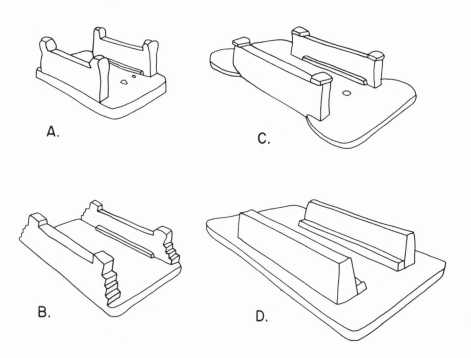

Figure 5.5. Plans of small, open-ended ballcourts derived from ceramic models found in shaft tombs in Nayarit.

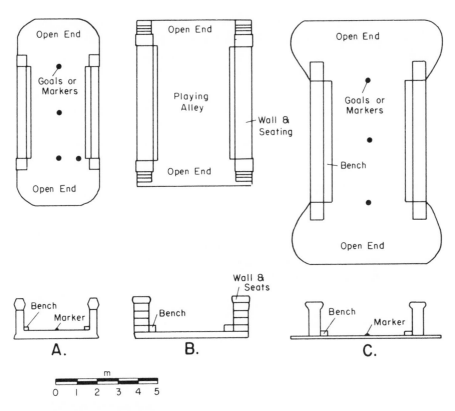

Figure 5.6. Reconstruction of ballcourt forms based on ceramic models found in shaft tombs and on the Schroeder site excavated structure.

ended ballcourts with those found archaeologically in Durango and Zacatecas, comparable floor plan sketches were drawn as were perspective sketches of the models with the players and spectators removed[9] (Figure 5.5). An approximate hypothetical perspective reconstruction of the Shroeder site ballcourt is also presented for comparison (Figure 5.6). In the shaft tomb models, courts are shown in two instances with three zonal markers placed longitudinally: one at the center and one at each end of the alley. All three courts shown have not only the raised spectators' benches or banquettes, but also a low interior bench along each side. That the courts are really of the open-ended type is shown by the placement of the spectators, who sit on both the lateral banquettes and the open ends of the court (two examples). In the ceramic models, there are four, five, and six players, and 16+, 19+, and 15 spectators. Playing balls are shown in two instances; in one case at least, the ball as shown is much larger than the head of the player.

The ceramic models of open-ended ballcourts from shaft tombs in Nayarit demonstrate the presence of this type at an early date in west Mexico; this may indeed represent the origin and cultural background for the small, open-ended courts. However, in published illustrations of sites of the Teuchitlán Tradition (the culture to which the shaft tombs belong, at least in Jalisco), Weigand has illustrated only the transitional type of ballcourt, varying from small, open-ended courts with detached temple platforms at the ends to long, narrow courts with associated temple structures at the ends (Weigand 1985:Figs. 2.12 and 2.13).

Ethnohistorical Data

Although the Tepehuan are the putative descendants of the Loma San Gabriel Culture, with which the small, open-ended ballcourts have tentatively been associated, we have no accounts of ballcourts or the game among this group.[10] Fortunately, there are ethnohistorical descriptions of both courts and game among the Acaxee (and presumably among the closely related Xixime). Beals has summarized many of these data.

> The full name of this game, according to Perez de Ribas, was *pelota de ule*. According to Santaren, the ball weighed two or three pounds and was about the size of a man's head. It was made of the milk or sap distilled by certain trees, presumably rubber-bearing plants. The game was played in a prepared playing ground, which, according to Santaren, was the first thing to be built in a new village. Santaren calls the playing ground *vatey*; Perez de Ribas, *batey*.
> . . . The *vatey* or *batey* is a small plaza, very flat, and with walls at the sides approximately a yard in height and similar to a bench in form. The disposition of the entrances is not given. . . . The ball was not touched with either the feet or the hands, but only with the buttocks and right shoulder. . . . Wagers were made both on games played by teams within the village and on the more serious games played between villages. The things wagered were largely clothing, shoes, turquoises, mantles of cotton, bows, arrows, and silver . . .
> (Beals 1933:11–12)

Beals (1933:12–13) gives considerable detail regarding the contest between the visiting teams (some of them enemies) and the challenging team, and the associated rituals. The game was preceded by dances and rituals in which mock warfare was carried out between the visitors and the villagers, with the visitors playing the part of the attackers. Immediately after this mock battle, the actual battle of the ballgame began, with the visitors supplying the ball. As elsewhere in Mesoamerica, at the time the Acaxee ballgame actually was a ceremonial battle between opposing forces, in this case between local teams and visitors from other villages. Wilcox and Sternberg (1983:249) summarize that "Dispute resolution, peace keeping, and redistribution are the principal functions of the Acaxee ballgame," and add that similar functions may have extended to the Hohokam ballgame in the American Southwest.

The Acaxee represent a key group in northwestern Mexico, though they are archaeologically unknown. Their territory was centered on the Topia region of the upper Río Culiacan drainage where they could have controlled passage through the important Topia corridor between the west coast and the Durango highlands. Recall that Mason's Sotolitos sites, while located in Tepehuan territory, were actually close to the border of Acaxee–Xixime territory. There is reason to believe that Acaxee may actually have represented a Chalchihuites survival in the high sierra refuge area, but until Acaxee–Xixime archaeology is investigated this view can be regarded only as speculation. Finally, in view of the Acaxee use of the ballgame as a means of maintaining peaceful relationships with erstwhile enemies, the repeated occurrence of both Chalchihuites and Loma San Gabriel cultural remains at sites where small, open-ended ballcourts occur may be more than coincidental.

Notes

1. These excavations were carried out under the direction of J. Charles and Ellen Abbott Kelley. Funding included continuous support from Southern Illinois University, Carbondale, and research grants from the American Philosophical Society and the National Science Foundation. The research was authorized by permits from the Instituto Nacional de Antropología e Historia.

2. Alta Vista was the major known ceremonial center of the Suchil Branch of the Mesoamerican Chalchihuites Culture, and was an astronomical center as well as an extractive center. It is believed that the Chalchihuites Culture occupied the Río Suchil area from the first centuries after Christ until about A.D. 1000. The Alta Vista center may have been first established as early as the sixth century A.D. It was remodeled and expanded in the ninth century, and apparently was abandoned about A.D. 850–900.

3. CETENAL is the abbreviation for *Comisión de Estudios del Territorio Nacional*, a major mapping project of the Mexico government.

4. The Schroeder site, partially excavated in 1954, 1956, and 1958 under my direction by the University Museum of Southern Illinois University, Carbondale, was a peripheral Mesoamerican center of the Guadiana Branch of the Chalchihuites Culture. It was apparently founded by refugee villagers from the Río Suchil area, following the fall of Alta Vista. Excavations were financed by Southern Illinois University and by grants from the Wenner Gren Foundation for Anthropological Research, Inc., and were carried out under permits issued by the Instituto Nacional de Antropología e Historia, Mexico.

5. For a recent comprehensive survey of the Loma San Gabriel Culture see Foster (1985).

6. Another alternative is that the Canutillo phase actually evolved from the local Loma Culture under renewed influence from Mesoamerican cultures to the south and that the situation seen at Gualterio Abajo reflects this development. The Gualterio Abajo component does appear to be early in the Canutillo phase.

7. The site was discovered by avocational archaeologists and medical doctors Jaime. Ganot R., Jesus F. Lazalde, and Alejandro Peschard F. of the Universidad de Juarez del Estado de Durango, who drove us to the site and helped with our investigations. They were also responsible for the discovery of the Cacaria ballcourt.

8. In my introduction to the 1971 reprint of the Mason article (Hedrick et al. 1971: 130–131) I challenged the identification of these structures as ballcourts, equating them instead with Loma San Gabriel–type residential compounds. With much new data at hand, it is clear that I was in error and Mason was correct in his identification.

9. In some instances, rough dimensions of the model are included with the illustrations. Vertical measurements were obtained using the height of the players for comparison. The drawings accordingly are only approximations of the original models.

10. However, Pennington (1969:171) notes that the northern Tepehuan may have had both the ballcourt and the ballgame.

CHAPTER 6

The Mesoamerican Ballgame
in the American Southwest

David R. Wilcox

A problem domain shared by all the contributors to this volume is that of New World prehistory. Each of us is a specialist in a particular subfield, yet all of our findings contribute toward a greater understanding of the New World cultural system and its evolution. What is called the "unity or diversity" of New World prehistory has long been debated and the controversies connected to this problem focus are seminally related to the emergence of American anthropology as a discipline (Putnam 1895; Fewkes et al. 1912; Hay et al. 1940; Hallowell 1960; Wilcox 1976). If Clovis hunters were the first hominids to enter the New World (Greenberg et al. 1986; Greenberg 1987), a unity of origin for New World macro-Indian technocomplexes, languages, cosmologies, and social organization is indicated. Therefore, a central problem of New World prehistory is to explain how the subsequent differentiation into so many diverse cultural groups occurred in a mere 11,000 years.

My basic premise is that Southwestern cultures evolved as little traditions interacting with the Mesoamerican great tradition, and thus they may be understood as participants in Mesoamerican civilization (Wilcox and Sternberg 1983; Wilcox 1986a, 1986b, 1987a). Basic similarities between Southwestern and Mesoamerican cultures may derive from the original unity of New World cultures. As Ronald Olson (1933:414) noted, "there is no reason why we should deny all but material traits to the people migrating to the New World." Shamanism, vision quests, cosmological concepts of an Earth Mother and Sky

Father, moiety divisions, and the conception of a cosmic whole formed from the relations of an underworld and an upperworld are strong possibilities in this regard (Olson 1933; Underhill 1948). Innovation in Mesoamerican ritual systems may have generated waves of change as versions of various ideas diffused, with local interpreters further redefining ideas to suit their own circumstances.

In searching for Southwestern–Mesoamerican connections, we should not expect to find many close similarities. The reality was polythetic and we must adapt our methodologies to that fact (see Needham 1975; Clarke 1978). The implication of this approach is that variation is expected to increase with greater distance between units of comparison. However, if causal connections exist, they can be traced by examining the continuities in the wave process.

As least two alternatives to this approach have been postulated. On the one hand, it can be argued that after certain basic traits were introduced from Mexico, Southwestern societies experienced an autochthonous development wholly due to internal factors (see Kidder 1924; Vivian 1970; Martin and Plog 1973). On the other hand, a direct intervention in Southwestern societies analogous to the Spanish invasion has been hypothesized, whereby traders from Mesoamerica are supposed to have entered the area in search of rare resources required by elites in the Mesoamerican metropolis (Ferdon 1955; Di Peso 1974; Kelley and Kelley 1975; Weigand et al. 1977; Weigand 1978, 1979a).

Criticism of both of these extreme positions is necessary. Excavations at Snaketown in the 1930s dealt the isolationist position a severe blow when a plethora of evidence was found that documented numerous cultural connections with northern Mesoamerica, both stylistic and substantive. Most dramatic was the presence of what were inferred to be ballcourts in Hohokam and other Southwestern sites (Gladwin et al. 1937; Wilcox and Sternberg 1983; see also Woodward 1931, 1941). Charles Di Peso's (1974; Di Peso et al. 1974) excavations at Paquimé further documented the case for significant causal connections between Mesoamerican culture and the evolution of Southwestern societies. Ballcourts, in this case I-shaped like many in Mesoamerica, were again an important element in this evidence. Nevertheless, there exists little support in these data for direct intervention of outside people (McGuire 1980; Pailes 1980; Plog et al. 1982; Wilcox 1986a, 1986b, 1991). A copper metallurgist may have come from West Mexico to Paquimé where a local elite sponsored his craft production. The most striking fact about the artifactual material in the Southwest from Mesoamerica, and vice versa, is its rarity. Chemical turquoise may be an exception (Weigand et al. 1977), but there are more parsimonious ways to explain its abundance in Mexican sites that do not require *pochteca* or *trocoderos* (Wilcox 1986b).

The purpose of this paper is to show how the study of the Mesoamerican ballgame and its distribution may be used to shed light on the importance of macroregional systems in the evolution of New World societies. My focus is the American Southwest, particularly the Hohokam and Sinagua populations; the data on Paquimé outlier courts are reviewed by Thomas Naylor (1985). First, the hypothesis that a class of features found in Hohokam and Sinagua sites is ballcourts is examined. Second, the data currently available are summarized and their classification is discussed. Certain empirical generalizations are then inferred. Finally, this information is applied to develop a general model of the evolution of the Hohokam regional system in the context of the greater macroregional system(s).

Current Status of the Hohokam Ballcourt Hypothesis

The hypothesis that oval, earthen bowl-shaped features found in Hohokam sites were "ballcourts," where a version of the Mesoamerican ballgame was performed, was first proposed by Emil W. Haury during Gila Pueblo's excavations at Snaketown in 1934–1935. Haury had just completed his doctorate at Harvard in 1934, where he had learned about Maya ballcourts from Alfred Tozzer. The parameters of those courts were remarkably analogous to attributes of the large Hohokam court at Snaketown. High parallel embankments flanked a playing alley within which were three "markers"; one in the center and one at each end (Haury in Gladwin et al. 1937). Soon Haury (1937) also showed that rubber balls, probably made from *guayule*, had been found in the American Southwest. When experts like A.V. Kidder, Sylvanus Morley, and later Linton Satterthwaite lent their support to the hypothesis, the revolutionary idea that ballcourts existed in the American Southwest (some 2400 km from the Maya Lowlands) became dogma.

A generation of students was intrigued by the question of Southwestern–Mesoamerican connections implied by this hypothesis (Gladwin 1938; Corbett 1939; Chard 1940; Haury 1945; Schroeder 1949). Only Donald Brand (1939:100) held out for the idea that the Hohokam courts were dance plazas, a local invention. Soon after Roger Kelly (1963) synthesized the Hohokam court data, Edwin Ferdon (1967) took up the issue, arguing elegantly that basic morphological differences between Mesoamerican and Hohokam courts existed and that it was equally likely that the courts were analogous to Papago *wiikita* dance grounds. Whereas the playing alleys in Mesoamerican courts were rectangular with flat floors, the Hohokam courts were oval with slightly concave floors. To many Southwestern archaeologists, Ferdon's argument implied that the larger question of Southwestern–Mesoamerican connections was moot (Martin and Plog 1973).

My monograph *Hohokam Ballcourts and their Interpretation* (Wilcox and Sternberg 1983) was designed to answer the arguments raised by Ferdon. If it is the ballgame rather than ballcourts per se that diffused from Mesoamerica, the formal differences in court morphology may be a consequence of independent invention. What is essential to the ballcourt hypothesis is that the Hohokam courts are *functionally* suitable as arenas for a version of the ballgame. I was thus faced with two problems: (1) to show that it is possible, plausible, and likely that the ballgame diffused northward during the Preclassic or early Classic periods of the Mesoamerican cultural sequence; and (2) to show that the functional parameters of Hohokam courts match those of Mesoamerican ones. The first problem required the construction of a new model of Southwestern–Mesoamerican interaction, called the "Tepiman Connection" (Wilcox and Sternberg 1983:225–228; Wilcox 1986a). It differs substantially from alternative models, equally denying what have been called the "isolationist" and "imperialist" positions (Plog et al. 1982; Wilcox 1986b). Basically, what I postulate is that the emergence of sedentism, dependence on agriculture, and pottery making (which were in place from Zacatecas to the American Southwest by ca. A.D. 200 [LeBlanc 1982]) served also to differentiate the proto-Tepiman (Tepehuan and Piman) dialect chain from proto-Tarahumaran and proto-Cahitan. This communication network linked the Chalchihuites culture area east of the Sierra Madres to Sonora and then southern Arizona west of the Sierras, thus defining a "route" through the mountains. Differential rates of innovation and differences of adaptation between Tepimans and their neighbors perpetuated cultural contrasts, but also fostered the north–south alliance networks. Ideas and high-status ritual paraphernalia, like iron-pyrites mirrors, copper bells, macaws, and strombus trumpets, moved northward on an intermittent but more-or-less continuous basis. Meanwhile, other ideas together with stone axes, slate palettes, and various other ritual items passed southward (see Kelley 1971; Wilcox 1986a, 1986b). An important mechanism facilitating this interaction may have been the playing of a version of the Mesoamerican ballgame.

The Tepiman model is highly speculative, though testable. Its principal value is that it focuses attention on specific problems whose solutions would advance general knowledge. Yet it is a fact that no court is needed to play the game (Leyenaar 1978), and certain Hohokam clay figurines dating to the early Pioneer period may portray ball players (Haury 1976:265; Wilcox and Sternberg 1983:61). Evidence that the game was played in the Middle Formative is no less widespread than the earliest villages (Lowe 1977b; Grove 1981;

Scarborough et al. 1982; Wyshak et al. 1971; Coe 1981) and the game played in formal courts had great social importance in west Mexico by the El Arenal (350 B.C.–A.D. 200), Ahualulco (A.D. 200–400), and Teuchitlán I (A.D. 400–700) phases of Jalisco (Weigand 1985, this volume). The game could thus have diffused northward along the Tepiman route without leaving physical traces in the form of ballcourts. The late prehistoric courts in the Casas Grandes area (Di Peso 1974; Naylor 1985) coupled with the ethnographic record (summarized in Wilcox and Sternberg 1983:55–92) support the claim that populations in northern Mexico have played the game continuously for the last thousand years (Leyenaar 1978). The first Hohokam courts were built during the early Colonial period, about A.D. 700 (for a discussion of the problems of Hohokam chronology see Wilcox and Sternberg 1983; Cable and Doyel 1985; Wallace and Craig 1988). They could have been independently invented there. Thus my contention that the ballgame rather than the ballcourt diffused to the Hohokam remains plausible, fits current data, and provides interesting test implications, but remains uncertain.

That Hohokam courts are functionally suitable as playing areas for performances of a version of the Mesoamerican ballgame is similarly plausible, testable, and uncertain. Their size, symmetry, smooth stop surfaces, and bowl-like character compare well with the functional parameters and range of variability in Mesoamerican courts. It also seems reasonable that a ball would respond predictably when bounced on them (Wilcox and Sternberg 1983: 175–188). What is most needed are experimental approaches—we need to play a version of the game in a court and observe the outcome. The dangers involved (Stern 1949), the expense in reproducing a court, and the absence of a strong tradition of experimentation in Southwestern archaeology are inhibiting factors, but the prospect is still possible.

Haury's hypothesis that Hohokam courts are ballcourts has thus been supported and the objections to it raised by Ferdon have been answered. Nevertheless, the issue has not been settled. The principal importance of the ballcourt hypothesis lies in its implications for Southwestern connections with Mesoamerica. Yet it is also important for Hohokam archaeology. Unequivocally, Hohokam courts are public architecture that probably functioned as ritual facilities. Their comparative study and distribution afford an excellent opportunity to identify the structural parameters of the Hohokam regional system and to model change in that system from its emergence to its disappearance. This is true whether the courts are ballcourts or not. If they are ballcourts, however, something is implied about the ritual process and the kind of exchange flows associated with it. The following discussion assumes that the ballcourt hypothesis is the correct one, and explores what implications this has for modeling the evolution of the Hohokam regional system.

Table 6.1. Colonial/Early Sedentary Period Hohokam Courts (ca. A.D. 700–1000)

Site Number	Site Name	Confidence	Crest to Crest (m)	
			Length	Width
Gila Bend				
T:13:9 ASM	Rock Ball Court	1	26.0	14.5
T:14:19 ASM	Enterprise Ranch	2	59.0	24.0
Phoenix Basin				
T:12:37 ASU	Los Solares	1	–	–
U:9:41 ASU	Los Hornos	3	–	–
U:13:1 ASM	Snaketown	1	62.6	31.7
U:13:27 ASM	Hospital-Turnkey	1	29.5	–
Agua Fria				
NA 4372	Jones Ranch	3	46.0	28.0
Middle Verde				
U:6:91 ASM	—	2	55.0	18.7
NA 3528	Verde Valley	2	64.1	26.5
NA 3528	Verde Valley	2	34.5	25.0
Upper Verde				
AZ N:4:12 (ASU)	Perkinsville	2	57.0	24.0
NA 10519	Wagner Hill	2	31.0	14.7
AR 03-07-01-127	Sycamore Point	2	33.0	15.0
Buttes				
U:16:4 ASM	Buttes Dam	1	28.5	13.75
Globe				
V:19:4 ASM	Ranch Creek	1	24.5	18.5
Point of Pines				
W:9:10 ASM	Stove Canyon	1	25.0	15.0
San Pedro				
BB:2:2 ASM	Big Ditch	2	38.0	29.0
BB:2:2 ASM	Big Ditch	2	63.0	32.0
BB:11:1 ASM	Redington	2	83.0	31.0
BB:15:1 AF	Tres Alamos	1	57.9	22.8
Tucson Basin				
AA:8:18 ASM	—	3	26.0	(19.5)
AA:8:21 ASM	Suffering Wash	2	29.3	17.7
AA:11:12 ASM	Robles Wash	2	22.4	15.2
AA:12:18 ASM	Hodges	1	61.5	30.9

Depth (m)	Orientation N of E		Rock Construction	Type	Age Estimate
0.5	43°30′,	223°30′	X	A	early Colonial
?	(95°),	(275°)	0	D	pre-Late Sedentary
?	124°,	304°	?		Colonial
–	EW/EW		?	D	early Colonial
5.8	105°,	385°	0	B	
1.0+	0°,	180°	0		early Sedentary
	SE/NW		?	C	Colonial?
1.0+	160°,	348°	0	D	Colonial
?	178°,	358°		D	Colonial?
?	0°,	180°		B	Colonial?
1.0	105°,	385°	X	D	A.D. 800–1000
0.5	118°,	298°	X	A	A.D. 950–1025
0.2	106°,	286°	X	B	A.D. 950–1025
0.3+	164°,	344°	X		late Col./early Sed.
0.8+	114°,	294°	(X)	A	Colonial
0.5+	45°,	225°	X	A	late Colonial
?	149°,	329°	0	C	Colonial/early Sed.
?	154°	334°	0	D	Colonial/early Sed.
2.7	54°,	234°	?	D	Colonial/Sedentary
?	156°,	336°	?	D	early Sedentary
0.3	30°,	210°	0	A	Colonial to early Col.
0.6	163°,	243°	0	A	Colonial to early Col.
0.7	80°,	261°	0	A	early Col. to early Cl.
2.2	105°,	285°	0	D	early Col. to Sed.

Table 6.1. *Continued*

Site Number	Site Name	Confidence	Crest to Crest (m)	
			Length	Width
AA:12:?	Derrio Wash	3	26.5	16.6
AA:12:57 ASM	Los Morteros	2	64.0	27.4
AA:16:49 ASM	Dakota Wash	1	–	–
BB:5:5	Rainbow's End	2	20	14
BB:9:1 ASM	Romero	2	54.2	27.0
BB:9:1 ASM	Romero	2	25.3	14.2
BB:9:88 ASM	Honey Bee	3	30.5	15.5
BB:9:104 ASM	Sleeping Snake	2	46.0	25.0
BB:13:15 ASM	Valencia	1	58.5	21.7
BB:13:16A	Punta de Agua	3	(35.0)	(15.5)
BB:13:16C ASM	Punta de Agua	2	34.5	18.5
BB:13:232	—	3	51.0	–
Avra Valley				
AA:16:94 ASM	Water World	1	23.3	12.3

Patterns in the Current Data for Hohokam Courts

In my monograph (Wilcox and Sternberg 1983), I assembled data on 193 courts at 154 sites. This nearly doubled the sample previously reported by Chester Chard (1940), Albert Schroeder (1940), and Roger Kelly (1963). Since then, new courts have been discovered, several others have been shown *not* to be courts, some have been tested, and many more have been recorded in much greater detail (Ferg 1984; Wilcox 1984, 1985; Effland 1985; Doelle 1988; Elson and Doelle 1987; Wallace 1987; Paul Fish pers. comm. 1987). Two courts included in my original sample, the Santa Cruz site in Sonora and SAR 62H:5 in New Mexico, now appear to be fourteenth century courts related to the Casas Grandes regional system (Wilcox 1991, n.d.). Altogether, the current sample of Hohokam courts now consists of 207 cases at 166 sites, all of them in Arizona. The spatial dimensions of this universe are 400+ km north–south by 330+ km east–west.

The most important result of recent work, in addition to better documenting the dimensions, orientations, and distribution of the Hohokam courts, is the clarification of their chronology. The construction data and life history of

Depth (m)	Orientation N of E		Rock Construction	Type	Age Estimate
1.0	12°,	192°	0	A	Colonial to Sedentary
1.5+	130°,	310°	0	D	late Col. to Sed.
–	NS/NS		?	B	late Col. to early Sed.
0.3	45°,	225°	0	A	late Col. to mid. Sed.
0.6+	49°48′,	229°48′	X	D	late Col. to Sed.
?	23°47′,	203°47′	X	A	late Col. to Sed.
0.3	32°,	212°	0	A	late to early Colonial
0.4	157°,	337°	0	C	late Col. to mid. Sed.
0.5	163°10′,	343°20′	0	D	late Col. to late Sed.
	171°,	351°	0	B	early Col. to Sed.
0.5+	77°,	257°	0	B	late Col. to Classic
–	NS/NS			D	Colonial to Sedentary
1.0	84°,	264°	0	A	Colonial

Hohokam courts are difficult to establish in the best of circumstances. Ceramic associations are often equivocal, as the best evidence is the record of intrusions. No independent means of dating any of the courts has been found. Three factors, however, have helped to refine current knowledge of their relative chronology: (1) it now appears that Snaketown was abandoned between A.D. 1075 and 1100 (Haury 1976; Gregory pers. comm. 1987); (2) all but two of the Flagstaff courts were built following the eruption of Sunset Crater in A.D. 1064, and these two may also have been late (Wilcox 1986c)—this means they probably were used if not built *after* the abandonment of Snaketown during what I will call the "early Classic" period; and (3) the excavation of several courts has established their relative age. Accordingly, it is now possible to group the courts into three chronological sets (see Tables 6.1–6.3).

Those courts that date to the Early Classic period (Table 6.3) were probably built after A.D. 1075. Those dated to the Colonial or early Sedentary (Table 6.1) were probably built before A.D. 1000 but after about A.D. 700. The remainder are the least certainly dated (Table 6.2), but most appear to relate to the late Sedentary, A.D. 1000–1075. Some of the courts built earlier than this may have continued in use during the late Sedentary and, similarly, some of

Table 6.2. Late Sedentary Period Hohokam Courts (A.D. 1000–1075)

Site Number	Site Name	Confidence	Crest to Crest (m)	
			Length	Width
Gila Bend				
T:13:2 ASM	Citrus	1	60.9	28.3
T:2:1 ASM	Gatlin	1	36.6	20.4
T:14:14,15 ASM	Three-Mile	1	24.0	16.0
T:14:14,15 ASM	Three-Mile	1	23.7	9.5
T:14:16 ASM	HiVu Ranch	2	29.0	18.3
T:14:16 ASM	HiVu Ranch	2	25.9	18.3
T:14:19 ASM	Enterprise Ranch	2	30.0	21.3
T:14:19 ASM	Enterprise Ranch	2	26.0	16.0
T:9:1 ASM	—	2	(30.0)	(18.1)
Lower Salt				
NA 11441	Van Liere	2	37.2	25.0
NA 15798	Coldwater	2	32.6	22.3
NA 14722	La Cienega	2	30.5	19.4
NA 14690	Cashion	2	32.9	24.7
T:12:7 ASM	Villa Buena I	1	74.0	32.0
T:12:7 ASM	Villa Buena I	2	31.4	21.8
T:12:7 ASM	Villa Buena I	3	30.0	22.0
T:12:4 PG	Las Cremaciones	2	84.0	34.5
T:12:4 PG	Las Cremaciones	1	30.5	19.4
U:9:38 ASM	Las Ruinitas	2	30.5	18.3
Middle Gila				
T:16:9 ASM	Hidden Ruin	2	32.9	16.5
T:16:9 ASM	Hidden Ruin	2	?	?
U:13:1 ASM	Snaketown	1	25.0	15.0
U:13:6 ASM	—	2	33.5	24.7
U:14:8 ASM	Santan	2	34.0	23.0
U:14:15 ASM	—	2	31.4	20.5
—	Chee Nee	2	30.0	15.5
U:14:54 ASM	—	2	30.0	22.0
U:15:52 ASM	Poston Butte	2	24.4	15.8
U:13:2 PG	Casa Blanca	2	64.0	30.5
U:13:95,99 101,103 ASM	Sweetwater	2	61.9	23.8
U:13:95,99 101,103 ASM	Sweetwater	2	30.5	23.5
AA:2:2 ASM	Grewe (Casa Grande)	2	33.5	21.3

Depth (m)	Orientation N of E	Rock Construction	Type	Age Estimate
–	121°, 301°	X	D	late Colonial/Sedentary
0.7+	162°, 342°	0	B	late Colonial/Sedentary
1.9	178°, 358°	0	A	Sedentary
1.4+	121°, 301°	0	A	Colonial/Sedentary
1.8+	NS/NS	0	A	?
1.5+	NS/NS	0	A	?
2.5+	NS/NS	0	B	Sedentary/Classic
low	NS/NS	0	A	Sedentary/Classic
1.0	NS/NS	?	B	?
2.4+	NS/NS	0	B	Sedentary
1.5+	NS/NS	0	B	?
0.7+	NS/NS	0	B	?
1.8+	NS/NS	0	B	Colonial/Sedentary
2.7+	104°, 284°	0	D	Colonial/Sedentary
1.5+	0°, 180°	0	B	Colonial/Sedentary
0.8	177°, 257°	0	B	Colonial Sedentary
?	1°, 181°	?	D	?
1.2+	176°, 356°	0	B	late Colonial/Sedentary
0.6+	NS/NS	?	B	?
1.4+	4°, 184°	0	B	Colonial/Classic
?	EW/EW	0	D	Colonial/Classic
0.5+	15°, 195°	0	A	Sedentary
0.9+	NS/NS	0	B	?
1.5	61°, 241°	X	B	Colonial/Classic
2.0	1°, 181°	0	B	Sedentary
–	10°, 190°	?	A	?
–	NS/NS	?	B	Sedentary
1.4+	NS/NS	0	A	Colonial/Sedentary
0.8+	SE/NW	0	D	Colonial/Classic
0.5+	EW/EW	0	D	Colonial/Classic
0.8+	NS/NS	0	B	Colonial/Classic
0.7+	112°, 292°	0	B	Colonial/Sedentary

Table 6.2. *Continued*

Site Number	Site Name	Confidence	Crest to Crest (m)	
			Length	Width
AA:2:63 ASM	Pueblo Bisnaga	1	34.2	21.9
SW Flank, Superstition Mountains				
U:11:1 ASU	—	2	27.5	18.0
—	Christenson	2	31.0	18.0
U:11:2 ASU	—	2	28.0	18.5
U:15:1 ASM	—	2	27.3	18.8
U:15:55 ASM	—	2	27.3	16.0
Florence 8:1 GP	—	2	33.3	17.2
Buttes				
U:16:29 ASM	—	2	25.7	16.4
U:16:78 ASM	—	2	25.0	12.0
U:16:95 ASM	—	3	22.0	15.5
U:16:119 ASM	—	2	24.2	14.2
V:13:58 ASM	—	2	30.0	15.0
V:13:8 ASM	Kearney	3	20.0	14.0
Safford				
CC:1:4 ASM	Eden	2	24.5	16.0
CC:2:3 ASM	Buena Vista	2	70.0	(30.0)
Prescott				
N:10:1 PC	Hays Ranch	2	57.0	19.4
N:10:2 PC	—	2	33.3	15.5
N:10:2 PC	—	2	30.0	16.3
N:10:2 PC	—	3	53.8	17.4
AR03-09-03-38	De Spain	2	30.0	15.8
Miscellaneous				
FF:7:2 ASM	Leslie Canyon	2	72.5	22.0
BB:15:3 AF	—	1	33.5	18.3
T:4:10 ASM	—	2	25.9	10.1
—	Robles	2	22.4	15.2
EE:2:105 ASM	—	1	24.8	12.0

the late Sedentary courts may have been used in the Early Classic. Based on the opinion of William Doelle (1988), I show all of the Tucson Basin courts in Table 6.1, but suspect that many of them lasted into the Middle Rincon phase, what I am here calling the "late Sedentary period." As for the Late Classic,

Depth (m)	Orientation N of E	Rock Construction	Type	Age Estimate
0.8	178°, 358°	0	B	Colonial/Sedentary
0.5+	7°, 187°	X	A	late Colonial/Sedentary
1.5+	172°, 352°	0	B	late Colonial/Sedentary
0.3+	16°, 196°	0	A	Colonial/Sedentary
1.2+	10°, 190°	0	A	late Colonial/Sedentary
1.5+	73°, 253°	0	A	late Colonial/Sedentary
1.0+	2°, 182°	0	B	late Pioneer/Sedentary
0.1	175°, 355°	X	A	late Pioneer/Sedentary
0.5	NS/NS	X	A	late Colonial/Sedentary
0.25	SSE/NNW	0	A	late Colonial/Sedentary
0.4	75°, 255°	X	A	late Pioneer/Sedentary
–	NS/NS	0	A	early Colonial/Classic
–	?	?	A	?
0.4+	13°, 193°	X	A	?
–	105°, 285°	0	D	?
1.0+	115°, 295°	0	D	late Colonial/Sedentary
1.0+	104°, 284°	0	B	?
10.0+	0°, 180°	0	A	?
0.5+	94°, 274°	0	D	Colonial?
0.5+	99°, 279°	0	A	late Sedentary?
–	3°, 183°	?	D	?
–	178°, 358°	?	B	Sedentary?
–	NS/NS	X	A	?
0.7+	80°, 261°	0	A	Colonial/Sedentary?
0.5+	35°, 225°	0	A	Colonial/Sedentary?

no evidence directly shows that any courts persisted into this period; it appears that all Hohokam courts were abandoned by about A.D. 1200–1250 (Wilcox and Sternberg 1983; Gregory pers. comm. 1987). The groupings shown in Tables 6.1–6.3 are in part hypothetical and will no doubt be modified as new data become available. Yet they do provide a reasonably reliable basis for assessing trends in the changing role of the courts in the Hohokam regional system. Data on three courts in the Upper Verde shown in Table 6.1 were recorded in the summer of 1990 but these data were not added to the summary figures.

The relationships of length to width and crest to crest in the current sample of 108 measured cases is shown in Figure 6.1. In my monograph, five classes of Hohokam courts are defined. Remeasurement of the sample from the lower Verde, however, showed that one class was specious because the measurements reported (Canouts 1975) were not taken crest to crest (Wilcox

Table 6.3. Early Classic Period Hohokam Courts (ca. A.D. 1075–1250)

Site Number	Site Name	Confidence	Crest to Crest (m) Length	Width
Flagstaff				
NA 15,349	Loflin	2	26.7	18.3
NA 3669	Ridge	1	40.0	28.5
NA 3687	Ridge	1	38.5	28.5
NA 2132	Winona	1	31.2	24.2
NA 5212	New Caves	?	?	?
NA 72	Old Caves	2	37.1	21.2
NA 4008	Doney Park	2	33.2	22.2
AR03-04-02-2166	Camp	2	36.9	21.8
NA 1893	Wupatki Road	2	31.5	19.1
NA 804	Juniper Terrace	1	34.2	20.4
NA 3254	Second Sink	2	34.5	20.8
Middle Verde				
NA 4643	Watter's Ranch	2	30.5	16.5
NA 4626	Sacred Mountain	1	32.0	23.8
Phoenix Basin				
T:12:9 ASM	Villa Buena II	2	36.0	25.0
T:12:9 ASM	Villa Buena II	2	31.4	22.8
T:12:10 ASM	Las Colinas	1	–	–
U:9:7 ASM	Pueblo Grande	1	–	–
U:9:41 ASU	Los Hornos	1	–	–
AA:2:17 ASM	Casa Grande	1	46.6	25.3
U:15:1 ASM	Adamsville	1	28.0	18.5
U:13:27 ASM	Pueblo del Monte	2	32.0	22.8

1985). Figure 6.1 shows that two distinct size classes are present, just as Haury (in Gladwin et al. 1937) long ago recognized. The smaller class may be arbitrarily subdivided into three subclasses. When the temporal distribution of the cases (Tables 6.1–6.3) by size is examined, additional patterns are apparent. These may be summarized as follows:

1. The earliest courts vary the most in size. Many are among the smallest known, but they also include the largest and a series in between.
2. The courts thought to date to the late Sedentary period are tightly clustered into two classes, small and large. Many of the largest courts were first constructed during the Colonial period, but they were often rebuilt

Depth (m)	Orientation N of E	Rock Construction	Type	Age Estimate
(1.5)	1°, 181°	0	A	?
	163°, 343°	X	C	early Classic
	169°, 349°	X	C	early Classic
2.7	172°, 352°	?	B	late Sed./early Classic
?	?	?	?	early Classic
(1.5)	34°, 214°	X	B	?
(2.0)	0°, 180°	X	B	late Sed./early Classic
(1.0)	40°, 184°	X	B	late Sed./early Classic
(1.5)	8°, 188°	X	B	early Classic
2.1	3°, 183°	X	B	early Classic
(1.5)	165°, 345°	X	B	?
?	9°, 189°	X	A	?
(1.0)	10°, 190°	X		early Classic
1.5+	NS	?	B	Classic
1.5+	NS	?	B	Classic
–	0°, 180°	?	(A)	early Classic
–	7°, 187°	?	(B)	late Sed./early Classic
–	0°, 180°	?	B	late Sed./early Classic
1.8+	178°, 358°	0	C	late Sed./early Classic
0.8+	165°, 345°	0	A	Classic
1.4+	162°, 342°	X	B	Sed./Classic

and it appears likely that many of them continued to be used into the late Sedentary (Wilcox and Sternberg 1983). Wasley and Johnson (1965:84), for example, showed that the large court at the Citrus site was built in the Sedentary period. The large one at Snaketown was rebuilt at the very end of the Colonial period (Gladwin et al. 1937:40). The small Sedentary courts may be arbitrarily subdivided into two subclasses.

3. None of the large courts appears to date to the Classic period. Two sites, Casa Grande and Ridge Ruin, have courts much larger than the norm for small courts. The Casa Grande court was the first to be reported in the archaeological literature (Johnson 1848) and is one of the first to be professionally investigated (Pinkley 1981 [1918]). Haury (in Gladwin et al. 1937) thus chose to refer to the small courts as the Casa Grande type. Quantification of court sizes shows, however, that the Casa Grande is somewhat unusual. It was one of the largest courts extant during the Classic period.

Figure 6.2 summarizes the data on court orientation in terms of the three chronological periods. Figure 6.3 shows the distribution of courts dating to

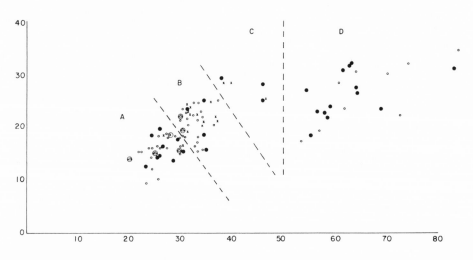

A-D   size classes
●   early Colonial/early Sedentary
×   early Classic
○   late Sedentary
⊖   early Col./early Sed. and late Sed.
⊗   early Col./early Sed. and early Classic

Figure 6.1. The relationship of crest-to-crest length to width, in meters, in measured Hohokam ballcourts.

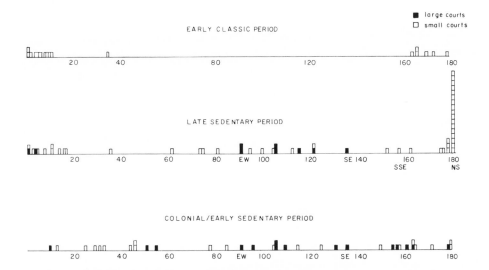

Figure 6.2. Hohokam ballcourt orientations by temporal period.

the Colonial and Sedentary periods. The wide range of variability apparent in court orientation was first remarked by Wasley and Johnson (1965) and is discussed in my monograph (Wilcox and Sternberg 1983). My earlier analysis found that in all local areas where sufficient data are available this wide variability was repeated. Documentation of court orientation in both the lower Verde Valley and Flagstaff areas confirms this basic pattern (Wilcox 1985; Tables 6.1–6.3).

Once the data are organized by temporal period, however, a more complex pattern emerges (Figure 6.2). All currently known courts dating to the early Colonial period fall in the middle range of orientation values from N43.5°E to N135°E. This sharply contrasts with the Early Classic orientations in which courts are concentrated at either extreme between N0°–34°E and N163°–178°E. When the data are grouped in 20° intervals, the orientations by the late Colonial period are distributed quite uniformly, being rare or absent only between N60°–80°E and N120°–140°E. Remarkably, by the late Sedentary period, one of those last intervals is preferred to the adjacent one of N20°–60°E. Significantly, the extremes around north–south also become much more popular. The whole middle range of N40°–160°E drops out by the Early Classic period.

Figure 6.3 shows the spatial distribution of large courts, all of which appear to be Preclassic in age, in relation to other Preclassic courts. The basic pattern of diversity in court orientations within local areas is similarly exhibited by

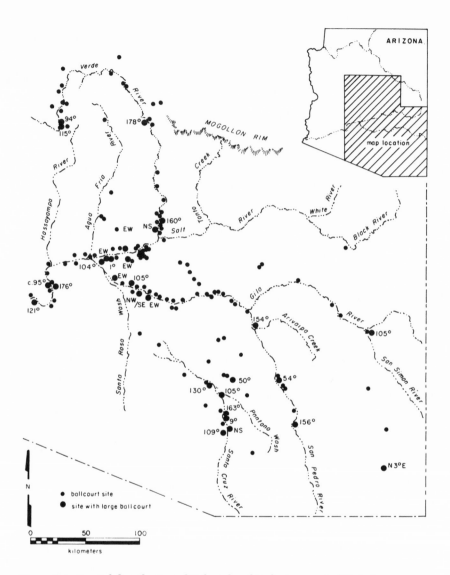

Figure 6.3. Spatial distribution of Colonial and Sedentary period Hohokam ballcourts.

the large court orientations. There is also a tendency as one moves up- or downriver for large court orientations to alternate between north–south and east–west. What, we may ask, do these various patterns mean, if anything?

One possibility is that court orientation is a random event, an outcome of decisions about site selection that have nothing to do with orientation per se.

James Holmlund has recently prepared detailed topographic maps of the Valencia and Romero sites in the Tucson Basin. His analysis (in Elson and Doelle 1987:133) suggests that:

> One characteristic of this [large Romero] ballcourt, which has been noted for other ballcourts, recently, is the fact that it was built perpendicular to the local slope. This seems to serve a dual purpose: 1) it significantly reduces the amount of excavation necessary to actually build a ballcourt, and 2) it deflects downslope water and sediment movement if a small upslope berm is maintained.

This is a plausible hypothesis that may fit other cases as well. At Snaketown, for example, the large court was built more-or-less parallel to the strike of a low ridge (see Wilcox et al. 1981). I wonder, however, if the Hohokam were capable of *both* taking advantage of local topographic conditions *and* orientating their courts as they wished. This possibility has not yet been excluded. More work like Holmlund's is needed to test alternative hypotheses, as are exact measurements of court orientations that take into account the local horizon as well as topographic and cultural features.

In an effort to explain the pattern of variability in Hohokam court orientations, I have previously postulated that each orientation has a specific ideological or mythological referent, and that they were complementary in their function. "Court orientation may then have been keyed to an annual progression of calendrical ceremonies designed to keep the universe moving smoothly through its annual cycle" (Wilcox and Sternberg 1983:212). This hypothesis was the foundation for my model of the Hohokam regional system in the Sedentary period (Wilcox and Sternberg 1983; Wilcox 1987a), and it also led to hypotheses about Mesoamerican court systems.

Franz Tichy (1981) has shown that the orientations of Aztec temples fall into regular equivalence classes that are evenly spaced 4.5° apart. Collectively they form a normal curve anchored by the solstice orientations. Assuming that the gods of each temple faced the direction from which the sun was supposed to rise (Tichy 1981; see also Carrasco 1982:97), important annual ceremonies on those dedicatory dates may be hypothesized. A round of ceremonies among differently oriented temples is thus indicated, forming an integrated ritual-economic system of exchanges (see also Ingram 1971). Although Mesoamerican ballcourts are often discussed as being oriented "north–south" or "east–west," in fact much wider variation is present (Blom 1932; Smith 1961). I wondered, then, whether a system similar to that proposed for the Aztec temples may have at an earlier time included ballcourts. One of the possibilities this hypothesis suggests is that Mesoamerican economies were structured by complex ceremonial exchange systems (see Dalton

1977) rather than by market systems for a much longer period than some authors have proposed (see Blanton et al. 1981).

If Hohokam court orientations, or equivalence classes of them, do correlate with astronomical or mythological events, changes in orientation patterns may indicate changes in belief systems. If a large range of orientations did in fact drop out during the Early Classic period, it is interesting to note that this is correlated with significant changes in ritual paraphernalia associated with death and burial practices (Doyel 1980; Wilcox 1987a; Gregory pers. comm. 1987). This is also the time when platform mounds become important. There are some intriguing hints that the rituals associated with the platform mounds may have taken over the role of the east–west courts.

Beginning as circular features in the Sedentary period, with earlier circular antecedents back to the end of the Pioneer period (Haury 1976), Hohokam platform mounds were successively transformed during the Early Classic period, becoming increasingly rectangular and oriented north–south (Gregory and McGuire 1982; Gregory pers. comm. 1987; Wilcox 1987b). By about A.D. 1250 (Gregory pers. comm. 1987), coursed-caliche structures were built on top of them for the first time; they were probably elite residences (Wilcox 1987b). These structures had courtyards on the east side and thus may be said to be east facing. Unfortunately, reliable orientational data are not available for most of these features.

Measurements are available in one case, however. The Casa Grande is a special case of a Middle Classic platform mound, lacking courtyards, but having its first story filled in (Wilcox and Shenk 1977). Two other similar structures have recently been identified, one at Pueblo Grande (Cushing 1893; Wilcox 1984), and one at La Ciudad (Wilcox 1987b). John Molloy (1969) and others (Evans and Hillman 1981) have measured the angles of the diagonals for a series of specially constructed holes in the Casa Grande walls. Two holes are oriented north–south, but the rest provide a way to observe the eastern or western horizon. Significant astronomical events are apparently correlated with the azimuths of these diagonals (Molloy 1969; Evans and Hillman 1981; see Table 6.4.).

No azimuths of Hohokam courts or most platform mounds have been measured. All current orientations are based on hand-held Brunton compass bearings converted to true north. Nevertheless, the data from the Casa Grande provide striking support for the hypothesis that platform mounds replaced courts as loci for measuring or celebrating certain astronomical or mythological events. Five of the holes in the Casa Grande afford a sighting line along an azimuth of N105°–107°E. The most frequent single true north orientation associated with east–west court data is also N105° (or 285°). Furthermore, this orientation is present in five different areas and in several of the largest

Table 6.4. Casa Grande Hole Orientations

Hole	Location	Orientation	Correlation
1	Tier C, S wall	NS	
2	Tier C, W wall S	EW	Spring Equinox
3	Tier C, E door	126.5°	
4	Tier C, W wall N	106.5°, 286.5°	
5	Tier C, N wall	NS	
6	Tier C, E wall up N	90.9°	other diagonal 105–107°
7	Tier C, E wall up S	88°	other diagonal 105–107°
8	Tier C, E wall lo N	90.5°	Spring Equinox 105–107°
9	Tier C, E wall lo S	94.5°	Spring Equinox 105–107°
10	Tier C, E wall S	EW	Spring Equinox
11	Tier E, W wall	113.5°, 293.5°	sides N174°–175°E
12	Tier B, W wall	66.5°, 246.5°	and (125.5°, 305.5°)
13	Tier A, W wall	118.2°, 298.2°	Summer Solstice; sides N174–175°E

courts, and within four of the largest and most complex sites (Snaketown, Hodges, Buena Vista, and Villa Buena I). Courts with this orientation were among the first built in Arizona in about A.D. 700 (Wilcox and Sternberg 1983). This date correlates well with the end of the Classic period in Mesoamerica (Wolf 1976).

Remarkably, the Classic site of Teotihuacán is laid out on an east–west azimuth of 285°, as are many other sites in Mesoamerica (Aveni 1980; Malmstrom 1981). Opinion varies as to why this orientation was chosen; Aveni (1980) suggests a correlation with the helical rising of the Pleiades and Malmstrom (1981) argues that it had a sacred significance associated with the 260-day almanac that he believes was developed at the Olmec site of Izapa. Associated with the grid layout of Teotihuacán are pecked crosses composed of 260 cupules (Aveni 1980). No comparable pecked crosses are known in the American Southwest (Donald Weaver pers. comm. 1985), but it is noteworthy that several are documented near Alta Vista, Zacatecas, that appear to date before the eighth century A.D. (Aveni et al. 1982).

While I cannot explain how the Hohokam might have deliberately and accurately established the N105°E orientation, its correlation with a widespread and highly significant orientation in Mesoamerica cannot be easily dismissed as mere coincidence. It tends to support the hypothesis that a cycle of annual, calendrically based rituals were associated with Hohokam courts. That this may have involved a 260-day almanac is a fascinating, if presently untestable, possibility. Another implication is that calendrical ceremonialism may already have emerged in the Hohokam area by the Colonial period, a century or more before I had previously thought (see Wilcox and Sternberg 1983; Wilcox 1987a).

The Evolution of the Hohokam Regional System

The Hohokam concept was invented in the 1930s by Harold Gladwin (1931) and others to explain a set of archaeological data in southern Arizona. They showed that an interaction sphere existed that was characterized by red-on-buff pottery and other traits. Archaeological remains on the Colorado Plateau and other adjacent areas sharply contrasted with the red-on-buff remains. Gladwin (1930; Gladwin and Gladwin 1935; Gladwin et al. 1937) inferred that the populations responsible for the red-on-buff distribution were part of a folk culture with a cultural tradition independent of those in surrounding areas. He postulated a model which envisioned a "pioneer" occupation in the Phoenix Basin, "colonial" expansion into outlying peripheral zones, a stable or "sedentary" period, and a final retraction back into the Phoenix Basin during the "classic" period. The Hohokam were envisioned to have been invaded by Salado populations from the upper Salt River drainage during the latter period. Emil Haury (1945) supported this theory in his dissertation, and in subsequent work continued to advocate what I have called the "Gladwinian model" (Haury 1976; Wilcox 1980). Haury's principal modification was to argue that the Hohokam migrated to the Phoenix Basin from Mexico at the beginning of the Pioneer period, bringing irrigation technology with them.

The Gladwinian model dominated Hohokam archaeology for many decades. Textbooks (McGregor 1965) proclaimed it, younger scholars treated most of it as fact (denying only the Salado migration), and the latest textbook on southwestern archaeology is still influenced by it (Cordell 1984). The pace of Hohokam archaeology, however, has greatly accelerated; the amount of data available has grown enormously, and today most of the assumptions of the Gladwinian model appear doubtful, if not altogether false. Controversy about chronology and the general characteristics of Hohokam cultural history will continue, though the struggle to formulate more realistic models has been joined.

My own approach (Wilcox and Shenk 1977; Wilcox 1979a, 1980) has been to redefine the Hohokam concept as a regional system of interacting populations. One is then free to ask questions about the nature of these interactions without the constraints of specific hypotheses about them which the Gladwinian model postulates. At the same time, the Gladwinian hypotheses can be retained and tested against alternatives that we may now proceed to formulate. One may also move back and forth from household to settlement to local system to region and on to macroregional fields without prior assumptions about how populations on each scale are related to one another.

Recent research on the Archaic period in southern Arizona has led Bruce Huckell (1984) to recommend that the concept of a "Cochise culture" be abolished in favor of a broader notion of a network of Archaic populations fluidly interacting over much larger spaces than previously conceived. Rock art data support this position (Schaafsma 1980; Wallace and Holmlund 1986). I suggest that Clarke's (1978) concept of polythetic technocomplexes suitably describes the reality of the Archaic assemblages that Huckell discusses. When stream aggregation began anew in southern Arizona in the second millennium B.C (Huckell 1988; see also Waters 1987), *cienagas* formed. Late Archaic populations gravitated around these rich patches of economic plants, living in small hamlets and growing cultigens (Huckell 1988). Pottery first appeared in the early centuries A.D (LeBlanc 1982; Cable and Doyel 1985; William Marmaduke pers. comm. 1988). By about A.D. 300, what have traditionally been recognized as Hohokam populations became visible in the archaeological record of the Phoenix and Tucson basins. The earliest good evidence of irrigation technology dates to the end of the Pioneer period when a general settlement shift from cienaga-edge to floodplain-edge also is apparent (Wilcox and Shenk 1977:180–181; Wilcox 1979a; Cable and Doyel 1985; Huckell 1988). Haury's (1976) hypothesis that the Hohokam were a people who migrated from Mexico seems increasingly untenable.

A "colonial" expansion also seems increasingly unlikely (Doyel 1984). Instead, *in situ* demographic growth and changes in the nature of interaction on all scales of organization characterize Hohokam populations. Population density increased differentially following the introduction of irrigation technology, and the riverine sectors of the Phoenix and Tucson basins rapidly exceeded their neighbors in size. These changes in the regional density distribution of population probably had a profound effect on the operation of exchange networks and the flow of valuables within them. It was in this context that the Hohokam ballcourts first appeared (Wilcox and Sternberg 1983). Interestingly, they seem to date no earlier in the Phoenix Basin than in numerous outlying areas (Table 6.1). Formalization of the ballgame, then, may have been a social mechanism to adjudicate the new realities of exchange flows in southern Arizona, following the success of irrigation agriculture and population increases (Wilcox and Sternberg 1983:228–232; Wilcox 1987b).

Because most New World populations lacked beasts of burden, transporting relatively large quantities of goods across any distance in a short time required the mobilization of large numbers of people. Ceremonial exchange systems are a way of accomplishing this task by supplementing the exchanges contingent on kinship connections. Formalization of the ballgame and the construction of ballcourts at fixed locations apparently brought such a system into existence (Wilcox 1987a). Together with significant changes in death ritual that were adopted in the Colonial period (see Wilcox and Sternberg 1983:232–235), the innovations in the ballgame sharpened cultural differences on a macroregional and then a regional scale. Thus new systemic boundaries were created that tore apart the old polythetic networks of the past.

Distinct core areas emerged with several kinds of peripheries supporting them. Ballcourts make one of these systems archaeologically visible (in southern Arizona). Great kivas mark similar systems whose core zones were Chaco Canyon (Lekson 1987) and the Mimbres Valley (LeBlanc 1983; Anyon 1984; Anyon and LeBlanc 1984), respectively. All three of these regional systems experienced a major crisis at the end of the eleventh century, and each apparently collapsed. Local settlement systems then formed, whose cultural identities and boundaries were sharply defined, in part, by conflict (Wilcox 1979b, 1988, 1989). The ballgame continued to play a role on a local scale in certain areas (Table 6.3), but new forms of organization soon replaced it. In the Phoenix Basin, a network of platform mounds was created that marks the emergence of an elite, presumably involved in decision-making and increased social complexity. Similar transformations were occurring elsewhere in the Southwest (Upham 1982). Interestingly, in one case (and the most complex one) at Paquimé in northwestern Chihuahua, I-shaped ballcourts were adopted (Di Peso 1974). A regional system centered on Paquimé, and defined by the predominance of Chihuahuan polychromes, apparently was integrated, in part, by a ballcourt network (Wilcox n.d.). Thus, it appears that the ballgame was a valuable mechanism in a variety of nonstate level societies, but not in all types. Why some societies manifested the game and others did not is a matter requiring further research.

Without insisting that the issue is settled, I have argued that a version of the Mesoamerican ballgame diffused northward as far as southern Arizona where Hohokam populations found it to be a useful social mechanism for region-scale integration. As a "little tradition" of the Mesoamerican "great tradition," Hohokam culture adapted innovations from the south to serve local purposes. Hohokam ballcourts were thus independently invented to solve organizational problems that emerged following the adoption of irrigation technology and subsequent differential demographic increases.

I propose that the ballcourt network marks the presence of a ceremonial exchange system that choreographed and regulated regional exchange flows among a set of contiguous local populations, populations that shared in the creation of a Hohokam cultural identity (Wilcox 1987a). These people cremated their dead and used ritual paraphernalia that was derived in part from a macroregional field outside the Hohokam regional system. Pyrites mirrors (some with pseudo-cloisonné Tezcatlipoca images on the back; Woodward 1941), copper bells, macaws (and probably their feathers), and shells are included among these items (Nelson 1986). We still know almost nothing about how that macroregional "system" worked (for various speculations, see Mathien and McGuire 1986). The coincidental collapse of three southwestern regional systems, ca. A.D. 1100, may be due to the chance conjunction of internal environmental and cultural factors (e.g., Vivian 1970; Wilcox 1987a). Or it may be explicable, in part, as an outcome of changes in the external macroregional system, such as the severing of the Tepiman connection (Wilcox 1986a).

In later centuries, Paquimé rose to power in the International Four Corners area by establishing a monopoly over the valuables of copper bells, macaws, and shells (Di Peso 1974; Wilcox 1991, n.d.). Meanwhile, on the Colorado Plateau and in the Rio Grande Valley, Pueblo populations accessed shell from the Pacific Coast via a local settlement system along the Mohave River (Warren 1984). Thus, in the late prehistoric period, the structure of macroregional systems and the relationships of the American Southwest to Mesoamerica were considerably different than they had been in previous centuries. Paquimé adopted a new version of the Mesoamerican ballgame to serve its own purposes; the Puebloans did not. Failure of the Paquimé macroeconomy led to regional abandonment in the fifteenth century, creating a geographical gap between the Puebloans and Mesoamerican populations in Sinaloa and points south (see also Riley 1982; Reff 1987). The impression of autochthonous development by the Pueblos may have been produced by this historical process. No doubt debate and fresh investigation of these issues will continue for many years before a satisfactory resolution is achieved. As that happens, New World archaeology will be enriched and we will be able to address even more fundamental questions about the unity and diversity of New World populations.

Note

Thanks go to Philip Thompson, director of the Museum of Northern Arizona, for his support and to Dolly Spaulding for drawing the figures. Much of the research reported here was originally sponsored by the Western Archeological and Conservation Center, National Park Service, under contract with the Arizona State Museum, University of Arizona. The support of Raymond H. Thompson, director of the Arizona State Museum, is warmly appreciated.

PART II
Southern Mesoamerica

Courting the Southern Maya Lowlands: A Study in Pre-Hispanic Ballgame Architecture

Vernon L. Scarborough

> The view of architecture as equipment—the sum of individual needs—denies the traditional, larger function of architecture; to be an artificial and built representation of the collective. (Lerup 1977:19)

The architecture of the Lowland Maya was a transitory medium, like the jungle ecology from which it arose. The complicated and somewhat fragile life cycles of the tropics were the immediate backdrop for this grand cultural landscape. In a manner similar to the way the Maya continuously interacted with the ever-changing natural world, as reflected in their "dispersed compacted" settlement design (Scarborough and Robertson 1986), architecture became a more plastic medium of expression than perhaps found in some other Mesoamerican societies. Generally, early buildings in the Lowlands only became the scaffolding for later architectural expression. The Maya ballgame, however, played on a masonry court, was an architectural exception.

The Maya viewed architecture as a transitory medium. From pyramids and acropolises to house mounds and plaza space, architecture underwent numerous building events and frequent orientational changes. The North Acropolis at Tikal may best typify the complexity of these events: beginning with the emergence of Maya civilization to its ultimate demise, as many as 100 individual buildings lie buried within its mass (Coe 1967:41).

The cultural landscape was a blending of physical and social environments. In the dispersed residential zones, few attempts at establishing permanence were assumed. It was only with the development of authoritarian elites that the central precinct and city architecture arose. As frequently stated, the city in the Maya area was a different construct than noted in the Highlands (Haviland 1970). It was not supported by the dense population aggregates associated with textbook definitions of urbanism, nor was it a vacant ceremonial center without the craftpersons, merchants, and laborers that maintained the structure of a city. Borne somewhere between, the Maya city was an open expression of an established elite interacting with the natural and cultural tides. The longevity of the civilization may in part be attributed to this adaptability.

Ballcourts

Within this context, the rubber-ball game played on a masonry court was institutionalized. The game was a social, political, and religious manifestation of the above interactivism. In the southern Maya Lowlands, ballcourts were forums for expressing political alliance and religious doctrine. In addition, the game was a public spectacle drawing the diversity in society under one ideological standard.

The ballcourt provides a single analytical unit for cross-societal comparisons. This unique architectural form permits a view of society that straddles the household and the temple. Because the game operated to integrate society, the distribution and form of the court reveal some of the forces at work within and between society. Although the form and function of the game may have changed with time and space, it was an enduring institution which helped define "Maya," and more generally Mesoamerica. Why should a game played with a rubber ball on a masonry court have such appeal? It unified the social and ideological fabric of a complex society.

Temporal Dimensions

Given the continual evolution of Maya architectural design within a community, it is of interest that ballcourts appear to remain intact, permanent features in the developing cultural landscape. Seldom has a ballcourt been buried by subsequent construction and only then as a consequence of a major reorganization, such as that ordered by Cauac Sky, great Lord of Quiriguá (Sharer 1978). (It has been suggested that a defensive plan to the central precinct in part precipitated the construction events at Quiriguá [Jones in Sharer 1978], when a new ballcourt was placed immediately north of the acropolis.)

Most courts have an extended period of use and reuse. At the lithic craft specialization center of Colhá (Hester et al. 1980, 1982), two ballcourts were superimposed one over the other in the main courtyard area (Eaton and Kunstler 1980). Though other courts reveal superposition believed associated

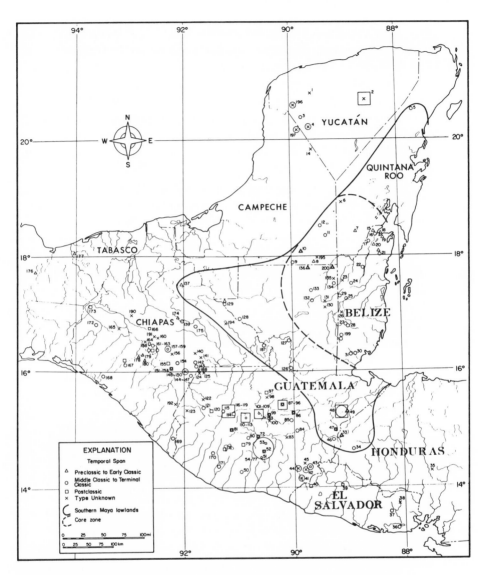

Figure 7.1. Temporal distribution of ballcourts in the Maya area. Symbol size indicates relative number of ballcourts for a particular period by site or site area. These data were taken primarily from sources in A. Smith (1961), Clune (1963), and Taladoire (1981). New data from highland Guatemala and Chiapas have not been incorporated (cf. Agrinier this volume; Fox this volume; Parsons this volume; Kurjack et al. this volume). The names of the sites and associated ballcourt characteristics are identified by site number in Scarborough (1985).

with major refurbishing operations, the Colhá courts are separated by nearly half a millennium. No other courts are found at this well-sampled community, and an Early Classic depopulation is suggested. The fact that a court would be reconstructed at the same identical locus as an earlier abandoned one suggests the enduring quality of the masonry court.

The dating of ballcourt architecture is no less difficult than other contexts within a Maya center. Excavated courts frequently provide marker stones and cache offerings which can be cross-dated. However, only a few of the known courts have been excavated and simple identification of a court can go unnoticed, given their unassuming appearance. Because limited resources allow many centers to be only pace-and-compass mapped, many unseen small mounds shrouded by the jungle canopy go unreported. Even the great pioneer of Maya studies, Sylvanus Morley, appeared unaware of the ballcourt structure 1B7 in the main courtyard at Quiriguá (Morley 1935).

Still, ballcourts *are* datable, though many times by association with adjacent structures. The earliest securely dated courts in the Maya Lowlands come from Cerros (Scarborough et al. 1982) and Colhá (Eaton and Kunstler 1980) in northern Belize. These courts appear to be morphologically similar (the playing wall batter descends to the alley floor without a break) and share alleyway dimensions of comparable size to those reported later.

Figure 7.1 indicates the temporal distribution of ballcourts in the Maya Lowlands. These data suggest that courts are not only earlier in northern Belize and along the Río Hondo/Río Azul corridor, but that most courts in the southern Lowlands expectedly date to the Early and Late Classic periods. Courts dating to the Early Classic are well documented only on the western and southern periphery of the Lowlands at Palenque (Rands 1977) and Copán (Stromsvik 1952). Both of these examples are likely to have had a long period of reuse.

In a previous article (Scarborough et al. 1982), we speculated that the courts on the edge of the Lowlands represented an isolated throwback to the late Preclassic game; a game postulated to have been supplanted by ancestor worship. The game was argued to have had a public ritual focus which was replaced during the Early Classic by private ancestor worship. The reappearance of figurines (believed associated with private ritual) in the Early Classic period, following their absence during the Late Preclassic and their abundance during the Middle Preclassic, suggested that household ritual was again the rule. Furthermore, the empire expansionism of Teotihuacán and its influence on the Lowlands during the Early Classic also affected the game.

Today this scenario seems less convincing given the probable appearance of Early Classic ballcourts in the core area of the southern Maya Lowlands. Although dated by structure association only, nine additional courts are

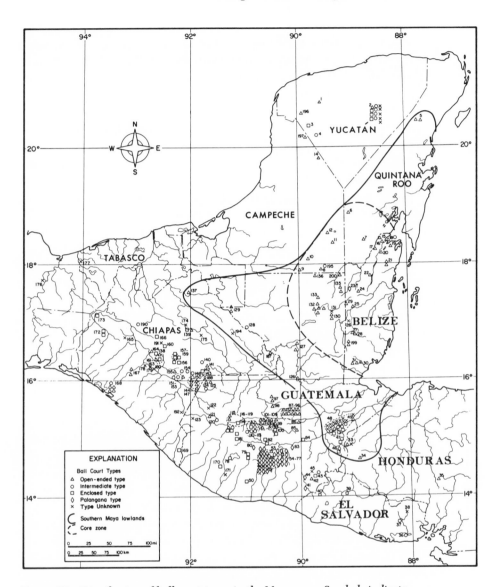

Figure 7.2. Distribution of ballcourt types in the Maya area. Symbols indicate number of ballcourts by type in the greater Maya area. Site numbers generally define individual archaeological sites with the exception of site area 48, representing a collection of non-Maya courts along the upper Motagua. These data were taken primarily from sources in A. Smith (1961), Clune (1963), and Taladoire (1981). New data from highland Guatemala and Chiapas have not been incorporated (cf. Agrinier this volume; Fox this volume; Parsons this volume; Kurjack et al. this volume). The names of the sites and associated ballcourt characteristics are identified by site number in Scarborough (1985).

suggested, eight of which rest in the core area. The current work at the Early Classic community of Río Azul should permit confirmation of one of these centrally located courts (Adams 1984). It would appear that the poorly understood Early Classic period manifests a ballgame presence commensurate with its developmental and temporal position. Predictably, the Late Classic period presents the strongest showing of courts for any time or place.

The Postclassic game is seldom documented in the Maya Lowlands. No courts are defined in the south and only Chichén Itzá can be argued to have Early Postclassic ballcourts from the north. However, even the courts at Chichén Itzá may be earlier, given the recent controversy generated by the "total overlap," "partial overlap," or "sequential" dating models (Ball 1979; Andrews and Robles 1985; Lincoln 1986). Postclassic courts in the Guatemalan Highlands will be treated by Fox (this volume), but in this Highland context the Postclassic court was well established and more strongly represented than in earlier periods, with the exception of Classic period Kaminaljuyú (Parsons this volume).

Ballcourt Form

Ballcourts indicate permanency and ritual importance. Although the game was surely played on informal earthen playing surfaces ("dusty court" from the *Popol Vuh*), of which little remains except for a few possible "marker posts" (Borhegyi 1980), formal masonry courts suggest sanctioned corporate labor projects.

Unlike many ballcourts in Mesoamerica, the masonry courts of the Lowlands were primarily open ended and without ring markers. Open-ended courts have undefined end zones and might be seen as manifesting less restricted access to a public gathering of spectators. Although flanking buildings sometimes defined the open ends of a court, these structures functioned in part to elevate the spectator rather than to act as stop surfaces (cf. Satterthwaite 1944). As shown through the pioneer work of Smith (1961) and Clune (1963), open-ended courts differ from: (1) intermediate courts constructed with only one distinguishable end zone or end zones with ill-defined walls; (2) enclosed courts with well-defined end zones and a typical "I" shape; and (3) palangana courts with no end zones but well-defined rectangular playing alleys surrounded by walls of even height.

The distribution of ballcourts using this typology has been plotted for the greater Maya area (Figure 7.2). Although the number and type of courts located on the margins of the southern Maya Lowlands are not anticipated precisely to reflect the most recent work reported in this volume, mapping of courts for comparative purposes was necessary. These data are preliminary and are drawn primarily from available secondary sources.

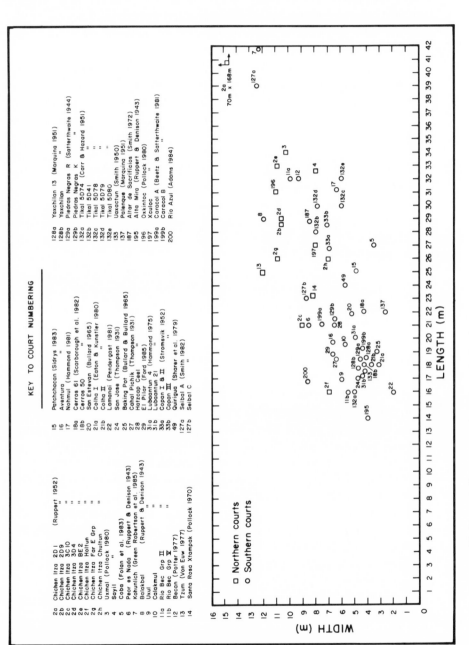

Figure 7.3. Sizes of ballcourt alleyways in the Maya Lowlands.

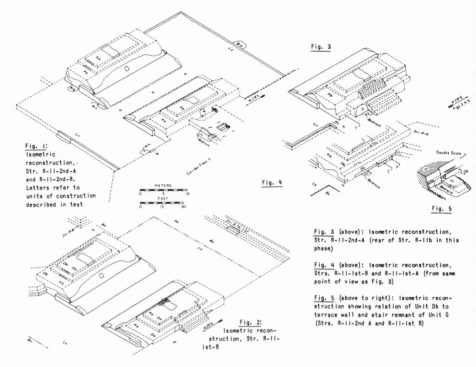

Piedras Negras Structure R-11   (Satterthwaite 1944)

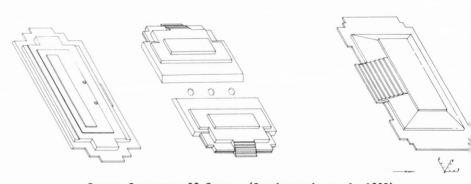

Cerros Structure 50 Group   (Scarborough et al. 1982)

Figure 7.4. Similarity of architectural form between a Late Classic ballcourt at Piedras Negras (ca. A.D. 622) on the western flank of the Lowlands and a Late Preclassic court at Cerros (100 B.C.–A.D. 100) on the eastern margin of the Maya realm.

Figure 7.3 presents the playing alley dimensions for open-ended courts in the southern Maya Lowlands. Although many researchers have focused their attention on the form and angle of the playing side walls which forced the rubber ball upward (and some excellent studies exist [Satterthwaite 1944; Acosta and Moedano 1946; Smith 1961; Clune 1963; Quirarte 1977]), there is a great deal of ambiguity in typology.

An examination of the size and shape of the playing alleys of Lowland courts indicates that limited space was made available for the playing of the game. Although variability seems to occur, some of it may be a consequence of scaling error during the collection of these metric data from small-scale maps. (Much of the data comes from carefully mapped but unexcavated alleyway measurements.) However, even accepting the variability in alleyway dimensions, masonry ballcourts in the southern Lowlands appear to accommodate a small number of players. Although the form and angle of the walls vary, and probably made a court "faster" or "slower," the number of players on the field appears to have changed little. It should be noted that the Great Ballcourt at Chichén Itzá was nearly 25 times larger than the next largest ballcourt alleyway in the Lowlands. Coupled with the monumental side structures, this court takes on a different function from the other courts. It appears to have been an effigy ballcourt, a monument to the ballgame institution.

The observation that most courts in the southern Lowlands were open ended and constructed with playing alleys of limited size suggests a major degree of standardization in the game. This standardization appears to span the entire southern Maya interaction sphere, and range the temporal gamut of the civilization. This is most evident when comparing ballcourt Structure R-11 at Piedras Negras with the Structure 50 group at Cerros (Figure 7.4); their involved forms are remarkably similar. These courts are on the eastern and western margins of the Lowlands, respectively, and are separated by more than half a millennium.

Intrasite Architectural Relationships

The Maya central precinct, in which nearly all recorded ballcourts rest, was an imposing setting with at least somewhat closed access to certain areas (see Quiriguá/Motagua drainage ballcourts as exceptions). The disposition of sunken plazas, raised acropolises, and directed causeways could cordon off access to privileged zones. The ballcourt, however, occupied open courtyard space. Courts were seldom found in traffic-restricted areas (once access to the central precinct was made) and never on top of the broad expanse of an acropolis. Although courts were centrally located in the core of a community, less restricted access to the game seems apparent.

Complementing the relative accessibility of the ballcourt is its low-lying appearance and clear visibility from more elevated surrounding structures. Given the degree of terraced architecture in the central precinct of a Maya center and the sometimes elaborate high risers associated with axial stair-cases, it is apparent that "grandstand" or audience floor space for a sizable group was readily available. If the game were an open ritual spectacle as much for kings and their deities as for the public at large, its many viewers could be comfortably accommodated by the versatility of the monumental architecture.

An examination of available site maps indicates that most ballcourts were oriented north–south along a broad medial axis within or between courtyards or acropolis groups. Although variability exists, the only sites to categorically reject this orientation were Seibal (Willey et al. 1975; Smith 1982), Quiriguá (Sharer et al. 1979), Baking Pot (Bullard and Bullard 1965), Río Bec and Balakbal (Ruppert and Denison 1943), and Kohunlich (Pacheco et al. 1981). Topographic conditions severely constrained the layout of Seibal with an exaggerated east–west directionality dominating the location of the major ar-chitectural complexes. (The early establishment of the Group D architectural complex on the hillock immediately above the Pasión River would have greatly influenced later city planning.) Both ballcourts at Seibal are oriented east–west and court Structure C-9 rests in a spatially mediating position on a principal causeway between the two major architectural groups. Except for Quiriguá and Seibal, the other courts mentioned are located in communities that warrant considerably more attention. Topographically, the orientation of these ballcourts may be controlled by the physical landscape and the orienta-tion of the associated centers.

Geographic considerations also appear to have altered the orientation of ballcourts at Piedras Negras and Yaxchilán. Particularly at Yaxchilán, the Maya captured the topographic relief and the orientation of the Usumacinta River in establishing the center (Andrews 1975:140). Each site has two ball-courts and each of the courts appears in an opposing architectural complex. The courts take on a 45° angle from north, in keeping with the orientation of the centers. Of the five well-mapped sites along the Usumacinta drainage, three represent the most unconventional court orientations recorded in the southern Lowlands. This may be a consequence of the somewhat isolated "buffer zone" location of these sites and the reduced effect of core zone build-ing conventions. Quiriguá, defining the southeastern Lowland boundary, also manifests this unconventional orientation.

Some evidence suggests that when ballcourts were placed between major architectural complexes, the game functioned as a mediating force. Both Michels (1979) and Hammond (1981) indicate that districts or acropolises can be identified with special interests or factions within a Maya center. Best represented at Seibal, and apparent at both Nohmul (Hammond 1973, 1975b; Hammond et al. 1987) and Uaxactún (Smith 1950), these ballcourts are located on or adjacent to a linking causeway.

At other major centers the ballcourt is found in the center of the major acropolis group. Centers having two or more courts, such as Caracol (Beetz and Satterthwaite 1981), Piedras Negras (Satterthwaite 1944), Yaxchilán (Marquina 1951; Andrews 1975), Tikal (Coe 1967; Carr and Hazard 1961), Lubaantún (Hammond 1975a), Yaxhá (Hellmuth 1976), and Río Bec (Ruppert and Denison 1943), have courts associated with the sites' major architectural complexes. Only Seibal and Cerros, both with two ballcourts, have courts located away from the major concentration of architecture. In the case of Cerros, a Late Preclassic community, a less concentrated volume of architecture was placed in the main acropolis area (central precinct) than is apparent in later centers. Coe (1977) notes a similar architectural openness in Olmec centers. It may relate to early experiments in administrative centralization.

Ashmore (1989) has most recently suggested that elites of a civilization attempt to assert their power or authority by manipulating building space within an administrative center. The location of various structures can be as important as their individual size and form. In the large centers, ballcourts were always placed within the protected reaches of the major architectural complexes and were likely associated with specific interests and activities carried out in these districts. However, the notion that the rigidity and permanence of architecture clearly reflect the motivations and interests of an elite must be tempered. Chronological control for a group of structures in a center for any one point in time is extremely difficult. Moreover, to disentangle the architectural messages emanating from a well-mapped center, when the elites frequently manipulated an earlier spatial design to complement a new order, may be beyond the current limitations of our discipline. However, I look forward to the epigraphic breakthroughs that may define this notion of a "cosmogram" for a Maya center (see Townsend 1979; Coggins 1980; Freidel 1981b).

Court Distribution

Figure 7.2 illustrates the extent of reported ballcourts in the Maya area. Some of the reported distribution of ballcourt masonry can be attributed to sample bias. A core area, including nearly all of Belize, northwest Petén, southeast Campeche, and southwest Quintana Roo, defines the greatest concentration of centers with masonry courts. This comes as little surprise, given the amount of archaeological work carried out in this area as opposed to the limited amount of survey conducted between its boundary and the better-understood Usumacinta drainage (see Rice and Puleston 1981).

The southern Maya Lowlands were defined in a traditional manner, except perhaps for the corridor enclosing much of Quintana Roo and extending northeast as far as Cobá. The Cobá stela cult and architectural detail resemble the south more than the north (Thompson et al. 1932). Although preliminary survey carried out in the swamps of Quintana Roo confirms architectural similarities with the south (Harrison 1979), clear evidence for ballcourt architecture is lacking.

Some centers, however, simply do not have ballcourts. This is most evident in the north, where large centers such as Dzibilchaltún, as well as the many east coast communities, mark the absence of the court (Kurjack et al. this volume). At the carefully reported site of Altun Ha, Belize, no ballcourt was identified, though the site contained some of the richest cache offerings from the Lowlands (Pendergast 1969, 1979). Most sites that have been carefully mapped or excavated, however, have revealed at least one court. Even small centers have been reported with ballcourts (Hatzcap Ceel and Cahal Pichik [Thompson 1931], San José [Thompson 1939], and Aventura [Sidrys 1983]). For a site like Altun Ha not to have a ballcourt might suggest some form of alliance with another center to help satisfy any demand for the game.

Ballcourt communities along the Usumacinta drainage defining the western margin of the southern Maya Lowlands and the Motagua drainage flanking the southeastern margin reflect zones of interaction with non-Maya groups. The geographic spacing of large cities with ballcourts is quite consistent along the Usumacinta (Figure 7.2) and may indicate the sphere of influence each of these communities had with regard to the game. It is somewhat speculative whether the standard spacing indicates a degree of local integration that served to filter out foreign influences. In this scenario, however, the game would have functioned to mediate conflict along an interregional boundary. During the Early Classic period (a date established for at least two of the most distant courts) and into a "Middle Classic" moment (Pasztory 1978b), these courts and the associated game would have engaged the sustaining population of the Maya and curbed the influence of any expanding Highland state. If any coercion was exerted by Teotihuacán and the Basin of Mexico on the Maya, it was not felt directly in the southern Maya Lowlands. This threat may have been realized in Highland Guatemala and Kaminaljuyú (Parsons this volume; Santley et al. this volume), but the Lowlands only appear to have incorporated what they wanted from these Highlanders though Teotihuacán influence was apparent. A similar suggestion has been noted in Oaxaca during Monte Albán II in which "significant imperial ventures outside the valley of Oaxaca" (Blanton et al. 1981) correlate with 11 of the 16 ballcourts in the valley located on the periphery (Kowalewski et al. 1983, this volume). Here the ballgame corresponds to the establishment of the Zapotec state.

The southeastern boundary of the Lowlands was even less affected by non-Maya state institutions. This border corresponds roughly with the margins of what is commonly considered Mesoamerica (this volume notwithstanding), and these non-Maya foreigners were less complicated chiefdom groups. The kind of interaction between Maya and foreigners in this area differed markedly from that on the "western front." The excavation and survey of Quiriguá may best typify the difference.

Sharer et al. (1979) have tentatively identified 22 plazuela/ballcourt groups within a 100-km² block enclosing Quiriguá and the adjoining Motagua drainage. The associated communities appear to be quite small and contain many non-Maya traits (Schortman 1986). Unlike the massive and powerful Usumacinta centers of Yaxchilán, Piedras Negras, Seibal, and Palenque, which were periodically challenged (economically if not politically) by societies of comparable complexity, Quiriguá was a relatively small center interacting with a noncentralized foreign frontier. Nevertheless, both Quiriguá and Copán controlled much of this frontier. The ballgame in this context appears to have been a mediating institution placed in the hinterlands to monitor these less organized communities. Direct confrontation with these less centralized groups would have resulted in much wasted energy. No major threat of force was required on this margin of Mesoamerica to define what was Maya, unlike imposing centers elsewhere.

It is also noted that the central Guatemalan Highlands as well as the northern Yucatán Peninsula manifested little boundary maintenance by way of ballcourt distribution from the southern Maya Lowlands. Given that Maya culture was clearly shared in these geographic regions, the mediating role of the game was less necessary.

The Ballgame

Recreational play was probably one reason for the continued popularity of the game, but the strongly ritualized character of the game for the resolution of disputes was most manifest in a community sanctioned masonry court. As an element of the successful mediation of conflict, the game acted as a forum for opposing groups to vie for social and political status. The forging of meaningful alliances during the contest would be expected and would have required a significant spatial and architectural investment in place. Decisions were legitimized in part by the architectural setting (cf. Lerup 1977).

Ethnohistoric accounts of the rubber-ball game reported in the Antilles by Oviedo and Las Casas (Alegría 1983) indicate spirited wagering by most in attendance, with the sacrifice of a human captive sometimes accompanying the event. Although played on much larger courts with many more players

(20–30 men per team), the community excitement associated with the game is believed analogous to that of the pre-Hispanic Maya. The epigraphy and iconography from the great centers indicate the importance of the game to the ruling elites (Schele and Freidel this volume; Cohodas this volume). However, the broad societal appeal of sport in most societies (Harris and Park 1983), coupled with the biased record left by only the controlling elites (Schele 1981), make an anthropological study of the effect games have had on other societies appropriate.

Public appeal for the game is presumed necessary given both the long history and distribution of masonry courts. Public gatherings during feast days or pilgrimages may have precipitated a lively match. Although the game clearly operated between elites to confirm social and political prowess, a broad audience representing the "sustaining population" of any center would have been actively involved.

At this lowest level, the game accommodated the spirited betting documented in the Antilles among the entire population. The game probably had an immediate though less consequential economic effect on the non-elite sustaining population. Ballgame ritual would have instilled an awareness of solidarity, while affirming the authority of the elite.

However, the rubber-ball game also functioned at the level of "status gambling" and alliance maintenance. It brought opposing groups together to vie for social and political status. Although the fate of a kingdom has been suggested to have rested on the outcome of a game in Highland Mexico (Durán in Stern 1949; Alegria 1983), it is unlikely that such stakes were ever honored. Still, wagers associated with the alliance network assumedly were high.

Geertz (1972) has analyzed "deep play" from the vantage of the Balinese cockfight. In his classic paper he discusses the ethnically irrational behavior associated with facets of the cockfight, but notes the moral meaningfulness of the event to the greater collective. Gambling is the social exchange Geertz focuses on to expose simple monetary wagering, but also status gambling. Here, as with the rubber-ball game, sport brings what is Balinese, Maya, or any other ethnic identity together. Operating in the economic sphere, small bets occupy much of the Balinese crowd. However, larger wagers take on a value in excess of their economic equivalent and clearly reflect status rivalries within or between communities.

At the highest level of abstraction, Gluckman and Gluckman (1983) provide a synthetic paper examining games, including a reference to the Maya ballgame. In it they define ritual as a set of prescribed actions or words that "involve beliefs in occult power" (197). They further differentiate sport from ritual in that sport involves more uncertainty and less appeal to the supernatural. Sport in this usage is generally associated with secular societies.

In the Maya ballgame, ritualized behavior associated with blood sacrifice was a dominant theme. Although the game may have had an oracular quality to it (Gluckman and Gluckman 1983:202), the outcome of the predicted event, not the game itself, was seldom in question. The governing elites extended the outcome of a match by appeasing displeased deities through post-ballgame ritual and human sacrifice, if the final result of the game were contrary to the predicted one. Sacrifice is not predicted to be a perfunctory act required at all ballgame performances, but a ritualized drama necessary only when the outcome of the game did not support the predicted event (cf. Schele and Freidel this volume).

The ballgame at this level of abstraction was an open expression of Maya ideology and group solidarity. To Durkheim (1954) the worship of God, through the totem, was the worship of society itself. If the totem were the ballgame, then the ultimate outcome of the game would never be in doubt. The elites in this design only acted as ministers or vehicles for the ideology.

The dart match among the Tikopia (Firth 1930) further suggests this sense of identity and belonging to the group. Firth indicates that deities of this less complex society were appeased and pitted against an opponent's in this display. The Tikopia drama is shown to be a forum for tying social alliances and reaffirming the collective as well as enhancing the prospect of a bountiful harvest, the latter a recurrent theme in the Mesoamerican ballgame and echoed by several authors (Parsons 1969; Pasztory 1972; *Popul Vuh*, Tedlock 1985; Cohodas 1975, this volume; Gillespie this volume). These matches also had their oracular qualities, but the final score again rested with group solidarity.

The ballgame then operated at (1) the recreational level of "shallow play," (2) the social status-role level, and (3) the ideational level. The enduring quality of the game is demonstrated by the longevity and distribution of the masonry court. Such longevity not only required the strictures of the elite, but the enthusiasm of the sustaining population.

Interactivism

Maya architecture, then, expresses a strong interaction with its surroundings. The central architectural complexes, and perhaps cities more generally, were in part forums to impose certain deities and policies on a constituency by an elite in power (cf. Lerup 1977). Given the ebb and flow within and between competing aristocracies as measured by architectural design and redesign, to say nothing about genealogy or marriage alliances reported in the epigraphy (Schele and Miller 1986), a degree of turbulence within the upper echelons is suggested. Maya warfare is a topic rapidly gaining wide acceptance after years of facile dismissal (Becker 1979; Webster 1977; Freidel 1986). With these forces pulling at any architectural detail, how do we account for the apparent stability and longevity of individual masonry ballcourts?

The answer lies in the unique nature of the ballgame and its establishment as an important institution to the group. Unlike the construction and razing events carried out on most structures, the ballcourt was an enduring structure with broad societal appeal grounded in tradition. To destroy a court was to challenge the underpinnings of society itself, while to modify or even level a previous ruler's accomplishments was anticipated and even acceptable in securing a constituency and publicly announcing one's control. Because the ballgame was a sacred institution at one level, it was one of the few structures less affected by palace intrigue, political networking, and the changing economic climate, though elite actors must have used the court as a theater for support. The importance of the ballcourt in the central precinct of a city cannot be overestimated. Unlike many courtyards and marketing areas, it had a ritual or sacred function; unlike the restricted access of temples and palaces, it also had a public or profane function. The game and the court operated in both worlds to unify the disparate forces affecting a great civilization.

The native American rubber-ball game played on a masonry court represents an important link in drawing together the similarities that make up greater Mesoamerica. At a time when provincialism and particularistic approaches are gaining ground in our disciplines, the opportunity to dissolve regional boundaries comes as a welcome change. The broad appeal of the game and the meaningful distribution of courts permit a developed statement about architecture and society.

The opening quotation from Lars Lerup may best capture the uniqueness of ballcourt architecture. By the Classic period, much of what was civic construction was an appeal to deities and other elites by powerful aristocracies. Lower status laborers or *milperos* had little access to these structures. The ballcourt, however, was a "built representation of the collective" which accommodated all segments of society. The court was a public statement of integration in which households, villages, and districts came together to reaffirm sociopolitical and ideological alliances.

Note

This paper was completed in part through the hard work of Kathleen Elmore. I would also like to thank my wife, Pat Mora, for discussing the clarity of my argumentation and its credibility. Irene Casas, Flo Dick, and Wilma George typed the manuscript. A longer version of this paper is on file at the Arizona State Museum Library, University of Arizona, Tucson.

CHAPTER 8

Ballcourts of the Northern Maya Lowlands

Edward B. Kurjack, Ruben Maldonado C., and
Merle Green Robertson

The question of pre-Columbian ballgame origins is a nineteenth century problem that has had a strong influence on contemporary explanations of Maya cultural development. In the past, scholars thought that the rubber-ball game spread from central Mexico. Today, most students emphasize Maya roots for the complex, though some authors believe various aspects of the game were relatively late importations. These new features, including rings, high vertical walls, and associated art depicting the slaying of a player, are considered part of an Early Postclassic "Toltec" horizon.

Controversy over the derivation of late art styles at Chichén Itzá replicates the question of ballgame origins. Most scholars think that the same invaders who brought the Mexican-type ballgame to Yucatán created a new art style at Chichén Itzá. Others have proposed Maya prototypes for key elements of that style. Positions taken on the genesis of both the ballgame and the art of Chichén Itzá are related to general opinions concerning the role of diffusion in the late history of Mesoamerica.

Those who contend that central Mexican invaders were responsible for the ninth century florescence of Chichén Itzá believe that the other important Yucatecan sites were abandoned shortly thereafter. Puuc sites such as Uxmal are thought to represent a Late or Terminal Classic period in local history while the "Mexican" occupation of Chichén Itzá constitutes the main component of an Early Postclassic period. The Mexican invasion argument, as applied to the origin of ballcourts, is difficult to combine with this chronology, because ballcourts at various Yucatecan sites, especially Uxmal, have rings and other late features. Some scholars, uncomfortable with the rigidity of the traditional chronological framework, have recently proposed various degrees of overlap between Puuc sites and the late occupation at Chichén Itzá.

Early identification of ballcourts in the Mexican Highlands played a dominant role in Mesoamerican archaeology. Stephens (1843) recognized that the Great Ball Court at Chichén Itzá matched descriptions of playing fields used by the sixteenth century inhabitants of central Mexico. Accounts of the rings utilized as goals by these Mexican players were particularly convincing, for one such ring was still in place at Chichén Itzá. A generation later, Charnay (1888:xxvii, 76–92) considered Mesoamerican civilization a single cultural tradition that was spread by a "Nahuan" people he called "Toltec." Charnay pointed out similarities between the ruins of Tula, his Toltec homeland, and Chichén Itzá. Ballcourt rings at both sites were a specific point of comparison. He believed that ballcourts were a Toltec characteristic and pointed to the Great Ball Court at Chichén Itzá as evidence for a Toltec presence.

By the end of the nineteenth century, students of American archaeology were convinced that the ballgame had come to the Maya Lowlands from central Mexico. Morley recorded the general consensus:

> The Ball Court is a purely Nahua importation. The game was originated and developed in the Nahua area, whence it spread to Yucatán at a comparatively late date, probably after 1200 A.D., as we have seen. Indeed, there is only one other certain occurrence of a Ball Court in Yucatán, namely at Uxmal. (Morley 1913)

For Morley, Chichén Itzá was the "connecting link" between the Maya and the Nahua, and the ballcourt was proof of that tie.

Tozzer (1930, 1957) incorporated much of this thinking in his influential concept of a Toltec invasion of Chichén Itzá. He first thought that the distribution of ballcourts marked the extent of Toltec territory. He believed that much of the art at Chichén Itzá commemorated a long struggle for Toltec supremacy over the indigenous Maya. This interpretation became a fundamental assumption in Mesoamerican archaeology.

Blom (1930, 1932) agreed that the Toltec built the high-walled courts with rings in Yucatán, but he challenged traditional outlooks by arguing that the ballgame had originated in the Maya area. While many historical descriptions of the ballgame survived the conquest of central Mexico, only the references in the *Popol Vuh* existed for the Maya. Blom, however, found a number of words associated with rubber, balls, and the ballgame in Colonial period Maya dictionaries.

The most convincing evidence in Blom's influential articles was a long list of Maya ballcourts. His survey indicated that courts with rings were found only in the northern Maya area, so Blom concluded that rings could have been a comparatively late Toltec feature. Stern (1949) repeated this idea. Borhegyi's (1961) maps showing distributions of ballgame equipment led him to similar conclusions, although he pointed to Veracruz as the place where many features originated (cf. Piña Chan 1969:20–21; Piña Chan et al. 1976: 216–217).

Blom's list included the two ballcourts with rings located by Thompson, Pollock, and Charlot (1932) at Cobá. After finding several supposedly late characteristics in early contexts at that site, Thompson disparaged the Toltec concept:

> if one follows the general theory . . . then the "Toltecs" dragged their way into Yucatán, loaded down with heavy *impedimenta* of square columns, Atlantean figures, feathered serpent balustrades, and other odds and ends usually ascribed to them, in the third quarter of Cycle 9. . . . If our first conclusion is correct, square columns, as well as ball courts and spear throwers, will have to be taken out of the knapsacks of this elusive people, who skulk in the shadows of Yucatecan history with their Pandora's box brimming with evils for archaeologists. (Thompson et al. 1932:199)

Thompson's own interpretations added complexity to Maya history by proposing several migrations rather than a single "Toltec" invasion.

By the time of his death, Tozzer (1957:16–17) had modified his views in response to these new data. Rather than a single conquest, he conceptualized the movement of central Mexican people into Yucatán as a peaceful intrusion that took place over a considerable period of time. Accepting the antiquity of the Maya ballgame, Tozzer contrasted early ballcourts and later ones at Chichén Itzá, Tula, El Tajín and Cotzumalhuapa. He pointed out that the late Tula-Toltec courts are associated with art depicting human sacrifice. While Tozzer once believed that ballcourts were the characteristic Toltec feature, by the 1950s he was arguing that the spread of these people was marked by a cult combining military ritual, ballgames, and human sacrifice.

The distinction between the Classic and Postclassic rests on the writings of these scholars. Most authors characterize the Early Postclassic in Yucatán as a period of overwhelming central Mexican dominance radiating from Chichén Itzá. The Mexican Toltec marked their intrusion by leaving a complex of foreign traits that they brought to the peninsular area over a relatively short period of time. Despite continuity in masonry techniques and other aspects of culture, scholars have emphasized contrasts between Chichén Itzá, viewed as a unique Early Postclassic component, and other Yucatecan settlements that are believed to be earlier. Sites that had previously been important are thought to have been either abandoned or to have lacked political and economic potential for monumental construction.

A century of interest in the Mesoamerican ballgame has left many problems. Two crucial questions stand out: (1) Did a Mexican-style ballgame forming part of a Toltec horizon once spread across Mesoamerica, and (2) What light can a study of ballcourts shed on positions that researchers have taken on the overlap between the historical development of Chichén Itzá and Uxmal? A review of available information about the northern Maya ballgame does not altogether conform with established views.

A Survey of Northern Maya Ballcourts

Despite environmental conditions that favor archaeological reconnaissance, recent exploration of the northern Maya Lowlands has not revealed many new ballcourts. The peninsula rests on flat bedrock that is barely covered by thin soil. Collapsed masonry forms heaps of debris on this level surface. The plantation fields and low scrub forest characteristic of northwest Yucatán do not conceal ruined architecture as completely as the tall forests encountered further south and east. Given such favorable conditions, additional courts should have been found if many more exist.

The surviving activity that has taken place still suggests a contrast between ballcourts in the north and the south. Differences are manifest in ballcourt distributions as well as ballcourt features such as the presence or absence of rings. Explorers have reported only 25 ballcourts at 12 sites within the huge area that lies north of the road crossing the base of the peninsula between Chetumal and Escarcega. Thirteen of these courts are in Chichén Itzá and two others are in Coba. By comparison, the relatively small region between the Chetumal–Escarcega highway and the Guatemalan border contains six sites (including Becán) with eight ballcourts.

Erroneous reports of ballcourts at some sites have been published. Ramon Carrasco (pers. comm.) states that detailed surveys conducted at Hochob revealed no ballcourts. Reexamination of the structure at Ake that Charnay (1888) thought was a ballcourt found no evidence to support that conclusion (see Roys and Shook 1966:36–37). Excavations at Edzná (see Andrews 1984: xxx–xxxiii, 100) showed that one structure was mistakenly thought to be a court, but recent research by Luis Millet (pers. comm.) has uncovered another playing field with an associated ring at that site.

Ballcourts are absent from settlements that were occupied immediately before the Spanish conquest of Yucatán. Years of research at Mayapán failed to reveal a ballcourt. Nor were ballcourts located at Tulum, Xel-Ha, Cancun, or

Ichpaatun, all Protohistoric sites on the eastern coast of Quintana Roo that
have been thoroughly explored. Surveys of Cozumel Island, a place well
known for conquest period activity, did not encounter a single ballcourt.
Thompson (1966b:149) believed that cessation of the game in Late Postclassic
times was part of a general cultural decline.

Blom thought that every important Middle American site had a ballcourt,
but large Classic sites without such structures are quite common in northern
Yucatán. E. Wyllys Andrews IV once joked tht lack of a court at Dzibilchaltún
was an embarrassment. His humor was taken seriously and the finding of a
formal playing field preoccupied surveyors. The elusive Dzibilchaltún ballcourt, however, evaded the mapping crews.

Exploration carried out in the course of the Archaeological Atlas of Yucatán
project (Garza and Kurjack 1980) encountered little additional evidence of
ballcourts. Very low parallel mounds were observed in aerial photographs of
Yaxcopoil, but only excavation will show if those structures constitute a court.
The clearing of agricultural fields that bared architectural details as small as
walls demarcating property boundaries in aerial photographs of Chunchucmil
did not lead to the identification of a ballcourt. The general architectural
forms of many other sites were made visible by aerial views taken during the
atlas project, but ballcourts were not detected. Since publication of the atlas,
however, structures identified as ballcourts have been reported by Peter
Schmidt at Kaua (atlas site 16Q-d(9):70), David Freidel at Yaxuná (site 16Q-
d(8):3), and Nicholas Dunning at Nohpat (site 16Q-d(10):3).

Many sites in the Puuc area were closely examined by Pollock (1980), but
he lists playing fields at only Uxmal, Oxkintok, Sayil, and Xculoc. Shook's
careful map of Kabah, a settlement linked by causeway to Uxmal, does not
include a ballcourt. However, Nicholas Dunning has recently reported a
court at Nohpat, a site situated along that causeway. Labná, Xcalumkin, and
Chacmultun are three other mapped ruins lacking structures of this type.

Brainerd, Roys, and Ruppert found a ballcourt at Santa Rosa Xtampak.
Their map showing the court's location and approximate dimensions was published by Pollock (1970).

Pollock believed that other ballcourts would soon be found in the hill country of Yucatán, but little data have been added to the record since his survey.
Afredo Barrera Rubio (pers. comm.) explored a pair of parallel mounds at
Uxmal, but his test excavations showed that this complex had no central floor
in what would have been the playing area.

Von Euw (1977) did find an open-ended ballcourt at Tzum. The two parallel
mounds that form the building are 25 m long, 13 m wide, a maximum of 2.5
m high, and from 6 to 8 m apart. In both form and proportions, this structure
resembles Pollock's (1980:382) illustration of the court at Xculoc.

Both of the ballcourts found at Coba have rings. Test pitting in the playing field of the Nohoch Mul Group at the end of Sacbe 4 yielded a cache containing obsidian, shell, pyrite, hematite, and jade (Benavides 1976:43). Most of the pottery from the excavations consisted of Late Classic and perhaps Early Postclassic materials.

No ballcourt rings were discovered at any of the eight playing fields reported from southern Quintana Roo and southwestern Campeche. Ruppert and Denison (1943) record the presence of ballcourts at Balakbal, Becán, Calakmul, Peor es Nada (a site situated some 40 km north of Becán), Río Bec Groups II and V, and Uxul. Pacheco et al. (1981:280) describe the open-ended ballcourt at Kohunlich (Clarksville). This structure includes an east–west playing area measuring 42.4 m long and approximately 12 m wide.

Archaeologists working in the northern Maya Lowlands have also found artistic renditions of the ballgame. Ceramic players from Jaina demonstrate the popularity of the game, although Piña Chan's (1968:31–34) identification of a ballcourt on the island has yet to be confirmed by excavation. Two sculptured panels (see Figure 8.3) from Ichmul (atlas site 16Q-d(9):80) are believed to have come from a ballcourt, but the location of that court is not known.

The catalog of ballcourts in the northern Lowlands indicates that these structures are relatively rare by comparison with the south. Ballcourts have not been found at any of the thousand or so smaller ruin groups that have been recorded on the peninsula. Nor is such architecture present at protohistoric or Late Postclassic ruin groups. Ballcourts are even absent from many large Classic centers.

Rings are associated with most of the northern ballcourts. However, the concentration of sites with playing fields in southern Quintana Roo and western Campeche seems to lack rings.

Chichén Itzá

The 13 ballcourts at Chichén Itzá (Ruppert 1952; Lincoln 1985; Peter Schmidt pers. comm.) are a significant exception to the scarcity of this construction type in the northern Lowlands.

Elite extended families constructed courts adjacent to their dwellings at Chichén Itzá. Lincoln (1985) notes that the plan of the building group where he found a small ballcourt (complex 5D5, on the same platform as Ruppert's [1952] 5D1, 5D2, and 5D3) resembles the layout of the buildings on the huge platform at the center of Chichén Itzá. In other words, the organization of the most significant monumental structures at the site replicates the plan of a residential group.

Figure 8.1. East and west panels from the Casa Colorado (Red House) ballcourt, Chichén Itzá.

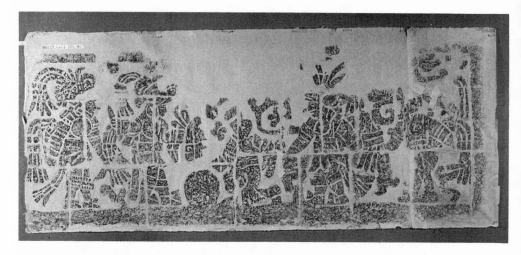

Figure 8.2. "Maya" and "Toltec" players from the west-central panel of the Great Ball Court, Chichén Itzá.

The proliferation of ballcourts at Chichén Itzá is associated with a unique art style that has strong affinities to central Mexico. Absence of hieroglyphic inscriptions at the courts of Chichén Itzá is an important area of contrast (but see Lincoln 1986:161–163) with earlier architecture. Ballcourt iconography at Chichén Itzá often depicts players watching a decapitation. Six panels on the sides of the Great Ball Court and the two existing panels of the Red House Ballcourt display this theme (Figures 8.1 and 8.2).

Tozzer (1957) believed that these ballcourt panels depict a series of games between the original Maya inhabitants of the area and the group of Toltec from central Mexico, who invaded Yucatán and established themselves at Chichén Itzá. According to Tozzer, the two taller sets of carved players at the center of the Great Ball Court benches show victorious Maya decapitating a Toltec player. The four panels at the ends of the benches represent Toltec winners taking Maya heads. The Maya win twice and the Toltec win four times.

Tozzer describes the characteristics of Maya and Toltec ball players on the east-central panel of the Great Ball Court:

> At first glance it looks as if the two groups of players on each of the six panels belong to the same ethnic background: all wear essentially the same habiliments associated with the game. But in other features of their dress they differ in such a way that, as has been suggested, they may represent Maya and Toltec.
>
> The Maya characteristics are the panache of feathers hanging from the shoulders and displaying beads strung near the ends of the plumes. The

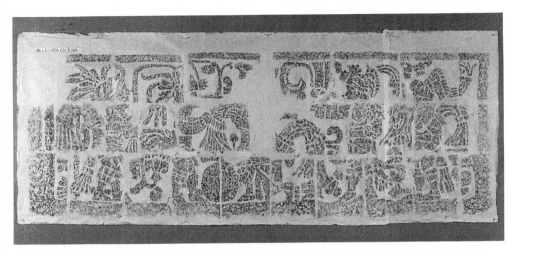

mosaic or stone cape or collar and the box-like headdress with the beaded front are worn by all of the figures on this side. In several cases, the top of the hat ending in feathers above the "box" is similar to the headdress worn by the Maya in Cenote disk M who also wears a panache.

The six figures on the side of the one who has lost his head, making seven in all, are almost certainly Mexican, although not the typical warrior of this class who appears so consistently at Chichén Itzá and Tula. The most significant characteristic of the dress of the players on this side is the shell design, sometimes within a star, worn as a pectoral by five of the figures. This is a sign of the Toltec Quetzalcoatl. Another Mexican feature is the turban worn by four of the group. It appears with or without an interwoven serpent. (Tozzer 1957:139).

In other words, interpretations of Maya and Toltec playing ball at Chichén Itzá rest largely on the presence of shell ornaments and turbans on some players and beaded feathers on others. Instead of representatives from distinct tribes or ethnic groups as proposed by Tozzer, the players could just as early have come from different factions within the same community.

Tozzer (1930) thought that most of the art at Chichén Itzá commemorates a prolonged Toltec–Maya conflict. He maintained that the human figures that were carved or painted at Chichén Itzá could be recognized as either Maya or Toltec (see Figure 8.1). Antagonism and strife between these distinct ethnic groups are, according to Tozzer, readily evident in the art.

Tozzer's arguments contended that: (1) the two groups of players facing each other in the ballcourt panels contrast in their dress and ornaments, and

(2) the identifying characteristics of one group are typical of earlier art in the Maya region while the features found on the other group have central Mexican antecedents. Our own overview of the Great Ball Court panels supports Tozzer's first conclusion but not the second.

The players that Tozzer considered Maya have the following characteristics: (1) beaded capes; (2) caps covered with beads; (3) mosaic headbands; (4) disk-shaped ear plugs with long beads; (5) back feathers from rear shields flowing first upward and then downward to the floor; (6) beads at the ends of feathers; and (7) lotus blossoms often on headdresses. These players always wear long nose bones or beads, never crescent nose pieces. Animal masks and large round-ended feathers in the headdress are also absent.

Feathers displayed by Tozzer's "Toltec" players include: (1) pectorals; (2) large feathers with rounded ends on headdresses; (3) back feathers always flowing downward; (4) some face-hugging animal headdresses; (5) some bouffant turbans; (6) large tubular ear pieces without dangles; and (7) some crescent nose pieces. These players never wear beads at the ends of plumes or back feathers that flow upward. Beaded capes are never present.

Almost all of the distinguishing features on both groups of players can be considered Maya in origin. Bouffant headdresses and the large, round-ended feathers are both found in Lowland Maya contexts. Animal headdresses, worn by only one person on each panel, are also characteristically Maya.

Shell pectorals are present in both groups. Other common apparel consists of the large variety of sandals depicted, handstones, articles of dress, shields, knee pads, and arm protectors. While two distinct "teams" can be conceptualized, interpretation of the contrast between these groups as ethnic differences does not seem justified.

Tozzer maintained that the theme of carved panels at the Great Ball Court was the same as that of other courts at Chichén Itzá. The relief carvings of the two central panels of the Red House Ballcourt (Structure 3C10) show a sacrificer facing the headless kneeling victim over a large ball (see Figure 8.1). Three other individuals are present, one behind the sacrificer and two behind the victim. All of the figures on both sides, however, seem to wear "Maya style" beaded back feathers (with the possible exception of the victim on the west side). Contrasts between the teams are clearly a less important part of the message than at the Great Ballcourt.

Excavations at the Uxmal Ballcourt

The temporal relationship between the ballcourts at Chichén Itzá and Uxmal constitutes a key part of the problem. Scholars consider Uxmal earlier than the Mexican Early Postclassic occupation of Chichén Itzá, but feathered serpents and Tlalocs at Uxmal suggest some overlap. A combination of feathered serpents on the facade and typical Maya hieroglyphs on the rings adorns the Uxmal ballcourt, but these features could have been late additions to an already existing structure.

Research at the Uxmal ballcourt began with the visit of Stephens (1843[I]:176) in 1941, who described the structure and excavated a tunnel into the east side. He thought that rooms were buried in the body of the construction, but his excavations encountered only fill.

Stephens was the first to suspect that the heavy stone rings of the Uxmal ballcourt had been deliberately broken up. He found the rings in pieces with only the tenons anchored in the walls. About half a century later, Case (1911:114) stated that vandals had purposely destroyed the rings. When Morley (1941:296) explored the ballcourt, he recorded 12 ring fragments. In 1948, Alberto Ruz L. (report in INAH Archives) observed only three of these pieces, one of which was part of the ring from the east side of the court. At that time, workers stated that Morley found this piece in rubble fill on the west side of the court.

Ruz (1958:635–636) exposed the main outlines of the ballcourt by clearing the entire playing area and benches. The stairs behind the west side of the complex and the two buildings on the sides of the court were tested. Ruz completed his Uxmal project in 1956.

Maldonado C. (1979:233) was assigned the task of studying and stabilizing the ballcourt in 1977. By that time, the sides of the structure were in danger of collapse. Complete clearing and consolidation of the complex were necessary to stop deterioration.

During the course of this fieldwork, two additional ballcourt ring fragments were uncovered on the east side of the complex behind the east bench. Evidently two or more people had, with considerable difficulty, moved these heavy pieces to the outside of the court. Again the evidence indicates vandalism at some time in the remote past.

The finding of these fragments made it possible for David Kelley (1982:15) to prepare new interpretations of the hieroglyphic inscription on the east ring. Kelley feels that the full date is probably 10.3.15.16.14.2 Ix 17 (written 16) Pop (January 13, A.D. 905).

While most of the archaeological evidence, including ceramic fragments encountered during the clearing operations, indicates a Late Classic context for the Uxmal Ballcourt, caches within the structure suggest an Early Postclassic date of construction. The majority of the sherds recovered from the ballcourt can be classed with Robert E. Smith's (1971[I]:134) Cepech Ceramic Complex, which represents the period between A.D. 800 and 1000. Pottery types from the lots collected in the course of the excavations include Muna

Slate, Sacalum Black on Slate, Holactun Black on Cream, Teabo Red, Balan-
can Fine Orange, Yokat Striated, and Halacho Impressed. The Muna Slate
was the most abundant; others were found in small quantities.

The figure of a serpent was incised on one sherd encountered in the excavations. This fragment was from the bottom of a plate that apparently can be
classed with the Dzitas Slate Group, type Xuku Incised. This type is often
decorated with the outlines of serpents. Smith (1971) considers the Dzitas
Slate Group part of the Early Postclassic Sotuta Ceramic Complex, dating
between A.D. 1000 and 1200.

Several sherds of Xcanchacan Black on Cream were also found in the ballcourt; Smith (1971:35) places this material within the Hocaba Ceramic Complex of Mayapan. This type, belonging to the Peto Cream Ware, indicates a
date between A.D. 1200 and 1300. At Dzibilchaltún the type was considered
transitional between the Early and Late Postclassic (Ball 1978:117). A similar
stratigraphic position for the ware was observed at Coba. Robles (pers.
comm.) reports that considerable quantities of this ceramic have been encountered at Isla Cerritos, where it has been dated around A.D. 1000.

Alberto Ruz (report in INAH archives) stated in 1948 that to definitively
identify the antiquity of the Uxmal ballcourt, excavations in the structure
would be necessary to find pottery sealed in an offering. Two such significant
caches were encountered during recent excavations.

The first cache was found in fill just outside the court, near the south wall
of the east bench and above the lowest floor that surrounded the complex. It
consisted of half a Muna Slate tripod plate which appears to have been purposely broken and the supports removed. A flint scraper was on the plate.
Ball (1978:103) reports that this type dates from approximately A.D. 700–1000
at Dzibilchaltún.

The second cache contained a Silho Fine Orange tripod plate, type Kilikan
Composite, that according to Smith (1971) is associated with the Sotuta Ceramic Complex. The plate was found within the body of the east side of the ballcourt, behind the second course of veneer stones at the base of the south wall.

Ball (1978:102) notes that the most accepted date for the Early Postclassic
period, for which Silho Fine Orange is a diagnostic type, is A.D. 1000–1200.
However, he does suspect that this material may have first appeared one or
two centuries earlier. How could Muna Slate, considered an earlier type, be
taken from a context stratigraphically above the ballcourt, and Silho Fine
Orange, a later pottery, be buried within the construction itself? The finding
of the caches supports Ball's position that Silho Fine Orange has an early
inception.

Silho Fine Orange is found in greater abundance at Chichén Itzá and Mayapán, although the ware was manufactured closer to Uxmal. Ball (1978:103)

believes that this pottery was produced on the northwest coast of the peninsula, possibly on the shores of the state of Campeche.

These data serve to elucidate the chronological position of the ballcourt at
Uxmal. The pottery and caches indicate the later period for its construction.
We have pointed out that only a few other formal playing fields are found near
Uxmal. Seriation of form, dimension, and height of these Puuc ballcourts sug-
gests a sequence that approaches the characteristics of the Great Ball Court
at Chichén Itzá. The Uxmal court appears transitional between the high-
walled Great Ball Court and lower structures at Sayil, Oxkintok, Tzum, and
Xculoc.

Conclusions

Three terms—Classic, Postclassic, and Toltec—epitomize conventional thinking about pre-Columbian Yucatán. Classic recalls both the high standards in
artistic expression and the inferred religious orientation of early Maya society.
Postclassic implies that new forms of social and economic organization were
characteristic of late Maya phases. Postclassic innovations are often called Toltec. In the context of Yucatecan archaeology, Toltec refers to the rapid spread
of a Postclassic complex that included ballcourts and a vigorous new art style.
Early Postclassic influence, including the ballgame, flowed from Chichén
Itzá, the only consequential Toltec site in Yucatán. Together these terms suggest that rapid diffusion resulting from ethnic migration was a key mechanism of culture change. Discontinuity in northern Maya cultural patterns is
emphasized.

The Mesoamerican ballgame is regarded as one aspect of discontinuity.
Comparison of ballcourt sculpture from Chichén Itzá (see Figure 8.2) with
that of Ichmul (Figure 8.3), a site situated less than 30 km to the northeast,
illustrates the traditional meaning of Classic versus Postclassic art. The
Ichmul panels contrast with the ballcourt reliefs and are similar to ballgame
representations in the southern part of the peninsula.

Many Mesoamericanists inferred that ballcourts with rings were "Mexican"-style features brought to Yucatán by Postclassic Toltec. These ballcourts
should indicate the presence of substantial Postclassic components. Tozzer,
Stern, Borhegyi, and even Blom all concur with this position. Knowing that
the ballcourt at Uxmal was decorated with feathered serpents and had rings
marked with Maya dates, these scholars would not have been surprised to
find the associated Toltec pottery.

Construction of ballcourts at Puuc sites such as Uxmal implies that other
buildings were erected as well. Ceramic evidence associated with this late
occupation consists of both types characteristic of Toltec Chichén Itzá and

Figure 8.3. Ichmul reliefs showing ball players. The left sculpture is now in the Merida Mission Hotel and the right is in the Merida museum.

wares that are usually considered earlier. It is no longer novel to suggest a degree of contemporaneity between occupation of Puuc sites and Toltec Chichén Itzá; researchers in Yucatán now debate only the duration and significance of the overlap.

Tozzer considered the main features of the Toltec art style and Mexican-style ballcourts to be parts of a complex that diffused as a whole. The two phenomena are clearly linked at Chichén Itzá.

Toltec art is found in association with the ballcourts at various places outside of Yucatán; on the peninsula the art is concentrated at Chichén Itzá, while ballcourts with rings are spread from Coba to Edzna. Toltec art is very restricted geographically and northern Maya ballcourts are widespread.

Viewed this way, the same features that have been used to argue the case for discontinuity in northern Maya history may be considered evidence for the endurance of earlier patterns. Evidently, a vigorous late occupation distinct from that of Chichén Itzá was characteristic of many areas. Even resistance to the spread of influence from Chichén Itzá is indicated. The subsequent imitation of architectural forms from Chichén Itzá at protohistoric Mayapán and Tulum was the aftermath of local development and success over several centuries.

CHAPTER 9

"Bois Ton Sang, Beaumanoir": The Political and Conflictual Aspects of the Ballgame in the Northern Chiapas Area

Eric Taladoire and Benoit Colsenet

During the fourteenth century, war between English and French armies was raging on most French territory. Troops and mercenaries from both countries were rampaging everywhere, bringing havoc and destruction. In 1531, a French nobleman, Jean, Lord of Beaumanoir, offered to his English foes an opportunity to settle the quarrel. Thirty warriors from each side were to fight to the death in a closed field, the losers' friends being banished or ruled over. On March 27, 1531, the English leader, Bembro, Lord of Ploermel, was killed, and the English army withdrew in defeat. This part of France then knew peace for some time.

The above event illustrates how two powerful Western European states locked in irreconcilable conflict were able to resolve their differences through symbolic public display and individual sacrifice. The story is recounted to clarify the analogous role served by the Mesoamerican ballgame in quelling conflict and conserving human resources. However, before this parallel can be developed, an introduction to the Mesoamerican ballgame, and more specifically to its appearance in northern Chiapas, is presented.

An Introduction to Mesoamerican Ballgames

It is common practice among Mesoamerican archaeologists to talk about *the* ballgame, as the very title of the volume indicates. To begin with, it seems necessary to point out two facts. First, there existed several quite different games in pre-Hispanic Mesoamerica, as suggested by available iconographic, archaeological, and ethnological data. Second, the best known of the games, Tlachtli, was described by many witnesses of Aztec times and is currently understood to have been associated with the ballcourt, but it too involved several different aspects of play.

At least two other ballgames can be identified in addition to Tlachtli. "Pelota Mixteca" is still played in the state of Oaxaca and has been described by several authors (Sweezey 1972). In his studies of the Dainzú ball player panels, Bernal (1969a) suggested a strong relationship between the way these ball players were attired and depicted and the present-day Oaxacan game. Yet, through recent studies of medieval European games, the antiquity and Meso-american origin of Pelota Mixteca has been challenged (Gillmeister 1987).

Another possible ballgame is represented on the Tepantitla murals of Teoti-huacán and has been described by Caso (1942) and other authors. It differed greatly from Tlachtli since it necessitated the use of sticks and specific markers which have been compared to the La Ventilla stela. Similar stelae have been identified on other sites (Cepeda Cardenas 1972), while a ballgame was still practiced in recent times in Michoacan (Corona Nuñez 1946) that presented strong affinities with this specific Teotihuacán occurrence. It should be noticed that a ballcourt was depicted on the Tepantitla murals, indicating that Teotihuacaños were aware of both games (Taladoire 1979, 1981; see Agrinier this volume).

A second fact emerges when considering only Tlachtli: there existed several different ways to play. This ballgame, the focus of this volume, lasted for more than 2000 years and extended over the entirety of Mesoamerica and the American Southwest. Its apparent uniformity suggests that there existed a strong cultural and symbolic unit to the game (Scarborough this volume). Nevertheless, considering the numerous differences between types of ball-courts, their sizes, plans, and proportions, as well as associated sculptures (e.g., stone rings, tenoned heads, panels, and markers), it is apparent that there existed distinct versions of the game through time and space. Miller and Houston (1987) even propose that the game was played in other architec-tural contexts than ballcourts. Leyenaar's (1978) studies of the present-day game in northwest Mexico confirm the existence of such variety.

The many differences between ballcourts from distinct regions of Meso-america further argue for this variability. The ballgame has changed its rules and meaning through time and has not met with the same significance everywhere. For example, more than 300 ballcourts have been surveyed or excavated in the Guatemalan Highlands, while only some 100 courts are ac-counted for in the Maya Lowlands. Although investigations remain incomplete in both areas, such a difference is too striking to be dismissed.

The existence of different games as well as the internal evolution of Tlachtli proper must be taken into account. This does not mean that a comprehensive and synthetic study of native American ballgames is unapproachable or somehow impossible (Stern 1949). Such an orientation may reveal a common mythical substratum, insisting on general significance (e.g., fertility, structural duality). More precisely, the Tlachtli has been called a Pan-Mesoamerican Tradition (Borhegyi 1969); this is what makes it so essential to Mesoamerican archaeology. However, it would be dangerous to underestimate its specific regional and chronological meanings, since only through such restricted approaches can we understand the game's significance to the people who played or rejected it.

Most studies tend to focus on the analysis of the best-known game, again Tlachtli. Writers and investigators such as Seler (1963) or Krickeberg (1966) have proposed solar and astral symbolism for the game, based on ballcourt orientation and the ball as a solar symbol. Others have proposed a distinct interpretation for the game as related to fertility cults (Knauth 1961). Recently these general interpretations have been modified due to more systematic research and new discoveries.

The ballgame has been variously interpreted as a representation of fertility rituals (Baudez 1984), a cult tied to trade (Pasztory 1972), a manifestation of social structure and antagonism (Fox 1980), or an institution tied to political influence and activities (Kowalewski et al. 1983). Quite often these interpretations are not mutually exclusive. Baudez' hypothesis, for instance, develops the fertility aspect of the game as representative of the cosmic forces at war with each other. He states that "the victory of the vital forces of the universe (which the King incarnated) over those of death, enabled the ball (symbol of the sun) to leave the Underworld, and light the heavens, and the earth to bear fruit, especially maize" (Baudez 1984:151). Baudez continues with other associations, such as astral symbolism and political connotations (it is the King who plays), as well as additional allusions to conflict and unrest.

The recent diversity of interpretation in ballgame symbolism stems primarily from greater attention to regional detail. Present studies are usually restricted to regional or chronological units, such as the Oaxaca Valley (Kowalewski et al. 1983), the Maya Highlands (Fox 1980, 1981), or the Middle Classic period (Parsons 1978; Pasztory 1972). This approach permits a realistic view of the ballgame, being all the richer for the diversity; however, it tends to limit sweeping generalizations and to make comparative studies more comprehensive. For example, there is a lack of agreement about what is to be taken into consideration when describing a ballcourt. If we are to compare data and avoid misunderstandings or erroneous interpretations, descriptions

Table 9.1. Tentative List of Features to be Described for Ballcourt Identification

1. Site location and identification
2. Location of ballcourts in the site
3. Type of site: ceremonial, residential, military, etc.
4. Plan
5. Profiles: width, length, slopes
6. Axis, orientation, central features
7. Architecture and building techniques
8. Associated sculptures: rings, tenoned sculptures, markers, disks, panels
9. Caches, burials associated with ballcourt
10. Other ballgame features found in the site: sculpture, ballgame paraphernalia
11. Associated structures: stairways, drains, superstructures
12. Related structures: palaces, courts, sweatbaths, tzompantli
13. Superpositions and rebuilding evidences
14. Chronological placement
15. Remarks

of surveyed or excavated ballcourts must be as uniform as possible. General agreement should be made about ballcourt terminology. A short list of entries such as the one proposed in Table 9.1 and Fig. 9.1, based on Ledyard Smith's study (1961), could be used.

Moreover, several other types of evidence should be considered. Figurines, sculptures, iconographic evidence, and ballgame paraphernalia have been used to describe the function and meaning of the game. These sources of information can become particularly useful data sets where ballcourts may be absent. For instance, no ballcourt has yet been found at Teotihuacán, though yokes have been discovered at the site (Palacios 1939). Further, a ballcourt is represented on the Tepantitla murals, and a possible ball player is depicted on a vase from Teotihuacán. This demonstrates that the game was known to the Teotihuacaños, but that its value there was different from that at other sites, even at sites under Teotihuacán influence.

In addition, problems arise in regard to the ambiguity of much ballgame-related evidence. Despite the iconographic evidence, yokes and the game may not always be synonymous. There exists without doubt a connection between them, but its meaning is still unclear since yokes have been discovered in other contexts or associations such as funerary offerings. It seems dangerous to infer from the presence of yokes at a site or in a specific area that they represent ballgame accoutrements without considering other possible implications.

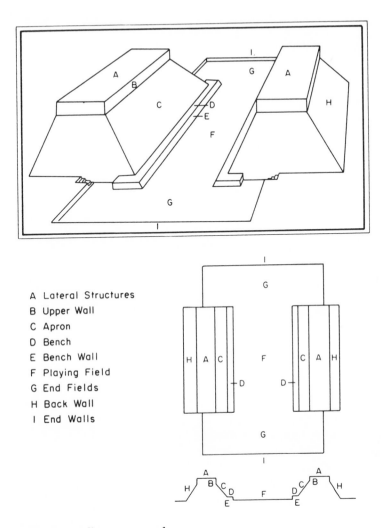

A Lateral Structures
B Upper Wall
C Apron
D Bench
E Bench Wall
F Playing Field
G End Fields
H Back Wall
I End Walls

Figure 9.1. Ballcourt terminology.

Another possible example of this discrepancy between the ballgame proper and ballgame iconography can be found in recent argumentation by Miller and Houston (1987). They use for their analysis the Yaxchilán steps, where ball players represented in full attire are engaged in ceremonial activities and sacrifice. Architectural elements seen on these steps resemble a stairway more than a ballcourt lateral structure. From this they propose that the ballgame could have taken place outside the ballcourt in certain ceremonial contexts, principally on temple stairways. While this hypothesis cannot be re-

Table 9.2. Known Ballcourts in Northern Chiapas and Adjacent Areas

Site	No.	Type	Date	Axis	Alley	Sculptures	References
Altar de Sacrificios	1	NC(II)	LC	NS	8.65×28.8	1(D)	Smith 1972
Cancuen	1	NC(O)	LC	EW	10×40	1(D)	Blom 1932; Tourtellot et al. 1978
Chacpuyil	1	NC(E)					Blom 1932
Las Tasas	1	NC					Piña Chan 1971
Mosil B	1	I	LC	EW	3×16.5		Becquelin and Baudez 1982
Ojo de Agua	1	VII	LC				Blom arch.
Palenque	1	II	LC	NS	2.7×22		Ruz L. 1961
Petulton	1	VII	LC	EW	7.6×21.5		Becquelin and Baudez 1982
Piedras Negras	1:K6	I	LC	NE-SW	6.65×21.3	1(P)	Satterthwaite 1933
Piedras Negras	1:R11	II	LC	NE-SW	3.5×18.1	5(D)	Satterthwaite 1933
San Gregorio–Na Balam	1	VII	LC-EP	EW			Culbert 1965
San Gregorio–Na Balam	1	NC	LC-EP	EW			Culbert 1965
Seibal	1:A19	II?	LC	EW	12×39		Willey and Smith 1970
Seibal	1:C9	VII?	LCT	EW	9×24		Willey and Smith 1970
Sultana	1	NC					Blom arch.
Toniná (H6:2–3)	1:H6	VII	LC	NS	29.4×5.9	15(3M,6TS,6P)	Becquelin and Baudez 1979
Toniná (G5:1–2)	1:G5	II	LC	EW	20×7.6		Becquelin and Baudez 1979
Toniná Nord	1	NC(O)	LF	NE-SW	10×17–19		Becquelin and Baudez 1982
Xoc	1	NC	LC	EW	10×30		Ekholm 1973
Yaxchilán	1:St14	II	LC	NE-SW	4.5×19	5(D)	Blom 1932
Yaxchilán	1:Str 67	II	LC	NW-SE	5×18		Blom 1932

Note: NC, not classified; LF, Late Formative; LC, Late Classic; LCT, Late Classic Terminal; EP, Early Postclassic; D, markers or disks; TS, tenoned sculpture; P, panels. Type I: open-ended ballcourt, without lateral benches. Type II: open-ended ballcourt, benches on the sides of the playing field. Type VII: enclosed ballcourt with benches and dissimilar end fields.

jected, another interpretation is possible. Ceremonial activities tied to the ballgame, such as sacrifice, need not have been performed on the ballcourt. Ball players or ball-player impersonators could take part in ritual activities prior to or following the game in other architectural contexts. Although many kinds of evidence related to the ballgame must be considered, these data should be analyzed with the utmost care, and always within the local, chrono-logical, and cultural context.

Northern Chiapas

There have been relatively few ballcourts identified in northern Chiapas, though this is probably a consequence of limited archaeological investigations rather than any pre-Hispanic cultural pattern. The absence of a ballcourt at Bonampak may be due to the fact that no complete map of the site exists. Prior to excavations by the French Mission in Mexico (1971–80), only one court had been reported by Blom (1932) at Toniná in the Ocosingo valley. Five ball-courts have now been identified and excavated in the valley, two at Toniná and three more in small sites of the valley (Toniná North, Mosil B, and Petul-ton) including one Late Formative court (Becquelin and Baudez 1979–1982). Nevertheless, it is unlikely that future investigations will discover numerous additional examples.

Currently, northern Chiapas proper accounts for only 15 ballcourts (Table 9.2). This small number can be slightly augmented by including ballcourts from neighboring areas, such as the Usumacinta Valley or the Pasión drain-age, which provide a total of 21 ballcourts. When compared with the number of courts in southern Chiapas (Agrinier this volume), northern Chiapas is ob-viously less well represented. Moreover, Table 9.2 includes data that have not always been counterchecked. For example, the ballcourt at Chacpuyil is probably the same as the one called Monteria Vieja de Dolores (Blom 1932). Cancuen's ballcourt, identified by Blom (1932) and Morley (1938), has not been confirmed through more recent survey (Tourtellot, Sabloff, and Sharik 1978). (It should be noted, however, that these latter investigators suggest that other structures from the same site may form a ballcourt.)

Several sites in northern Chiapas present close linkages with those from southern Chiapas (Agrinier this volume). This is most apparent at Chinkultic, Tenam Puente, and Tenam Rosario. They are referenced here because of their shared iconography. Recent investigations by Universidad Nacional Autó-noma de Mexico in the northwestern Maya Lowlands have identified addi-tional ballcourts in that area. At least seven ballcourts are now reported from the Tabasco–Campeche area, though none of them have been excavated (Ochoa Salas and Pincemin pers. comm.). While these courts do not seem to

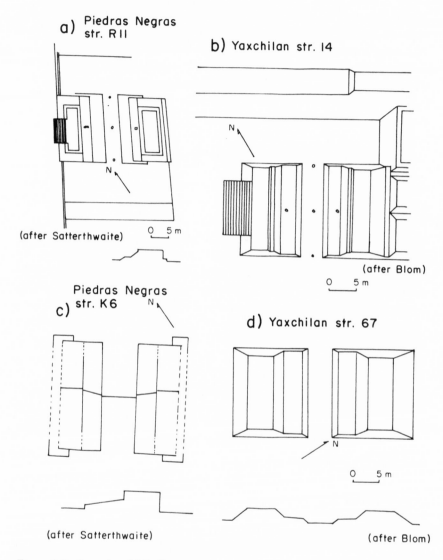

Figure 9.2. *Types I and II ballcourts.*

belong in the same context as those identified in northern Chiapas, their proximity suggests at least some relationship between the two zones.

While several ballcourts presented in Table 9.2 are still unclassified, most
courts in the area belong to three main types (Taladoire 1981). There are open-
ended ballcourts and enclosed ones. Type I ballcourts (Mosil B and Piedras

Negras Structure K6; see Figure 9.2c) are open ended, and their lateral structures do not have benches. They resemble in profile the Copán ballcourt, a
type most frequently associated with the Late Classic Maya Lowlands.

Type II is well represented in the area with at least six confirmed examples
and one additional court at Altar de Sacrificios which is very similar (Table
9.2; see Figure 9.2a, b, d). They are open-ended ballcourts, identified in part
by low benches along their lateral structures. The type is dated to the Late
Classic period in the Maya Lowlands (Piedras Negras, Palenque, Yaxchilán)
as well as a portion of the Chiapan Highlands (Toniná Structure G5:1–2).

The third kind of court is Type VII ballcourts; they are enclosed, though
their end fields are unlike most enclosed courts. In most cases, one end field
at a court is larger than the other. This is apparent at Toniná (Structure H6:2–
3, Figure 9.3), Ojo de Agua, San Gregorio, and in the southern Chiapan Highlands at Chinkultic and Tenam Puente. Moreover, the lateral structures include benches in their profiles. There are perhaps five occurrences of this
ballcourt type in northern Chiapas. It appears during the Late Classic period
at Toniná, and lasts into the Terminal Classic at Seibal and the Early Postclassic period in the Highlands (Figure 9.3a, c).

The orientation of ballcourts and their locations within a site have not been
considered here, as there are too few examples and too many differences.

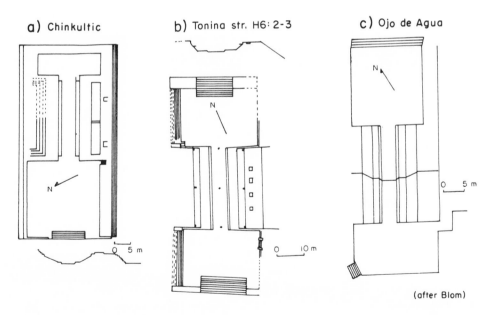

a) Chinkultic   b) Tonina str. H6: 2-3   c) Ojo de Agua

(after Blom)

Figure 9.3. Type VII ballcourts.

Table 9.3. Types of Sculpture and Associated Representations Identified with Ballcourts and the Ballgame

Sites	M-A	P	TS	S	ST	D-W	C	BP	RA
Altar de Sacrificios	X								
Piedras Negras 1		X			X			X	
Piedras Negras 2	X(5)								
Tenam Puente			X(2)				X		
Tenam Rosario 1	X(8)					X			X
Tenam Rosario 2	X								
Toniná H6:2–3	X(3)	X(6)	X(6)			X	X		
Yaxchilán	X(5)					X			
Cancuen	X							X	
Chinkultic	X					X		X	
Dos Pilas				X					
Itzan					X	X		X	X
La Amelia					X			X	X
Seibal					X(2)	X		X	
Yaxchilán Str. 33				X(13)		X		X	X
Usumacinta Area	X							X	
Site Q		X(7)						X	

Note: M-A, markers or altars; P, panels; TS, tenoned sculpture; S, steps; ST, stelae; D-W, dignitaries or warriors; C, captives; BP, ball players; RA, ritual activities. The upper portion of the table includes sculpture found in ballcourts. The lower part tabulates representations of ball players or ballgame-related activities in other contexts. Glyphic representations of ballcourts are not included here.

Little pattern can now be established (see Table 9.2). At Toniná, for instance, the main ballcourt (Str. H6:2–3) is located on one side of the main plaza, while the smaller one is positioned in front of the Acropolis. One court is oriented north–south, while the other is east–west. Nevertheless, there does exist one pattern worth noting. At each of the three sites containing two ballcourts, one court belongs to the Type II variety and the other to Type VII. This same pattern is repeated in other sites from the Highlands, both in southern Chiapas (Tenam Puente, Tenam Rosario) and Guatemala.

When considering the number of ballcourts in northern Chiapas, the ballgame does not seem to have been a major activity, especially when compared to southern Chiapas (Agrinier this volume) or the Guatemalan Highlands (Fox this volume). However, another data set indicative of the ballgame must be consulted before minimizing the import of the game in northern

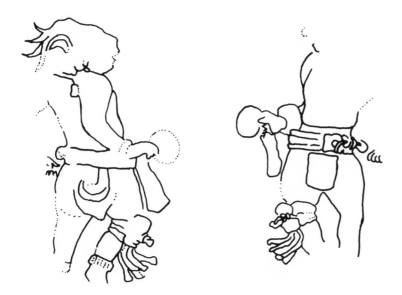

Figure 9.4. Sketch drawing of the Piedras Negras ball-player panel.

Chiapas. Associated sculpture and related ballgame representation are available from several contexts (Table 9.3). Colsenet is presently working on an inventory and study of all ballgame-related monuments in the Maya Lowlands. He has established a list of 135 monuments directly associated with ballcourts (i.e. markers, tenoned sculptures, panels), and 46 monuments with ball-player iconography, the latter without ballcourt architectural associations. Of all these monuments, 37 from the first list and 28 from the second list are located in northern Chiapas and adjacent areas (Table 9.3). Most monuments come from sites which have more than one ballcourt. The main ballcourt from Toniná accounts for as many as 15 examples, with 18 from the site of Yaxchilán.

The relative lack of ballcourts is then largely compensated by the amount and richness of ballgame iconography. Much of this iconographic evidence is frequently derived from architectural contexts other than ballcourts, such as the Yaxchilán Structure 33 stairway, or the panels identified from what Mathews calls Site Q (Taladoire 1976). Nevertheless, the spatial distribution of the monuments considered here fits almost perfectly the spatial distribution of known ballcourts.

Table 9.3 presents the contexts of these ballgame representations, first by monuments and then by iconographic theme. The main theme apparent from most depictions is the representation of ball players. These players are either engaged in the game, as in the Piedras Negras panel (Figure 9.4), or they are

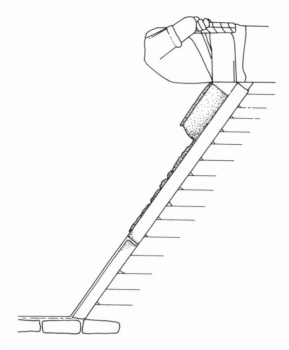

Figure 9.5. Tenoned captives from the Toniná ballcourt, H6:2–3.

richly attired and involved in ritual or ceremonial activities, as on the Yaxchilán steps (Graham 1982; García Moll 1977), or on the panels from Site Q.
Without additional information it may be premature to define the actual nature of these latter activities. It should be noted that it would be difficult for
players to practice the game attired in the manner indicated by the render-
ings. Further, in many instances such as on the steps from Yaxchilán, ball
players are associated with other beings. Dwarves, dignitaries, and victims
have been found elsewhere in association with ballgame iconography (e.g., at
Naj Tunich: Stuart 1981), but all remain somewhat enigmatic. If indeed these
nonplaying individuals are ball players, they are seen as symbolic manifestations rather than as active participants. Most probably, these individuals are
not ball players, but ball-player impersonators.

Two other prominent features must be mentioned. First, captives are presented in association with ballcourts at both Tenam Puente and Toniná. On
the main ballcourt at Toniná, 12 out of 15 monuments picture captives (Figure
9.5). Second, dignitaries are associated with ballcourts and ballgame iconography. At Toniná the central marker (M69) shows a dignitary. According to
Greene Robertson (1972), Stela 7 from Seibal represents the rise to power of a

chief dressed as a ball player in A.D. 771. Pictured on the steps from Yaxchilán Structure 33 is the name of Bird Jaguar, along with several emblem glyphs. At Tenam Rosario (Agrinier 1976) warriors or individuals standing for war are portrayed on the ballcourt markers. It should be noted that if the hypothesis by Miller and Houston (1987) suggesting that certain glyphs represent ballcourts is accepted, then Toniná, Yaxchilán and Seibal, as well as Tortuguero and El Perú, represent heightened ballcourt activity. Most examples of this glyphic evidence come from these sites, well within the general study area.

Although several of the above iconographic themes can be defined at other sites outside the northern Chiapas study area, they tend to be isolated occurrences; for instance, at Copán the king (a dignitary) is playing in a ritual context (Baudez 1984). Captives are represented on panels within one of the ballcourts at Coba. But nowhere are the number of different ballgame themes as well documented as in northern Chiapas. Clearly a discrepancy exists between the apparent richness of iconographic evidence and the relative lack of architectural examples.

A Model

In an attempt to explain this apparent discrepancy we propose the following model, the validity of which may not be proved in other areas. As in most parts of Mesoamerica, the ballgame in northern Chiapas and in the Usumacinta Valley appears grounded on a shared ritual and religious substratum. Elements of this tradition include an expression of duality (e.g., the representation of players in different attires as shown on panels from Site Q, or the opposition between individuals as depicted on the Tenam Rosario markers), a relationship with cosmic forces and fertility cults, and a conflict between life (as represented by chiefs and dignitaries) and the Underworld (associated with trophy heads worn by some players, dwarves, etc.). However, this common tradition surely had more specific meanings peculiar to the various regional settings within the subcontinent.

Northern Chiapas and the Usumacinta Valley constitute a frontier zone between the Maya core area and the northwestern Chontalpa (Thompson 1970). The arguments proposed by Thompson to explain the Putún expansion in the Usumacinta drainage need not be repeated here; suffice it to say that the fall of Maya cities such as Palenque or Yaxchilán or the takeover of cities like Seibal by new dynasties characterized the Late and Terminal Classic of the region. Warfare and conflict were decidedly part of life in that area, probably more than in other parts of the greater Maya area. The presence of the Bonampak murals attests to this state of war. The importance of the captive motif in the area should be understood as well (Baudez and Mathews 1979). The captives at a site like Toniná are considered as prisoners more than as future victims for sacrifice. Further, the violent fall of Toniná (Becquelin and Baudez 1979–1982) may suggest a military siege. War and militarism were certainly pronounced characteristics of the area.

Among numerous complex societies around the world, "games" are documented as ways of resolving conflict. When confronted with conflictual situations, many people settle the matter by resorting to a duel patronized by supernatural forces which takes place in a closed court between the opposed parties or their representatives (the David and Goliath biblical encounter may be the most familiar to western audiences). The supernatural forces do not act as judges, but as patrons of the group who are fighting for the "just" cause. Victory confirms that a winning team acted on behalf of these supernatural forces. There have been many different applications of these duels, and Beaumanoir's fight as described in the introduction is one such case. We suggest that in northern Chiapas and in the Usumacinta Valley the ballgame was played in a similar way.

In the prevailing war-like setting of the study area, we suggest that the ballgame was used as a substitute and a symbol for war. It acted to resolve conflicts between Maya cities, and between the Maya and other neighboring peoples. This would help explain the dignitary (chief no. 7) standing in the middle marker of the Toniná ballcourt surrounded by captive representations. It would also explain the importance of captive iconography in other sites, such as Palenque or Tenam Puente, and the war and peace motifs on the Tenam Rosario markers.

This interpretation provides a unity to the different themes represented on monuments associated with ballcourts and the ballgame: warriors, ball players, dignitaries as war chiefs, captives, and scenes of sacrifice. It also helps explain the relative scarcity of ballcourts in the area. If the ballgame had acquired a war-like and political meaning, it may have been restricted to prominent sites and capitals. Ballcourts would then be built only at major sites or in communities where political or military activities were especially important (cf. Santley et al. this volume). This link between ballgames and militarism is underscored elsewhere in this volume (Kowalewski et al.; Fox) and can be exemplified in other contexts (in Michoacan for example; Michelet pers. comm.).

The above model must be counterchecked through additional study of the available iconography. It does not preclude the existence of a more general symbolism to the ballgame. It does give the game a new dimension which in some ways resembles the meaning of the ballgame as it was used by the latter Aztecs: as a method of conquest and expansion.

CHAPTER 10

The Ballcourts of Southern Chiapas, Mexico

Pierre Agrinier

The significance of the following report rests in the sheer number of unpublished or little known ballcourts of southern Chiapas. Most of these 181 ballcourts were identified by the New World Archaeological Foundation between 1955 and 1983 and in salvage archaeological surveys of the Instituto Nacional de Antropología e Historia. These surveys have recorded the highest density of ballcourts for any region in greater Mesoamerica. Southern Chiapas includes the Pacific Coastal Plain, the Central Depression of Chiapas, and most of the Central Chiapas Plateau Highlands.

Ballcourt distribution across southern Chiapas is summarized in Figure 10.1 and Tables 10.1–10.8. Brief descriptions of ballcourt characteristics and distribution by major chronological period will be introduced in the text. More detailed descriptions will be given of a few outstanding examples which have been more thoroughly explored. These courts have a long history, starting with the Middle Preclassic period and ending in the Early Postclassic period.

The Middle Preclassic (900–400 B.C.)

The three earliest ballcourts belong to the sites of Finca Acapulco, El Vergel, and San Mateo, on the right bank of the Grijalva River. These sites date from the late Middle Preclassic period and are believed to have been regional cen-

Figure 10.1. Map of ballcourt sites in southern Chiapas.

ters abandoned at the close of the Escalera phase around 500 B.C. (Lowe 1977b:226). The three corresponding ballcourts are the oldest known in Mesoamerica, except for the uncertain examples from La Venta (possibly dating to the early Middle Preclassic) and San Lorenzo (dating to the Palangana phase and approximately contemporary with our Chiapas examples [Beristáin Bravo 1983:213–215; Figure 10.1a]). The three Chiapas courts are of the open-ended type with a small, separated platform placed at each end of the playing field. Two of them, Vergel and San Mateo, had a roughly circular slab placed at the center of the playing field. In both instances, these slabs were raised about 30 cm above the floor and covered with an encasing layer of very hard black mud.

Architectural details are not well known. The flanking range and benches were made of packed dirt, faced with uncut stones and covered with mud

(Mora 1971). At San Mateo, Gareth Lowe (pers. comm. 1985) found a whitish sandy material filling the center field and suggested that it may be the eroded vestige of a superstructure which was washed away from the top of the range. The three ballcourts had a north–south alignment with an eastern deviation of 13–25°.

The only southern Chiapas ballcourt that has been definitely dated to the latter part of the Middle Preclassic is at La Libertad, a major site at the extreme end of the Central Depression on the Mexico–Guatemala border. The court is located on the north side of the central architectural complex, a huge acropolis, to which its southern range is attached. The surviving portion of the ballcourt reveals benches made of clay, faced with roughly hewn stones. The 6-m-wide playing field was covered with small gravel and crushed limestone (Miller 1976:15). The north range was 9 m wide and 27 m long, while the southern range formed a projecting part of the acropolis' basal platform and sustained a secondary platform. This ballcourt is of the open type, as far as can be judged from the limited excavation undertaken. It is oriented 65° west of magnetic north.

The Late Preclassic (400 B.C.–A.D. 100)

Three Chiapas ballcourts possibly date from the Late Preclassic period: Santa Rosa (Lowe 1959; Delgado 1965) in the Upper Grijalva Basin; Santa Cruz in the Acala subregion (Lowe 1959:34); and Rancho Alegre on the Chiapas coast near Pijijiapan (Lowe pers. comm. 1985). All are open-type ballcourts; Santa Cruz has a small separate structure located at each end of the playing field.

The Early Classic (A.D. 250–450)

The Early Classic in Chiapas is represented by the ballcourts of Ocozocoautla in the western Central Depression, Ojo de Agua in the Upper Grijalva Valley, and El Recuerdo and Mújica in the central Chiapas plateau near the town of Comitán. Unfortunately, none of these structures has been sufficiently explored to offer a detailed description. They were all of the open-ended type. The Ocozocoautla ballcourt consisted of two parallel and rectangular 1.50-m-high platforms, 22 m long and 14 m wide, with a sloping playing wall and an absence of benches. The core of the structure was made of dirt and uncut travertine blocks; the exterior was faced with cut travertine. The narrow, 3.75-m-wide playing alley was paved with limestone and oriented 40° west of magnetic north.

At Ojo de Agua, the Early Classic ballcourt was covered by a later construc-

Table 10.1. Distribution of Southern Chiapas Ballcourts by Period

	Coast				Highlands				W. Cent. Dep.			
	O	**I**	**T**	**U**	**O**	**I**	**T**	**U**	**O**	**I**	**T**	**U**
Postclassic												
Late Classic	1	1			5	7			10	17		3
Middle Classic	4	1										
Early Classic					3				1	1		
Late Preclassic	2											
Middle Preclassic												
Undated	7				1				3			1
Total	14	2			9	7			14	18		4

Key: O = open-ended; I = I-shaped; T = T-shaped; U = U-shaped

tion dating to the Late Classic, raising the possibility that more Early Classic examples lie buried below the numerous Late Classic courts reported from Chiapas. The Ojo de Agua ranges were terraced, forming three steps 50–70 cm high and 40–50 cm wide. They were faced with cut limestone slabs and had an orientation of N40°E (Bryant 1982).

The Middle Classic (A.D. 450–650)

Probably the most spectacular site of the Middle Classic period in Chiapas is Los Horcones, between the towns of Tonalá and Pijijiapan. It is located on the northern flank of a rocky escarpment called Cerro Bernal which overlooks the Pacific Ocean (Navarrete 1986). The Horcones site extends over 2 km of partly leveled ridgetops reaching a maximum elevation of 115 m. It forms a chain of stone structures, including several platform-and-plaza complexes, four stelae in Teotihuacán style, and five ballcourts. One of the courts was associated with two of the stelae. The site is believed to have been a Teotihuacán settle-

E. Cent. Dep.				Upper Tributaries				Middle Grijalva				Row Totals
O	I	T	U	O	I	T	U	O	I	T	U	
	1			1		2						4
10	7		2	37	19	6		6	9		3	143
												5
												5
2												4
3					1							4
				11	3	1		1	1			29
15	8		2	50	22	9		7	10		3	194

ment controlling the commercial route between Kaminaljuyú and Teotihua-cán (Agrinier 1975; Navarrete 1974).

If so, the presence of ballcourts would be unusual since none was found at Teotihuacán, despite the secondary evidence there of the mural painting at Tepantitla and the marker at La Ventilla. The Los Horcones ballcourts might indicate a dominance of local, native desiderata. Another large court is also located near the highway, west of Los Horcones. The uncommonly large number of courts at Los Horcones seems to mark the unusual importance of that site as a controlling regional center. The absence of other reported Middle Classic ballcourts in coastal Chiapas does, however, raise the possibility that the trait was brought here by Teotihuacán through one of its zones of influence, possibly Veracruz.

It is worth noting that Middle Classic Mirador, in the Western Central Depression, which also shows an unusual Teotihuacán stylistic influence, does not have a ballcourt. There were, however, one or two courts at nearby Miramar, of undetermined but probable Middle or Late Classic date.

Table 10.2. Western Central Depression Ballcourts

Site		Early Classic				Late Classic				Not Dated			
		O	I	T	U	O	I	T	U	O	I	T	U
OCZ	Guayabilal					X							
OCZ	Guayabilal					X							
OCZ	El Encanto II		X										
OCZ	El Encanto I											X	
OCZ	El Eden (no info)												
OCZ	Ocozocoautla	X											
JIQ	La Florida						X						
CINT	Villa Morelos (in info)												
OCZ	Bajo San Cosme									X			
OCZ	El Porvenir (no info)												
OCZ	El Guayabal (no info)												
OCZ	El Campamento (no info)												
OCZ	El Canelar (no info)												
OCZ	Rancho Santa Laura						X						
JIQ	Miramar I					X							
JIQ	Miramar II					X							
JIQ	Cerro Campanario						X						
JIQ	Site J					X							
JIQ	El Refugio						X						
JIQ	Ocotlan					X							
BER	El Ocote (no info)												
CINT	Varejonal I						X						
CINT	Varejonal II						X						
CINT	El Sueño					X							
CINT	Santiago (no info)												
CINT	Pueblo Viejo (no info)												
CINT	Rancho Macuilapa												
SUC	San Pedro Buena Vista					X							
V.CO	Veracruz II 1										X		
	Veracruz II 2										X		

The Late and Terminal Classic (A.D. 650–1000)

Ballcourt popularity in southern Chiapas reached its highest level during the Late Classic period. The Late Classic accounts for 85.5 percent of the dated ballcourts. The highest density is found in the Upper Grijalva Tributaries re-

Sweat House	Atypical	Orientation	References
			Peterson n.d. unpublished
			Peterson n.d. unpublished
			Peterson n.d. unpublished
		EW	Peterson n.d. unpublished
			Peterson n.d. unpublished
		40W	R. Lowe, in prep.
			Peterson n.d. unpublished
			Peterson n.d. unpublished
	X		Peterson n.d. unpublished
			Pailles 1988
			Pailles 1988
			Piña Chan & Navarrete 1967
			Taladoire 1981
X			Agrinier 1972
		40E	
		30W	
		WNW-ESE	Peterson 1961 vol. 1
			Peterson 1961 vol. 1
			Peterson 1961 vol. 1
		30W	
			Pailles 1988
		32E	Agrinier 1969a
		25E	Agrinier 1969a
	X		Peterson n.d.
			Peterson n.d.
			Peterson n.d.
		50W	Lowe 1959; Navarrete 1966
		50W	Navarrete 1960

gion, which contains 50 percent of all reported Late Classic ballcourts. The open-ended type is by far the most numerous (51%), followed by the enclosed I-shaped type (40%). Two other types, the T-shaped and U-shaped, share 5 and 4 percent of the total, respectively; the U-shaped type is limited to the Central Depression. Two unusual double ballcourts were reported at San

Table 10.3. Middle Grijalva—Malpaso Dam Basin Ballcourts

Site	Late Classic				Not Dated				Attached
	O	I	T	U	O	I	T	U	
Chico El Magueyal		X							
Tec El Raudal I (no info.)									
Tec El Triunfo (Precla; no info.)									
Tec Colonia López Mateo					X				
MP2 La Reforma						X			
M65 Brazo Piedra	X								
MP11 Estación RH 806				X					
MP20 San Isidro	X								X
MG23 No name	X								
MG30 Estación RH-364-65				X					
MG65 Banco Nieve	X								
MG70 El Laurel	X								
MG71 El Progreso				X					
MG86 San Antonio IV (no info.)									
MG89 San Vicente Agua Fría		X							
MP26 Santa Cruz	X								
MG31 La Pampa		X							
MG40 Totopac		X							
MG42 La Vega del Laurel		X							
MP22 San Antonio		X							
MG49 El Coyol		X							
MP11 El Achiote		X							
Río Hondo		X							

Isidro in the Middle Grijalva Mal Paso Dam basin (Matos Moctezuma 1966) and San Gerónimo in the Upper Grijalva Tributaries region (Lee and Blake in prep.). A sweathouse was associated with the ballcourt at San Antonio and possibly at Santa Laura. Both sites are located within the area of the Mal Paso Dam basin.

Fifteen sites had a ballcourt attached to a temple platform: Tenam Soledad, Tenam Poco Vinic, TR-76, San José Las Canoas, Naranjo, Jomanil II, La Papaya, Santa Inés, Guajilar I, and Piedra Labrada, all situated in the Upper Grijalva Tributaries region; Chinkultic and Copanaguastla in the Comitán area; Varejonal and San Isidro in the Western Central Depression and the

Sweat House	Atypical	Orientation	References
			Beutelspacher 1982
			Piña Chan 1967
			Piña Chan & Navarrete 1967
		NS	Piña Chan & Navarrete 1967
	X	75W	Lee & Navarrete n.d.
		40E	Lee & Navarrete n.d.
		45W	Lee & Navarrete n.d.
		22W	Lee & Navarrete n.d.
		20E	Lee & Navarrete n.d.
		45W	Lee & Navarrete n.d.
		75W	Lee & Navarrete n.d.
		NS	Lee & Navarrete n.d.
		65W	Lee & Navarrete n.d.
			Lee & Navarrete n.d.
		EW	Lee & Navarrete n.d.
		NS	Lee & Navarrete n.d.
		NS	Lee & Navarrete n.d.
		EW	Lee & Navarrete n.d.
		NS	Lee & Navarrete n.d.
		75E	Lee & Navarrete n.d.
		22W	Lee & Navarrete n.d.
		75W	Lee & Navarrete n.d.

Mal Paso Dam basin, respectively; and Izapa on the Coastal Plain.

Nine of these sites are considered to have been regional centers. Direct association of stelae or sculptured altars, as opposed to ballcourt markers, are rare in Late Classic southern Chiapas. They are found on the Coastal Plain at Izapa but seem to have been reused as displaced Protoclassic monuments (Lowe et al. 1982:233).

At Chinkultic several carved Maya stelae were associated with the ballcourt. Two stelae seem also to have been located on the Tenam Puente ballcourt, at each corner of the southern range (see plan by Blom and La Farge 1926[II]:Fig. 356).

Table 10.4. Eastern Central Depression—Acala Sub-region Ballcourts

Site		Late Preclassic				Late Classic				Post-Classic			
		O	I	T	U	O	I	T	U	O	I	T	U
AC.3	Ruiz Site									X			
AC.	Santa Cruz	X											
AC.7	San Luis El Alto					X							
AC.9	San Francisco Angostura I					X							
AC.9	San Francisco Angostura II					X							
AC.13	Laguna Mora												
	Late Classic (no info.)												
SO.	Las Posadas					X							
Ve.3	Chachi A15					X							
Ve.	Chachi Panteon					X							
Ve.7	Paso de la Vega I							X					
Ve.7	Paso de la Vega II												

Table 10.5. Eastern Central Depression—Chapatengo-Chejel Sub-region Ballcourts

Site		Middle Preclassic				Late Preclassic				Late Classic			
		O	I	T	U	O	I	T	U	O	I	T	U
CN.1	Las Maravillas									X			
CN.9	Niños Heroes									X			
CN.9	Portatenco I											X	
CN.9	Portatenco II									X			
CN.10	Santa Rosa					X							
SO.3	Chapatengo I										X		
SO.3	Chapatengo II										X		
SO.5	Poblason										X		
SO.6	Laguna Francesa										X		
SO.	Las Delicias									X			
SO.	San Francisco									X			
	Acapulco	X											
	Vergel	X											
	San Mateo	X											
	Mojon de Mazapan											X	

Not Dated					
O	I	T	U	Orientation	References
				NS	Lowe 1959
				60E	Lowe 1959
				20E	Lowe 1959
				70W	Lowe 1959
				70W	Lowe 1959
					Lowe 1959:148
					Sorenson 1956:14
				65W	Martínez plan 1973, unpub.
				55W	Gussinyer 1972a
				?	Gussinyer 1972a
				50E	Lowe 1959
X				NS	Lowe 1959

Marker*			
C	P	Orientation	References
		20E	Lowe 1959
		50W	Martínez 1972 plan; unpub.
		60W	Martínez 1972 plan; unpub.
		25E	Martínez 1972 plan; unpub.
		20E	Lowe 1959
		60W	Lowe 1959; Gussinyer 1972b
X		60W	Gussinyer 1972b
		68W	Lowe 1959
	X	20E	Lowe 1959; Con Uribe 1981
			Gussinyer 1972b
			Gussinyer 1972b
		26E	Lowe 1977b
	X	25E	Mora 1971: field notes; unpub.
	X	13E	Lowe 1977: field notes; unpub.
			Lowe 1959; Martínez 1972 plan; unpub.

*C = Carved; P = Plain

Table 10.6. Upper Grijalva Tributaries Sub-region Ballcourts

Site		Middle Preclassic				Late Classic				Not Dated			
		O	I	T	U	O	I	T	U	O	I	T	U
TR-2	Castellano					X							
TR-9-I	Tenam Rosario I						X						
TR-9-II	Tenam Rosario II	X											
TR-44	Tenam Soledad						X						
TR-45	Tenam Concepción						X						
TR-46	Rodríguez Site						X						
TR-50	Tenam Pojo Vinic							X					
TR-55	San José Las Canoas							X					
TR-63	El Laurel					X							
TR-70	Jomanil I					X							
TR-71	Jomanil II					X							
TR-74	Bolsa Plátano					X							
TR-76	No name						X						
TR-77	Naranjo								X				
TR-79	El Zapote									X			
TR-81	El Recreo					X							
TR-86	El Jicaral					X							
TR-112	San Gerónimo I						X						
TR-112	San Gerónimo II					X							
TR-99	Lagartero					X							
TR-118	Tres Cerritos						X						
TR-123	La Trinitaria						X						
TR-127	El Porvenir						X						
TR-128	Cuajilote					X							
TR-142	El Rosario					X							
TR-152	Ojo de Agua					X							
TR-153	El Pijiji						X						
TR-167	Cerro Iguanero					X							
TR-181	Santa Rosa–La Union						X						
TR-186	San Antonio Zapotal					X							
TR-109	No name									X			
TGR-90	San Agustin									X			
TR-122	San Antonio Playa Grande					X							
TR-157	La Libertad				X								
TR-171	La Papaya						X						
TR-172	Potrero Mango					X							
TR-189	Camcum					X							
TR-225	Las Canoitas Tsutson					X							

Attached	Double	Orientation	References
		N-S	Lee & Blake n.d.
		50W	Lee & Blake n.d.
		45W	Lee & Blake n.d.
X		65W	Blom 1932
			Lee & Blake n.d.
		60E	Lee & Blake n.d.
X		65E	Rivero 1983, vol. 1
X		50W	Lee & Clark 1980
		30W	Lee & Clark 1980; Rivero 1983, vol. I
		30W	Lee & Clark 1980; Rivero 1983, vol. I
X		40W	Lee & Clark 1980; Rivero 1983, vol. I
		50W	Lee & Clark 1980; Rivero 1983, vol. I
X		40W	Lee & Clark 1980; Rivero 1983, vol. I
X		60E	Lee & Clark 1980; Rivero 1983, vol. I
		E-W	Lee & Clark 1980; Rivero 1983, vol. I
		30W	Lee & Clark 1980; Rivero 1983, vol. I
		60W	Lee & Clark 1980; Rivero 1983, vol. I
		45W	Miller & Lowe 1977
	X	60W	Miller & Lowe 1977
		45W	Ekholm 1976
		40W	Lee & Blake n.d.
		E-W	Lee & Blake n.d.
		N-S	Lee & Blake n.d.
		25W	Lee & Blake n.d.
		45E	Lee & Blake n.d.
		40E	Lee & Blake n.d.
		15W	Lee & Blake n.d.
		60W	Lee & Blake n.d.; Rivero 1983, vol. I
		60E	Rivero 1983, vol. I
		45W	Lee & Clark 1980
		E-W	Lee & Clark 1980
		N-S	Lee & Clark 1980
		60W	Lowe 1959; Rivero 1983, vol. I
X		65W	Lowe 1959; Miller 1976
X		45E	Lee 1975; Rivero 1983, vol. I
		E-W	Lee 1975; Miller & Lowe 1977
		50W	Lee & Blake n.d.
		55W	Lee & Blake n.d.

Table 10.6. *Continued*

Site		Middle Preclassic				Late Classic				Not Dated			
		O	I	T	U	O	I	T	U	O	I	T	U
TR-226	Marroquín					X							
TR-237	Ampliación Guerrero Cipres					X							
TR-240	Jocote Colorado	X											
TR-?	San Felipe	X											
TR-	Tierra Blanca I	X											
TR-	Tierra Blanca II		X										
TR-	Santa Inés			X									
TR-	Zorrillo	X											
TR-	Meson de Piedra		X										
TR-	La Mesa				X								
TR-	Desconsuelo						X						
TR-	El Rosarito (no info.)						X	No shape					
TR-	San Gregorio		X										
TR-43	Barrio Santa Rosa	X											
Co. 2	Guapinole						X						
Co. 3	Cuxu							X					
Co. 7	Costa Rica						X						
Co. 17	San Joaquin						X						
Co. 23	El Guanacaste						X						
Co. 51	San Antonio Playa Grande								X				
Co. 14	No name						X						
Co.	La Ceiba	X											
Co. 55	San Caralampio Tampisque								X				
Co. 58	Encierre del Estoraque I		X										
Co. 58	Encierre del Estoraque II		X										
Co. 59	Guajilar I			X									
Co. 59	Guajilar II		X										
Co. 15	Aquespala		X										
Co. 63	Sta. Maria Equistenango						X						
Co. 65	No name			X									
Co.	Laguna Candelaria		X										
Co. 12	No name		X										
Co.	Los Cimientos			X									
Co. 67	Encierro La Chaperna			X									
Co.	San Caralampio		X										

Attached	Double	Orientation	References
		N-S	Lee & Blake n.d.
		56W	Lee & Blake n.d.
		50W	Lee & Blake n.d.
		70W	Lowe 1959
		No info.	Lowe 1959
		No info.	Lowe 1959; Rivero 1983, vol. I
		45W	Lowe 1959; De Montmollin 1985
		45W	De Montmollin 1985
		70E	De Montmollin 1985
		65W	De Montmollin 1985
		30W	Blom & Duby 1957:44–45, Fig. 8
			Blom 1932
			Shook 1956; Rivero 1983, vol. I
		65W	Lee & Blake n.d.
		20E	Lee & Blake n.d.
		E-W	Lee & Blake n.d.
		30E	Lee & Blake n.d.
		70E	Lee & Blake n.d.
		55E	Lee & Blake n.d.; Rivero 1983, vol. I
		10E	Lee & Blake n.d.; Rivero 1983, vol. I
		70E	Rivero 1983, vol. I
		40E	Rivero 1983, vol. I
		60E	Lowe 1959; Lee & Blake n.d.
		25E	Rivero 1983, vol. I; Lowe 1959; Lee & Blake n.d.
		25E	Rivero 1983, vol. I; Lowe 1959; Lee & Blake n.d.
X		60E	Rivero 1983, vol. I
		NW-SE	Rivero 1983, vol. I
		E-W	Shook 1956; Taladoire 1981; Rivero 1983
		60W	Lee & Blake n.d.
		75E	Lee & Blake n.d.
		60E	Rivero 1983, vol. I
		45W	Rivero 1983, vol. I
		30E	Rivero 1983, vol. I
		50E	Rivero 1983, vol. I
			Culebro 1939; Shook 1956; Piña Chan 1967

Table 10.6. *Continued*

Site		Middle Preclassic				Late Classic				Not Dated			
		O	I	T	U	O	I	T	U	O	I	T	U
Co. 69	El Jocote	X											
Ch. 9	Piedra Labrada		X										
Ch. 16	Tujú	X											
Ch. 23	La Pinta I									X			
Ch. 37	No name							X					
Ch. 3	Potrero Terrenal 2	X											
Ch. 20	No name	X											
Ch. 66	Zapotalcito										X		

Table 10.7. Central Highlands Ballcourts

Site		Early Classic				Late Classic			
		O	I	T	U	O	I	T	U
CM. 3	Cerro de la Lanza						X		
	Chinkultik						X		
CM. 11	Mújica	X							
CM.	Tenam Soledad	X							
CM. 5	Tenam Puente						X		
CM.	Durazno-Las Cruces (no info.)								
CM. 4	Yerba Buena	X							
CM. 7	El Recuerdo					X			
	Bolonchac					X			
CV. 1	No name						X		
	San Ton						X		
AM. 1	Rancho San Nicolás						X		
SC. 3	Moxviquil					X			
SC. 3	Cerro Ecatapec					X			
SC. 3	San Cristóbal								

Attached	Double	Orientation	References
			Shook 1956
X		60E	Lee & Blake n.d.
		70W	Lowe 1959
		25W	Lee & Blake n.d.
		20E	Lee & Blake n.d.
		E-W	Lee & Blake n.d.
		20W	Lee & Blake n.d.
		E-W	Lee & Blake n.d.

Attached	Sunken Atypical	Orientation	References
		25W	Lee & Blake n.d.
X		25W	Agrinier 1969b
		41E	Adams 1970
		?	Rivero 1979
		55W	Blom & Duby 1957
			Taladoire 1981
		E-W	Culbert 1965
		50W	Rivero 1983, vol. I
		NW-SE	Piña Chan 1967; Taladoire 1981
		55E	Adams 1970
		30E	Adams 1970
		42W	Culbert 1965
		20W	Taladoire 1981
			Adams 1970
	X		Taladoire 1981

Table 10.8. Coastal Plain Ballcourts

Site	Late Preclassic				Middle Classic				Late Classic			
	O	I	T	U	O	I	T	U	O	I	T	U
TON Tiltepec												
TON La Chincuya												
TON Los Horcones 1					X							
TON Los Horcones 2						X						
TON Los Horcones 3					X							
TON Los Horcones 4					X							
TON Los Horcones 5					X							
HU. Huixtla												
DIJ. Rancho Alegre	X											
TAPA. San Antonio												
TAPA. Los Toros												
TxCH. Omoa	X											
TxCl. Izapa										X		
Front. San Joaquin												
SUCH. El Campito									X			

At Chapatengo, a ballcourt built with very carefully cut limestone had a marker at the center of its playing field. It is a limestone disk, 79 cm in diameter and 26 cm thick, carved on one face. The design consists of an 11-cm-wide glyph band circling the edges of the stone. The center design, if it existed, has been obliterated by erosion.

An offering of several Late Classic pottery vessels, some of them Maya, was located underneath the marker. One of the vessels contained several marine shells and a few stone beads (Gussinyer 1972b[4]:Figs. 3, 4).

A Late Classic ballcourt floor marker was found at Laguna Francesa, the major center on the Upper Grijalva River (Con Uribe 1981:42–44, Figs. 29, 30). A sculptured drum-like marker was located at the center of the playing alley of the Ojo de Agua ballcourt in the Upper Grijalva Tributaries region. In the neighboring site of Tenam Rosario, Ballcourt I had seven carved stone disks.

The Ojo de Agua ballcourt is an I-shaped stone structure with ranges measuring approximately 44 m × 15 m, with a narrow 5-m-wide playing field.

Not Dated							
O	I	T	U	Monumental	Attached	Orientation	References
X						65W	Navarrete 1969
X				X		27E	Navarrete 1969
				X		30E	Navarrete 1969
						32E	Navarrete 1969
						50E	Navarrete 1969
						40E	Navarette 1969
						E-W	Lowe, pers. comm.
X						40E	Navarrete 1969
							Lowe pers. comm.
X						E-W	Agrinier 1969c;
							Navarrete 1969
X						50E	Navarrete 1969
X						40E	Navarrete 1969
				X	X	10S of E	Lowe et al. 1982
X						13W	Navarrete 1969
							Navarrete 1969

The southern end field is delineated by a low, 50-cm-high wall, 13 m deep and 35 m wide. The other end field is slightly deeper and is bordered by two small platforms on the eastern and western sides and a larger one (23 m × 20 m) at the northern extremity. All three are joined by a low wall. A sculptured drum-like marker was located at the center of the playing field.

The Izapa ballcourt is situated on the northernmost part of the site. At its western extremity, it is attached to the largest and most complex structure of Group F, Mound 125. Its eastern end is formed by a low, double terraced rectangular platform, Mound 128. The total length of the court is 42 m from end field to end field, with a playing alley 26 m long and about 5 m wide; the alley is delimited by two identical long-structures about 2.40 m high and 8 m wide. The structure's profile includes slightly inclined benches with 50-m-high vertical faces, a vertical upper zone over 1 m high, a 3.60-m-wide range top and stepped rear range sides. The end fields are open on the north sides, giving access to the Group F plaza. Its long axis is oriented east–west with a 10° deviation to the south.

Located at the east end of the ballcourt was a stone ring with a stone ball set in its center and placed at the base of Stela 60, a reused monument.

At the western end was found a monolithic stone seat with four square legs and a flat top, bearing a damaged relief effigy head on its front (Throne 2). At its base was placed a shallow stone basin with another stone ball and a stone serpent head with tenon (Lowe et al. 1982:233).

The Postclassic (A.D. 1000–1450)

Only four Postclassic ballcourts have been reported; one in the eastern Central Depression (Acala subregion) at the Ruiz site, and three at La Mesa, Cuxu, and Ch. 37 in the Upper Grijalva River basin (see Table 10.6). It is probable that the Postclassic period saw the end of ballcourt construction if not of the ballgame itself. No report of the game being played during the Colonial period has ever been known for Chiapas.

CHAPTER 11

The Ballgame in the Southern Pacific Coast Cotzumalhuapa Region and Its Impact on Kaminaljuyu During the Middle Classic

Lee A. Parsons

The southern Pacific coast region of Mesoamerica (Chiapas–Guatemala–El Salvador) supported one of the most spectacularly dramatic elaborations of the pan-Mesoamerican ballgame complex during its Classic period "Cotzumalhuapan" era (Figure 11.1). Despite an impressive and prolific monumental stone sculptural tradition, permeated with ballgame symbolism, the region's culture and style have been curiously neglected in Mesoamerican syntheses (however, see Parsons 1967, 1969). The southern phenomenon cannot be understood without reference to the Mexican gulf coast region and the parallel development of the "Classic Veracruz" culture and sculptural style. I have defined this whole continuous region, joined by the Isthmus of Tehuantepec, as the "Peripheral Coastal Lowlands" (Parsons 1978). Throughout this ecologically uniform coastal belt contacts were maintained between the greater Mexican Highlands and the Maya Lowlands from Olmec times onward. Innovative and interrelated art styles emerged in this region during the Preclassic from the non-Maya Olmec (just north of the Isthmus) to post-Olmec, to Izapan and the contemporary proto-Maya Miraflores–Arenal styles (the last centering at Kaminaljuyú in the Guatemalan Highlands; see Parsons 1986). During Classic times the Classic Veracruz style coalesced in the north, as did the Cotzumalhuapa style in the south. This florescent ballgame era was essentially inaugurated by the spread of the Teotihuacán "horizon style," and will be the major focus of this paper.

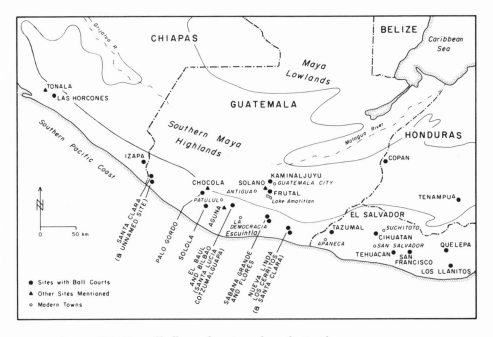

Figure 11.1. Map of ballcourt locations along the Pacific coast.

Paralleling the highland chain of volcanoes, the southern Pacific coastal strip varies from 20 to 50 km in width. Bordering the ocean is a broad low alluvial plain crosscut by numerous north–south river courses. Inland, between about 300- and 500-m elevation, is the piedmont which in turn grades into the steep volcanic slopes. The well-watered piedmont is the cacao-growing ecological zone which the Aztecs called the Soconusco (from Chiapas to western Guatemala). In the pre-European period much of the coast was characterized by rain-forest flora. Edwin Shook's survey (1965) counted some 200 archaeological sites in Pacific Guatemala alone. The large 200-mound site of Kaminaljuyú (located in modern Guatemala City in the highland Valley of Guatemala) was intimately linked, both economically and culturally, throughout its history to the Pacific coast, via Lake Amatitlán and a pass leading down to the tropical Department of Escuintla, and the cacao zone. Kaminaljuyú, therefore, must be considered critical in an analysis of coastal ballgame manifestations. Kaminaljuyú had equally convenient access to the Caribbean coast via the Motagua River Valley, and thus to the prime sources of obsidian and jade.

Evidence of the ballgame in our delimited region ranges from architectural ballcourts, to monumental stone sculpture bearing explicit ballgame iconography, to portable ballgame paraphernalia replicated in stone, to thematically decorated pottery. Initial ballgame themes appear during the Late Preclassic and Protoclassic (500 B.C.–A.D. 200), intensify as a trait complex during the Teotihuacán contact period at the outset of the Middle Classic (ca. A.D. 400), and continue to the end of the Late Classic. During the Postclassic there is an absence of ballgame data on the coast, though they persist in the adjacent highlands.

More of a mytho-religious ritual than a sport, the game usually culminated in human sacrifice—normally decapitation. The cult may have served for purposes of divination and the prognostication of extraterrestrial events (and the attempted control of them through "sympathetic magic"); through time, however, it was increasingly manipulated for worldly political purposes as well. Esoteric meanings attached to the movements of the rubber ball, the layout of the courts, the action of the players, the outcome, and post-game sacrifices fundamentally pertained to concepts of primary cosmic cycles—equinoxes as well as seasonal agricultural fertility. Emphasized were the pervading dualities of dry season–rainy season, sky–Underworld, day–night, sun–moon, morning–evening Venus, and most especially death–rebirth. There was a preoccupation here with the Underworld, including the passage and transformation of sacrificed ball players, which primarily symbolized the diurnal death and rebirth of the sun (and correspondingly the moon). The sacrifice of the sun in the west through the guise of a "privileged" ball player assured the sun's successful Underworld passage and its ultimate transformation and rebirth in the east. This act was metaphorical, being crucially equivalent to the regeneration of maize, vegetation, and life itself. Classic ballcourt layouts, often with I-shaped playing alleys, essentially represented the surface of the earth, the four cardinal directions, and the symbolic entrance to the Underworld within its center. Furthermore, a typical vertical cross section of a ballcourt graphically portrays the stepped "jaws of the earth," and again the entrance to the Underworld. In this paper there is no need to elaborate further on the complexities of ballgame symbolism, much of which is cryptically presented in the Quiché-Maya *Popol Vuh*, the content of which is probably much more ancient than the extant document.

The underlying symbolism of the game is primary and very ancient in the Mesoamerican co-tradition (Parsons 1964), even though all the components did not consolidate and floresce until the Classic period. Therefore, the question may be raised as to whether or not all the essential elements of the developed ballgame complex originated in the same place. Different components may have different histories, though we have insufficient evidence to determine precise trajectories (Barbara Price pers. comm. 1985). Presently, we operate on the premise that the core of the Classic complex had its roots in the gulf coast "rubber lowlands," despite the fact that ball-player figurines are very early in the Mexican Highlands. However, much of the pertinent iconography seems to have evolved by way of the Late Preclassic Maya on the southern Pacific coast and adjacent Highlands, and then was elaborated upon throughout these coastal Lowlands during the Classic.

In the south, the Preclassic ballgame evidence comes mainly from monumental stone sculpture (see Parsons 1986). According to present information, formal architectural ballcourts do not appear here until A.D. 400. Prior to that time a version of the game may have been played on impermanently demarcated fields. Deplorably, few ballcourt zones have been intensively excavated to determine their earliest stages. Despite the suggestive evidence of developing ballgame ideology in the southern Maya area during the Preclassic (space prevents documentation here), it is only during the Middle and Late Classic that we have overwhelming evidence of the entire complex—much of it apparently derived from the gulf coast. It reflects, in part, the expansion of Teotihuacán.

The Middle and Late Classic (A.D. 400–950)

Whereas all architectural ballcourts in the southern Pacific coast region were at one time considered to be Late Classic, recent evidence from Kaminaljuyú (a site with a total of 12 courts [Figure 11.2]; see also Parsons 1986:Map 4) indicates that there was an early Middle Classic variety as well, beginning by A.D. 400 (Brown 1973). Four of the Kaminaljuyú courts are of the early type. Of the 16 documented ballcourts on the Pacific coast from Izapa, Chiapas, to Quelepa, El Salvador, at least two appear to belong to this early variety (in addition, Los Horcones, Chiapas, may have a cluster of such early courts [Agrinier this volume]). The Classic period ballgame complex appeared not only with formal courts but with associated horizontally tenoned stone effigy scoring markers, ceremonial stone ballgame equipment (chiefly plain yokes and effigy thin stone heads or *hachas*), and a prolific monumental stone sculptural style that emphasized ritual ballgame content. These permanent new forms herald altered rules and perhaps patrons of the game. Nevertheless, the iconography continues to suggest retention and probable intensification of widespread Preclassic symbolism.

Curiously, the immediately preceding Early Classic period (A.D. 200–400) seems to have witnessed a hiatus in the production of stone sculpture at both Kaminaljuyú and on the coast (Parsons 1986), as well as a paucity of site construction (Shook 1965:186). This evidence may have a bearing upon the northern Mexican opportunistic intrusions at the outset of the Middle Classic as defined by the Teotihuacán horizon style, A.D. 400–600. If the indigenous

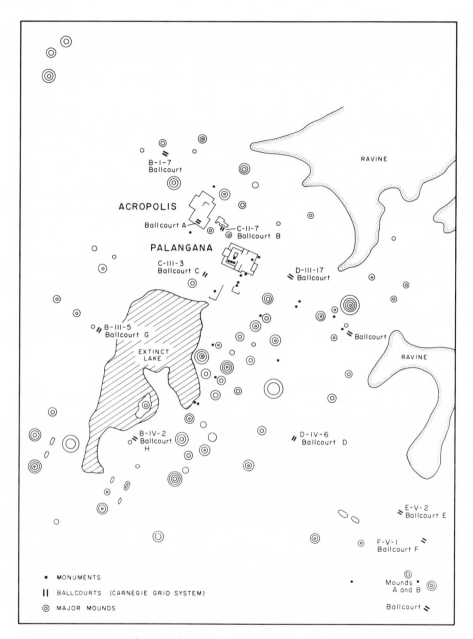

Figure 11.2. Site map of Kaminaljuyu.

Maya traditions had weakened, as the apparent lack of sculptural and building activity implies, the incoming foreigners may have encountered a relative lack of resistance.

By at least A.D. 400, Teotihuacán entrepreneurs, probably in the guise of merchants and warriors, had moved into the southern Pacific coast region. The principal motive may have been economic, with the establishment of a port of trade at Kaminaljuyú (Brown 1977) in order to secure access to the expanding northern markets of the Lowland Maya area. One of the more overt manifestations of this foreign presence in the south was the renewed ballgame cult. The associated complex, including ceremonial yokes and hachas, seems to have crystallized on the gulf coast, from which it may have been introduced to the Pacific coast under the aegis of Teotihuacán. Interestingly, this highly developed version of the ballgame was not established at the urban site of Teotihuacán.

This paper employs a bipartite Classic chronology, simplified from an earlier, more detailed presentation (Parsons 1969). The earlier Teotihuacán period (A.D. 400–600) is stylistically diverse and eclectic, with archaizing traits, and can be viewed as an incipient form of the later Cotzumalhuapan style. The subsequent Cotzumalhuapan period (A.D. 600–950) reached its maximal florescence on the Pacific coast during the Late Classic and became thoroughly non-Maya. Simultaneously, during the seventh century (the end of my Middle Classic) Kaminaljuyú witnessed the withdrawal or absorption of the Teotihuacanos. Kaminaljuyú was effectively abandoned by A.D. 800. Although this compressed scheme may seem to deemphasize the distinctiveness of the Middle Classic period, these divisions correspond to the two varieties of ballcourts at Kaminaljuyú, both intimately associated with Teotihuacán occupation. After excavating the north–south ballcourt B-III-5 at Kaminaljuyú, and analyzing some 50 ballcourts throughout the Valley of Guatemala, Brown (1973, 1977) determined that the north–south open-ended courts were earlier (beginning ca. A.D. 400) and the east–west enclosed courts were later (beginning ca. A.D. 600).

Whether this orientational pattern will hold for other regions remains to be established, though information is accumulating that this may be a viable hypothesis. At Kaminaljuyú two north–south courts and two east–west courts have been professionally excavated or tested (documented in Parsons 1986); unfortunately, very few ballcourts have been excavated on the coast and compass orientations and overall dimensions have often gone unpublished. Information from the coast will be summarized on the basis of (1) architectural courts, (2) monumental sculpture, (3) portable stone paraphernalia, and (4) representations on pottery. Each category reflects differential expenditures and the elaboration of the complex, from greatest to least cultural significance.

Architectural Ballcourts

Although the southern coastal ballcourt complex was probably not indigenous, one cannot look to metropolitan Teotihuacán as the origin of the ballgame "package." Even though one famed Teotihuacán polychrome mural at
the Tepantitla residential compound depicts a stepped profile of a side range
or viewing terrace of a ballcourt, none has been excavated at the site. Also
cached at Tepantitla was a gulf coast-type stone yoke and a human trophy
skull. At Teotihuacán we simply have the portable composite La Ventilla ballcourt marker carved with gulf coast-derived scroll decoration. A pair of such
markers is precisely depicted in the same Tepantitla mural. These were apparently used in open playing zones, if not in precincts of the main avenues.

However, we do have remains of four Middle Classic architectural ballcourts elsewhere in the central Mexican Highlands, though these do not
seem to date earlier than A.D. 500 (see Santley et al. this volume). One court
with Teotihuacán style *talud-tablero* terracing is reported from Tingambato,
Michoacan (Weaver 1981:221, Pl. 30; citing Piña Chan). Chalcatzingo, Morelos, also has a Middle Classic ballcourt representing Classic period reoccupa-
tion, and there are also two at Manzanilla, Puebla, near Cholula. This particular Highland court complex may have been adapted from somewhat earlier
manifestations in central Veracruz. Significant gulf coast–central Mexican
contact is further shown by Tajín-style interlaced scroll motifs applied at both
Teotihuacán and Cholula.

From the gulf coast itself, the proposed area of origin for the southern
Pacific coastal ballgame complex, more early Middle Classic evidence than
now exists would be desirable. The core metropolitan site of El Tajín, like
Kaminaljuyú, had at least 11 ballcourts by the end of the Late Classic. While
García Payón indicated that the first courts at El Tajín may date as early as the
fifth century (1971:527), more recent information suggests that several of the
small north–south sloping-benched courts at El Tajín, as well as one east–
west vertical-walled court, may truly be Early Classic and date approximately
to the fourth century (Wilkerson pers. comm. 1985, this volume). Farther
south in the Los Tuxtlas, Lake Catemaco zone of the gulf coast we have additional Middle Classic evidence. The site of Mata de Canela (Matacanela) has
a north–south ballcourt partially enclosed on the north by a large mound, and
on the south by a low platform (Coe 1965a:683). That site also has three monumental stone basins with border designs in Teotihuacán-derived style (Parsons 1969:Pl. 57h–j), suggesting the early Middle Classic epoch there. The
nearby site of Matacapan, known to have Teotihuacán talud-tablero style architecture, also has a small Middle Classic north–south oriented ballcourt
(Robert Santley pers. comm. 1985). Santley, who is currently working at that

site, believes that this zone was an economic way-station midway between Teotihuacán and the Petén or Kaminaljuyú.

Similarly, we apparently have another important Teotihuacán way-station on the direct route to Kaminaljuyú at the recently reported site of Los Horcones, south of Tonala, on the Pacific coast of Chiapas. This single site supported *five* Middle Classic ballcourts which are approximately north–south in orientation (Agrinier this volume). Furthermore, they are associated at the site with four carved stone stelae in a demonstrably Teotihuacán-derived style. Thus, a concrete pattern of north-to-south diffusion of the ballgame complex is beginning to emerge, especially if some of the El Tajín courts are to be dated as early as A.D. 300.

Pierre Agrinier (this volume) announced a total of 11 sites with architectural ballcourts on the Pacific coast of Chiapas, including Izapa. Therefore, for the entire southern Pacific coastal Lowland region, from the Isthmus to the southeast Mesoamerican frontier, we can list 26 sites with ballcourts. Nine courts can now be documented on the Pacific coast of Guatemala (see Shook's survey map [1965, facing page 184] for the locations of the six he knew about 20 years ago); surely more will be discovered. Moreover, there are six courts reported on the coast of El Salvador. Geographically from west to east, the relevant sites in Guatemala are as follows: Santa Clara (plus a nearby unnamed site to the south), Solola (Tiquisate), Palo Gordo, El Baúl, Sabana Grande, Flores, Nueva Linda, and Los Cerritos. In El Salvador, ballcourts are reported in Tazumal, Cihuatán, Tehuacán, San Francisco, Quelepa, and Los Llanitos. These sites are remarkably evenly spaced on the southern coast, averaging some 30–50 km apart. The location of the majority of these courts at sites of the higher piedmont is economically significant: they occupy the cacao-growing zone. Also significant is the fact that the majority of ballgame-related stone sculptures are distributed along the same piedmont zone. The north–south oriented ballcourts at Palo Gordo and Nueva Linda may well represent the earlier contact period, if we accept Brown's evidence in the Valley of Guatemala. These two were accompanied by early-looking horizontally tenoned death's head sculptures functioning as scoring markers (discussed below). Space does not permit describing these coastal courts in detail.

Monumental Stone Sculpture

The following brief survey of Classic ballgame sculpture begins with the more monumental forms, and initially with the tenoned sculptures often incorporated in the side ranges of ballcourts which functioned as scoring markers during the game. These artifacts are particularly diagnostic of the southern Maya region and extend to Copán, Honduras, in the form of vertically tenoned parrot heads on ballcourt benches; however, the sculptural forms themselves have antecedents at Teotihuacán.

The overwhelmingly predominant class of Middle Classic sculpture at Kaminaljuyú is the Teotihuacán horizontally tenoned heads. There are 16 examples at Kaminaljuyú, of which half were reliably excavated. The latter were only slightly displaced within the centers of both early and late variety ballcourts (Parsons 1986). These specialized tenoned stone heads, whether laterally flattened or full round, depict serpents, parrots, jaguars, monkeys, or humans (living and skeletal). The first two types often reveal a human head in their open mouths. They tend to be carved in matched pairs for opposite sides of a ballcourt, though we do not have good information on how many were used simultaneously in one court (Copán notwithstanding, where three opposing pairs were documented).

The large site of Frutal, south of Kaminaljuyú, also had a north–south ballcourt with an associated horizontally tenoned parrot head (Brown 1977). Similar sculptures have been reported elsewhere in the Valley of Guatemala. All of these pieces reflect the extensive inventory of large tenoned sculpture so widely distributed on the south coast (see Parsons 1969:Fig. 53ff, for many examples). Some of the Cotzumalhuapan tenoned heads represent the Mexican deities Xipe and Quetzalcóatl-Ehécatl, both associated with ballgame ideology in Mesoamerica. However, on the coast we know only *in situ* examples of this sculpture type from the early Palo Gordo and Nueva Linda courts, though the probability is high for finding them at the late El Baúl ballcourt. At El Baúl they were also tenoned into the bases of staircase balustrades (Thompson 1948:Fig. 21).

For the possible origins of this sculpture type we can only look to central Mexico. While horizontally tenoned serpent heads are a hallmark of Teotihuacán prior to A.D. 400 (tenoned into pyramid terraces and staircase balustrades), one pair of short-tenoned, laterally flattened death's heads, as well as a tenoned full-round jaguar head (Parsons 1969:Pl. 55d, g), particularly resemble the early Cotzumalhuapan (Teotihuacanoid) corpus in style. Furthermore, a pair of stone serpent heads from Teotihuacán, now in the Denver Art Museum, may have served in a composite assemblage with a circular disk as a portable ballgame marker according to the reconstruction of curator Robert Stroessner (1973). Significantly, a Cotzumalhuapan-looking horizontally tenoned serpent head, with a human face in its jaws, is also known from Xalapan, Veracruz (Parsons 1969:Pl. 57a, b). This particular ballgame feature must have diffused south at the onset of the Middle Classic by way of the gulf coast tropical rubber Lowlands, where permanent courts and ceremonial yokes and hachas were added to the complex.

On the southern Pacific coast the emerging Cotzumalhuapan art style constituted a distinct and eclectic synthesis of influences from Teotihuacán, the gulf coast, and Oaxaca, plus probable narrative archaisms deriving from the local Izapan heritage. The specifics of subject matter in Cotzumalhuapan monumental art also parallel those of contemporary Classic Veracruz art, though the styles are far from identical. Vividly evident in Cotzumalhuapan stone sculpture, both in low relief and full round, and both in the Middle Classic Teotihuacán and Late Classic florescent phases, is the profound emphasis on ballgame ritual. This is especially apparent with regard to death and sacrificial images. This prolific tradition is distributed from Tonala, Chiapas, to western El Salvador, penetrating as well the Antigua Valley in Highland Guatemala, and including as its major manifestation at Kaminaljuyú the Teotihuacán tenoned heads. Bilbao, El Baúl, and their immediate neighbors in the Department of Escuintla are central-type Cotzumalhuapa sites with a local concentration of over 200 monumental stone sculptures by the end of the Late Classic.

Selected foreign features of this new, decidedly non-Maya, Cotzumalhuapan art style include Teotihuacán-type tabbed speech scrolls, derivative Teotihuacán reptile eye glyphs, a unique glyphic system with circular cartouches and disc-like numerical counters resembling late Oaxacan usages, and such diagnostic Mexican deities as Tlaloc, Xipe, Quetzalcóatl-Ehécatl, and Huehuéteotl (see Parsons 1978:32–34, for an exhaustive inventory of shared foreign traits). Dynamic ball players are portrayed wearing U-shaped effigy waist yokes, effigy gloves, knee pads (or a single calloused knee), and one or two square-toed sandals. Subsidiary flowering vines and anthropomorphic cacao pods invoke agricultural fertility, if not mercantile symbolism. Ritual scenes elaborate themes of human sacrifice, ball players offering sacrifices to "diving" celestial sun and rain deities, and "sun vultures" carrying off the trophies. Death manikins and severed human trophy heads abound. Expressions of sacrificial death are not limited to decapitation, but include heart removal and frequently the complete dismemberment of bodies. Replicas of amputated human limbs are even carved "in the round" at Bilbao and show the protruding bones. This cluster of themes and motifs seems to pertain to pre- and post-game ceremonies and attendant mythology.

A full analysis of the obviously rich and complex ballgame symbolism expressed in the Cotzumalhuapa region would entail detailed comparison with carved panels in Veracruz, Chichén Itzá, and elsewhere, and would clearly comprise another paper. (See Parsons 1969 for full discussion and illustration; note particularly Bilbao's Monument 21 [frontispiece], the eight large ball-player stelae that flanked the Monument Plaza [Pl. 32–34], and the immediately associated carved panels [Pl. 41–42].)

Portable Stone Paraphernalia

Although the ceremonial stone yoke-hacha-palma ballgame complex surely originated on the gulf coast, it was also strongly manifest on the southern Pacific coast, probably beginning by A.D. 400 with the first ballcourts and a host of other Mexican-derived traits. While the functional association between portable stone paraphernalia and the necessary equipment for the game can no longer be questioned, it remains unclear whether the replicas themselves were worn during an active game. Although the surviving stone objects do fit surprisingly comfortably sideways above the hips, they may have been worn only during post-game sacrificial ceremonies, which perhaps took place outside the ballcourts.

I favor the hypothesis that the U-shaped objects actually worn about the waist during the game normally were carved of wood or fabricated of wicker and leather, as would have been the hachas or palmas lashed to those yokes. The wooden prototypes would have been notched for precise attachment. In nine recorded instances, the surviving carved stone objects were ritually cached with human burials or, appropriately, with the actual sacrificial trophy skulls. This interment pattern may have allowed dead ball players to continue their cosmic contest into the Underworld (see the *Popol Vuh* [Tedlock 1985]). Further, stone yokes were often ceremonially cached with hachas and palmas in direct association (eight recorded instances). Thus far, I know of no examples in which these objects have been excavated from ballcourts per se.

Other than serving as practical midriff padding and as a solid ball deflector, the U form of the yoke esoterically symbolized the "mouth of the earth" and the "cavelike entrance to the Underworld," and conceivably the crescent moon. It has been suggested that players wearing yokes were symbolically positioned half in the Upperworld and half in the Underworld. In continuity with Preclassic symbolism, the frontally attached hachas were primarily trophy-head surrogates, while the derivative palmas were primary fertility symbols (featuring watery scrolls, spurting blood, or growing vegetation). Although hachas and palmas probably had little practical function in the execution of the ballgame, they may have had important heraldic significance for the individual players or teams. Specifically, effigy yokes often represented toads, reptilian/feline earth monsters, or double-headed serpents. Carved hachas represented human heads or skulls, monkeys, and a variety of other animals and birds associated principally with the Underworld. Palmas additionally represented all forms of ballgame sacrifices including standing humans, death figures, or warriors as well as avian or saurian creatures. Palma iconography is especially elaborate, and proliferated toward the end of the Late Classic.

Stone yokes, and particularly effigy hachas, are abundant on the southern Pacific coast, but are mostly known from private collections without documented site provenience. The vast majority of these yokes are plain, while the hachas are of the thin stone head variety with their southern expressions having some distinctive features as well. Previously, it was argued (Parsons 1969) that the apparent absence of palmas in Guatemala suggested the introduction of the complex during the Middle rather than the Late Classic. More recent evidence, however, indicates that communication between the gulf and Pacific coasts remained open well into the Late Classic, when squat palma forms were added to the Middle Classic corpus on the Pacific coast. One, which was apparently found on the coast (Borhegyi 1980:17), is reported from a collection in Quetzaltenango, and another short palma has "appeared" as a donation to the municipal museum at La Democracia, Escuintla (noted after the conclusion of our Monte Alto project there). In addition, there are currently six effigy palmas known from El Salvador (Andrews 1976:172), including the two excavated at Quelepa which were interred in a remarkable cache containing one hacha and three plain yokes intentionally placed in an interlaced pattern (Andrews 1976:28, Fig. 52).

In the adjacent Highlands at Kaminaljuyú yokes and hachas are also recorded. One unusual plain yoke with convex outer side and perforated ends for attachment was found in Mound C-III-11, near early Ballcourt C (Borhegyi 1980:Fig. 18). Interestingly, yokes and hachas in diagnostic Pacific coast style have been discovered at the Maya site of Copán, Honduras, where Webster and Abrams (1983) reported a Late Classic deposit consisting of one plain yoke coupled with two effigy hachas on the floor of an elite residential structure. At Copán, the first north–south ballcourt is dated to the fifth century, while a superimposed court has the Highland-derived vertically tenoned bench markers. Ballgame features at Copán thus seem to be derived in part from southern influences.

Pottery

To conclude this survey, there is evidence of the ballgame from the ceramics of the southern Pacific coast during the Middle Classic. Most of the pottery illustrating ballgame themes has been recently reported from the Tiquisate zone and much of the coastal alluvial plain of the Department of Escuintla (Hellmuth 1975b, 1978). This iconography mainly occurs on mold-impressed, Teotihuacán-influenced, cylindrical slab-tripod vases. Ceramic molding technology itself seems to have originated at Teotihuacán. Like the Cotzumalhuapa stone sculptural style, the style and motifs are eclectically inspired from metropolitan Teotihuacán, the gulf coast, and possibly Oaxaca. Mold-impressed bowls from the south-central Veracruz Río Blanco region (see Borhegyi 1980:Fig. 10) are particularly closely related in style and subject matter to the Pacific coast inventory (see also von Winning 1965). These narrative ceramic scenes commonly represent Tlalocs, processions of fully accoutered ball players, or half-kneeling players facing a central ball, as well as decapitation scenes.

Despite indications of an indigenous proto-Maya version of the game, substantive evidence supports the Mexican origins of the particular Middle and Late Classic ballgame complex in the southern Maya area. Bolstering this hypothesis are Middle Classic Teotihuacán way-stations, complete with ballcourts and stone sculptures, in the geographically intermediate Los Tuxtlas, Veracruz zone and at Los Horcones in coastal Chiapas. Significantly, Los Tuxtlas is approximately halfway between Teotihuacán and Kaminaljuyú, while Los Horcones, in turn, is halfway between Kaminaljuyú and Los Tuxtlas. Additionally, an unusual cluster of six ballcourt sites in the Izapa zone is approximately halfway between Los Horcones and the target site of Kaminaljuyú, although most of these have not yet been dated.

The Middle Classic Impact on Kaminaljuyu (A.D. 400–700)

Teotihuacán horizon markers were first manifested along the Pacific coast of Guatemala in the form of structural ballcourts and associated stone sculpture, as well as foreign pottery styles, including composite incense burners. Teotihuacanos established themselves in the Valley of Guatemala soon after, especially at the important long-occupied site of Kaminaljuyú. Kaminaljuyú reveals not only ballcourts, stone sculpture, and Teotihuacán-derived pottery, but impressive pyramid-temple complexes with talud-tablero profile imitating Teotihuacán architecture at the north-central Acropolis and Palangana (Sanders and Michels 1977). In the far southeast corner of the site were the elaborate burial mounds A and B with elite tombs containing both Mexican and Maya pottery types (Kidder et al. 1946). Teotihuacán expansionist motives were both economic and political. Although Kaminaljuyú may not sustain an interpretation as a true colony, it is perhaps classifiable as a port of trade linking the Peripheral Coastal Lowlands with the central Maya Lowlands via the Motagua River Valley. In fact, the contact situation at Kaminaljuyú was characterized by considerable Mexican-Maya syncretism (see full discussion in Parsons 1986). After Teotihuacán withdrawal (or possibly "Mayanization") by A.D. 700, the final century of Kaminaljuyú's occupation was marked by a "Maya resurgence" (Cheek 1977). This discussion, however, concentrates only on the implications of the Mexican-derived ballgame complex.

Of the 12 recorded ballcourts at Kaminaljuyú, four are roughly north–south in orientation and eight are oriented approximately east–west relative to the

declination of the site's axis (Parsons 1986:Map 4). In conjunction with Sanders' Kaminaljuyú Project, Brown (1973) excavated the north–south, open-
ended ballcourt G (B-III-5) on the west side of the now-extinct shallow lake.
This court was about 30 m long, with an 8-m-wide playing alley flanked by
narrow benches. The actual declination was 26° east of magnetic north (the
site declination being about 20° east of north). Excavations determined that
it was constructed in the early A.D. 400–600 Teotihuacán-contact period (Es-
peranza-Amatle 1 phase).

After analyzing other courts at the site and in the valley, Brown suggested
that the east–west, enclosed ballcourts were Amatle 2 phase, beginning in
the seventh century. All of the Kaminaljuyú courts, early and late, are very
comparable in overall size. Courts G (B-III-5), B (C-II-7), C (C-III-3), and D
(D-IV-6) are of the early north–south type. Courts G and B each yielded one
horizontally tenoned ballcourt marker. Court B, previously excavated by
Borhegyi, confirmed the earlier dating, complete with talud-tablero features
(Parsons 1986). It is centrally located in the plaza between the Acropolis and
the Palangana, while court C is located just south of that zone but also on the
north–south centerline of the site. Court D is to the east of the lake, halfway
between court G and the Teotihuacán burial mounds A and B.

Among the later east–west enclosed ballcourts, two (A or C-II-4; and F or
F-V-1) were previously tested by Ledyard Smith and both had several *in situ*
horizontally tenoned heads (documented in Parsons 1986). Court A is located
at the southern margin of the C-II-4 Acropolis in an upper level, stratigraphically overlying a prior talud-tablero temple complex. Almost no information
is recorded concerning the remaining six early Late Classic courts at Kaminaljuyú, which have now disappeared under suburban Guatemala City. Like
ballcourt F, they were more peripherally distributed at the site. Three were
clustered around mounds A and B. The large "Palangana" basin itself did not
function as a ballcourt, as was so often presumed prior to excavation. In Teotihuacán times it contained a central residential compound, and during its terminal phase it was converted to a monument plaza for resurrected Preclassic
Maya stone sculpture (Parsons 1986).

Intriguing processional questions are raised by these data and a few tentative conclusions may be suggested concerning the historical events of the
Middle Classic. The foregoing data from the coast and Kaminaljuyú, taken in
conjunction with a seemingly distinct Teotihuacán-derived ceramic complex
that included large composite incense burners, may help in the reconstruction of cultural patterning for the period.

Teotihuacán-derived ceramic censers have been recently reported in great
quantity along the lower coastal Escuintla region and at Lake Amatitlán, on
the pass between Escuintla and Kaminaljuyú (Hellmuth 1975b, 1978; Berlo

1984). These censers duplicate the style of the elaborate examples with attached moldmade *adornos* known from Teotihuacán itself, although their expressions in the south are more specialized. Berlo (1983, 1984) states that the
Escuintla incense burners emphasize "warrior-butterfly" symbolism, whereas
a mixture of Maya and Mexican raingod (Tlaloc) symbolism pervades the
iconography of the Amatitlán lake offerings. This lake was a pilgrimage center
for rain-god cults in Maya times, with offerings customarily cast into the water
from the south shore (Borhegyi 1959). At Kaminaljuyú, such incense burners
are rare. Their particular manifestation on the lower coast may suggest an
initial martial component to Teotihuacán intrusions, and thus supports the
idea that merchants and warriors probably marched hand in hand. Taking this
linkage one step further, Pasztory (1972) has astutely explained a functional
relationship between merchants and warriors and the ballgame cult.

I suggest that this incense-burner complex, clearly based on selected components of the Teotihuacán state religion, became increasingly a folk cult and
a mechanism for introducing foreign ideology to the local populace. The
Teotihuacanos not only took over and syncretized the pre-existing pilgrimage
cult at Lake Amatitlán but also took over and revised the pre-existing proto-
Maya ballgame cult in other zones. The influence of Teotihuacán took on very
different aspects in the southern Maya region, perhaps in part depending
upon resistance or lack of it. The ritually competitive and powerful "ballgame
cult" may have been employed and manipulated in areas with stronger local
resistance and coveted economic resources (such as those associated with the
piedmont), while the "folk cult" approach to influence would have been adequate in areas of lesser resistance and with fewer strategic resources, such as
on the alluvial plain. However, where they could not conquer they pacified,
as at Kaminaljuyú. The Teotihuacanos may be regarded as sensitive diplomats
within the boundaries of their cultural ethos.

In support of these suggestions, the evidence of a nearly mutually exclusive
distribution of ballcourts and incense burners within the Pacific coast region
is especially striking. Courts appear mainly on the higher piedmont, and the
Teotihuacán-contact pottery, including the cylindrical tripod vases, occurs on
the lower alluvial plain. All of the evenly distributed piedmont sites that accepted the new ballcourt and sculpture complex have strong indigenous Preclassic traditions, demonstrating their uninterrupted long-term economic
and political importance. For example, Palo Gordo, Bilbao-El Baúl, Sabana
Grande, the Nueva Linda and Tazumal zones, and even Quelepa all have
significant Preclassic stone monuments. Furthermore, these ballcourts sites
are intimately associated with the limits of the cacao-producing zone. Because
this commodity was a major elite trade item sought by the Teotihuacanos, it
was probably a major determinant for the course of what might be termed

Teotihuacán foreign policy, and may explain why the foreign elite expended greater efforts to secure this piedmont region.

While the alluvial plain formerly supported even more Preclassic sites, by the time of Teotihuacán arrival most of those sites had apparently waned in importance. The far south coast may therefore have served as a convenient, easily overcome, initial staging ground for infiltrating the highly desirable piedmont, and eventually the more difficult targets such as Kaminaljuyú. Those established zones with greater social complexity were perhaps more acculturated than conquered. The lower alluvial plain itself, however, was not without its commercial attraction, in that it was ecologically suited to the cultivation of cotton, as it still is today.

The earliest phase of ballcourts on the Guatemalan coast is probably represented at Palo Gordo and Nueva Linda. Both of these north–south courts have several contact-period horizontally tenoned death's head stone markers. Of further significance in this proposed route of foreign influence is the intermediate site of Frutal between Lake Amatitlán and Kaminaljuyú in the Valley of Guatemala (Brown 1977). It has a north–south ballcourt incorporating a Teotihuacanoid tenoned stone head. The fact that Frutal also has considerable Middle Classic pottery of diagnostic *coastal* types suggests that the court and the sculpture complex were transmitted to Kaminaljuyú via this site.

An anomaly in this developing model of Mexican–Maya contact and syncretism in the Valley of Guatemala is that the large site of Frutal lacks Mexican-inspired talud-tablero architecture. Paradoxically, the nearby contemporary rural site of Solano expresses that foreign architecture, but lacks a ballcourt. Solano may have been more easily influenced than the established Frutal which maintained its indigenous architecture and, like the coastal piedmont sites, could only be influenced through the ballgame. Clearly, there are many more problems to resolve in this contact situation.

At Kaminaljuyú, the integration of Teotihuacanos was principally expressed in (1) the Acropolis-Palangana, temple-plaza, talud-tablero zone; (2) the elite burial *barrio* isolated in the southeast sector; and especially (3) the four central north–south ballcourts with their sculptural markers. From a base established at Kaminaljuyú, the Teotihuacanos set their sights on the Maya Lowlands; Copán was the first influenced. This entire initial phenomenon, from south coastal penetration to central Maya penetration, probably required only a few generations of Teotihuacán entrepreneurial effort.

I propose that those strategically and centrally placed ballcourts at Kaminaljuyú represent a deliberate strategy by the Teotihuacanos to establish their political and religious authority in the central Guatemalan Highlands. Doubtless other economically based tactics were employed as well to assure some degree of control over a region that produced and distributed so lucrative a range of resources. This particular ballgame, albeit with altered forms and patrons, was easily adopted by the local Maya, given that the fundamental symbolism had already been established there. The Middle Classic game became a formal expression of a demanding state religion, and a sanctioned ritual means for selecting qualified human sacrifices as well. One trophy skull in mound B, tomb IV (Kidder et al. 1946:Fig. 165), which could well have been from a sacrificed ball player, was decorated with a carved Mayoid profile serpent motif. This implies that *this* victim may have been a Maya nobleman.

Prior Maya sociopolitical and religious structures in the Highlands seem to have revolved around competitive ranked lineages, each worshipping their own ancestors (Parsons 1986). Indeed, this became the basic pattern for the Classic Lowland Maya as well. In contrast, by Middle Classic times, Teotihuacán had developed a centralized ideology, which must have been capable of exerting a profound level of social control when selected aspects of it were imposed on the south, an area where state systems were not yet formulated. Thus, one essential cohesive ideological factor that facilitated the political and religious legitimation of Teotihuacán presence at Kaminaljuyú, and its surveillance of the local economy, may well have been the gulf coast–derived cult of ballgame ritual. The Tlaloc pilgrimage cult at nearby Lake Amatitlán would have offered secondary religious reinforcement and support.

Meanwhile, the south coast was completely converted to the Mexicanized regional Cotzumalhuapa culture that continued to the very end of the Late Classic. No doubt reciprocal communications were maintained with El Tajín in the northern Peripheral Coastal Lowlands through the regular interchange of iconographic concepts (Parsons 1978). Developing Cotzumalhuapa or Classic Veracruz ballgame ideology by A.D. 600 may have prompted the symbolic shift in ballcourt orientations from north–south to east–west as a more appropriate mark of death and rebirth for the sun and Venus. This change was also reflected at Kaminaljuyú during its declining seventh century. Further, during the Late Classic, ballcourts proliferated throughout the Highlands with far greater concentrations than on the coast. Over 50 courts are reported in the Valley of Guatemala alone (Brown 1977). This distribution conforms to the situation in the adjacent Chiapas Highlands.

At the close of the Late Classic the widespread stone yoke-hacha-palma tradition expired in Mesoamerica. During the Postclassic, the ballgame complex disappeared from the southern Pacific coast. Nevertheless, the complex was resumed at strategic Highland sites along with the late Mexican-inspired tenoned ballcourt markers. In the Guatemala Highlands the Postclassic ballgame reflects renewed Toltec, Mixtec, and Aztec expansionist activities, lasting to the Spanish conquest. These activities followed the pattern first established by Teotihuacán a millennium before.

Note

I wish to acknowledge the editorial advice offered by Barbara J. Price, though I did not incorporate all of her intellectual insights. I am further grateful for the productive interchange of information from other members of the Tucson symposium. The present paper is a 50 percent abridgment of the original.

CHAPTER 12

The Lords of Light Versus the Lords of Dark: The Postclassic Highland Maya Ballgame

John W. Fox

The Quichean Kinship-Political Network

The Quichean peoples of the Postclassic Guatemalan Highlands built more ballcourts at this time than anywhere else within the Maya world. Virtually every Quichean *tinamit*, or fortified site where conquest-minded lineages huddled together for mutual protection, maintained its own court. The Quiché state was also the major polity situated on the southern cardinal point of the Maya world, conceptually the locus of the Underworld. It is therefore befitting that the Quiché authored the *Popol Vuh*, with its rich mythological account of twin divinities engaging the Lords of the Underworld in this ritualized sport. The Quiché also maintained four ballcourts at their capital, Greater Utatlán, with each court positioned in the center of the four major political segments. The combination of abundant archaeological evidence for ballcourts, coupled with the mythology and reconstructed political organization from extant texts, provides a fertile interplay for abstracting varied meanings of the ballgame for the Postclassic Highland Maya.

For the Quiché, the ballgame ritual stood at the very center of sociopolitical organization. Cosmically it interfaced the Middleworld and Underworld. Sociopolitically, it functioned to bring together otherwise opposing kinship groupings, each economically autonomous and ritually associated with a specific point in the elliptical-shaped quadripartitioned world.

Settlement patterning of the early Quichean sites in Highland Guatemala matches that in the Lowlands along the Río Usumacinta, the Petén, Acalán, and Yucatán. Such patterning supports inferences from the documents for a common Putún ancestry, for ties to Chichén Itzá with its north–south oriented Great Ballcourt, and therefore, tangentially at least, ties with the Toltec.[1]

As the Quiché held the south cardinal point, Chichén Itzá occupied the north cardinal point. The correspondence in settlement patterning is particularly strong between Highland Guatemalan radial-temple centers, like Chuitinamit in Sacapulas (Tuja). Significantly, Tuja maintained ritual and kinship ties with the nearby Quiché south at Hacawitz, as well as ties with distant Chichén Itzá (Fox 1980). In ethnohistory, not only is it formally recalled in the Relaciones de Yucatán (1898:120–121, 176) that the Guatemalans recognized Chichén Itzá as the font of Lowland authority during what would be the Early Postclassic, but later generations of Quiché perpetuated the proper name Itzá within a princely lineage (Carmack 1981:136, 150). By extension, this all-embracing kinship network also extended into northern Mesoamerica to the sites of Tula, Xochicalco, and Cacaxtla, which once contained contingents of Putún Maya called Nonoalca.

With the centrality of the Quiché ballgame nested within kinship matrices, it is perhaps noteworthy that among most of Putún-derived peoples cast throughout Mesoamerica, the ballcourt assumes an enclosed I-shape (Table 12.1, Figure 12.1).[2] However, the form and degree of slope of the inside playing walls varied from region to region and through time. With the nearly vertical talud-tablero–shaped playing walls, the Quichean I-shaped enclosed ballcourts manifested a greater similarity with the perfectly right-angled playing walls at Chichén Itzá and El Tajín than to the obliquely angled ($<40°$) playing walls at the Lowland Late Classic Maya sites of Copán, Tikal, and Palenque.

Furthermore, the imagery of decapitated players and sacrificial scenes inscribed on ballcourt playing walls at El Tajín and Chichén Itzá supports the western origin of the ballgame carried by the Putún-descended peoples, when they relocated north to Chichén Itzá and south to the Guatemala Highlands. It is equally noteworthy that no ballcourts occur in the Quiché basin and adjoining mountains prior to the intrusive site of Hacawitz during the Early Postclassic. Therefore, the ballgame figured into a new political organization which was coincident with the Putún horizon at Chichén Itzá, Tuja, and Hacawitz—an organization that was militarily successful in fostering conquest of foreign peoples in distant territories.

Some political functions of the ballgame become evident by examining the ballcourt locations at sites within the Quiché state, especially when accompanied by ethnohistoric narrations of political alliances (cf. Carmack 1981).

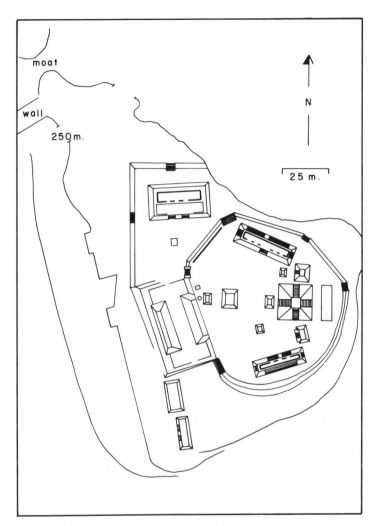

Figure 12.1. Site map of Chutixtiox (after Smith 1955). By permission of the University of New Mexico Press and Cambridge University Press.

Specifically it is proposed that ballcourts were placed along moietal lines. Quiché lineages were ascribed spatial positions within the color-coded four cardinal directions, based on the transfiguring counterclockwise rotation of the sun.

The Third Creation of the *Popol Vuh* deals largely with the mythology accompanying the ballgame. In this drawn-out cosmic litany, it becomes possible to discern the meshing of a solar-focused calendar with normative behav-

Table 12.1. Ballcourts of Postclassic Highland Guatemala

Site	Approx. Orientation	Length (m)	References
I. Quiché			
Hacawitz	E–W	35–37	Figure 12.2
Ismachí	NE–SW	40	Fox 1978
Utatlán	E–W	47	Figure 12.3
Chisalin	E–W	40	Weeks 1983
Resguardo	E–W	32–35	Fox 1978
II. Sacapultec			
Chuitinamit	E–W	50	Smith 1955
Chutixtiox	N–S	35	Figure 12.1
Xopacol	N–S	40	Smith 1955
Pacot	N–S	37	Smith 1955
III. Other Acropolis Sites			
Chamac (Uspantan)	E–W	43	Fox 1980
Chuitinamit-Atitlan	?	?	Guillemin 1977
IV. Sites within Quiché State (or groups controlled by the Quiché)			
Tenam (Balamija)	E–W	40	Fox 1978
Pueblo Viejo Malacatancito (Malacatan)	E–W	43	Fox 1978
Los Cimientos (Zahkabaja)	E–W	42	Smith 1955
Sija	NE–SW	35	Fox 1978
PaMaca	E—W	35	Fox, field notes 1978
Pueblo Viejo Camilla (Xoyabaj)	NE–SW	35	Fox 1978
Comitancillo	E—W	33	Smith 1955
Zaculeu	NW–SE	48	Woodbury and Trik 1953
Cucul	N–S	28	Fox 1978
Vicaveval	NE–SW	32	Smith 1955
V. Rabinal/Eastern Agaab			
Tzameneb	E–W	37	Fox, field notes 1978
Chuitinamit	N–S	32–35	Figure 12.6
Cawinal	NW–SE	37	Fox 1978; Ichon et al. 1980
VI. Cakchiquel Sites			
Iximche	NW–SE	40–45	Guillemin 1967, 1977
Jilotepeque Viejo	N–S	45	Figure 12.5; Smith 1955; Lehmann 1968

iors of segmentary lineages. In mythic guises, the Quiché replicated the roles of the infamous culture twins, Hunahpu and Xbalanke. A thematic undercurrent throughout the Third Creation is the solar-generated light of the true warriors, represented by Hunahpu, counterpoised against alien peoples. The heroes are paired for combative purposes, like the Quiché themselves. Their mythical foes are the Lords of the Underworld, or darkness, or those bereft of the "solar light." Historically, the Quiché enemies were largely indigenous Maya who opposed the solar-focused religion held in common by the Lowland-originating Putún. Physiographically, the local Maya enemies were situated during the Early Postclassic period on level plains to the south, east, or west of the Quiché; that is, along the edges or within the ritual geography ascribed to the Underworld.

Segmentary Lineage Massing and Migration According to the Solar *Tun*

At the time of the Spanish conquest in 1524, the Quiché of Utatlán were organized in 51 principal lineages (Carmack 1981:162). These in turn were variously grouped into major lineages, moieties, and then confederacies. Lineage houses (*nim ha*), or long structures, were scattered throughout the site. The ballcourt, however, was situated on the southwest side in the single plaza at the center of Utatlán (see Figure 12.3). For the Quiché, west represented the sun's disappearance into the Underworld and south was the direction of the Underworld proper; that is, for the sun at nadir. This reverses the directions for the entrance to the Underworld: north during the Classic period (Schele and M. Miller 1986:277) to south during the Postclassic period, unless there was a direct drop from north to south along a vertical *axis mundi*.

However, the moietal line actually bisected the ballcourt (Wallace 1977), and therefore bisected the entire settlement of Utatlán. In fact, the palace complexes of the Cawec and Ajaw were symmetrically situated 15 m north and south of the ballcourt, respectively (see Figure 12.3). The ballgame thus bound together the centripetal lineages which otherwise were autonomous land-holding bodies that coalesced into uneasy political alliances of various sizes and levels, and generally in response to the pressures of conquest or rebellion (Fox 1989:Table 1). Accordingly, political bonds varied in intensity: "Complementary opposition creates the structure; without opposition the higher segments do not exist" (Sahlins 1961:333). So too, when outside pressures ameliorated, confederation often unraveled (Sahlins 1961). The documents, accordingly, tell of coups and migrations upon victory and the subjugation of long-opposed enemies.

Therefore, relations between segments tended to be balanced between the seemingly contradictory conditions of competition and cooperation. For example, two units might cooperate by pooling their efforts to acquire additional lands. Ultimately, political lineages involved confederacies of three or four kinship-based units for the Quichean peoples. Basically, three kinship groups related to three principal heavenly bodies—the sun, the moon, and Venus—spaced according to the cardinal directions. A fourth kinship segment was added later, thereby achieving ritual and political balance (Fox 1989). However, relations between units varied between rivalry at one time and mutual assistance at another. Thus, the political formations reconfigured and even collapsed as the sun, the ultimate metaphor, transfigured into the small and malnourished Venus prior to the dawn.

When in Acalán, Yucatán, or Guatemala, these kin groups occasionally referred to themselves as the Amak Tun or Putún (Chontal Text [1567] 1968:398; Perez 1949:29, fn. 15; Edmonson 1982:5); that is, "lineages (*amak*) of the solar year (*tun*)," and "place or people of the tun." Drawing upon Landa's notations, as corroborated by the twelfth century *Codex Dresden*, Carlson (1981) argues that the solar-year Uayeb ritual articulated with the quadripartite spatial layout of Chichén Itzá and Mayapán. The central focal point was the radical temple at Tuja, an *axis mundi*, with four stairways pointed to the four world directions and to outlying peoples. This temple functioned to enjoin rural warrior lineages, such as the Quiché at Hacawitz, 20 km to the south (Totonicapán 1953:181; C'oyoi 1973:289; Xajil 1953:64–66). Barbara Tedlock (1982) shows that some present-day Quiché communities persist in quadripartitioning their territories, each fourth with its own patron saint. However, in the center of the community is the principal altar (Paclom in Momostenango) that unifies, like the radial temple of Postclassic Quiché sites, the four altars and barrios on mountain tops at the cardinal points (Tedlock 1982:101).

To reiterate, during the Early Postclassic the Quiché lineage occupied the south cardinal point of wider alliances, the direction of the Underworld "battleground." Just as the radial temple represented the skyward focus of the wider settlement system, the ballcourt represented the nether half. Together the two buildings were often aligned, but in binary opposition. Accordingly, Sacapulas (Tuja) is referred to as "the middle of the sky and the middle of the earth" (Sacapulas 1968 [1551]), in reference to the site's apex/nadir layout. Sacapulas was also brought the "Tun [stone] called Lacadona" (Sacapulas 1968 [1551]:18), which was probably the calendar stone.[3]

Associating the ballcourt as the "other half" of the radial temple complex with the world directions is indicated by painted colors signifying the cardinal directions (red = east, blue/green = vertical, yellow = south, black = west, and white = north; see Villacorta 1962:17, 98, 223; also the *Codex Dresden*). Short successive stripes appear on the plastered ballcourt playing walls at

Tenam (Balamija) and Pueblo Viejo Malacatancito (Smith 1955:16; Fox 1978: 134, 246). For the Quiché, each of the colors had overriding qualities: north (white, skyward), south (yellow, downward, and vegetation), east (red, power, and direct heat from the sun), and west (black, cold) (Carmack 1981:77–78).

Early Postclassic Intra-site Settlement Patterning

In each of the two tiers of sites, those with radial temples and what might be termed warrior sites like Hacawitz, the ballcourt occupied a pivotal spatial position. For radial temple sites, predictably, the ballcourt was largely oriented north–south in tandem with the site's zenith—the temple (Table 12.1)—and occupied the lower terrace, a spatial manifestation of the Underworld (Figure 12.1). The lower-lying ballcourt may have represented ritualized opposition to the "people of darkness" by the "people of light," later allied under the aegis of Nacxit, a spokesman and apparent descendant of the Feathered Serpent.

To follow this line of reasoning, alliance for conquest calls for the massing of lineages through complementary opposition. The ballcourt's largely north–south orientation (15° E of N) at the Great Ballcourt at Chichén Itzá might therefore relate to this skyward/Underworld directionality.[4] So too, it was probably significant that the ballcourt at Tuja, Sacapulas, was oriented some 15–17° off east–west cardinality since the Toltec lineage dominated the alliance at Tuja, and this approximates a "Toltec" alignment. At the second ranked site, Chutixtiox, Sacapulas, 3 km west of Tuja, the ballcourt is also oriented 15–17° off north–south cardinality (Figure 12.1) like Chichén, but the remainder of the site displays close or absolute cardinality. Together, the matched ballcourts at Tuja and Chutixtiox intersected both north–south and east–west cardinal axes.

A series of carved panels on playing walls of Chichén's Great Ballcourt (Cohodas this volume: Figure 14.2) depicts the much-celebrated 14 Lords of the Underworld, in full ballgame regalia (e.g., yokes, palmas) identified by their skull "death symbol" protruding upward from each player's belt (Folan 1980:70–75; e.g. "Skull Staff"). Paralleling the Quiché's version in the *Popol Vuh* (Tedlock 1985), the head of the "athletic" contest's decapitated loser transforms into a perfectly spherical ball (Tozzer 1957:Fig. 474). Six serpents plus a sprouting tree (calabash or green reeds) project from the headless player's neck, suggesting Hun-Hunahpu. In the mythico-literary account, Hunahpu, the son, eventually ascends victorious from similar purification trials.

The small outlying sites like Hacawitz (together with Amak Tam and the Uquín Cat) of the first Quiché settlement, and contemporaneous Tzameneb of the Rabinal, have three architectural groupings of two plazas each, literally

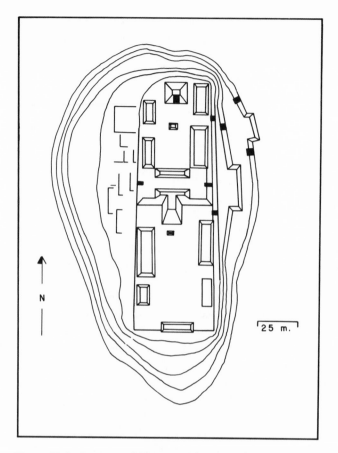

Figure 12.2. Site map of Chitinamit (Hacawitz). By permission of the University of New Mexico Press and Cambridge University Press.

reflecting lineage coupling through complementary opposition. In contrast to the radial-temple sites, the ballcourt comprises the very heart of both nucleated settlements (Figure 12.2). Accordingly, only one temple is placed at the end of each enclosed plaza rather than in the center, as at the radial temple sites. At Hacawitz, itself at the center of a tripartite nucleation (together with Amak Tam and Uquín Cat on either of its sides), the ballcourt actually divides the two main plazas. The plazas were the seats,[5] respectively, of the Ajaw and Cawek "moieties" (Carmack 1981).

Since the Ajaw adhered to the patron deity Hacawitz, as Venus/Hunahpu, and the Cawek upheld their patron Tojil, the sun (a legacy God GII of the Classic period), the two plazas on a single elongated platform (headed by Venus [GI] and the sun [GII]) conceptualized the two-headed sky monster,

K'ucumatz (Fox et al. in press). Therefore, in the center of this serpentine sky monster, oriented south to the dark Underworld, was the ballcourt, which cosmically interfaced the Middleworld and the Upperworld. Importantly, the Temple of Hacawitz was a beacon of the first morning light and was viewed as Venus emerging from the Underworld's night. The Temple was actually attached to the southern range of the ballcourt (Figure 12.2). In Quichean mythology, the sun was carried by the two-headed serpent, K'ucumatz, as a young traveler from the west across the daytime sky (DeLeon, cited in Carmack 1981:275).

The only comparable attached temple-ballcourt complex known so far is at Chichén Itzá, where the Temple of the Jaguars is attached to the Great Ballcourt, and at Guaytán in the middle Motagua Valley, which is of late Classic/ Epiclassic vintage (although dating is still problematic). As at Hacawitz, the ballcourt at Guaytán is enclosed I shaped, surfaced in adobe, and still has attached ballcourt markers, each with a single human head protruding from the opened jaws of a serpent (cf. Smith 1961:119, Fig. 5); that is, the young sun as the traveler carried by the sky serpent, K'ucumatz.

To return to the political function of the ballcourts juxtaposing allied lineages, the Rabinal "drawing center," Tzameneb, also manifests an equal-sized, I-shaped ballcourt at the very center of the site (Ichon et al. 1982:73). Thus, the centrality of the game was shared by other Quichean peoples.

Since the proxemics are different between radial temple and warrior communities, they may have assumed distinctive roles within the tun-centric alliances. It is proposed that at the small sites like Hacawitz and Tzameneb, the ballgame served as a political mechanism for uniting through complementary opposition the fairly egalitarian and inherently fractious lineages; and that the ballgame/radial-temple complex at the larger sites like Tuja functioned to bind outlying warrior lineage communities into regional alliances.

As an ideology for social linkage, the ballgame myth of the *Popol Vuh* may have presented the requisite ideational umbrella to unite continually advancing Putún-derived peoples. As we have seen, the early Quiché warriors massed together in a single nucleated community with the ballcourt as the centralizing point. This group in turn was linked to their next neighbor in distance, Tuja to the north, within the kinship-based network of the "warriors of the solar calendar (tun)."

Capitals of the Late Postclassic States

With the Late Postclassic period, beginning in about A.D. 1100, the ballcourt retained its spatial and political centrality within a more centralized and hierarchic Quiché segmentary state. The Quiché state followed the collapse of

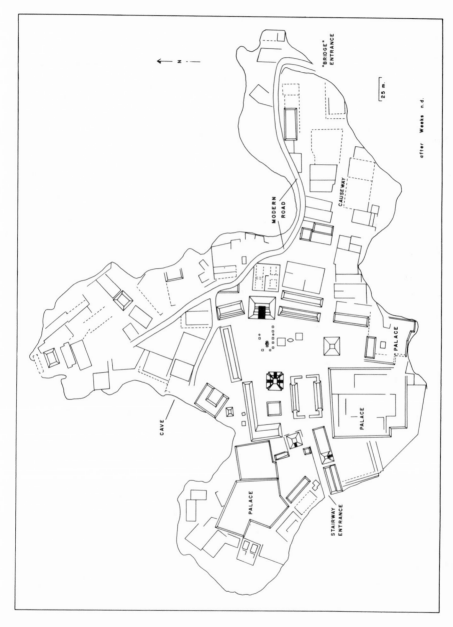

Figure 12.3. Site map of Utatlán. By permission of the University of New Mexico Press and Cambridge University Press.

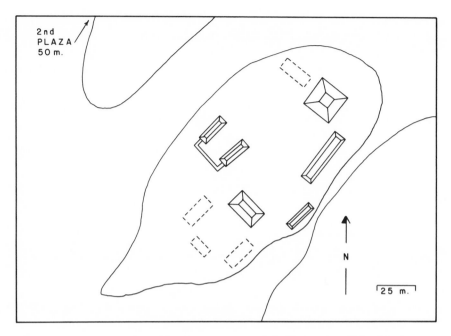

Figure 12.4. Site map of Ismachi. By permission of the University of New Mexico Press.

the confederacies at Chichén Itzá and apparently at Tuja, Sacapulas, coincident with the end of the Early Postclassic period. To illustrate, at the Quiché capital of Utatlán, following Hacawitz, the north range of the single ballcourt seems to have been associated with the Cawek and the south range with the Ajaw (ahau) major lineages. That is to say, the community's moietal cleavage actually bisected the playing field (Figure 12.3) (Wallace 1977).

Indeed, the moietal line is even more dramatic at the Tamub's Contact Period center of Ismachí within Greater Utatlán (Figure 12.4). Here, the two ballcourt ranges were laid out at slightly variant angles; each range was aligned to one of the plaza's two temples, and thereby each was associated with one of the Tamub's two moieties, the Kakoja and Ekoamak. Thus, the slightly distinctive angles of the two ranges graphically underscore this duality. In all, Greater Utatlán displays four ballcourts—perhaps denoting the complement of the four world directions of the calendar. Within Greater Utatlán three additional confederates were attached to the Nima Quiché core confederate: the Tamub and Ilocab, the traditional allies of the Early Postclassic period, and a new confederate, the Achí, shown in a pictorial from the *Título Totonicapán* (see Carmack 1981:Fig. 17).

By comparison, at Iximché, the capital of the Cakchiquel state, the two ballcourts are situated on the south side of two of the three civic plazas, bespeaking both complementary opposition and the tripartite aggregating principles. Quite dramatically, both courts are sunken below the plaza surface. They are reached by stairways in the end zones that descend two tiers and seemingly nine stairs in all, apparently for the nine levels of the Underworld (Guillemin 1967:28). A stone yoke and a spherical stone ball were recovered at Iximché in a single burial. These may have been heirloom pieces from either the Gulf homeland or perhaps the local Cotzumalhuapan enclaves, also of Gulf coastal origins (Guillemin 1977:243).[6]

For more distant comparisons in time and space, at El Tigre (Itzamkanac), the principal site of Acalán in the Gulf Lowlands, a small open-ended ballcourt is situated directly in the plaza center amid three pyramidal temples. Therefore, both El Tigre and Palenque, on the western periphery of the Maya world, display a fundamental Mayan trinity of deities/temples mediated by a ballcourt, like Utatlán (Fox et al. in press). In diametrical opposition on the eastern periphery of the Maya geopolitical orbit, the single ballcourt at Copán provides a passage between the two major complexes, the Great Plaza to the north and the Acropolis to the south, recalling the ballcourt as a midpoint and vehicle of transformation between the two halves, as also suggested at Uxmal (Schele and Miller 1986:247).

Ballcourts in the Provinces of the Quiché State

From Utatlán, the Quiché conquered and settled among the peoples throughout the Guatemalan Highlands, the piedmont, and the coast. These colonies comprised the dendritic tentacles, fastened through kinship ties to the capital of the segmentary state, Utatlán. From the priority of cardinal directions within the tun, the Quiché expanded outward: first north (Sacapultec/Tujalja), south (Tzutujil), then east (Akajal),[7] and finally west (Mam) (Fox 1987:Ch. 6).

Appropriately, the Quiché first subjugated the higher-status seats of the tun (radial-temple centers), mostly to the north, east, and south. Colonial scions of the higher-ranked Quiché lineages are reflected at these sites; archaeologically separate civic plazas were constructed adjacent to earlier radial-temple plazas. This two-plaza coupling of new and old plazas bears out spatially the balanced symmetry of forced complementary opposition. Generally, the Quiché plaza was built on a terrace lower in elevation than the radial-temple plaza, befitting the Quiché's status as former warrior lineages. This duality is readily evident at Tenam (see Fox 1978:Fig. 21; 1987:Fig. 6.5). An initial plaza for the Balamija lineages occupied the site's zenith, and the later Quiché plaza was modeled on the Utatlán plaza, oriented east–west, and replete with one temple for Tojil of the Cawek-led moiety, and one temple for Awilix of the Nijaib-led moiety. But pointing to syncretism between the Balamija site organization and the Quiché plaza organization, the single ballcourt lies on the lower terrace (true to the radial-temple configuration) though with the correct positioning within the Quiché plaza scheme. Therefore, the site's only ballcourt was apparently shared by the Balamija and Nima Quiché factions at Tenam, and fit both groups' plaza patterns. Here, the ballgame was literally the institution of enjoinment.

Nima Quiché lineages also established large colonies on defensible mountain tops overlooking broad and fertile upland basins, both east and west of Greater Utatlán. These latter Quiché colonies therefore reflected more east–west cardinality (e.g., at the sites of Sija, PaMaca, and Xoyabaj) than the north–south cardinality of the first wave of expansionism. Like the Early and Late Postclassic sites, these colonies manifested a single ballcourt in the midst of lineage houses surrounding a single plaza. In similar fashion, the ballcourt lies at or near the site's center at Sija and Pueblo Viejo-Canilla (cf. Fox 1978, 1987; Ichon et al. 1982).

As a point of contrast, along the eastern frontier of Mesoamerica during the Late Postclassic, ballcourts are not known beyond the boundaries of the Putún-derived polities (e.g., those of the Quiché, Cakchiquel, and at Naco). This further suggests that the game functioned to cement political linkages between fairly autonomous lineages who shared a common belief system and ancestry.

At a number of outlying Quichean sites, ballcourts appear to have been built upon the takeover of more distant Putún-derived "brethren" (e.g., the Akajal, Pokom, and Agaab; Fox 1981). For example, excavations of the Agaab site, Cawinal, indicate that the single ballcourt was first built during the last construction phase, coincident with Quiché political domination known ethnohistorically (Ichon et al. 1980:188). Moreover, at Jilotepeque Viejo (Chaupec Quecajol Nimabaj), the last Akajal center to have been subjugated by the Cakchiquel, two north–south oriented ballcourts were late additions. However, the ballcourt facades were covered in lime plaster and appended onto the two Akajal plazas (Figure 12.5, plazas A and B). These Akajal plazas were otherwise devoid of plaster, in contrast to buildings of the two Cakchiquel plazas C and E, which were lavishly coated in lime. The ballcourt of plaza B also lies near the moietal line separating the counterbalanced Cakchiquel and Akajal halves of the settlement.

This fundamental duality through structured opposition may have been borne out by the game itself, with matched (though opposite) playing walls, end zones, markers, and even numbers of players.

One final site along the eastern perimeter of the Quiché state, Chuitinamit

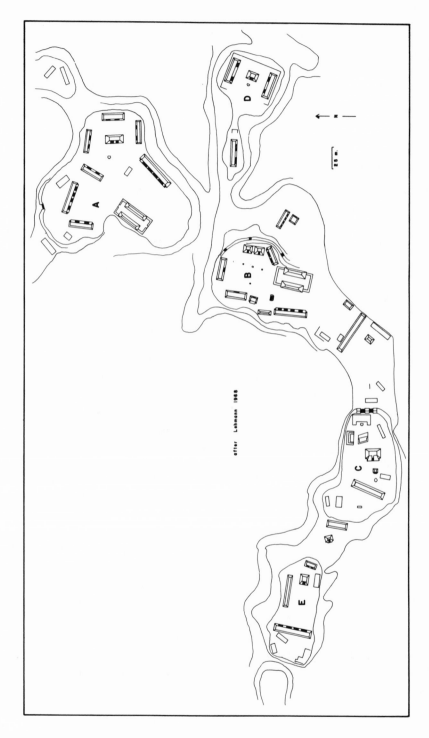

after Lehmann 1968

Figure 12.5. Site map of Jilotepeque Viejo. By permission of the University of New Mexico Press and Cambridge University Press.

of the Rabinal continued its role as a largely warrior lineage community closely coupled with the Quiché of Utatlán. By literally transposing the implications of the segmentary lineage model spatially, each of nine plazas at Chuitinamit is separated by considerable distance. And this spatial separation underscores the autonomy of individual principal lineages. Moreover, aggregating cleavages through complementary opposition are also borne out spatially: Chuitinamit divides into moietal groupings, an eastern half with three plazas and a western half with six (i.e., two subsets of three "warrior lineages").

The function of the ballgame linking moieties is indicated by the two more highly ranked plaza lineages situated at Chuitinamit's midpoint, each containing a north–south oriented ballcourt for the respective moietal groupings (plazas H and C; Figure 12.6). The tripartite clustered yet fractious lineages also reflect diachronic continuity from the earlier Rabinal site, Tzameneb. To reiterate, the earlier community had an east–west oriented ballcourt in the center of three plaza groupings. Later, Chuitinamit displayed three multiples of three (nine), apparently from lineage fissioning. Overall, the centrality of ballcourts again emphasized alliance through complementary opposition. Duality was inherent in opposition. But with the interregional ranking of communities across the Quiché state premised on ascribed positions to cardinality, the status of the Rabinal may have changed somewhat from their first site, Tzameneb, with an east–west oriented ballcourt, to the later Chuitinamit, with its two north–south oriented ballcourts.

But it must be remembered that the distributions of Late Postclassic ballcourts ceased with the state boundaries. Immediately east of the Rabinal was said to be the land of Xibalba, with the Underworld symbolism enduring from the Classic through the Postclassic periods.

The Ballgame Myth as Ideology for the Sun's Advancing Warriors

Inasmuch as scenes identified at Chichén Itzá (Cohodas this volume; Figure 14.1) may be associated with the *Popol Vuh*, the ballgame becomes not just a Quiché myth, but one shared by Mayan peoples from one end of southern Mesoamerica to the other. The basic meaning of the *Popol Vuh*'s mythic structures was apparently at the heart of social life. By sheer length alone, the ballgame epic comprised the full "Third Creation" and was the most vital of Quiché cosmic tales. By extension, it was apparently central for all Putún-descended peoples.

The ballgame ritual has long been considered to relate institutionalized conflict in one form or another. Tozzer (1957:139) looked to the armed military conflict between "Mexicanized" Putún (Itzá) and local Yucatecan Maya. After all, the ballcourt temple at Chichén (Upper Temple of the Jaguar) portrayed

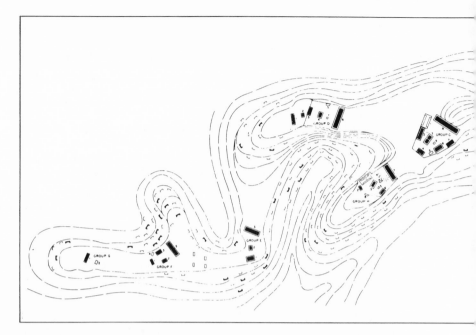

Figure 12.6. Site map of Chuitinamit (from Smith 1955). By permission of Cambridge University Press.

detailed battle murals. Expanding upon this idea, Federico (1973) considered the *Popol Vuh*'s myth to be an expression of class conflict between a Mexicanized elite and an indigenous Maya populace. However, in the more general sense, for any myth to retain longevity, it must provide sufficiently basic symbols to be rearranged in new situations (e.g. Cohen 1976). Therefore, the meaning of the mythic contest probably varied from one set of circumstances to the next, but it held basic "truths" for a variety of situations. Now that it is recognized that Putún expatriates were organized into segmentary lineages, it is possible to consider that the myth provided ideology for massing through complementary opposition at any of the levels of political organization.

It is therefore argued that the basic mythic structure of the ballgame applied to the principles of linkage, from the "coupling atom" of one principal lineage with that of its immediate neighbor, and eventually, one moiety with another. On a higher level of massing, the Quiché pitted themselves against the local Maya. In Yucatán, for instance, the Itzá opposed the Puuc (e.g., the A.D. 918 invasion of Quiché; Thompson 1970), although the Putún/local Maya eventually joined in pluralistic communities.

More fundamentally, however, the myth may have eased inherent tension among divisive lineages either massed together horizontally or vertically. The

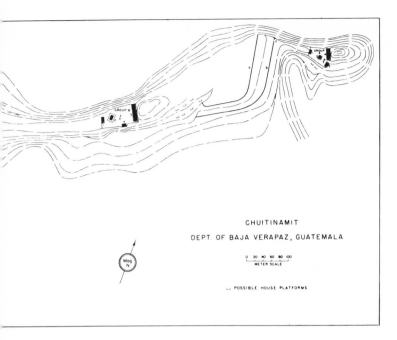

CHUITINAMIT

DEPT. OF BAJA VERAPAZ, GUATEMALA

0 20 40 60 80 100
METER SCALE

⌐⌐ POSSIBLE HOUSE PLATFORMS

basic polarities are seen in numbers associated with the ballgame myth, especially the duality of two as the overriding pair (e.g., Hunahpu and Xbalanke)
as well as the seven and fourteen lords of the Underworld. Both seven and
fourteen may have been key calendric nodes, for the interaction with both
friends and foes. For example, Hun-Hunahpu's brother was Vuqub Hunahpu
(Seven Hunter)—a close kinsman—whereas the indigenous enemies of the
Quiché during the Early Postclassic were the Vukamak—the "Seven Clans/
Lineages."

Now that some political and ritualistic functions of the ballgame are correlated with segmentary lineage principles, it becomes possible to address the
more nebulous mythic symbolism within the historical sequences of Putún
peoples expanding across the political landscape. From the vantage of binary
opposition the *Popol Vuh*'s official ballgame myth is the middle or Third Creation of four or five creations (depending upon Edmonson's or Tedlock's translation). Therefore, the Third Creation mediates the volume's mythological
(Creations 1–2) and historical parts (Creations 3–4), as the ballgame mediated
two social segments spatially and politically.

More widely, the Quiché collective conscience (in the Durkheimian sense)
was the experience of migrating to new localities. Thus, they migrated from
the Gulf Lowlands to the Guatemalan Highlands, and subsequently eastward

on the very margins of Mesoamerica. It is possible to muster some archaeological support to relate the Third Creation of the *Popol Vuh* to peoples encountered historically within southeastern Mesoamerica.

The plot of myth involves trials and tribulations of paired Quiché culture heroes in torturous, dreamlike ballgame contests against Lords of the Underworld (Xibalba). As offspring of the originators (Xpiacoc and Xmucane), two elder brothers (Hun Hunahpu and Vuqub Hunahpu, translated One Hunter and Seven Hunter) descend into the Underworld, first passing through rivers of churning spikes, blood, and pus, and then undergo seven purification trials that result in mishaps and death. Upon a "hybrid" mating between Hun Hunahpu and X'kik, daughter of an Underworld lord, symbolically paralleling the coupling through marriage of the immigrant Quiché warriors to local Maya women, the next generation of twin culture heroes Hunahpu and Xbalanke are begotten (*Popol Vuh*, Tedlock 1985:105, 106).

The twin brothers are versed in the much-prized military way (e.g., *Popol Vuh*, Tedlock 1985:105, 106) and parallel, at least metaphorically, the intrusive ancestors at Hacawitz and Tzameneb. The myth also recounts that the twins felt free to invade and generally cause havoc in lands controlled by allies (the Kulaja) as well as in the realm of the Underworld lords (*Popol Vuh*, Tedlock 1985:106, 107). This may mythologize the original Quiché warriors during their Early Postclassic expansion against the local Maya. Perhaps the initial setback of the twins couches allegorically the arduous siege and defeat by the Vukamak (*Popol Vuh*, Tedlock 1985:195, 196), and even the destruction of Hacawitz (Fox 1989; Brown, pers. comm.).

Within the cosmologic model, the Early Postclassic Quiché were situated on their mountain-top fortress, at Hacawitz in the Sierra de Chuacus range. The Vukamak were situated below them to the south and west in nondefensible, more open locations on the broad and level plains of the Quiché basin. Simply, the vertical contrast between the two sites may reflect the myth's binary opposition of upward "mountain," which Hacawitz translated as "Open Mountain," and downward "Underworld," for the indigenous Vukamak. With the relocation to Ismachí/Utatlán and the incorporation of the Vukamak as vassals during the Late Postclassic period, the new settlement on the fortified plains of the Quiché basin seems emblematic of the mediation of sky (mountain at Hacawitz) and Underworld (Vukamak), and especially mythologically with the marriage of Hunahpu to X'kik. So Utatlán, topographically intermediate between the defensible mountains and indefensible open plains, itself mediated settlement types.

Returning to the myth's litany, the larger-than-life Hunahpu pays tribute to his slain father Hun Hunahpu (as fruit now hanging in the calabash tree). Hunahpu next uses the head of his father as the game ball. This sequence of

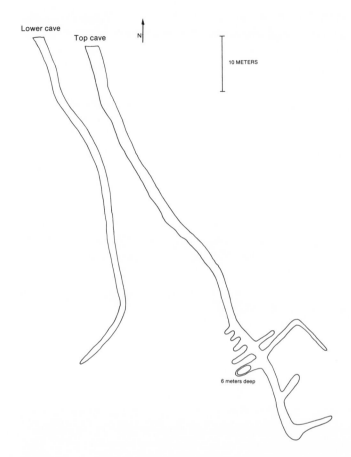

Figure 12.7. Caves of Utatlán: A, Lower Cave, which terminates near the Temple of Tojil; B, Upper Cave, which terminates near the Temple of K'ucumatz.

events paralleled the historical Quiché father-and-son pair, the rulers K'ucumatz and Q'uic'ab, who followed one another in their conquests of the northern and western Mam (*Popol Vuh*, Tedlock 1985; Carmack 1981; Fox 1987). Like the alien Lords of the Underworld, the indigenous Mam killed K'ucumatz in battle, as Hun Hunahpu was slain in the myth. Q'uic'ab paid homage to his father by collecting his father's bones from the Mam, paralleling the calabash tree scene, and then vanquished the Mam as the Lords of the Underworld were finally outwitted and defeated. In this regard, the Quiché, like their Lowland Mayan counterparts, apparently calibrated sequences of historical events that were embedded within repetitive calendrical cycles.

The pivotal events of the ballgame's mythic plot may be encapsulated. The hero twins, Hunahpu and Xbalanke, after descending past perilous canyons and bloody rivers of the Underworld, eventually triumph over the death lords; finally Hunahpu rises to become the sun. His twin, Xbalanke, moves in both the Middleworld and the Underworld as the moon is visible in both the day and night skies. However, his associations with the dark were stronger, as this moon was brighter than the pale and malnourished daytime version (*Popol Vuh*, Edmonson 1971:159).

Therefore, the myth follows the sun's counterclockwise daily trajectory that underpinned the solar calendar and political ordering (see Carrasco 1981; Graulich 1981). Accordingly, the departure of the twin heroes for the Underworld follows the setting of the sun. Their trials and tribulations in the Underworld houses (e.g., Houses of Razors/Knives, Cold, Jaguars, Fire, and Bats) represented places of the dead. At Utatlán, the upper of two long tunnels hewn in corbelled shapes runs below the main plaza and terminates immediately before the Temple of K'ucumatz (Figures 12.3 and 12.7).[8] Nine short side chambers may relate to the nine levels of the Underworld, as postulated by James Brady and Duncan Earle (pers. comm.).

Regarding the Putún descendants as the principal protagonists within a geographically advancing political system, the tale conveys a lurid tribal-centric message of "our lineages" united under the aegis of the sun deity (of the east and the apex of the sky; cf. Gods GI and GII of the earlier Palenque Triad) and the Feathered Serpent of the Postclassic for joint action against the alien lords. In the strict sense that segmentary lineages coupled to oppose foes, the location of the ballcourt on a lower terrace at radial-temple sites and between plazas at the upland "warrior sites" (e.g., Hacawitz, Tzameneb) may have been conceptualized as the road to Xibalba or, in political terms, the ritual battleground. For the warrior peoples of Hacawitz, Tzameneb, or later Utatlán, the ballcourt was oriented east–west. As suggested by caves at Utatlán, Xibalba was reached by traveling from the west to the east. But for many of the radial-temple sites, as the seats of the tun for the Early Postclassic confederacies, the ballcourt was more prevalently oriented north–south. As with the vertical *axis mundi*, the north–south axis represented the vertical drop to Xibalba, in contrast to its edges beyond the east and west cardinal positions.

As in any overarching myth, the ballgame episode undoubtedly pertained to symbols for social formations. Carmack's (1981:195–196) ethnosemantic analysis singles out meanings of conflict and blood, so necessary for acquiring new lands by the confederated segmentary lineages.

> As the lords descended into the ballcourt, they recreated descent to the Underworld of the hero twins, Hunahpu and Xbalanke. Like the game played by those heroes, the contest was against death itself. Some blood sacrifice of the

losers was probably always part of the game. The ball, *quic* ("blood"), was
the personification of blood. As it bounded underground, it represented
Xbalanke, the moon, night, menstrual blood, and the female principle. As it
sailed in the air, it represented Hunahpu, the sun, the light, sacrificial blood,
and the male principle. It symbolically united day and night, the Underworld
and earth's surface, male and female principles. This gave the game a ritual
role that was symbolically equivalent to the mythic role played by Xquic
(Blood Woman) in the *Popol Vuh* tales. (Carmack 1981:195–196)

X'kik (Xquic), to reiterate, was the mate of Hun Hunahpu and thereby the
hero twin's mother. The game unified separate social units in play by opposing teams of two, four, or more individuals; in essence, complementary opposition. It is noteworthy that every generation within the pedigree of the
culture heroes is paired, as coupling defines segmentary lineage joining.
Moreover, the journey of the twin culture heroes to the Underworld, where
they become locked in protracted conflict with the local lords, may be the
mythic analogy of migration, warfare, victory, and eventual unification with
the enemy, which characterized Quichean political history.

In the latter episodes of the *Popol Vuh*, it becomes clear that the victorious
sibling *dramatis personae* are the Quiché themselves. Hunahpu (the sun)
and Xbalanke (the moon) are Nima Quiché reincarnates, the two principal
moieties (Cawek/Sakic vs. Ajaw/Nijaib) of the later segmentary state. The
Nima Quiché were a party of two, like the mythical characters: the Cawek
moiety (Tojil = sun, east and north) and the Nijaib/Ajaw moiety (Awilix =
moon = Xbalanke, west; Ajaw = Venus = Hunahpu, south).

The Quest for the "East"

In overview, the Quiché were like the hero twins pushed forever eastward
from a homeland in the west (Gulf Lowlands) and upward from the Underworld toward Venus and the sun, where power and heat derive. Venus appears first as the morning star, which was the patron of warriors. Historically,
the Early Postclassic intrusive Quiché warriors were represented cosmically
by Venus (the morning star) at Hacawitz 20 km south of Tuja. As Hacawitz
was emblematic of Venus, Tuja exemplified imagery of the sun. The Quiché
transformed (with Hun Hunahpu's progeny) into the day (Cawik plus Sakic)
and night (Ajaw plus Nijaib) moieties following the formation of the segmentary state with the advent of the Late Postclassic period. Both the Sakic
major lineage, from Tuja, and the Nijaib, from local Vukamak stock of
Chujuyup, coupled, respectively, with the original Cawek and Ajaw pairing.

In any of the newly invaded territories where local Maya, without the
"fire" or "light," opposed the peoples of the tun or solar calendar (Putún), the

former were conceptualized as ignominious denizens of darkness/death—that is of Xibalba. These foes provided sacrificial blood to propel the sun and moon in counterclockwise daily journeys.

While prototypes of the hero twins may be identified during the Classic Period in the Lowlands (Coe 1973), it should be kept in mind that the Classic period Maya ballcourt itself changed apparent meaning as well as architectural form; from open-ended to the Postclassic sunken floor, and from shallow-sloped to steep-sloped playing walls. For example, the playing walls at Copán's court sloped less than 40°, but at the two courts at Late Postclassic Chuitmanit (Figure 12.6) each angled 70 and 78°, respectively. Because Postclassic Quichean ballcourts manifested sunken enclosed playing fields, they apparently provided a more dramatic arena for the ritualized conflict of the game. In contrast, the more open-ended courts of the Classic period with playing floors at the same level as the adjoining central plaza, reflect a less dichotomized ballgame. Therefore, the ballgame's meaning undoubtedly metamorphosed, perhaps with the formation or resumption of more fluid segmentary lineages.

The ballgame markers correspondingly switched from depiction of birds, jaguars, and even the ball players Hun-Ahau (Hunahpu) and his borther to a serpent (K'ucumatz) with a human face. A sanguine ballgame complex with hachas (symbolic of trophy heads from decapitated bodies, like that of Hun Hunahpu), palmas, and yokes (together with scenes of human sacrifice) originated along the western gulf coast in Veracruz, near El Tajín, as the western flank of the Maya world. This complex was first transplanted eastward into Guatemala and Honduras with the Middle or Late Classic Cotzumalhuapan traditions. Later, during the Late Postclassic period, with the last of these west-to-east migrations, ballcourts extended only to the borders of the Quiché and Cakchiquel states. They seemingly marked the easternmost limit of confederated segmentary lineages at Naco and Cihuatán.

As reflected in the ballcourt's intermediate position between rival kinship factions within single "linguistic" communities (e.g., Cawinal), or even between intrusive and local peoples (e.g., Cawinal among the Akajal at Jilotepeque Viejo), the ballgame continued to serve mediational functions. Interestingly, only in the easternmost province of the Quiché and Cakchiquel do ballcourt markers actually picture Hunahpu and his twin, Xbalanke, as human faces protruding from an open-mouthed feathered serpent (e.g., at Jilotepeque Viejo). Marqusee (1980) suggests that Hunahpu is depicted in a nagual-like state of transformation, as Venus (Hunahpu) transformed daily into the sun. To reiterate, Carmack (1981) suggests that the sky serpent, K'ucumatz, simply was the vehicle of transport for Hunahpu as the young ascending sun.

In explaining the north–south orientation of the ballcourts in these eastern provinces, it is noted that the sun's shadow first passes the east ballcourt marker (Hunahpu) and playing wall and later in the day crosses over the west marker (Xbalanke). The second half of the day (Xbalanke) is thus the mirror opposite of the first half (Hunahpu). However, the Quiché lineages proper at Hacawitz and later Greater Utatlán may have built east–west ballcourts, because the overarching sky serpent K'ucumatz mediated the east and west in the sun's daily trajectory. K'ucumatz was thereby juxtaposed conceptually and spatially between Hunahpu (Tojil) and Xbalanke (Awilix). At Utatlán the small circular Temple of K'ucumatz was positioned precisely in the center of the plaza, intermediate between the Temples of Tojil and Awilix. As we have seen, K'ucumatz, the green Feathered Serpent, was said to carry the sun between its jaws as a young traveler across the eastern sky and then, as an older traveler, west to the Underworld. Importantly, however, no ballcourt markers, whether circular or of human face-serpent mouth design, are known within the Quiché state proper, except in the eastern provinces facing Xibalba.

In Quiché political geography and cosmology, the entrance to the Underworld was said to be reached by taking the "black road" to the "drop off," toward the north star (*Popol Vuh*, Tedlock 1985:110–111; Thompson 1970:372) within the northeasternmost province of Verapaz. Perhaps this is related to the persistent north–south orientation of the ballcourts within the eastern-most provinces of the Quiché and Cakchiquel states. Remember, the stairways on the north and south end zones ritually descended into the Underworld. Also recall the north–south cardinality of ballcourts during the Early Postclassic period at radial-temple sites and that these were built in newly settled territories, conceptually in the "east."

For the Quichean groups, therefore, the entrance to the Underworld may have been the north slope of the Sierra de Alta Verapaz, near Coban, where both the Río Negro/Chixoy eventually descends into the Chontalpa, via the Usumacinta, and where the Río Polochic eventually drops due east to the Caribbean. The karstic hills of Verapaz contained innumerable surreptitious caverns, often kilometers long, that may have provided, quite hypothetically, another possibility for the various "houses" of the Underworld, where the twin heroes underwent trials (*Popol Vuh*, Tedlock 1985:111–113, 137–144). In fact, the natural protruding stalactites and stalagmites may have been equated with the House of Knives/Razors and its row upon row of knife blades (*Popol Vuh*, Tedlock 1985:113).

So too, the House of Bats in which the twins were momentarily overcome may pertain to the late military penetration in the eastern provinces by the Cakchiquel, whose emblem was a bat, who usurped the Quiché here. Whether coincidentally or not, mythically the entrance to Xibalba for the

Quiché, Pokom, and Kekchi lay near Tucuru ("owl"), a town at the entrance to the Río Polochic thoroughfare. The community Tucuru successfully held off Quiché military onslaughts within this eastern territory, known cryptically as Tecucistlán, or "land of war." In the ballgame myth, Tucuru was referred to as an owl messenger from Xibalba (*Popol Vuh*, Tedlock 1985:109). Similarly, Holom, the name of an Underworld Lord ("Skull Staff" in the *Popol Vuh*), also was a neighboring Pokom community that was temporarily conquered (Xajil 1953:99). Relating to the region as Xibalba in general, owls and bats are nocturnal airborne animals. Bats return to their caves and owls roost with the dawn, apparently with political metaphor.

Looking to antecedents, the fabled Tulán of the east, proposed as Copán by Tedlock (1989), also manifested the bat in its emblem glyph (an earlier House of Bats?) and maintained a paired north–south-oriented ballcourt and radial-temple in the northern Great Plaza, and ballcourt markers portraying Hunahpu (as its Classic phonetic equivalent Hun-Ahau [Ajaw], Schele and Miller 1986:251). While monumental construction ceased at Copán about A.D. 870, the ceremonial center endured into the Early Postclassic period. If Copán was the *Tulán* of the east later visited by the Quiché, then Palenque may have been the primordial *Tulán* of the west, near the Putún homeland where the Quichean groups first organized for their migration east. A strong ritualistic east–west cardinal axis apparently endured and was embedded in Quiché political geography. If so, then Kaminaljuyú would have been a candidate for the *Tulán Xibalba*, the great city of the Underworld (Xajil 1953:45) on the south cardinal direction. Later Chichén Itzá, with its Great Ballcourt, apparently was the *Tulán* of the north. In contrast, Kaminaljuyú once boasted a still more massive palangana-type ballcourt plus dozens of smaller courts throughout the Valley of Guatemala (Lothrop cited in Smith 1961:116). It is worth considering that the many ballcourts of the Postclassic Quiché may have reflected the south cardinal point in the Maya world associated with the Underworld, as well as their fractious segmentary lineage organization. Together south and east have nocturnal imagery of Venus for the Putún, as do bats and owls for the people they opposed.

In overview, the Quiché world view was dualistic: two aspects of a greater whole. Certainly political events were framed within the solar-based calendrics, with the two diametrically opposed sets of paired cardinal directions: the vertical (north–south) and the horizontal (east–west) axes. Not only did the broad sequencing of their political expansionism relate to this ideational framework, but so did their segmentary sociopolitical organization, with particular lineage groups ascribed to specific directions. The ballgame, played in the center of their communities, ritualized opposing factions, or when one Putún-descended group coercively "allied" with another group. Therefore, the always-changing Quichean political alliances paralleled the fundamental ballgame myth of the *Popol Vuh*. As Hunahpu of the Hero Twins was reborn into the youthful sun, the alliances of the Quichean political order were continually reformulated. Even the segmentary states died and were reborn, as Chichén Itzá and Utatlán replaced the *Tuláns* of the Classic period.

Notes

1. Brown (1983, 1984, 1985) disputes a Lowland ancestry of the Quiché. Tedlock (1989) offers that the Quiché originated on the opposite frontier of southern Mesoamerica, at Copán.

2. It is at present difficult to assess the temporal priority of the ballcourt's enclosed I shape, although it is often assumed to have been a "Mexican" architectural form. Smith (1961) encapsulates the range of variation in measurements for enclosed I-shaped ballcourts in Postclassic Highland Guatemala which is included for comparison:

> These ball courts have high walls defining end zones from which stairways lead out. The ranges are always higher than these end walls and measure from 3 to 5 m in height. The end walls are about 1 to 2.10 m. . . . The width of the playing alley from bench face to bench face may be anywhere from 6 to 9.50 m across, and the ranges vary from 20 to 30 m long. End zones measure anywhere from about 9 to 19 m across and 2.50 to 7.50 m in depth. The plan of the enclosed ball court, with its long narrow playing alley and expanded end zones, takes the form of a "capital I." The profile consists of a vertical bench face, a level bench top, and a sloping playing wall with a vertical upper molding that projects a few centimeters from the playing wall and rises from .45 to 1 m above the playing wall. . . . The slope in the playing wall varies from 64 degrees at Chutixtiox to 85 degrees at Mixco Viejo [Jilotepeque Viejo]. (Smith 1961:110)

3. The tun or stone of the Lacadona could mean the solar calendar from either Acalán itself or its namesake along the upper Río Usumacinta; the latter was called Lacadona well into early colonial times (Thompson 1970:26–27).

4. To illustrate the "vertical" dimension of the radial-temple sites, the temple on Chamac's summit at Uspantan is connected to the ballcourt by a stairway descending 80 m (see Fox 1980).

5. In their earlier statements, Majewski and Brown (e.g., 1983, 1985) and Brown (1983, 1985) alternate between accepting and rejecting the presence of a ballcourt at Hacawitz. However, identification is confirmed by Ichon's delineation of an equal-sized east–west oriented I-shaped ballcourt at Tzameneb.

6. Smith (1961:120) calls attention to circular (quadrafoil?) shaped "drains" in the center of the playing floors at two ballcourts elsewhere, which may have served for the continuation of the "mythological" passage of the hero twins through the Underworld, Xibalba, which the game enacted.

7. However, the Akajal at Ochal were conquered and then colonized, complete with a Quiché-designed plaza, during the first wave of Quiché expansionism. The Akajal were situated northeast of the Quiché, in what is today San Martin Jilotepeque.

8. Separate investigations of the two caves on the west barranca of Utatlán were undertaken by Brady (1989), Fernandez (1990), Duncan Earle (pers. comm.), and myself. Fernandez (pers. comm.) recorded oral tradition that the caves were dug in the late nineteenth century by French treasure hunters. However, the location of the lower cave some 40 meters below the plaza surface would suggest a prehispanic construction. Nonetheless, blackened walls especially in the side chambers suggest continued use in Maya ritual, even in the present day. Ethnographic identification in the galleries with the houses of the Underworld has not yet been attempted.

PART III
Iconography and Symbolism

CHAPTER 13

Ceramic Figurines and the Mesoamerican Ballgame

Susanna M. Ekholm

Introduction

Our knowledge of ancient Mesoamerican ballgames began with conquest accounts written by Europeans who saw the games being played in many areas. These descriptions varied greatly in the amount of detail provided (Stern 1949). The conquerors saw only the end of a 2,000-year-long tradition of ball playing which in some areas, as among the Maya, was no longer at its greatest level of elaboration and importance.

Ever since the earliest settled Mesoamericans began working clay, they made ceramic figurines. These still enigmatic objects have played a major role in giving us a glimpse of when the pre-Hispanic ballgame began, where it flourished, what it was like, and what equipment was part of it. They raise questions about variations in the ballgame as well as their own distribution. They make us reflect upon the nature of the society that made them, used and enjoyed them, and discarded them in various ways.

The following presentation is not intended to be a description of all Mesoamerican ballgame figurines, but a reminder of the role ceramic figurines have played in our knowledge of the ballgame. At the outset, the limitations of figurines should be well understood. A particular difficulty in dealing with figurines is that most of them—and almost always the best and most complete—are not from controlled archaeological excavations or known proveniences.

Figurines in Determining the Beginnings and Distribution of the Ballgame

For many areas and time periods, our knowledge of the ancient ballgame is entirely limited to figurines. The figurines of central Mexico that date from as early as 1000 B.C., and wear what have long thought to be ball player costumes, have been known for some time (Porter 1953). These hand-modeled figurines have been found in the spectacular cemeteries of Tlatilco, where they were placed as mortuary offerings for several centuries. The ball players were simply dressed in belts with hand and knee protectors (Piña Chan 1955: Lám. 7). Their heads were sometimes wrapped, giving a helmet-like effect (Coe 1965: Figs. 108–111). Masks may have been worn (Coe 1965b: Fig. 100), including both protective masks and ceremonial masks such as small round clay ones (Type D1, Coe 1965b: Fig. 165). The same tradition was found at Tlapacoya, with even more elaborate padded belts, ornate headdresses, and the use of masks (Coe 1965b). Ball player figurines were being buried at Las Bocas, Puebla, and in Morelos as well.

Similar representations have been found at San Lorenzo (Coe and Diehl 1980) on the gulf coast. From Xochipala, Guerrero, come some of the most naturalistic of the figurines (Griffin 1972). The tradition continued through the Late Preclassic in such Highland sites as Ticomán (Piña Chan 1969: Fig. 2) and Cuicuilco (Matos M. 1968). An example from Cuicuilco wears a belt that is suspiciously like the yokes that are later known to have been worn by ball players of the gulf coast.

The above figurines have long been considered evidence that the ballgame existed in areas in which there were no known ballcourts found for these early periods. They match Conquest period descriptions of players and their garb, while conforming to individual artistic traditions and styles. Because of these similarities, figurines give us an accurate glimpse of what a ball player looked like. We now have confirming evidence of ballcourts from as early as the Middle Preclassic in Chiapas (Agrinier this volume), and by Late Preclassic times ballcourts are known from many regions.

Although Middle and early Late Preclassic figurines represent ball players, and the ballgame was indeed being played, it has been uncritically assumed that the courts associated with the game simply have not yet been discovered. It seems more likely that at Tlatilco, Tlapacoya, and other early sites, a game was played that did not require a court, or at most one that had only perishable or movable boundaries and markers. Ethnohistoric and ethnographic descriptions of a number of different games exist and their variety can be used to help explain not only the ballgame itself but its social, political, and economic aspects. Closer description and study of the ballgame figurines will be helpful in such an endeavor.

Ceramic Figurines as Tools in Reconstructing the Ballgame, its Accoutrements, and its Ceremonies

Although ancient Mesoamericans obviously played several types of ballgames—some with their hands, their feet, and with sticks—the game that seems to have risen to the most universal ceremonial and religious height was that played within special courts by hitting the ball with the hips, thighs, and buttocks. The accoutrements for that game, especially of the Classic period, have been best identified through an examination of ceramic figurines.

The archaeological discovery and investigation of ballcourts have a long history. Sculpture found associated with ballcourts, especially carved panels at such sites as Tajín and Chichén Itzá, reinforced and expanded ethnohistoric descriptions of ballgame ceremonies. It was then that figurines played a major role in relating what was depicted on the sculptures to other portable artifacts.

Stone *yugos* or yokes that appeared primarily on the Mexican gulf coast and in the Highlands of Guatemala were for a long time items of speculation (Strebel 1890, 1893). When Lothrop (1923) suggested their association with the ballgame, it was principally on the evidence of a hollow ceramic figure (Weaver 1981:252), apparently a reclining or falling ball player, from near Santa Cruz del Quiché in Highland Guatemala. The figurine convinced him that the personages identified as ball players on the stelae of Santa Lucía Cotzumalhuapa also wore yokes. Thompson (1941) disagreed, believing that the yokes that Lothrop had identified must have been manufactured of something other than stone, and he inferred that the heavy stone yokes with elaborate carving might not have had any necessary connection whatever with the ballgame, either as apparel or equipment. He equated the yoke of the Quiché figurine with the garments of two of the six ball players on the three Copán ballcourt markers (Pasztory 1978a:Fig. 26), who wear what appear to be wrapped and tied "deflectors" (Hellmuth 1975a) high on their torsos. He did, however, identify all of these garments as the *bate* (rings) listed as ballgame equipment of the hero twins, Hun Hunahpu and Xbalanke, in the Quiché *Popol Vuh*.

Lothrop's idea that the stone yokes were ballgame equipment and were worn about the waist was revived by Ekholm (1946). Again, the evidence in support of the idea included a number of ceramic figurines: a modeled Huastec figurine from Pánuco (Ekholm 1946:Pl. 3) wearing an open-sided yoke that was compared with the many similar figurines that wear simple heavy, low belts along with knee pads and hand guards, and are assumed to be ball players (Parsons 1974:Fig. 165; *Historia de México* 1974 [1]:152; Borhegyi 1980); a beautiful mold-made Late Classic figurine from near the Tuxtlas, Veracruz that wears a heavy belt definitely in the shape of a yoke and even bears a design similar to that of known yokes, as well as other ballgame garb (*Fondo*

Editorial 1964:Fig. 105); and a similar one from Campeche. Ekholm did not rule out the use of stone yokes as ritual replicas of wooden belts that were in fact used, but the identification of stone yokes with the ballgame was assured. Ekholm (1961) carried the identification further with the "stone collars" of Puerto Rico.

Two other stone artifact classes, usually carved in many forms, were encountered in the same areas as the yokes: *palmas*, or palmate stones, and *hachas*, or thin stone heads. By comparing them with relief carvings on the ballcourts of El Tajín, Ekholm (1949) showed that palmas or wooden prototypes could have been carried upright on the front parts of heavy belts or even stone yokes. When he turned to a discussion of the possible use of hachas, Ekholm again used as major evidence a ceramic figurine from the Tuxtlas, Veracruz, that shows an hacha attached to a belt. Along with sculptural evidence from Finca Arevalo, Guatemala (Ekholm 1949:Fig. 7), and physical evidence that hachas had been inserted into something, hachas were shown to have functioned with yokes in ballgames or associated ceremonies. Their association with yokes was confirmed by ceramic vessels in the form of hachas attached to yokes.

Borhegyi (1961) undertook to explain the ancient use of the loop-handled stones that had a distribution similar to that of the yokes, palmas, and hachas. After inspection of ballcourt-panel sculpture, decorated palmas, and ceramic figurines, Borhegyi suggested that these stones functioned as ballgame handstones to deflect the ball and, in some way, to protect the hand. Through the study of a number of ball player figurines, he determined that the use of such handstones probably originated in central Veracruz and spread to Highland Guatemala and Yucatán; in other areas during the Classic period, figurines showed that arms were protected by wrapping.

Kemrer (1968) has more recently suggested two additional classes of stone artifacts that may also be associated with the ballgame: Preclassic "kneeguards" shaped like small open yokes, and masks. The kneeguards he compares with those of a mold-made figurine (Clancy et al. 1985:Fig. 144) and a Jaina figurine with a thick pad-like belt high on the chest (Acosta and Moedano Köer 1946:Fig. 1). The shapes are not comparable; the kneeguards on these latter two Late Classic figurines are likely made of leather, as they would have to have certain flexibility and comfort. For evidence of masks, Kemrer cites figurines of the Middle Preclassic of Tlatilco and the mention of a ball player's mask in the *Popol Vuh*. Kemrer's work is nonrigorous and a less successful attempt to identify stone artifacts as ballgame accoutrements on the basis of figurines. Dockstader's (1968) identification of stone arm bands is more successful, as he shows miniature stone arm bands and can make an analogy between them and the miniature yokes and hachas.

The foregoing history of our recognition of various artifacts made of stone as integral parts of the pre-Columbian ballgame was given to point out how some of our ideas of the Classic period ballgame came about and the role that figurines had in that development. The association of yokes, hachas, palmas, and handstones with the game seems obvious now, and there are many figurines to verify the identifications that began so painstakingly nearly 70 years ago with very few available figurines.

Two Maya Ballgame Costumes as Reflected in the Figurines

In the investigations described in the preceding section some obvious problems arose, but were not recognized by the earliest of the authors discussed. As more figurines became available for study, it was Borhegyi (1969) who pointed out differences in the apparel of ball players. Gulf coast area ball players wore what could be described as yokes, while those of the coast and inland areas of Campeche, Yucatán, and Quintana Roo wore another variety of costume (*Historia de México* 1974 [2]:30). In the central Lowland Maya area, they wore heavy body padding and belts (Rands and Rands 1965:Fig. 30; Joyce 1933:Pl. V, top two at upper right), but in the southern or Highland Maya area they wore open-ended "yokes" or heavy belts tied over layers of protective padding (*Kunst der Maya* 1967:Fig. 67).

These distinctions have been simplified into a dichotomy by Hellmuth (1975a), mainly on the basis of the many newly available polychrome vessels from the Maya area. He also proposes that the ballgame in the gulf coast and related areas was played differently from that in the "traditional Classic Maya" area; the former played the ball from the hip with their yokes, while the traditional Maya hit it high on the chest with what Hellmuth calls a deflector to distinguish it from gulf coast yokes.

The gulf coast was certainly the center of a spectacular development for the ballgame and its ritual and "cultic" aspects, with El Tajín in central Veracruz as the center of this elaboration between A.D. 400 and 700 (Wilkerson this volume). This is reflected in the long history of the ballgame as seen in figurines. By the Terminal Preclassic, modeled figurines show the use of yoke-like belts (Parsons 1980:Fig. 65); by Middle Classic times, mold-made figurines (Drucker 1943:Pl. 48) wearing yokes (Piña Chan 1969:Fig. 9; Drucker 1943: Pl. 51) and other accoutrements are common there. The Late Classic saw a great range of styles in different parts of Veracruz: north (Taladoire 1981:Pl. 26), north-central (Borhegyi 1963:Pl. 12; Bushnell 1965:Fig. 61), and south-central (Bolz-Augenstein 1975:Pl. 80; Parsons 1974:Fig. 101c).

This strong ballgame cult with its particular dress and ceremonies apparently spread, by late Middle Classic times, through the Peripheral Coastal

Lowlands (Parsons 1978), along the Pacific coast of Central America (Hellmuth 1978:Figs. 8–11), and also along the gulf coast into Tabasco (Borhegyi 1980), Campeche, and Yucatán (Kubler 1962). This is not the place to discuss how and why the ballgame cult diffused; the appearance and distribution of the figurines are simply noted.

The Campeche coast has the greatest confusion of figurines. This has resulted because (1) the greatest number of figurines exist in Campeche, due to the unusual practice of burying them with the dead at Jaina and other nearby sites, and (2) excavation data are missing for most contexts. The "Jaina Complex" has been examined from various points of view, but it still remains uncertain which figurines are contemporary and from which surrounding areas they specifically come. It will do here simply to point out the coexistence in the Jaina region of two major ball player styles: that of the gulf coast Tajín-centered cult (Corson 1975:Figs. 22b, c; Piña Chan 1968:Lám. 19) with yokes (Corson 1975:Fig. 33d), hachas, and handstones (Corson 1975:Fig. 9a), both mold-made and modeled (Hellmuth 1975a:10, 17; Anton 1970:No. 20) (the "yoke," if it can be called that, is sometimes reduced to a bare minimum); and the other style that relates to the central Maya Lowlands (Toscano 1945:Fig. 1b), again both mold-made and modeled (*Historia de México* 1974 [2]:30), whose ball players wear the ball deflectors high on their torsos (Norton 1984: Fig. 348). Beyond the Campeche coast, there is meager figurine evidence for the two styles; here the evidence of polychrome pottery generally dominates. One small figurine from Moxviquil in the Chiapas Highlands, however, does show a yoke-wearing ball player (Na-Bolom Museum, San Cristóbal de Las Casas).

For the southern Highland Maya there exist detailed visual descriptions (i.e., figurines) of Late Classic ball players. The example from Alta Verapaz (*Tesoros Mayas* 1974) of the Guatemala National Museum's Dieseldorff Collection, published in 1967, was the first of a number of similar figurines that now allow a good description of ball player figurines and ball player accoutrements of that area. Borhegyi (1980) discovered more of the Dieseldorff Collection in the Guatemala Museum. I recently searched for his published examples in the *bodegas* there; I found only three of them but found three more that Borhegyi had missed. The ball players of the Alta Verapaz wore three layers of padding high on the torso and a heavy half-belt or deflector tied over one side, above the hip, on top of one extra small pad. The belts were probably of wood or leather. Some appear to be carved with glyphic bands. The figures wear arm wrappings, especially on the side on which they wear the deflector. This type of Highland ball player figurine is amplified by others in the Popol Vuh Museum which are more complete and show the knee pads, as do some from private collections (Hellmuth 1975a).

Ball player figurines of the central Maya Lowlands are more difficult to describe, as few examples exist. There seems to be great standardization and conservatism. Excavated examples, usually not from burials, are in poor condition. Where figurines were peculiarly abundant and graphic, as at Lubaantún (Joyce 1933), more data are available. Looted and therefore selected examples (Guatemala Museum) provide the best information. Like the southern Highland Maya, the central Maya costume is also high wrapping with a final narrow deflector of heavy material for striking the ball. With this large area of similar ballgame players, however, a few examples of gulf coast style players remind us of the complexity of the situation: a vessel with excellent yoke and hacha (*Rediscovered Masterpieces* 1985) and a simple standing figure from the Lost World Pyramid at Tikal (Guatemala Museum).

The ballgame figurine costume in the Maya area provides clues to kind and degree of interaction. The central Maya Lowlands and southern Highlands were surrounded by gulf coast influence affecting the Maya during the Middle and Late Classic periods. While the uniformity of ballgame accoutrements within the central Maya area may be partly an illusion based on figurines representing a limited sample from within a certain pervasive style, their differences from the gulf coast examples are real. Figurines are more realistic than polychrome vessel paintings and may represent the ordinary underpinnings of more telling events; consequently, they help in understanding the major interregional events depicted on such sculptures as the ballcourt markers of Copán. Here, a central Veracruz style player faces a central Lowland Maya player as depicted on the center marker (Benson 1967), while central Lowland Maya players face off on the other two end markers.

There is a desperate need for more detailed figurine studies and greater interaction between figurine, polychrome, and sculpture studies. Together they can elucidate such problems as what an unathletic dwarf figurine is doing with a ball (Borhegyi 1980:Fig. 14) when we have sculpture evidence for his possible participation in ballgame rites (Stuart and Stuart 1977), or whether headdresses represent vying lineages or a greater political arena (see Kurjack et al. this volume). Given what is understood of the varying functions of the ballgame, as primarily evidenced by the ballcourts themselves, figurine studies can aid in elucidating many aspects of the game.

How Were Mesoamerican Ballgame Figurines Used?

Ceramic figurines particularly aid in reconstructing costume and equipment of the ballgame because they depict ball player figures entirely or partially in the round. This is particularly useful in identifying yokes, palmas, hachas, and handstones. Players represented on polychromes and other vessels are often distorted, as the painter attempts to show more than one would actually see if looking at a live player; artistic license allows garments to hang in unnatural positions, headdresses to take on impossible sizes and attributes, and the players to assume graceful and artistic but impractical or impossible poses. While some of this distortion also occurs on the figurines, it does so to a much lesser extent.

Ceramic figurines also depict the players of the ballgame and their equipment more realistically than vessels or monuments because of the different uses to which the artifacts were probably put. Ball players on monuments presumably represent elite or ruling personages in historical acts, functioning as monuments to these acts and made as elegant statements of propaganda. Ball players on Maya polychrome vessels are usually elaborately outfitted with more costuming that can be imagined for the presumably athletic action of the game. The players are often named in glyphic texts and apparently are rulers, deity impersonators, or deities. The scenes show events, though greatly stylized and glorified, taking place in real life or in mythical history. The final function of these vessels appears to have been as burial offerings for the elevated elite.

Ball player figurines, on the other hand, are of a more generic nature. They usually depict real ball players, perhaps professional players, who are not obviously identified as individuals; in fact, in later periods the figurines are mold-made and produced in great numbers. In some places they do represent ball-playing deities, but that is not always distinguishable.

The *final* function of figurine ball players differs too; except in special situations such as the cemeteries of Tlatilco and Jaina, figurines do not figure strongly as burial offerings. They occur in refuse of various kinds; the *apparent* paucity of figurines in most non-cemetery areas reflects their generally casual disposal and their more serendipitous discovery. Most figurines are found in general household refuse.

When figurines are found in burials, as at Tlatilco and Jaina, there is as yet no discernible reason as to who is buried with whom. Women can be buried with ball player figurines; the deceased may also be buried with a variety of figurines.

Why, then, were they made, and why were they used as burial offerings in certain areas? The lifetime of a figurine probably included several functions. Many of the Classic period figurines are *ocarinas* or whistles, and so had one obvious function as music or noise makers. Some kinds of figurines, especially of deities, probably functioned much like modern Catholic saints on household altars. Figurines probably took part in crèche-like scenes and dramas or in processions like modern saints. A figurine may have done all of these things before it was broken, discarded, or buried.

Mesoamerica, of all ancient culture areas, was one of the greatest producers of ceramic figurines. Ceramic art is very much a Mesoamerican characteristic. Besides recognizing a predilection for ceramic art, it should be remembered that we are investigating cultures that are understood as civilizations and which embodied a high degree of social, political, and economic sophistication. Society included a "middle class" which presumably was interested in objects, in beautiful and interesting things for their own sake. Perhaps we are often too hasty to assign tags of "fertility" and "religious" or even the ubiquitous "ceremonial" to objects such as figurines.

The ballgame was played for many reasons, not simply to settle wars or to move planets. Ballgames were extremely important in the lives of almost all Mesoamerican peoples, but they were played for fun as well.

Perhaps the ceramic ball player figurines can be viewed as almost souvenirs of teams, or of deities that manipulated the ballgames, or of specific games. They were available to most "middle-class" people, who *may* have used them in various "ceremonial" ways. They were possibly buried as offerings of fine and beloved pieces, perhaps with religious connotations.

Most important, ceramic figurines are the closest we have to real portraits of the players of the Mesoamerican ballgame.

CHAPTER 14

Ballgame Imagery of the Maya Lowlands: History and Iconography

Marvin Cohodas

Scope of the Present Analysis

At least three types of ballgame were known during the Classic period in the Maya Lowlands. Masonry ballcourts were constructed for the hip-ball game, in which players struck a large and heavy rubber ball with a protected right hip. They also wore padding on one forearm and knee to prevent scrapes when bracing against the court floor to return the ball with a rotation of the hips.[1] The half-kneeling posture required for this hip shot is frequent in Maya depictions of the ballgame (Figure 14.1). As reported for the post-conquest Aztec, players were restricted from holding or hitting the ball with their hands.

A contrasting handball game appears in some Lubaantún figurines, as well as on El Baúl Monument 27 and the Dainzú reliefs.[2] Players wear a heavy, visored helmet, leaving hips unprotected, and they hold a small ball in a heavily bound hand. The action of this game is shown with violence consistent with the extreme protection—some players appear to stumble and fall in defeat. There is no evidence that masonry courts were constructed for the handball game.

A third game which may have been played in the Maya Lowlands is the stick-ball type represented in the Tepantitla murals (Pasztory 1976:Fig. 39) and the Codex Borgia (p. 42), in both cases associated with Venus. Although no Maya images of the stick-ball game have come to light, the discovery of a

Figure 14.1. Roll-out of design on painted funerary ceramic, 14.2 cm high. Rijksmuseum voor Volkenkunde, Leiden (Robiscek and Hales 1981:Vessel 143; Justin Kerr photographic roll-out No. 1551).

sculpture at Tikal[3] which is similar to the "markers" represented at Tepantitla and in the La Ventilla stela suggest Lowland acquaintance with this game.

Each of these three games appears to have involved a specialized type of ball, protective equipment, playing field, and rules. The ritual function of these games would presumably differ as well. Consequently, the interpretations presented here on the ritual function of the hip-ball game and the symbolism of its imagery cannot be presumed to apply to the other two ritual sports.

Even among artworks related to the hip-ball game, the diversity of form and context precludes a single interpretation. Classic Maya art and architecture erected to commemorate the hip-ball game represent a specialized regional complex, as distinct from the more widespread and generalized Mesoamerican type as football is from rugby. As the non-Maya approach climaxes in the coastal Lowlands, especially at El Tajín, Bilbao, and Chichén Itzá,[4] it will be referred to as the "Mexican" hip-ball game.

Ballgame images of the Mexican and Maya type are clearly distinguished by the costume of players and the event portrayed. While Classic Maya

Figure 14.2. Detail of central bench relief from the Great Ballcourt, Chichén Itzá (Cohodas photo).

players (Figure 14.1) wear bulky torso protectors of cloth and wood, coastal Lowland players (Figure 14.2) are shown with yoke-type hip protectors and *hacha*- or *palma*-type stomach protectors, and often a purse-shaped hand protector. While Classic Maya players appear in action, with the ball still in play, coastal Lowland scenes usually depict the post-game sacrificial ritual, sometimes in a ballcourt setting, with the ball decorated as a skull.

The form, decoration, placement, and symbolism of the ballcourt differ among these two varieties. While the Maya court is commonly furnished with a line of three markers set into the playing field, the Mexican court may feature a seven-part sculptural set, with six tenoned heads or relief panels (three on each side) and a central altar or relief, as at Chichén Itzá, Toniná, and El Tajín.[5] The use of rings tenoned into the playing wall is also most consistent in the Mexican courts.[6] While the playing field of the Maya court is open ended, the Mexican court often has enclosed end zones to create a capital I shape, and several are sunken below the plaza surface to further demarcate interior space.

While both types of courts are associated with large and centralized public spaces, they differ in placement within that space. The Maya court is generally placed near the center of the plaza on line with a pyramid or acropolis, as in the East Plaza at Tikal; or the court may be used to mark the plaza entrance, as in the Plaza of Seven Temples at Tikal. By contrast, the I-shaped ballcourt generally occupies the eastern or western side of the main plaza, as at Toniná, Chichén Itzá, and Monte Albán. Taken together, the axial orientation, absence of end zones, and line of three markers in the Classic Maya court emphasize architectural symbolism of the world axis which demarcates a cosmological passage through the earth's surface and into the Underworld; while the eastern or western placement, enclosed end zones, and seven-part sculptural scheme of the Mexican court symbolize the surface of the earth itself (Cohodas 1985:52). The four-color scheme used to decorate the playing field in I-shaped ballcourts represented in Postclassic and Postconquest codices supports this latter interpretation.

The chronological development of the Maya and Mexican elaborations of ballgame imagery and ritual is also distinct. While the Mexican type is known in the Mexican Highlands from Preclassic through Postclassic times, its development climaxes in the coastal Lowlands during the Middle Classic period.[7] By contrast, the Maya type is known only from around A.D. 400 to 900, and it climaxes in the first half of the eighth century, after coastal Lowland sites such as El Tajín, Bilbao, and Chichén Itzá may have already switched to the elaboration of warrior cult iconography (Cohodas 1978b:261–273). The differences in historical as well as cultural context for these two forms of hipball game imagery may be expected to affect their symbolic content.

Iconographic studies of the hip-ball game have always focused on the coastal Lowland monuments because the narrative style of reliefs such as those at Chichén Itzá allow more detailed interpretations. Krickeberg (1966) has shown that the two teams personify the forces of light and darkness, which meet in violent conflict when the sun sets or rises. At Chichén Itzá, either team may be shown winning or losing, suggesting that the game was played to ensure not only the setting and death of the sun, when the forces of darkness triumph, but also the rising and rebirth of the sun, when the forces of light emerge victorious. The victim in these post-game rituals, presumably the captain of the losing team, would then represent either the setting sun defeated by the Underworld lord, or the Underworld lord later destroyed by the rising sun (Cohodas 1975). The opposition of these two games appears not only in Codex Borgia (Krickeberg 1966:228–230) but also in the *Popol Vuh*, where the first game results in the defeat and death of the elder hero twins, while the second game leads to the destruction of the death gods and apotheosis of the younger twins.

Building on Krickeberg's analysis, I (Cohodas 1975) have also shown that these two games may be associated with the agricultural cycle, based on the analogous renewal of both sun and maize. The ballgame played in the dry season, perhaps at the vernal equinox, would be designed to force the sun into the Underworld shortly before the maize kernels are actually planted. The game played in the rainy season, perhaps at the autumnal equinox, would allow the sun to rise by ending the dominance of the earth gods, just as the first ears of corn begin to ripen. Aztec chants and myths graphically illustrate the association of the ballcourt with both the beginning and ending of this fertility cycle.[8]

Classic Maya ballgame scenes cannot be subsumed under the same interpretation applied to coastal Lowland narratives. With the game still in play, and the outcome as yet undecided, there is no winning or losing team, and no possibility of differentiating games associated with dry and rainy seasons. In Classic Maya art, dynastic and temporal transformations were accorded far more importance than agricultural renewal. As will be shown, these functions are better served by the image of a single game, with emphasis on its process rather than its result.

Before analyzing the iconography of Classic Maya ballgame images, it is necessary to narrow the scope of this discussion still further. The complex ceramic paintings and stone reliefs discussed here represent the second in a three-stage sequence of Maya ballgame imagery, preceded and succeeded by images which are far more limited in format, detail, and areal extent. These two simpler approaches will be briefly described in order to set off both the form and the context of the main body of artworks under analysis.

Ballgame imagery first appears in Maya art on cylinder tripod vessels of the early Middle Classic period (ca. A.D. 400–500) in the Petén. Players in the hip-shot posture are shown semi-reclining, with one arm thrust upward (Schele and Miller 1986:Pl. 97). The ball is usually decorated with feathers, and occasionally with other ornaments, giving the impression that it is also an object of veneration. Outside the Maya area, this early Maya format appears in the murals of Tepantitla at Teotihuacán (Pasztory 1976:Fig. 38), and it may be related to ballgame representations on contemporary cylinder tripods of the Escuintla region (Hellmuth 1978:Fig. 9).[9]

In the final development of Classic Maya ballgame imagery, the usual player is replaced by the image of a ruler wearing a reduced yoke or torso protection and a large knee pad. In this Terminal Classic approach, virtually limited to the Pasión region, the hip-shot posture is entirely absent. Rulers are shown with one heel raised and both hands pointing in the same direction, a standard posture both for ball players and dancers. The representation of two royal figures flanking the ball on the Cancuen altar (9.18.5.0.0 or A.D. 795)[10] precedes a brief fashion for depicting these rulers separated onto a pair of stelae or wall panels that flank a stairway, as at La Amelia. The paired relief panels at Seibal (9.18.10.0.0 or A.D. 800) and Itzan (undated) both flank the stairway of the eastern, three-part structure (Willey et al. 1975:Fig. 2; Tourtellot et al. 1978:244–247) in a modified Group E Imitation Assemblage, an appropriate setting for their function as period-ending monuments (Cohodas 1980:214).

In contrast, Lowland Maya ballgame images of the intervening second stage are widely distributed, occur in a variety of media, and are far more complex in symbolism. Ball players appear in terracotta figurines from Alta Verapaz to Jaina, and on painted or carved vases in both southern and northern Lowlands as well. In stone sculpture, ballgame scenes occur primarily on altars, ballcourt markers, and stairways, from Copán to Ichmul (near Chichén Itzá). Although the second stage may begin slightly before A.D. 600, if the date on the Chinkultic/La Esperanza sculpture is contemporary, the climax is reached in the half century between A.D. 710 and 760. During this time, several hierarchic ensembles of three ballgame sculptures were dedicated, including the sets of three markers at Copán (possibly 9.14.0.0.0 or A.D. 711) and Lubaantún (undated), and the stairway panels of El Perú/Site Q (possibly 9.15.5.0.0 or A.D. 736)[11] and Yaxchilán (9.16.6.0.0 or A.D. 757).

In the complex narratives of the second stage (Figure 14.1), two or more players flank the ball, which may be inscribed with a glyphic compound. The setting is indicated by a stepped platform shown clearly in profile or suggested by horizontal lines. In addition to the exaggerated hip protection and knee pad, players also wear elaborate animal or deity headdresses, or

Figure 14.3. Drawing of relief on central marker at Ballcourt II-B, Copán, 74-cm diameter. Instituto Hondureño de Antropología e Historia, Tegucigalpa. Drawing by Barbara Fash (Schele and Miller 1986:Pl. 102a; reprinted with permission of artist).

simple "bowler" hats of plaited fibers. When erect, players appear in the "dancing" posture with one heel raised and both arms pointing in the same direction, while players posing for the hip shot are depicted in a dramatic square-legged posture that is diagnostic for this stage.

Despite the naturalistic style, sculptures of this second stage depict a game that is more symbolic than real. The players' hip protection, like the ball itself, is exaggerated in size to emphasize its importance. In some reliefs (Figures 14.3 and 14.4), a player wearing the coastal Lowland yoke-and-hacha complex opposes one in Maya costume, providing an ethnic contrast that would jeopardize the skill of ball players if it were put into practice. The stepped platform, nearly ubiquitous in second-stage scenes, does not reflect either ballcourt architecture or the constructions that adjoin Maya ballcourts.[12] Tenoned heads recovered from courts in the Copán and Quiriguá region (Stromsvik 1952) do not show damage expected from actual use as goals. The markers in the court floor do show wear, but this could be from ritual activity rather than the game, since the carvings would pose an obstacle to running players. Finally, masonry ballcourts at most southern Maya sites

Figure 14.4. Drawing of ball-player triad from El Perú/Site Q, 43.2 cm long.
Figural portions of reliefs average 30 cm high. Top panel: drawing by Linda Schele
(Schele and Miller 1986:Pl. 101a and Fig. VI-12; reprinted with permission of
Kimbell Art Museum). Central panel: Art Institute of Chicago. Bottom panel:
reconstructed and redrawn after Ian Graham by Marvin Cohodas.

are too small for a sporting team competition. This combination of oversize ball and costume with undersize court suggests two possible explanations: either the sculptures represent the symbolic importance of the ballgame ritual rather than its realistic action, or they realistically represent a symbolic game in which a few heavily costumed nobles took perfunctory shots at an oversize ball in a small exhibition court, perhaps reenacting a cosmogonic myth.

Elements of the Ballgame Scene

In order to begin understanding the symbolic value of this Lowland Maya ballgame image, the elements which make up the stage-two compositions will be discussed individually.

The Ball

Despite the variety of hieroglyphs or images inscribed on the ball, its meaning remains consistently associated with Gods N and L, two prominent versions of the elderly male deity. God N is identified by a netted headdress and conch shell or turtle carapace attribute. The deer appears most often as his animal counterpart. God L wears a flat headdress bordered with eagle feathers, often with an eagle perched on top.[13] His animal counterparts include a cigar-smoking insect and a rabbit. Both of these supernaturals represent the setting sun, at the end of his life cycle, descending into the Underworld to mate with the earth-moon goddess, whereupon he will die and be reborn. This sexual union appears in several Jaina figurines, where the aged male deity may wear the headdress of a deer, jaguar, or vulture, or he may appear in naturalistic rabbit form.[14] This interpretation of the ball as an image of the setting sun is consistent with analyses of coastal Lowland ballgame narratives.

The ball is most consistently associated with God L, primarily through the hieroglyphic compound inscribed on it, as will be shown below, but also through the image of his animal counterpart, the rabbit. Schele and Miller (1986:Pl. 103) illustrate a ceramic bottle in which the ball is actually shown as a rabbit. Although the authors relate this image to a specific event in the *Popol Vuh* in which a rabbit pretends to be the ball, it is likely that the Maya recognized a general similarity between the hopping rabbit and the bouncing ball. The naturalistic rabbit head also appears as a coastal Lowland-type hand protector in some Jaina figurines as well as the central marker at Copán (Figure 14.3). In the latter sculpture, the same player also wears an hacha in the form of God L's head, with a bird image occupying the cranium.

Examples in which the ball appears to represent God N are fewer and less standardized. On one painted ceramic, an additional figure in the hip-shot posture appears above the confronting players on the stepped platform next

Figure 14.5. Rubbing of disk or marker from La Esperanza/Chinkultic, 55-cm diameter. Museo Nacional de Antropología, México (Navarrete 1984:Fig. 88).

to the ball, as if he were the supernatural counterpart of the ball. This player clutches a large conch shell, identifying him as an impersonator of God N (see Figure 14.10).

The head of God N may be inscribed on the ball from the Chinkultic/La Esperanza sculpture (Figure 14.5). The adjoining player wears a shell diadem which may designate him as the impersonator of the Shark God (GI of the Palenque Triad, and also the ancestor of the codical God B or Chaac). On the painted ceramics this sacrificial deity is sometimes shown destroying God N. While God N represents the aged and setting sun, the Shark God (GI) personifies the destructive and devouring potential of the watery underworld and its visible surface, the ocean, by combining attributes of marine predators such as the shark, stingray, and angler fish. The opposition of ball and player as setting sun and devouring ocean would then express the general relationship of victim to sacrificer. The hieroglyphic text on this circular sculpture may underline the dualistic opposition between ball and player as victim and sacrificer. Only two glyphs follow the date, constituting a verb that duplicates the dedication phrase from Primary Standard texts on painted ceramics but is here written as simple portraits of the Shark God (GI) and God N.[15]

The image of the ball as the sacrificed and setting sun is also apparent from the only major example in which associations with the old gods are absent: the central triad of ballgame reliefs from the steps of Yaxchilán Structure 33 (Figure 14.6). The bound prisoner destined for sacrifice may be derived from sacrificial altars at Tikal (Schele and Miller 1986:249), but its vertical descending position on the ball also recalls an acrobatic posture frequent in funerary arts, used to show the sun as a jaguar or human descending in flames.

The Ball Compounds

On sculptures carved after the Chinkultic/La Esperanza stone and the Copán markers, a standard compound appears that may name God L. The compound always consists of the same three components. The first component is a numerical prefix, which is generally nine throughout the Maya area. Exceptions occur primarily in the late stage-two sculptural ensembles at Yaxchilán and El Perú, where 12, 13, and 14 also occur. The second component is a superfix, almost always shown as T23, read *na*. The only exceptions are a bird image seen on a Chochola ceramic (Tate 1985:Fig. 12), an eagle feather on a ceramic from Codex Site A (Figure 14.1), and an eroded form similar to the eagles cere decoration on Step XIII of Yaxchilán Structure 33. The third component is the main sign, a variant of the *imix* glyph or T501, often personified. This versatile sign is usually read phonetically as *ba*, *b(a)*, or *naab*.

Various unsatisfactory interpretations have been proposed for this ball compound. The phonetic superfix and main sign have been read together as *naab* (na:b(a)), meaning water lily or standing bodies of water, but without relationship to the ballgame context. The numerical prefix has been interpreted separately as a possible score, or as the number of sacrificial victims at stake in the game (Schele and Miller 1986:252), but the repetition of a few select numbers makes either interpretation untenable. As yet no interpretation accounts for both the phonetic and numerical elements of this compound.

Fortunately, there is one reading of the ball compound which incorporates both the numerical and phonetic components, makes sense within the ballgame context, is consistent with the imagery of God L and the rabbit, and is supported through hieroglyphic usage in other contexts. The clue to this reading comes from ceramic paintings in the codex style by the Metropolitan Master, who often created several versions of a single narrative scene to which he applied a consistent verbal expression (Cohodas 1989a). His narrative of a deity flanked by youthful "headband gods" or other attendants, all shown in half-figure, appears with a repeated verbal expression in which the main sign

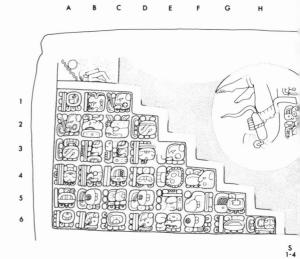

reveals a common substitution pattern of imix (T501), a snake head, and *quincunx* (T585). While this substitution pattern would normally indicate a reading of *be*, the Metropolitan Master indicates a different phonetic value by the inclusion of the suffix na (T23), a clarification that appears as well in the inscription of the same verb by another ceramic painter (Robiscek and Hales 1981:Catalog 186). The combination of snake head and na is invariably read as *chaan* (sky) or *chan* (snake), indicating by substitution that the same reading might apply to the equivalent imix (T501) and quincunx (T585) in the same context. In this light, the na element of the ball compound might also act as a phonetic complement to indicate a reading of the imix glyph as chaan.[16] Since the head of an eagle is a common substitute for the sky sign, the atypical bird and feather elements which replace na would act as semantic complements to indicate the same reading.

A reading of the phonetic portion of the ball compound as chaan would also facilitate explanation of the numerical prefix. God L, the deity most closely associated with the ball, is often named by compounds which include such prefixes. On the tablet of Palenque's Temple XIV, two portrait heads (A4-B4) of God L with long rabbit ears, which follow the glyph of the young moon goddess, are prefixed by the numbers 7 and 12, the latter found also on ball compounds. A closer parallel occurs in the headdress glyphs of three images of God L in which the sky sign is prefixed by the number 9 (Vase of the Seven Gods), 12 (Palenque Temple of Cross Jamb), or 13 (Vase with rabbit and God L), again typical of ball compounds. The headdress glyph and ball compounds are thus phonetically identical, and both appear to function as titles for God L.

*Figure 14.6. Drawing of central step (VII) from ballgame series on Yaxchilan
Structure 33, dedicated A.D. 757 (9.16.6.0.0), 1.65 m long. Drawing by Ian Graham
(Graham 1982[3]:160; reprinted with permission of Peabody Museum, Harvard
University).*

The reason for using two different compounds in these titles seems clear.
The headdress compound employs the sky glyph because it is associated with
the eagle counterpart of God L, which appears in his headdress. The ball
compound employs the imix glyph—which through phonetic similarity may
replace the T757 rodent sign—because the ball is associated with the rabbit
counterpart of God L.

Interpreting the ball compound as a title for God L and his rabbit counterpart, with a numerical prefix and phonetic elements read as chaan, would
make most sense of the information presently available. No other phonetic
reading for these elements has been suggested which may be associated with
either the ball or the game. Furthermore, there is much additional evidence
to interconnect the rabbit and God L with the ball compound.[17]

The Stepped Platform

The architectural setting featured in many of the stage two ballgame scenes
in the Lowland Maya region presents a different problem for analysis. Why
would the Maya reject the ballcourt image, common in coastal Lowland ballgame narratives as at El Tajín, in favor of a stepped platform? To explain this
conflict, Schele and Miller (1986:247–249) suggest that Lowland Maya
ballgame scenes illustrate a sacrificial event which takes place after the con-

Figure 14.7. Roll-out of painted Tepeu I funerary ceramic ballgame scene, 19.0 cm high. Pearlman Collection, Israel Museum (Coe 1982:Vessel 10; Justin Kerr photographic roll-out No. 1288).

clusion of the ballgame, when the victim is brought to a stepped platform, trussed up like the ball, and kicked around the steps. Their explanation is a literal interpretation of the scene on the central risers of Yaxchilán Structure 33 (Figure 14.6).

On the other hand, Maya artists may not have intended the stepped platform and the prisoner on the ball to be interpreted so literally. Stairways and stepped platforms are frequently associated with conquest and the sacrifice of prisoners of war, whether in narrative painting, as on the Bonampak murals, or in hieroglyphic writing. The Maya sometimes carved risers of actual stairways with hieroglyphic records of such conquests, both at the victorious and the defeated sites. An alternative explanation for the depiction of the victim in descending posture on the balls of the central Yaxchilán reliefs is that it might be designed to underline the parallel between the sacrifice of a prisoner of war and of a losing ball player, both of which would represent the descending sun.

This stepped platform is appropriate to both conquest and ballgame imagery in that it conveys the general meaning of the sun's sacrifice and descent through the earth's surface for entrance into the Underworld, analogous to

the architectural symbolism of the ballcourt itself. In the ballgame scene on a Tepeu I vase in the Pearlman collection (Figure 14.7), the stepped platform is decorated with cauac/witz markings, signifying stone and mountain as well as cave (Taylor 1979), a passageway into the Underworld. The opposed players are differentiated by red and black body paint.[18] In Late Postclassic art and thought, this juxtaposition of red and black represents the gateway in the western horizon through which the sun descends into the Underworld (Seler 1963 [II]:24). In the adjoining scene on this vase, the paired Headband Twins, similarly differentiated by red and black color, confront the aged God N (or D)[19] who sits atop a cauac monster head with gaping maw. Both scenes may represent descent through the symbolism of the surface of the earth at the western horizon (cauac monster; stepped platform), flanked by the red sky and black earth of sunset (Headband Twins; ball players.)[20]

The Ball Players

The opponents who meet in ballgame scenes do not possess a specific mythological identity. Various supernaturals or their impersonators may don protec-

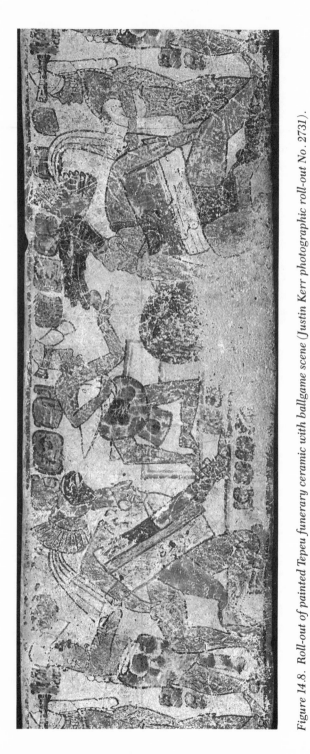

Figure 14.8. Roll-out of painted Tepeu funerary ceramic with ballgame scene (Justin Kerr photographic roll-out No. 2731).

tive costume and appear in the posture of a ball player. The wider symbolic function of these impersonators is indicated by their headdresses. On ceramics, most players wear the plaited bowler cap or deer headdress commonly worn by deer hunters. The functional equivalence of ballgame and deer hunting scenes suggested by this shared costume, and even by the blowing of a conch shell trumpet,[21] would explain why the ball was for a time associated with God N, and why the image of God N with a conch should appear as a ball player (Figure 14.8). Although a deer headdress usually indicates either a hunting or ballgame scene, it may also appear on warrior attendants in throne room scenes, and on the Jaina image of the Old God seducing the Young Goddess, both consistent with the symbolism of the sacrifice and descent of the sun.

As the ballgame is still in play, with winner and loser undecided, the confronting players are not differentiated in power or status. The two standing players painted red and black on the Pearlman vase show a clear equality, but this relationship is apparent even when one player is lowered in the hip-shot posture. Although animals of varying power may be chosen for their headdresses, there is no suggestion of dominance or submission. For example, neither the herbivorous deer nor the predatory eagle is consistently worn by players in either the hip-shot or standing ballgame posture. Neither are the players consistently differentiated from the ball on which they act, as both God N and God L may appear in the posture of a ball player (Tate 1985:Fig. 10). Similarly, in ceramic scenes of hunting, the hunters may wear the headdress of the deer as well as that of the predatory jaguar. As these animal headdresses do not serve to identify ball players as either victorious or defeated, they may not provide additional information, but simply elaborate on the general analogy of ballgame and hunting scenes to the descent and sacrifice of the sun.

Despite occasional parallels with the ball, the players generally function as paired opponents or sacrificers of the ball. Again, the Pearlman vase provides a useful example. The players of earth and sky who flank the cauac/witz platform representing the horizon are paralleled to a pair of sacrificial deities known as the Headband Twins, who confront the old god (Figure 14.7). As Schele and Miller (1986:51) note, the Headband Twins are the deities most closely connected with ballgame scenes, whether by juxtaposition or involvement. Another pair of sacrificial deities known as the Shark God (GI) and Jaguar God (GIII) appear among the players in the flanking panels of the El Perú triad (Figure 14.4). Although not players, a pair of dwarves is inserted into the ballgame scene on the central Step VII of Yaxchilán Structure 33. A dwarf and a hunchback usually attend a pair of dancing lords on a type of ceramic painting popular in the Naranjo-Holmul region (Reents 1985). The

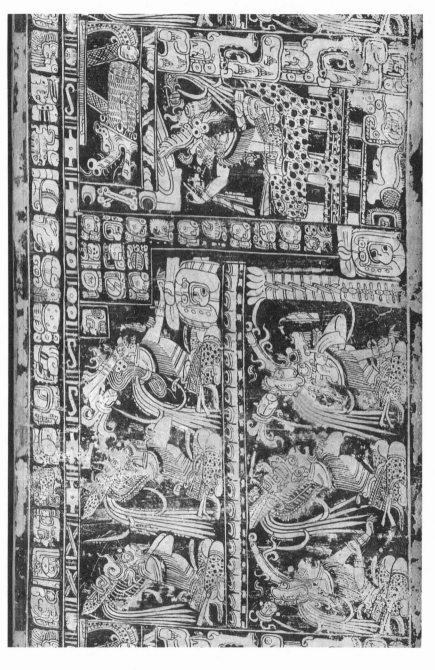

Figure 14.9. Vase of the Seven Gods, 27.5 cm high. Private collection (Coe 1973:109; Justin Kerr photographic roll-out No. 2796).

deformity of these individuals was probably interpreted as a shamanistic calling, whereby they could guide the soul of a deceased noble into the Underworld.[22] The Yaxchilán dwarves have Venus glyphs on their arms, recalling
the analogous role of the evening star which guides the sun into the Underworld. In contrast to the ball as the passive Gods L and N who personify the
setting sun, the pair of players thus takes on the active sacrificial role of earth
and sky which flank the sun as he descends through the horizon.

Context

Ballcourts and ballgame scenes do not compose a separate ritual complex in
Maya culture. Instead they constitute one motif within a broad ritual sphere
related to the sacrifice and descent of the sun. This broader context allows
ballgame imagery to be employed in period-ending monuments, such as Uxul
Altar 2, or on funerary ceramics, where it is combined with the analogous
imagery of deer hunting. Conversely, other images related to the mythology
of the setting sun may appear in the ballcourt setting, as in the Moon Goddess
and rabbit relief on the central marker of Tenam Rosario Court 2.

In Mesoamerica, the descent of the sun is the paradigm for the separation
phase that begins any transformational rite of passage, whether the funeral
that ends the life of a noble and begins his Underworld journey, or the bloodletting rituals used to end a temporal cycle so that a new cycle might begin.
As separation rituals involve the destruction of an old order or state of being
so that a new one may be created, images of destruction and disorder are
appropriate to this context. The ballgame is especially suited to the commemoration of separation rituals because its dramatic and dangerous action alone
suggests transformation and change, perhaps accounting for Lowland Maya
preference in showing the action of the game rather than the sacrifice at its
conclusion.

While ballgame scenes on funerary ceramics are most closely paralleled to
narratives of deer hunting or the confrontation of the aged deity, ballgame
scenes in monumental art share imagery and context with scenes of capture
and sacrifice. Stepped platforms and stairways used in ritual commemoration
and historical records of such military achievements also take on a major role
in ballgame imagery. The stepped platform is the standard setting shown on
stage two ballgame reliefs, which in fact came increasingly to be placed on
stairways—as at El Perú, Site Q, Yaxchilán, Dos Pilas, and probably Laguna
Perdida—rather than in ballcourts. This trend continued into the Terminal
Classic, as all three of the known stage three sculpture pairs were erected
flanking stairways. Similarly, ballcourts often functioned as the setting for
military imagery: prisoners decorate the courts at Cobá and Toniná, while the
marker of the Caracol court (Chase and Chase 1987:33) is inscribed with a

conquest record of the type usually appearing on stairways. As many Maya courts are too small for active team competition, they may have been constructed primarily as a symbolic setting for sacrifice, akin to the ballcourts in the Teocalli precinct of Tenochtitlán. The ballcourt and its stepped platform would thus function similarly as a symbolic setting, representing the earth's surface, for sacrificial rituals metaphorically related to the descent of the sun.

The Complex of Paired Sacrificer Imagery

The Maya appear to have elaborated ballgame images within a broader complex focusing on paired sacrificial deities, whether in figural or inscriptional form. These deity pairs may be introduced into various analogous scenes, including ballgame, throne room, hunting, canoeing, bloodletting, and sacrifice. Frequently two or more such scenes are juxtaposed, as in the Pearlman vase (Figure 14.7) and the Naj Tunich cave paintings (Stuart 1981:230–233). Alternately, a single scene or inscription may contain multiple elements of this iconographic complex, as in the paired stelae A and C at Quiriguá, the Vase of the Seven Gods (Figure 14.9), and the Tablet of Temple XIV at Palenque. The following discussion will serve to define the components of this paired sacrificer complex using these and other works of Maya art.

The Gods

Three deity pairs dominate the paired sacrificer complex in their frequency and standardization. Of these, the Headband Twins may be most important (Figure 14.10). These gods are identified by their youth and body markings. One twin has large black spots on his body. His portrait glyph reveals these to be snake spots, since it is characterized by chicchan markings at the temple, and is prefixed by the numeral one. The second twin has patches of jaguar skin on his body, and is represented by a portrait glyph with jaguar spots around the mouth, prefixed by the sign *yax*. Both are aspects of the God of the Number Nine, whose portrait glyph combines the snake markings at the temple, jaguar spots around the mouth, and yax prefix. The twin with snake spots is most important, often appearing alone, doubled, or with a generalized youthful deity, in both Classic art and the Postclassic codices. In addition to their ballgame association, these twins appear frequently as sacrificers, deer hunters, and bird hunters with blowguns.[23]

Coe (1973:13–14), who first identified the Headband Twins, associated them with the hero twins of the *Popol Vuh*, called Hunahpu and Xbalanke. This is a conclusion suggested not only by their blowgun hunting but also by the jaguar associations of the second twin's name (Jaguar Deer). While the similarity is undeniable, their roles and relationships changed dramatically

Figure 14.10. Codex-style plate with Young Lord and Headband Twins. Private collection (Robiscek and Hales 1981:Vessel 117; Justin Kerr photograph No. 1892).

between Classic and Postconquest times. In Classic funerary ceramics (Figure 14.10; Cohodas 1989a:221–224), the Headband Twins appear as adversaries to the deities named One Ahau and Seven Ahau, whereas in the *Popol Vuh*, these same deities are their fathers. This transformation makes it difficult to directly equate the Classic period ceramics with the *Popol Vuh*.

The Shark (GI) and Jaguar (GIII) Gods constitute a second deity pair most commonly juxtaposed on late Tzakol cache vessels apparently used for burial of sacrificial offerings.[24] They reappear in the Late Classic at the end of the inscription (D7-C8) on the Tablet of Palenque Temple XIV, the same text that featured the paired glyphs of God L.[25] This deity pair appears again as adversaries to God L on the Vase of the Seven Gods (Figure 14.9), where the Jaguar God leads the upper register with two blade-tongued gods as his attendants, while the Shark God occupies the center of the lower register flanked by paired attendants wearing skeletal headdresses.

The third pair, composed of the Old Jaguar God and Old Stingray God, is now frequently referred to as the Paddlers, as they transport their victim in a canoe on the Tikal bones and a vase in the Castillo collection. As Schele and Miller (1986:52) have shown, the Paddler Gods are closely associated with bloodletting rituals performed by the ruler at period endings, an equivalent sacrificial function. The pair may be noted in inscriptions by their portrait glyphs or by the signs *kin* and *akbal* in a special cartouche. The kin sign— meaning sun, light, and day—is associated with the Old Stingray God who shares the combination of aged face and solar squinting pupil with God D. The akbal sign—meaning earth, darkness, and night—represents the Old Jaguar God. The cartouche suggests the shape of a quatrefoil, a symbol of the sun's passage through the quadripartite surface of the earth.

These three deity pairs, as well as others less frequently shown, appear designed to represent the same opposition of earth and sky which structures the bench reliefs at Chichén Itzá and the ballgame scene on the Pearlman vase. The kin and akbal glyphs of the Paddler Gods suggest not only light or day sun versus dark or night sun but also sky versus earth. On Tikal stela 31—perhaps their earliest appearance in Maya art—their portrait glyphs (A15-B15) actually follow personifications of earth and sky (A14-B14).[26] Similarly, on the Vase of the Seven Gods (Figure 14.9), where the two-register format immediately suggests this cosmographic opposition, the names of the first two deities recorded in the secondary text are again earth and sky (Q3-R2). This opposition is also given cosmogonic context by the 4 *ahau* 8 Cumku date which begins the secondary inscription (P1-Q1) denoting the destruction of the previous cycle of 13 baktuns which allowed the creation of the present era.

The Headband Twins carry similar dualistic associations. While the jaguar is generally associated with the earth, Underworld, and night, the snake may function as a symbol of the sky, largely due to the related words for snake (chan) and sky (chaan). This earth–sky opposition is clarified on several examples of the Naranjo-Holmul dancer vase in which the associated animals, jaguar and snake, appear in the backracks of the young lords, and are named in the accompanying glyphs as "6 jaguar (*ix*)" and "6 sky (chaan)." Furthermore, the consistency of this opposition of earth and sky would explain why one member of each of these three sacrificial pairs is associated with the jaguar, a concept still retained in the *Popol Vuh* despite the alteration of roles.

To represent the sacrifice of the sun at the hands of these paired deities, Maya ceramic painters often depicted the twins confronting the elderly Gods N or D, or hunting their animal counterparts, the deer and bird.[27] God L is

Figure 14.11. Drawing of central marker from Toniná ballcourt. Monument 69, 70-cm diameter (Becquelin and Baudez 1979–82[3]:Fig. 141). Dedicated A.D. 775 (9.17.5.0.0), Chiapas Museum of Tuxtla Gutierrez.

less commonly shown as a victim of paired deities (the Vase of the Seven Gods is an exception), since he represents the descending sun by mating with the young goddess. A young lord also represents the setting sun, as in the Naranjo-Holmul dancer vases where he is attended by the dwarf-psychopomps, or the canoeing scenes in which he is transported by the Paddler Gods, or the seduction scenes in which his paired opponents are a pair of beautiful naked women. In Codex Style painting, the Metropolitan Master frequently depicted the Headband Twins confronting God N, holding a deer, and flanking or sacrificing the young lord (Figure 14.10). This painter clearly demonstrates the analogy among these scenes, and the equivalence of the old and young forms of the setting sun as victim, by freely interchanging the God N and One Ahau glyphs which name them—although he associates the Seven Ahau title more closely with the deer (Cohodas 1989a). The Metropolitan Master also appears to have used the title One Ahau for the victim in his rendition of a ballgame scene (Figure 14.1).

Number Symbolism

In Maya iconography, specific numbers may function as shorthand symbols for cosmographic relationships. Well-known examples include the number thirteen associated with the sky, the numbers seven, five, and four associated with the surface of the earth, and the number nine associated with the Underworld. However, within the context of the paired sacrificer complex, the number nine takes on a different meaning, expressing the relationship of the paired sacrificers of earth and sky to the setting sun. The God of the Number Nine is the clearest example, since his portrait combines the jaguar and serpent traits of the Headband Twins. In their major appearance in monumental inscriptions, these twins are actually associated with a 9 ahau date (Figure 14.11: J1-L1). Nine is also the general coefficient for the ball compound, and appears as well in the analogous "nine star earth" compound inscribed on a pair of bundles on the Vase of the Seven Gods. The star–earth compound not only represents an opposition of earth and sky, but it is also frequently employed in Maya writing to assert that a military raid has been planned for the capture of prisoners under the auspices of the evening star (Lounsbury 1982). In at least two major examples of this complex, the Vase of the Seven Gods and the Palenque Temple XIV Tablet (A9), the Shark God (GI) is named Bolon (Nine) Yocte.[28] The Bolon Yocte title reappears on Dresden 60a, with an analogous scene of youthful paired warriors who attack God N, while his deer counterpart cowers below.

The number six is also closely associated with the paired sacrificer theme. This number often appears in titles, as in the names Six Ahau and Six Jaguar (Ix) given to the Paddler Gods on the Tikal bones, or the names Six Sky and Six Jaguar (Ix) given to the snake and jaguar on the Naranjo-Holmul dancer vases. In ballgame contexts, the title Six Ahau appears above the player on a Chochola vase (Tate 1985:Fig. 12). On the central Copán marker, the portrait glyph of the Snake Spot Headband Twin appears to name the left player, while a Six Ahau title (possibly Wak Mitun Ahau, with the hand on jaw) names the right player. Finally, *wak ebnal* (Place of Six Stairs) appears below the ball-playing king on Seibal stela 5. Schele and Grube (1990:6) suggest that "*wac ebnal* could well be the sacred ballcourt where royal bloodletting takes place."

This number symbolism extends to six-part formulas, both in Lowland Maya elaborations of the paired sacrificer complex, and in coastal Lowland ballcourts. The best example of the latter category[29] is the Great Ballcourt at Chichén Itzá, in which six bench reliefs surround the central altar, carved in the shape of a ball passing through a ring (Mayer 1984:Pl. 126). On each of these bench reliefs, a team is composed of six players and a captain, while from the severed neck of the sacrificed loser sprout six serpents and a vine. A clear example in Lowland Maya art is the Vase of the Seven Gods, in which six deities confront God L.[30] All of these examples emphasize both the number seven, whose patron is the Jaguar God, and the number six, whose patron appears to be the Shark God (GI).[31] These two gods also constitute the sacrificial deity pair which forms the basis for the vase composition.

While the symbolism of the number seven, in relation to the passage of the sun through the horizon, derives from the penetration of the three-level *axis mundi* along which it travels through the quadripartite surface of the earth, the number six appears linguistically associated with the opposition of earth and sky. The word for six in Yucatec Maya (*wak*) also means to erect, set upright, or suspend vertically (Barrera Vasquez 1980:906–907). These connotations of a vertical axis reflect the underlying concept of the world axis that links earth and sky, the central theme of the paired sacrificer complex. As patron of the number six, the Shark God (GI) holds a special place in this iconographic complex. Thus his title (*bolon yocte*) directly follows the personifications of earth and sky which begin the series of six names on the Vase of Seven Gods (R4). Significantly, the event that begins this inscription takes place on the era date 4 ahau 8 Cumku, perhaps because the act of creation involves the vertical separation of earth and sky.

Time Cycles and Period Endings

Venus and its cycles constitute an important element in this complex. The star-earth compound noted for the bundles on the Vase of the Seven Gods also forms the verb on the Tikal bones, followed by glyphs of the Paddler Gods. Venus glyphs also appear on the dwarves of the central step from Yaxchilán Structure 33, emphasizing the importance of Venus as a psychopomp.

Several dates on this Yaxchilán inscription involve the Venus-solar cycle which equates five Venus periods to eight solar years. The historic ballgame event recorded in the right glyphic panel for the date 9.15.13.6.9 (M1-P2) begins an eight-year Venus-solar cycle whose completion is celebrated on the lintels of Structures 42 and 1, which with Structure 33 form a single triadic assemblage.[32] The date of this ballgame was contrived at a later time so that Bird Jaguar's inauguration (on 9.16.1.0.0) would fall 169 days (13 × 13) before the completion of this eight-year cycle. To place this span in cosmological context, the scribes recorded a distance number in the left hieroglyphic panel (D3-C5) which is 169 (13 × 13) eight-year cycles, plus 11 days.[33] Furthermore, the initial series date of the historic event is preceded by glyphs of eight additional time units higher than the baktun (I1-L2), each completed by the number 13. The choice of eight such completed periods refers to the larger Venus-solar cycle in which 13 eight-year cycles equal two calendar rounds.

The importance of Venus to this complex is easily understood. As an evening star, Venus could be considered responsible for the sacrifice and descent of the sun. Due to its manifestation as both morning and evening star, as well as its bondage with the sun, the Aztec considered Venus a god of twins. The Aztec Venus God was patron of the day wind, which in the Maya calendar is associated with the number six, and by extension the Shark God (GI), thus tying these two important elements into a single iconographic context.

Due to the importance of the number six, monuments which elaborate the paired sacrificer context are often associated with 6 ahau, including 6 ahau period endings (*hotun*, *lahuntun*, or *katun*), which can occur every 65 tuns. For example, the inscription on Copán stela 2 (D6-9B) cites the glyphs of the Paddler Gods in conjunction with the initial series date of 9.10.15.0.0 6 ahau 13 Mac. The Paddler Gods appear on Dos Pilas stela 25, dedicated to the katun ending 9.14.0.0.0 6 ahau 13 Muan, and again on Dos Pilas stela 8, in connection with an inauguration which occurred during the same katun 6 ahau.

Six ahau dates are also associated with ballgame imagery, often in conjunction with the Venus-solar cycle. The initial series on the Chinkultic/La Esperanza sculpture (9.7.17.12.14) is 186 days short of one Venus-solar cycle after the 6 ahau period ending on 9.7.10.0.0. In the inscription on Quiriguá Zoomorph M, a colossal version of the rabbit head seen as hand protector on the central Copán marker, the 6 ahau 18 Zac date is specified as occurring 3.2.0 since the katun ending of 9.15.0.0.0 (A1-B3). Unstated is the obvious information that this 6 ahau date is precisely one Venus-solar cycle (8.2.0) after the previous hotun ending of 9.14.15.0.0.

For nine consecutive 6 ahau period endings, comprising 585 tuns and encompassing most of the Classic period, the month coefficient was 13. The number 13 is associated not only with sacred completion, but also with vertical axes,[34] and thus complements the symbolism of the number six.[35] The significance of this numerical juxtaposition in 6 ahau period endings is underlined by two monument groups dedicated in 9.17.5.0.0 6 ahau 13 Kayab, the last period ending for over a thousand years in which this numerical configuration could occur. These are the Toniná ballcourt and the paired Quiriguá stelae A and C. Both configurations not only incorporate elements of the paired sacrificer context, but also place these in a unique transformational setting.

On the Toniná marker (Monument 69: see Figure 4.11), the 6 ahau 13 Kayab period ending is placed within a 260-day span designed to encompass a ritual transformation from the old time period to the new.[36] The nonhuman subject is clear from the name, Six Sky (E,O)—not a Toniná ruler but a concept typical of the paired sacrificer complex. As the first event is recorded as death (D),[37] the subsequent event at the completion of the 260-day cycle is probably rebirth (N). Although 260-day spans are typical of Toniná inscriptions, the scribes chose to place this example from the months Zac to Xul, consistent

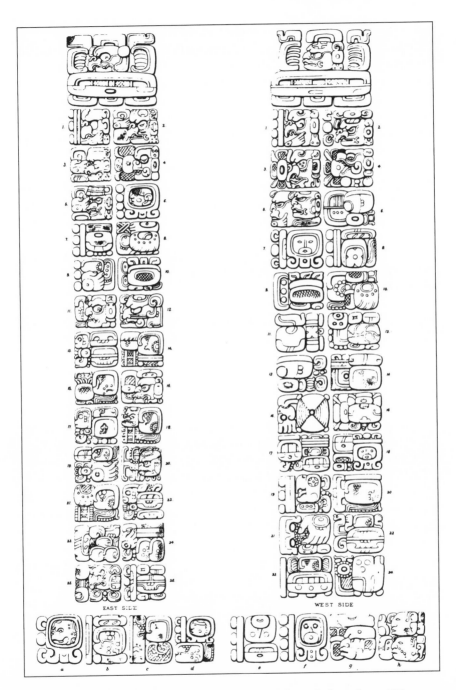

Figure 14.12. Drawing of inscription on Quiriguá stela C, dedicated A.D. 775 (9.17.5.0.0.) (Kubler 1974:Fig. 2, after Maudslay).

with evidence for an agricultural *tzolkin* and *haab* that were both fixed in relation to the solar year, and which operated simultaneously with the unfixed inscriptional calendars (Cohodas 1974).[38] In this way, the scribe drew a comparison between the long count transformation of the katun and the seasonal transformation of the sun and maize. The use of paired sacrificer imagery to engender temporal transformations is thus consistent both with the inscription on the central marker and the general dedication of the court to a 6 ahau period ending.

At Quiriguá, the simultaneous erection of two nearly identical stelae (A and C) immediately recalls the concept of pairing central to this iconographic complex. The dancing, destructive deities carved in low relief on the south side of each stela suggest the sacrificial pair of Shark and Jaguar Gods (GI and GIII). In the text on the east side of stela C (Figure 14.12), the Paddler Gods are mentioned as agents in the 4 ahau 8 Cumku event (A8-B8), and the passage ends with a reference to Six Sky (A15-B15). Similarly, on the Panel of the Cross (C9-C13) at Palenque, Six Sky may name the temple erected in the sky as part of the acts of creation (Schele in press).

The cosmological importance of the 6 ahau period ending is placed in dynastic context in the inscription on the west side of Quiriguá stela C, where rituals performed by the current ruler are compared to those performed by an earlier ruler, presumed to be the founder of the Quiriguá dynasty (Jones and Sharer 1986:29), in 9.1.0.0.0 6 ahau 13 Yaxkin. The third major deity pair, the Headband Twins, concludes the inscription at the base of stela C (L1), in combination with Venus and possibly lunar intervals,[39] and in association with a 9 ahau (J1) date. The paired stelae of Quiriguá thus illustrate the complex of paired sacrificer imagery in a most complete fashion, linking the 6 ahau period ending, symbolism of the number nine, and all three major pairs of sacrificial deities. The erection of paired stelae at Quiriguá and the Toniná ballcourt to commemorate the same 6 ahau period ending further demonstrates their parallel as expressions of a single symbolic complex.

Ethnicity and Archaism

The previous section treated those elements of ballgame ritual and symbolism which allowed it to be viewed by the Lowland Maya within a broader context of paired sacrificer imagery. The discussion will now consider elements which are more closely associated with the ballgame, and which therefore encouraged the selection of ballgame imagery from among other parallel themes for appropriate functions. Two specific features selected for this discussion share the quality of opposition: ethnicity represents a spatial opposition between local and foreign cultures, while archaism represents a temporal opposition between past and present.

The earliest Lowland Maya ballgame images suggest mediation between opposed ethnic and geographic entities. Ball (1983:133) suggests that the Petén cylinder tripods were developed for rituals sanctifying commercial ties between Teotihuacán and the Lowland Maya. The nature of this ritual may be indicated by the occasional citation of the last clause of the primary standard hieroglyphic text, which Stuart[40] (Schele in press) interprets as a reference to the vessel shape and its use in holding cacao drink. The ballgame, cacao, and perhaps even the cylinder tripod derive from the coastal Lowland region, as do the representations of interlaced scrolls and yokes that appear in connection with ballgame scenes. Perhaps coastal Lowland traders were responsible for mediating the ritual and economic interaction between Highland Mexico and the Lowland Maya during this early phase of the Middle Classic period.

Whereas the variety and complexity of ballgame images in the Late Classic obscure this underlying theme of mediating economic interaction, the Terminal Classic ball player images are once again virtually limited to a single format and concentrated in a small region distinguished by its importance in trading with non-Maya cultures. This depiction of rulers as ball players on paired stelae of the Pasión region appears earliest at Seibal, perhaps the most prosperous Terminal Classic polity and later the locus of an Itzá enclave from northern Yucatán.[41] Although these stelae lack suggestions of opposed ethnicity, they do coincide with a focus on long-distance trade, and they directly precede an intensive development of ethnic opposition in later Seibal sculpture.[42]

Commercial enterprise in Terminal Classic Pasión is also connected with the rise of Tula, as Toltec artists imitated Pasión sculpture on several occasions. Notably, these Highland artists produced versions of both the paired ball player panels (Tozzer 1957:Figs. 490, 491) and the earlier paired warrior stelae (Aguateca 2 and Dos Pilas 16) on which the later type was partly based. The revived importance of ballgame sculpture in Terminal Classic Pasión art may then relate to increasing commercial importance of this region linking cultures in the coastal Lowlands and Mexican Highlands.[43]

While the intervening Late Classic images lack this type of uniform association with long-distance trading foci, some are characterized by incorporation of coastal Lowland yoke-and-hacha–type torso protection. On the central Copán marker (Figure 14.3) as well as the central panel of the El Perú reliefs (Figure 14.4), a player wearing these foreign accoutrements confronts another wearing the Maya form of protection. Although the political or economic justifications for this ethnic contrast are not yet apparent, the greater emphasis on opposition than mediation is consistent with other aspects of Late Classic Maya ballgame imagery.

The player who wears a yoke and hacha on the El Perú panel also wears a specialized costume composed of Maya adaptations of Highland Mexican imagery, including the "Tlaloc," and "Teotihuacán serpent," as well as the sideways-skull chest pendant. The same Highland-affiliated costume, worn by Maya rulers as warriors conquering other Maya, appears on stelae at Piedras Negras and Naranjo, as well as on the paired stelae of Aguateca and Dos Pilas (Stone 1987). Together, these two images of the Dos Pilas ruler form a jaguar and eagle pair, which not only expresses the opposition of earth and sky, but also is characteristic of the Mexican warrior cult (Cohodas 1989b). The more equal opposition of Maya and Mexican ethnicity of the El Perú panel is more characteristic of Highland Mexican art and areas under its influence in the coastal Lowlands, as at Chichén Itzá.

While conditioned also by cultural and economic relationships and their symbolic expression, the overt symbolic function of this ethnic opposition is apparent from the bench reliefs of the Great Ballcourt at Chichén Itzá. In these, the opposition of Highland Mexican astral deities and Lowland Maya dynastic-fertility figures represents the mythic opposition of the Upperworld and Underworld as the forces of light and darkness. As sacrificers of the sky and earth, these Mexican and Maya players represent a Highland Mexican/coastal Lowland symbolic complex parallel to that of the paired sacrificers in Maya art (Cohodas 1989b). The artist who planned the El Perú relief and drew this parallel was not only responding to a fashion for Teotihuacán-derived costume then at its climax in the Petén, Pasión, and Usumacinta regions,[44] but was also elaborating on the underlying association of the ballgame with the articulation of cultural interchange.

In contrast to the ethnic opposition of Mexican and Maya, which was generally abandoned after A.D. 736,[45] the use of temporal opposition is retained through the span of the Late Classic ballgame image. All three major complexes of Late Classic ballgame sculpture, the Copán markers and the step reliefs of El Perú and Yaxchilán, feature an element of archaism in the central relief of a triad. Specifically, the right player with yoke and hacha on the central Copán marker appears in the half-kneeling posture of the preceding marker set, the right player on the central El Perú panel appears in the Early Classic semi-reclining version of the hip-shot posture,[46] and the central triad of ballgame steps at Yaxchilán is set off from the flanking ten panels by an anachronistic solid and static composition.

The text on the central step of the Yaxchilán complex suggests a rationale for this late example of archaism in a ballgame scene. As noted above, the ballgame ritual recorded for Bird Jaguar in 9.15.13.6.9 was contrived after his inauguration on the basis of appropriate calendric intervals. This ballgame ritual is one of several events invented to bolster Bird Jaguar's shaky genealogical claim to the throne (see also Bardsley 1987). This political manipulation is validated on the central step relief by the parallel with a series of supernatural ballgames occurring in the mythological era. The artist who planned this series of reliefs appears to have drawn on the appropriateness of the ballgame ritual—with its action, danger, and chance outcome—to illustrate primordial transformation, and thus to validate a rewriting of history. Nearly a millenium later, a Quiché Maya scribe used the same technique in compiling the *Popol Vuh*, inserting into the origin myth of the Quiché dynasty a separate and more widespread myth of the Hero Twins who play a ballgame with the lords of death. In the Yaxchilán relief, the archaic carving technique may be designed to enhance this sense of primordial transformation. Although there is as yet no evidence, it is possible that references to archaism on the Copán and El Perú reliefs likewise emphasize the transformational function of the ballgame in order to validate contemporary historical transformations.[47]

Summary and Conclusion

In contrast to the "Mexican" association of the ballgame with both the rising and setting sun, as on the ballcourt reliefs of El Tajín and Chichén Itzá and in the Codex Borgia, the primary association in Maya art is solely with the sacrifice and descent of the sun, as a paradigm for transformation. This association allowed the ballgame to be incorporated within a larger complex of Maya images characterized by paired deities who personify the earth and sky as sacrificers of the setting sun. As the ballgame motif represents only one of several available images in this context, its appearance is not specifically tied to ballcourt architecture. Whether in a ballcourt or on a stepped platform, the architectural setting of ballgame reliefs is designed for public viewing of dynastic rituals involving temporal renewal.

The manipulation of ballgame imagery to serve dynastic ends is characteristically Maya. Elsewhere in Mesoamerica, the game was a public ritual, tied to the seasons and to agricultural rejuvenation that was crucial to all levels of the population (Cohodas 1975, 1980, 1985; Scarborough this volume). The Maya adapted this ritual game by shifting the representation of ballgame imagery in sculpture away from the court setting to the triumphal stairways, by changing the ball player image from a deity to a ruler, by altering the ritual focus from seasonal to long count cycles, and perhaps by changing the event from ball player or prisoner sacrifice to royal bloodletting. The Maya also adapted the functional Mexican court to create a cosmographic setting for these dynastic rituals, moving the ballcourt to the plaza center or entrance, reducing its size, eliminating the end zones, lowering the playing wall while extending the bench, and adding a line of three sculptures on the court floor.

The use of ballgame imagery to serve other ritual ends also characterizes Highland Mexican art. Only in the coastal Lowlands, where it apparently originated in Preclassic times, does ballgame ritual function as an autonomous state cult (Pasztory 1972). At sites such as El Tajín, Bilbao, and Chichén Itzá, a significant proportion of architecture and relief sculpture is dedicated to ballgame imagery. In fact, Chichén Itzá is the *only* site in Mesoamerica that boasts a repeated association of ballgame imagery with ballcourts. Furthermore, Chichén Itzá exemplifies the traits of ethnicity and archaism which distinguish Lowland Maya ballgame images from other manifestations of the paired sacrificer complex, and may therefore be intrinsic to its meaning. Ethnic opposition achieves its grandest expression in the plan of central Chichén Itzá, where Mexicanized architecture in the North Terrace group contrasts with a more local Maya style in the Maya-Chichén group.[48] Temporal opposition of past and present is evident in the contrast of masonry technology between these two groups: whereas the Mexicanized structures feature the finest veneer masonry, the Maya structures were built in a cruder and outmoded masonry technique (Cohodas 1989a). As these structures were contemporaneous, the distinctions must be symbolic. The ethnic and temporal oppositions which animate several Lowland Maya ballgame reliefs may thus derive from coastal Lowland elaborations, as at Chichén Itzá.

Notes

1. The hypothesis that players hit the ball with elbows or knees no longer seems tenable.

2. See Parsons (1969:Pl. 52d) for El Baúl, and Bernal (1973) for Dainzú. The Lubaantún players appear in Joyce (1933:Pl. 7, 8). Examples occur in Jaina figurines and Tepeu painted ceramics as well.

3. Another composite "marker" has been found in coastal Veracruz (Robert Santley pers. comm. 1987).

4. Parsons' (1969) Middle Classic dating for the Chichén Itzá ballgame reliefs, accepted by Pasztory (1972:443), is also followed here.

5. This differentiation oversimplifies in order to highlight general trends. For example, two courts at El Tajín follow the coastal Lowland sculptural scheme but are not I shaped. Hybrid examples also occur in the Maya area. The Classic Maya courts at Copán also feature sets of six tenoned heads, while a line of three markers is introduced into the I-shaped Monjas ballcourt at Chichén Itzá. The synthesis is most astute at Toniná, where six sculptures of bound prisoners decorate the playing wall, but only the central marker of the triad is carved, in order to complete the set of seven sculptures.

6. Rings occur not only in northern Lowland courts, as at Uxmal, Chichén Itzá, and Cobá, but also in the Petén at Naranjo (Graham 1980 [2]:187).

7. The climax development is marked by the diffusion of an image in which the decapitated player spouts six serpents from his severed neck. The well-known example from Chichén Itzá bench reliefs is close to the fragment from Bilbao which Parsons (1969:Pl. 42c) incorrectly associated with the relief of a solar bird, mistaking the player's cape for a wing. Other examples are known from Aparicio and El Tajín (Kampen 1972:Fig. 19a) in Veracruz, and on the cylinder tripods of Escuintla (Hellmuth 1978:76–80). Although they share a geometric stylization of the serpent motif, they are probably contemporary with the Chichén Itzá and Bilbao examples.

8. The chant which Sahagún (1950–82 [3]:212–213) recorded for the Atamal-qualitztli festival associates the ballcourt with the mating of Pilzintecuhtli and Xochi-quetzal, an act analogous to the planting of the seeds which begins the fertility season, and supervised by the ball-playing Xólotl, the evening star. The opposing function of the ballcourt is recorded in a segment of the Aztec migration myth, in which Huit-zilopochtli decapitates his sister at the center of a ballcourt in order to end the rains and the season of fertility (Krickeberg 1966:220).

9. Those cylinder tripods in which players are represented in a pose similar to that of Early Classic Maya representations appear stylistically earlier, in shape and technique, to the ceramics that show the seventh century fashion for depicting six serpents spouting from the victim's severed neck.

10. Transitional stages leading to the development of this Terminal Classic type are known from the Usumacinta region in the late eighth century. The Yaxchilán ballgame steps of Structure 33, the final example of the major second-stage works, already show the figure in hip-shot posture to be a ruler first and a player second. The relief from ballcourt K-6 at Piedras Negras provides the confrontation between two standing ball players, an arrangement that would not be possible as long as the hip-shot posture was still in use.

11. As of this writing, the attribution of the looted "Site Q" reliefs to the site of El Perú is still under debate. Of the ballgame panels, one (Mayer 1978:Pl. 26) clearly does not belong with the others. The five stones that are related in style formed a three-panel group with the uncut Chicago panel (Schele and Miller 1986:Pl. 101) in the center. This center panel was flanked by the two-figure panel, which Schele (Schele and Miller 1986:Fig. VI 12) reconstructed from two fragments, and another panel which may be similarly reconstructed from the remaining two fragments (Mayer 1978:Pl. 27, 1980:Pl. 60). Although these ball player panels are not well dated, they may have formed part of a stairway ensemble with glyphic panels in the same style, and would then have been dedicated contemporaneously in 9.15.5.0.0.

12. The stepped platform at the north end of Copán's Court III was built after the image of the stepped platform in ballgame scenes had gone out of fashion. Also, the Copán markers, unlike most others, lacked this platform setting in the sculptural

scene. The Copán court supports the point that the stepped platform shown in ball-game scenes was symbolic, not real.

13. The bird and its feathers in God L's headdress have often been referred to as the Moan, a kind of owl; however, the large black area at the tip seems distinctive of eagle feathers. Apparently, recent scholars have confused the two elongated crest feathers of the Harpy Eagle, shown commonly in the art and glyphs, with the elongated feathers of the horned owl.

14. In the literature on Mesoamerican religion, the rabbit is often confused with the moon. Jaina figurines clearly show this animal to be male, as the seducer of a young goddess. Similarly, in the Codex Borgia the moon is shown as a water-filled vessel with the rabbit inside, suggesting a fetus within the womb. Apparently the sun could be shown as a rabbit both when he is old and mating with the goddess, and when he has been conceived again within her womb. Like the Jaguar and Eagle, the rabbit could represent both the setting sun and his sacrificer, and thus appears to steal God L's insignia when he appears with the Moon Goddess on several painted vases.

15. Selection of glyphs for both phonetic and symbolic value is characteristic of the Primary Standard texts (Cohodas 1989a:198–199). In these, the dedicatory phrase is often followed by a "completion of cycle" verb which would be appropriate in a funerary context where the interment of the deceased noble is likened to the descent of the aged sun into the Underworld. One wonders whether the composition of the hieroglyphic compound kan tun (precious stone) inscribed on the ball of the central marker from Copán (Figure 14.3) might also involve an indirect symbolic reference.

16. By comparison, the compound that is standard for bundles on both stone sculpture and painted ceramics is composed in identical fashion to the ball compound; again the superfix T25 (ca) functions as a phonetic complement for the main sign T507 (kan).

17. Variants of imix (T501) are not only associated with the rabbit through the phonetic value of *ba* but also through the prefix that identifies the portrait head of God L in the codices. Similarly, the sky sign is not only part of God L's headdress title, closely associated with his eagle counterpart, but is indirectly associated with the rabbit as well. Although the Maya do not designate the eighth day as rabbit, as did the Aztec, the god of the Number Twelve associated with that day is distinguished by the sky sign on his forehead. The number twelve, it will be recalled, appears in ball compounds at Yaxchilán and El Perú, and with the head of God L on the Palenque panel of Temple XIV.

18. In actual play, the two teams may have been differentiated by red and black body paint in order to represent the western horizon at sunset without involving deity impersonations that depend upon the outcome of the game.

19. God N has an entirely human face, with human eye, while God D is a more supernatural version with a large rectangular eye and the solar square-squinting pupil.

20. A third scene on this ceramic also appears analogous. The representation of a bird in a tree is a clear reminder of a common ceramic image in which one or both of the Headband Twins shoot the bird with a blowgun. In this image, the bird is equivalent to God N and the ball as the setting sun; the tree is equivalent to the cauac throne or stepped platform as the earth at horizon; and the Headband Twins again personify the earth and sky which flank the horizon.

21. In one unusual enema scene, the participants also wear deer headdresses. Since the enema ritual involves anal ingestion of a mind-altering substance—whether alcoholic or a tobacco infusion—it carries the symbolism of an entrance into the supernatural realm, the same general meaning as images like the ballgame and deer sacrifice which symbolize the descent of the sun into the Underworld.

22. A parallel function for these deformed figures appears in Aztec mythology, where they are specifically associated with Quetzalcóatl at the pass between the volcanos Popocatépetl and Iztaccíhuatl (Sahagún 1950–82 [3]:37). In this myth, Quetzalcóatl takes on the role of the sun entering the Underworld, and the pass represents the passage through the earth's surface.

23. The bird-hunting scene has been confused with another image of a bird in a tree which is its direct opposite (see Robiscek and Hales 1981:86). In Maya monumental art, the Principal Bird Deity sits atop a world tree which sprouts from the head of the Bicephalic Monster, all rebirth symbols (Cohodas 1982). In the funerary ceramics, a more naturalistic bird appears (with one exception [Robiscek and Hales 1981:No. 109]), and the tree grows from the head of the Pax God, a sacrificial deity with feline attributes. The hunting theme and Pax God both suggest death imagery.

24. The Shark and Jaguar Gods are now commonly referred to as God I and God III of the Palenque Triad, or simply GI and GIII. However, the Palenque Triad is a Late Classic phenomenon, first appearing on the steps of House C and in the tablets of the Temple of the Inscriptions (A.D. 683), then defining the layout of the Cross Group (A.D. 692); it remains characteristic only of this site. The Palenque Triad was developed by adding the Flare God (God K) to the older Shark and Jaguar God pair.

25. Schele and Miller (1986:273) are unable to translate either passage.

26. An intriguing aspect of this complex is the citation of several deities in a glyphic series. The Earth and Sky Lords begin a series of seven gods on Tikal stela 31, and six gods on the Vase of Seven Gods, while the Paddler Gods begin a series of five on Dos Pilas stela 8 as well as Ixlu Altar 1 (Mathews 1977). The three-deity list at Palenque which features the Shark (GI) and Jaguar (GIII) Gods may also be expanded to record seven deity names.

27. Some Tzakol phase stuccoed cylinder tripod vessels are painted with the design of fishing or composite birds with the head of God N on their bodies.

28. In the short inscription on this tablet, the number nine actually appears seven times: twice in the Bolon Yocte title, twice in a verbal expression, and as the tzolkin coefficient in three of the five calendar round dates.

29. Other examples include the Toniná court in which six prisoner sculptures surround the carved central marker, and the Tajín courts in which six wall reliefs surrounded a seventh set into the court floor (Wilkerson this volume).

30. The arrangement of the six deities in two groups of three also parallels the coastal Lowland-type ballcourt with three bench reliefs or tenoned sculptures on each side, or the victim on the Great Ballcourt benches with two sets of three snakes flanking the central vine.

31. The axe is diagnostic of both the Shark God (GI), who wields it, and the God of the Number Six, who wears it in his eye. The abstract variant of the number six is the Shark God's pectoral or belt ornament with its central knot.

32. Structures 1 and 42 are placed along a single straight line which passes through Structure 33, and they both face in toward it rather than toward the river. The lintels of Structures 1 and 42 actually record ceremonies held three and one days before the ending of this Venus-solar cycle, on 9.16.1.8.6 and 9.16.1.8.8.

33. The clause that follows this distance number (D3-H6) includes further elements of the paired sacrificer complex: the tzolkin date is 1 ahau, associated with Venus through time cycles and symbolism; nominatives in this clause include portrait glyphs of a youthful deity pair, as yet unidentified; and the distance number-introducing glyph which terminates the left panel includes the kin and akbal glyphs of the Paddler Gods. By comparison, the same variant of the distance number introducing glyph occurs on the Tablet of 96 Glyphs at Palenque, along with three other variants each involving dualistic oppositions, including the star-earth opposition noted on the Vase of the Seven Gods. The association of this Palenque tablet with the paired sacrificer complex is clear from the decoration of the flanking panels, with the pair of self-sacrificing nobles known as the scribe and orator.

34. Examples include the association of the number 13 with the eagle and the sky, and in Aztec art, the 13 pyramid steps on the Teocalli stone.

35. This emphasis on 6 ahau period endings may explain some anomalies in the inscription on the central Copán marker. First, instead of naming both Headband Twins, the scribe follows the name of the Snake Spot twin with that of a death god Six Ahau. Second, following the agency compound, the name of Lord 18 Rabbit is recorded as 13 Rabbit. On one level, the inscription may be approximately interpreted as "their prisoner (the ball or victim), Snake Spot Headband Twin and Six (Death) Ahau, under the auspices of 13 (18) Rabbit, King." On another level, the scribes may be indicating that the 6 ahau period ending (6 ahau 13 Muan: 9.14.0.0.0) was celebrated by 18 Rabbit through a ceremonial ballgame or ballcourt sacrifice.

36. The Toniná marker may incorporate elements from Tikal altar 5, dedicated on the previous 6 ahau period ending of 9.14.0.0.0, which combines images of paired sacrificers with an inscription involving a symbolic span of time: 28 tzolkin or 20 solar years minus one uinal.

37. Appropriate to the function of paired sacrificer imagery to destroy old time periods before the new one may be born, the representation of a royal figure on the marker is altered to express death symbolism. Both the loincloth and the ceremonial bar are changed from usual serpent and sun god imagery of rebirth to the representation of standard bloodletting costume ornaments.

38. Evidence from Landa, Duran, and the ethnographic Maya suggests a fixed tzolkin running from February to November, or from Zac to Xul if the months are preserved. This would explain the meaning of Xul as "end," and the subsequent month Yaxkin as "new sun." The beginning of a 260-day count specifically on 13 Zac each year would explain why the 13 Zac glyph appears for each 260-day cycle on Toniná monuments. Note that the scribes are recording the inscriptional calendar on this marker, and thus begin and end the 260-day cycle on 9 chicchan rather than 13 ahau.

39. In this basal inscription (E1-H1), the current 6 ahau period ending is connected to a calendar round date 148 days earlier. The eight-day interval (I1) that connects this calendar round to the 9 ahau event suggests Venus symbolism, since it both equals the period of inferior conjunction in which Venus is transformed from an evening to a morning star, and prefigures the eight-year Venus-solar cycle. Similarly, the 148-day interval is close to one-twentieth (146 days) of the Venus-solar eight-year cycle.

40. According to Stuart (Schele in press), the clause preceding this reference to shape and contents explains the technique of decorating, whether carving or painting.

41. The inclusion of Seibal within the Itzá sphere explains the later use of ballgame imagery on Itzimte stela 4 (von Euw 1977 [4]:13) in A.D. 879.

42. The quartet of stelae surrounding Seibal Structure A-III, dedicated at 10.1.0.0.0 or A.D. 849, involves two thematic pairs in which one member of each pair is given Mexican features (10, 11) while the other is Maya (8, 9). The cruder and later stelae erected in the context of the Itzá enclave are generally hybrids of Mexican and Maya symbolic ideas, although stela 17 may show a confrontation between ethnically opposed figures.

43. The eclectic sculpture of Seibal includes elements derived not only from Chichén Itzá but also from the Cotzumalhuapan style (Parsons 1969:185).

44. The major examples of this Teotihuacán costume in these regions occur within a single decade. They include Yaxchilán lintel 25 (9.14.15.0.0–9.15.0.0.0 or 726-731), Piedras Negras stelae 7,8,9 (9.14.10.0.0–9.15.5.0.0 or 721-736), and the Aguateca 2-Dos Pilas 16 pair (9.15.5.0.0 or 736). As explained previously (note 11), the El Perú panels may date contemporaneously (9.15.5.0.0). There are enough precise similarities both in costume and in the overlay of eagle and jaguar pairs on a Mexican–Maya opposition to suggest that the Cacaxtla Structure A murals date from about the same time.

45. The rejection of Highland Mexican costume elements in Maya art after A.D.

736 (9.15.5.0.0) may reflect the collapse of Teotihuacán, generally dated to the early or mid-eighth century.

46. As the older form of hip-shot posture appears to survive longer on the Yucatec slatewares, as at Chochola (Tate 1985), the artist may have also intended a further ethnic opposition.

47. The rewriting of history may be a more general function of the paired sacrificer complex. The early appearance of the Paddler Gods, along with personified forms of earth and sky and three additional deities in the inscription on Tikal stela 31, is associated with a similar form of propaganda. By beginning the inscription 130 tuns before the dedicatory date, Stormy Sky invokes supernatural authority for claiming legitimacy as a successor of Great Jaguar Paw. The paired warriors in Teotihuacán dress which flank Stormy Sky and occupy the sides of stela 31 also conform to tenets of the paired sacrificer complex.

48. The Mexican- and Maya-style structures at Chichén Itzá are now generally treated as contemporary both with each other and with Classic Puuc architecture. For a review of this chronological readjustment, see Lincoln (1986) and Cohodas (1989b).

CHAPTER 15

The Courts of Creation: Ballcourts, Ballgames, and Portals to the Maya Otherworld

Linda Schele and David A. Freidel

> And thus they honored him
> And left the heart of their father.
> "It will just be left at Dusty Court,
> And here you will be called upon
> In the future,"
> His sons then said to him.
> Then his heart was consoled.
> "First will one come to you,
> And first also will you be worshipped
> By the light born
> The light engendered."
>
> Edmonson 1971:143–144

The ballgame was a central focus of power and mystery to the pre-Columbian Lowland Maya. More than a game, it was a passionate play with intent to move the cycles of the natural and social worlds across the dangerous thresholds of oblivion (Cohodas 1975; Gillespie this volume). It was in the ballcourt of Xibalba, the Otherworld "Place of Fright," that the first twin brothers One Hunter/Hun Hunahpu and Seven Hunter/Vuqub Hunahpu were sacrificed and buried at Pucbal Chaah, "Place of the Ballgame Sacrifice."[1] The head of Hun Hunahpu was severed from his body before it was buried and hung on a tree that stood on the road next to the Place of the Ballgame Sacrifice (Tedlock 1985:113). It was this head which spat upon the hand of the X'kik to inseminate her with the Hero Twins, Hunter/Hunahpu and Jaguar Deer/Xbalanke. It was to this ballcourt that these offspring of the dead brothers ultimately returned to sacrifice each other and come back to

289

life, triumphing over the Lords of Death and establishing the cosmic relationship between eternally dead gods and regenerative human beings. It was to
this ballcourt that those human beings "of the light born, the light engen-
dered" would return, the Lords of the Maya. The ballgame was the pivot of
the cycle of creation (Tedlock 1985).

The *Popol Vuh* is a Highland Quiché Maya document, but it is surely a late
version of orthodox Lowland Maya theology of the Classic period and earlier
(Coe 1973, 1978; Tedlock 1985:63). The Classic Ancestral Hero Twins, Hun
Ahau/One Lord/Venus and Yax Balam/First Jaguar/Sun,[2] pervade the royal
pronouncements found on carved and painted monuments throughout the
Lowlands (Schele 1976:App. A). It is equally certain that the Classic Maya
played the game, that the Ancestral Heroes are implicated in ballgame ritual,
and that ballgame ritual had as its prime objective sacrifice and decapitation
(M. Miller 1986; Miller and Houston 1987; Schele and Miller 1986:Ch. VI). It
is our thesis that the ritual of ballgame sacrifice was a compelling illustration
of rebirth out of the wellspring of death—of kings, their communities, and
nature—in keeping with ballgame symbolism elsewhere in the Americas (Gillespie this volume). The masonry ballcourts found in the Maya area facilitated
the sport and no doubt served many ritual functions, but the high kings performed ballgame rituals on grand stairways. There these divine ahauob re-
created the Place of the Ballgame Sacrifice, which pierced through to its
analog in the Otherworld.

Ballgame Sacrifice

At the site of Yaxchilán in Chiapas, Mexico, an extraordinary Maya king
named Bird-Jaguar raised a building to celebrate the fifth-tun anniversary of
his accession to central power (Proskouriakoff 1964; Tate 1986). Prosaically
designated Structure 33, this building was a stage for the kinds of cosmic
rituals described above. As recently explained by Miller and Houston (1987;
see also Schele and Miller 1986:248–250; Schele and Freidel in press), the
elaborately carved blocks on the upper tread of the stairway fronting Structure 33 at Yaxchilán graphically display several key features of Maya ballgame
ritual and sacrifice (Graham 1982:Figs. 71–76; Cohodas this volume:Fig.
14.6).

The central step, number VII (Figure 14.6), shows king Bird-Jaguar kneeling in position to receive the ball as it bounds toward him. Several clues show
that this is royal theater and not a sporting event. First, Bird-Jaguar has put
the gear of the game, a heavy belt and knee pads, over elaborate costuming
not directly related to ball playing (including a massive back-rack with the
important fish-nibbling-waterlily motif). Second, the court, as observed by

Miller and Houston (1987), is actually a stairway rather than the expected sloped or vertical wall of a masonry ballcourt. Finally, the ball itself contains a bound victim whose contorted body is flying down to greet his doom at the hands of the king who awaits him (Schele and Miller 1986:251). The victim is the ball and the means of sacrifice is the Maya version of defenestration.

Bird-Jaguar's sacrifice in the guise of a ball player is part of a series of events confirming his accession as king of Yaxchilán, but it is also in commemoration of a series of events that took place at some time previously.[3] The inscription occurs on the lethal stairway to the viewer's left, and it relates three events that took place in a remote, but unspecified, time in the past. The historically present action portraying the king is inscribed on the right side and took place on 9.15.13.6.9 3 Muluc 17 Mac, which is written in the form of an elaborate Long Count[4] including the current positions of eight cycles above the baktun. The implication of this spectacular allusion to the great cycles is that the historical event is of a kind with many reverberations in the temporal cosmos. The distance numbers punctuating the events on the stairway inscription cover a period of at least 1468 years. Although we are not told how much time elapsed between the last of those events and the historical one on the right, they are undoubtedly mythical.

The last clause on the left informs us that these events happened in the portal to the Otherworld, in a location they called "the black hole" (Figure 15.1a) which Maya artists sometimes depicted as a Skeletal Maw. This location follows *uti* (or *ut-ix*), "it had happened." The location itself is written with the glyph for "black" and the sign used in the inscriptions and the codices to record "sink holes," "cenotes," and other types of penetrations into the earth. This is the exact location used to identify the Skeletal Maw of the Underworld on the Cosmic Plate (Schele and Miller 1986:310–311, Pl. 122). In this text, the "black hole" is followed by the number 6, the phonetic sign *nal* (which also occurs often with locational nouns), and the "shell-with-hand" zero sign. This glyph very likely specifies the location within the "black hole" where the action of the ballgame took place, which was no doubt on the other side of the Skeletal Maw.

On the panel that is set to the left of this main scene, Shield-Jaguar plays a game after his death. That location is also specified following an *uti*, "it occurred," glyph (Figure 15.1b). In that text, the location is written with the number five (pronounced *ho*), the "completion" hand, and either T74 or T140, both of which have the value *ma*. The affixes on the "completion" hand spell the word *hom*, which is glossed in Yucatec (Barrera Vasquez 1980:229) as "*zanja, sima, hoya*" or "*barranca oscura y hundimiento de tierra y cabo o quebrada que dejó algún aguaducho y caverno de tierra y atolladero*" (pit, chasm, abyss, hole, sink hole, cavern, etc.). This "abyss" is followed by *pitz ti*, "he played at ??? ballcourt."

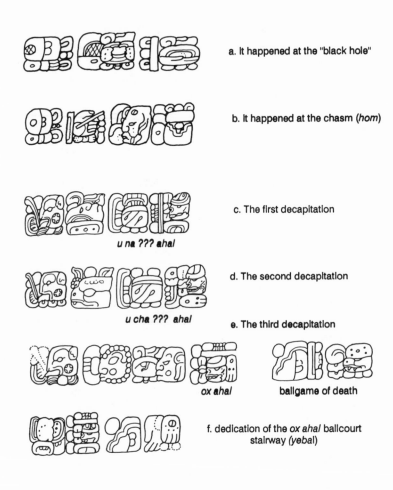

a. It happened at the "black hole"

b. It happened at the chasm (*hom*)

c. The first decapitation

u na ??? ahal

d. The second decapitation

u cha ??? ahal

e. The third decapitation

ox ahal   ballgame of death

f. dedication of the *ox ahal* ballcourt
   stairway (*yebal*)

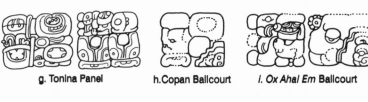

g. Tonina Panel   h. Copan Ballcourt   i. *Ox Ahal Em* Ballcourt

j. name of the Reviewing
Stand from Copan Templ e11

k. he played ball at *ox ahal em*

Figure 15.1. Maya glyphs.

The time frame and the location of the ballgame events from mythology and as played by dead ancestors, therefore, locate the site of play as down a deep abyss in the Otherworld of sacred experience and the afterlife. These scenes emphasize the importance of the mythos and the Otherworldly ballgame commemorated by Bird-Jaguar to his present world order.

The Ballgame Text

The primordial events are given in the glyphic passage inside the stairway court. We intend to explore this mythic text for clues to the meaning of the ritual action carried out by Bird-Jaguar as a ball player. These events are a threefold repetition of the same action (Figure 15.1c–e). In each repetition the passage beings with an "axe" event (T333.757:60 or 136[5]), which can refer to an astronomical event, to a war or battle related event, or to decapitation[6]. This decapitation action is precisely the mode of sacrifice recorded in the *Popol Vuh* myth discussed above. Most importantly it is the verb in pottery scenes such as on the famous Vase from Altar de Sacrificios (Schele 1988), where deities are shown cutting their own heads off with an axe. There is good reason to believe that this verb records, in fact, ritual sacrifice by decapitation.

In the first passage (Figure 15.1c), the subject is recorded as the head of a young male resting in what may well be a plate. Above his face is the sign Stuart (pers. comm. 1988) has identified as nal, which can mean "elote" and "mazorca" (ear of maize). We suggest that this image represents the ear of maize cut from the stalk as the sacrificed head of Hun Hunahpu. This exact scene is engraved on a lip-to-lip cache vessel (Schele and Miller 1986:195, 207). Taube (1985) has identified the Maize God of Classic period imagery as the prototype of Hun Hunahpu and Vuqub Hunahpu. We suggest this passage represents the decapitation sacrifice of the original set of twins.

The last part of this passage records an ordinal construction for "first" (*u na*) which is prefixed to a glyph meaning "successor," "replacement," or "node (as in a time)" (T1.4.676:140[7]). This is followed by a glyph consisting of T12 (*ah*), a knot prefixed to a skull sign (T60.1041), and T24 *li*.

In the second passage (Figure 15.1d), the "decapitation" verb is followed by the number one flanked on either side by a leaf. This odd suffix is over an animal head which appears to be a version of the Vision Serpent.[8] We have no suggestions about how this glyph relates to the *Popol Vuh* sacrifices, but it may perhaps refer to the death of the Hero Twins before their bones are thrown in the river. It is followed by "second" (*u cha*), the "successor" glyph, and the ah-knot-skull glyph described above.

In the third passage (Figure 15.1), "decapitation" is followed by Yax and a jeweled head, earth and an ahau head variant, which may read *Yax Xim Cab-*

nal Ahau.[9] This third passage also ends differently. The knot-skull glyph is preceded by a cardinal number, "three" (*ox*), rather than the ordinal forms used in the other passages. The entire sequence ends with the ballcourt verb suffixed with T12 ah and the "quincunx" death glyph (Lounsbury 1974), confirming that these are actions in a ballgame of death.

The text can be paraphrased in rough equivalents as follows:

> On 13 Manik 5 Pax, he was decapitated, the Young Maize Lord, the first successor, ah-knot-skull.
> 17 days, 0 months, 19 tuns, and 5 katuns later and then it came to pass 9 Kan 12 Xul.
> He was decapitated, Personage 2, the second successor, ah-knot-skull.
> 11 days, 14 months, 10 tuns, 8 katuns, and 3 baktuns later and then it happened 1 Ahau 13 Xul.
> He was decapitated, Yax Xim Cabnel Ahau, three ah-knot-skull.
> He played the ballgame of death (or the dead one.)
> It had come to pass at the Black Hole, Six ???? place.
> It changed as from day to night . . . (left side to right side inscription) . . . to the day
> 13.13.13.13.13.13.13.13.9.15.13.6.9 3 Muluc 17 Mac.

Although the three mythical events are separated by time from each other, they certainly constitute a ritual totality in the deep past. The event being carried out by Bird-Jaguar is a specific commemoration, and perhaps a reenactment, of these events announced on the stairs. Furthermore, three different entities or events take on the "ah-knot-skull" quality successively through their enactment of the "decapitation" ritual.

Time moves to a historical framework on the right side of the scene. Following the fancy Long Count date, the passage begins with a verbal glyph (Figure 15.1f) that we believe refers to a dedication. It is immediately followed by three-ah-knot-skull glyph, a sign for the ballcourt, and a glyph David Stuart (pers. comm. 1989) has successfully read as *yebal*, "the stairway of." The historical event is the dedication or use of a structure called "three-ah-knot-skull ballcourt," which is identified as a stairway. This association of a stairway with ballcourts is not just one found in Maya imagery (Miller and Houston 1987), but it is one confirmed at Copán. The inscription on the Reviewing Stand on the south side of Temple 11 calls it a ballcourt (Figure 15.1j), even though it is technically a hieroglyphic stair (Schele 1987a).

As Bird-Jaguar conducts the ritual at Yaxchilán that dedicates the Ballcourt-stairway, he materializes a Vision Serpent[10], perhaps through his own bloodletting or just as likely by means of the decapitation sacrifice of an important captive. Presumably this action is the one shown in the scene (Figure 14.6). Its function is both to dedicate the stairway and to recreate the "three-ah-knot-skull" quality recorded in the three mythological actions. The question is, what is the knot-skull glyph and how does it bridge the mythological and historical ballgame rituals?

The Knot-Skull Glyph

The knot-skull glyph in the text of this ballgame scene occurs in several contexts in the corpus of Maya glyphs. From the study of all these contexts, it is evident that the combined signs record a syllabic value of h + some vowel. This value can be specifically determined in two places: in substitutions in the *nahal* glyph of the Primary Standard Sequence (Grube in press) and in a passage from the middle panel of the Temple of the Inscriptions at Palenque. In the context of the Primary Standard Sequence (Figure 15.2a, b), nahal is a glyph that frequently follows the *tz'ib* "write" glyph. Normally composed of T23 *na* or one of its substitutions, T181 (or T683) *ha* and T178 *la*, nahal is most

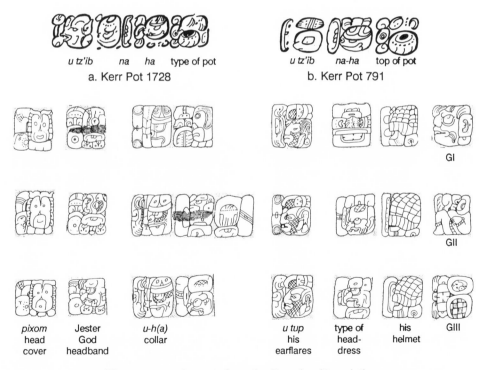

    u tz'ib   *na*   *ha*   type of pot   *u tz'ib*   *na-ha*   top of pot

          a. Kerr Pot 1728   **b. Kerr Pot 791**

GI

GII

GIII

| *pixom* head cover | Jester God headband | *u-h(a)* collar | *u tup* his earflares | type of head-dress | his helmet | |

c. The costume elements from the Temple of Inscriptions

Figure 15.2. Maya glyphs.

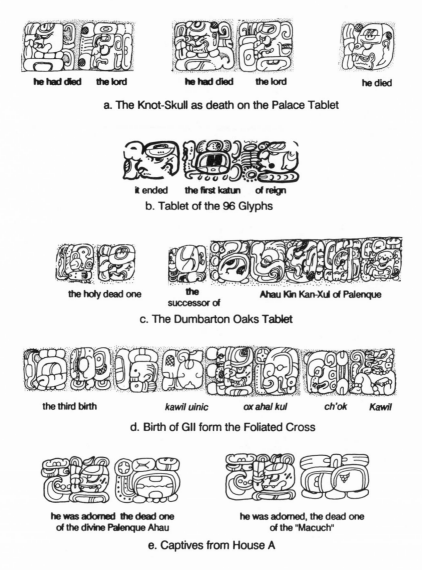

a. The Knot-Skull as death on the Palace Tablet

he had died   the lord

he had died   the lord

he died

it ended   the first katun   of reign

b. Tablet of the 96 Glyphs

the holy dead one   the successor of   Ahau Kin Kan-Xul of Palenque

c. The Dumbarton Oaks Tablet

the third birth   *kawil uinic*   *ox ahal kul*   *ch'ok*   *Kawil*

d. Birth of GII form the Foliated Cross

he was adorned the dead one
of the divine Palenque Ahau

he was adorned, the dead one
of the "Macuch"

e. Captives from House A

Figure 15.3. Maya glyphs.

likely some kind of verbal derivation (Krochock in press). In at least two examples, the knot-skull glyph replaces T181 *ha* in this context, thus providing evidence of its substitutability with an *h* + v syllable.[11]

The Temple of the Inscriptions context involves a series of phrases associated with the Palenque Triad as first noted by Heinrich Berlin (1963). Martha Macri (n.d.) provided the catalyst idea to understand what the phrases are doing. These repeated phrases occur with the katun endings 9.11 and 9.12 as lists of costume elements, either dedicated during the period ending rites or worn by the king. In the 9.12 passages (Figure 15.2c), these costume elements include a head wrap Macri identified as the word *pixom*[12], a Jester God headband, a set of earflares, a helmet specific to one of the gods of the Palenque Triad, and finally an object spelled with a sign recording the sound *u* and the knot-skull. If the knot-skull has the value *hv*, this collocation spells *uh*, the word for necklace or collar. Since this interpretation is in keeping with the other objects, we take it to confirm the *hv* value.

The knot-skull glyph occurs as a verb on the Palace Tablet at Palenque (Schele 1979) where it describes the posthumous state of the great kings Pacal and Chan-Bahlum either at or after their deaths (Figure 15.3a). On the Tablet of the 96 Glyphs from Palenque (Figure 15.3b), it is used to record the end of the first katun of reign in Bahlum-Kuk's reign (Lounsbury 1985:50). On the Dumbarton Oaks Tablet from Palenque (Figure 15.3c), the knot-skull glyph follows *u k'ul* in a clause reading "it is the god (or holy thing) Knot-Skull."[13] In turn the next phrase reads "he is the replacement for Kan-Xul" in a context where the second son of Pacal is apparently named the "replacement" for an ancestral king of the same name, ninety-two tropical years after his death (Schele 1988:310).

These contexts describe the state of being dead and of being a dead ancestor. The Dumbarton Oaks Tablet furthermore alludes to substitution and succession through sacrifice. In the scene (Figure 15.4), king Kan-Xul of Palenque is shown dancing out of the Otherworld as Chac-Xib-Chac (Schele and Miller 1986:275) and avatar of Venus, the eldest of Ancestral Hero Twins. This god is the axe-wielding executioner usually shown threatening a jaguar baby avatar of GIII, the sun, second born of the Ancestral Hero Twins, as on the Metropolitan Vase (Schele and Miller 1986:Pl. 117). Chac-Xib-Chac is also portrayed as Eveningstar rising from the black waters of the Otherworld (Schele and Miller 1986:310–312, Pl. 122).

The Dumbarton Oaks Tablet was raised at Palenque following Kan-Xul's capture by the people of Toniná, a nearby Maya capital (Becquelin and Baudez 1982). The text records both the ritual in which Kan-Xul was designated the replacement of his ancestor and his own apotheosis after his death. The first ritual occurred when Kan-Xul was twelve years old while his father Pacal reigned. The action is described as the "housing" as *balbil-ahau* of Chac-Xib-Chac followed by the "going out of the mountain"[14] of the divinity knot-skull's (presumably here an allusion to the ancestral Kan-Xul) successor (or replacement) Kan-Xul. The apotheosis of king Kan-Xul is recorded with an undeciphered verb, but again the protagonist is named as Chac-Xib-Chac. The scene shows the second Kan-Xul dancing in exactly this role. Kan-Xul became the replacement of his dead ancestor in the dance of the Sacrificer, Chac-Xib-Chac, when he was a child and then danced out of the Otherworld after his his own death as the same god.

In most of these death contexts above, T679 *i* is infixed into the skull and T24 *li* is suffixed below. We propose that the *i* sign functions to specify *i* as the vowel, and this gives a phonetic reading of the word as *hil*, a term glossed in proto-Cholan (Kaufman and Norman 1984) as "to rest." Nikolai Grube (pers. comm. 1989) pointed out this meaning to us suggesting that it is an appropriate metaphor for the state of being dead and for dying. However, modern Chol (Aulie and Aulie 1978:65) has an even closer entry: *jilel* is listed as "terminarse" and *jilib* as "terminación." Here is the root phonetic term under review used directly as "to come to the end" or "to be terminated." Certainly this proposed decipherment is commensurate with the status of the immediate predecessors of king Kan-Xul, Pacal, and Chan-Bahlum on the Palace Tablet and of the ancestral Kan-Xul on the Dumbarton Oaks Tablet. It also confirms Lounsbury's interpretation of the final three glyphs of the Tablet of the 96 Glyphs as "the end of 1 katun of reign."

Another association of the knot-skull glyph with death and sacrifice is found on the northern and southern alfardas of the Eastern Court of the Palace at Palenque (Schele 1982:268). Here hieroglyphic statements decorate the loincloths of submissive figures on what Baudez and Mathews (1979) have argued are conquest slabs depicting sacrificial victims. Following dates (Figure 15.3e), there is a *nawah* verbal glyph (Schele 1984), meaning "to adorn"[15] as with clothing or paint (Bricker 1986:158), with clear iconographic evidence that the context is sacrificial ritual. The knot-skull glyphs on the loincloths immediately follow nawah (Figure 15.3e), but in these texts, the glyph is preceded by T126 *ya*. We take this sign to represent the possessive pronoun, giving *yahil*, "the terminated one of." In one text, the possessor is a divine Palenque Ahau and in the other it is the "macuch" title. Thus the captives are being adorned as the "terminated one of" the lords who captured them, very likely the king himself. To call sacrificial victims "terminated ones of" their captors seems an appropriate description.

The three-ah-knot-skull glyph shows up in one other important context at Palenque; it is part of the name phrase of GII, the third born god of the Palenque Triad (Figure 15.3d). The birth of this god is recorded in the first half of the Tablet of the Foliated Cross (Kelley 1965; Schele 1977). The text uses the T740 birth frog preceded by the ordinal construction *uy-ox-tal(a)*, "third," to mark the action as the third of the third birth in the mythological sequence. After the birth verb, the name begins with an undeciphered glyph and a phrase naming the god to be *k'awi winik* (a person of the quality k'awi). This title probably refers to *kawil*, which David Stuart (1987:15–16) has iden-

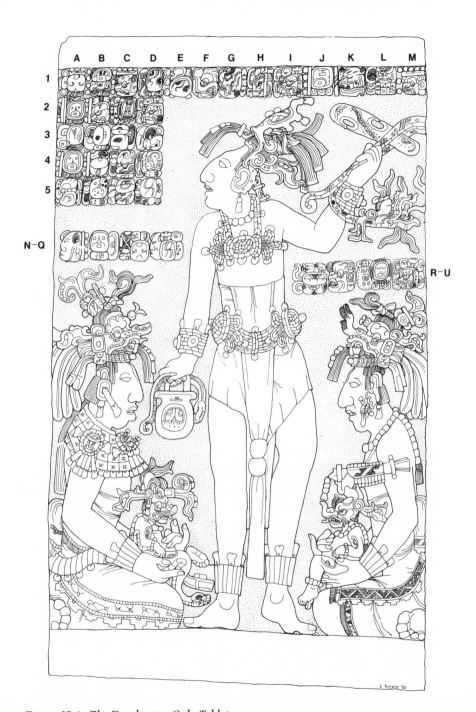

Figure 15.4. The Dumbarton Oaks Tablet.

tified as one of this god's names. This title is followed by "Three-Ah-Knot-Skull" and the God C glyph now known to record k'ul "divinity, holy thing." GII is then a "Three-Ah-Knot-Skull divinity." If we have correctly identified the *hv* phonetic value for knot-skull, then this title is (TIII.228:60.1041:24) *ox-aha-li*, to give *ox ahal* as the reading. GII is then as Ox Ahal K'ul, but what meaning does ahal have that is appropriate to this context and to the ballgame mythology at Yaxchilán?

Beyond the instance of Bird-Jaguar's stairway at Yaxchilán (Figure 14.6), the ox ahal glyph is associated elsewhere with ballgame ritual on grand stairways (Figure 15.1g–k). On the Naranjo Hieroglyphic Stairway (Figure 15.1g), *pitzah*, "he played ball" (Stuart 1987:24–25), is followed by ox ahal and a collocation including a uinal frog and the sign that has been read *mu*.[16] Nikolai Grube (pers. comm. 1989) has found good evidence that the uinal frog substitutes in phonetic contexts for signs with the value *e*. If this is the correct reading, then the collocation on the Naranjo Stair is pizah ox ahal em.

The Hieroglyphic Stairway at Copán, a monument recording the dynastic history of the kingdom in the context of war-related iconography (Fash 1988; Stuart and Schele 1986), Step 44 (Figure 15.1h, i) twice records the name of a ballcourt glyph. In the first example, it is called the "Copán Ballcourt," but in the second it has the same name as the Naranjo ballcourt, ox ahal em. This is surely the name of the great ballcourt which sits adjacent to this great Hieroglyphic Stair. Finally, a recently discovered panel stone from Toniná (Houston 1983) records the dedication of a ballcourt named the Ox Ahal Ballgame Edifice. The owner of the court then follows in the phrase "his ballcourt edifice, Ruler 3."

The knot-skull glyph is further associated with supernatural locations prominent in the Palenque inscriptions. To show this, we must return to the text recording GII's birth in the Tablet of the Foliated Cross. Recent work on toponyms by Stuart and Houston (n.d.) has identified a series of glyphs for geographical features and for locations within the larger polities. Among the toponyms they have identified are a series of supernatural locations that play an important part in the mythology recorded in the Temple of the Foliated Cross. The scene on the Tablet (Figure 15.5) shows objects or persons in three locations. First, Chan-Bahlum stands on corn plants sprouting from a cauac monster with a stepped-down fontanel that Stuart (1987:19) has shown is identified by the glyphs in its eyes as "Yax-Knot-Skull *witznal*" or "Yax Hal(i) Witznal" (Figure 15.5a). Second, Chan Bahlum's dead father Pacal is on the opposite side of the scene, standing on corn plants being drawn by a supernatural being into a shell identified glyphically as Kanab Matawil[17] (Stuart and Houston n.d.). This location (Figure 15.5b), presumably inside the shell, is the place where the mother of the gods resides, for in this text she is called a Kul

the mountain   the maize tree growing   the shell
                      from the Kan-Cross
                      Waterlily Monster

texts on the
locations

Yax Hal   Witz Nal   Kanab   Matawil
          a. Glyphs in the scene

it happened   Yax Hal Witz   Na Te Kan   "shell place"
at
          b. Locations where the mythological actions occurred

Lady "Beastie"   Kul Matawil Ahau
c. Name of the First Mother

Figure 15.5. The Tablet of the Foliated Cross with associated glyphs.

Matawil Ahau, "Holy Matawil Lord" (Figure 15.5c), a construction that parallels Emblem Glyph denotations of polity. All of her offspring, the three gods of the Palenque Triad, are also associated with *matawil*. Finally, the third location is the central tree, the Foliated Cross, which is called Na Te Kan, "First Precious (or Yellow) Tree."[18]

These same three locations appear in the passage that bridges from the mythological to the historical side of the Foliated Cross and locates where these actions occurred. It states: "Utiy ('it happened at') Yax-Hal Witznal, (at) Na Te Kanal, and at the shell place." The first location is a mountain from which sacred corn grows. The second is a World Tree in the guise of a maize tree emerging from the head of a Kan-cross Waterlily Monster. The third is a shell inside of which is the primordial sea and the place called matawil.

The Ox Ahal Glyph as the "Third Manifestation"

The question then remains how Ox Ahal and Yax Hal relate to all the different contexts described above. Nikolai Grube (pers. comm. 1989) provided us with the clue for understanding what is meant by this glyph. He noticed the pattern we have just described in his own studies and reconstructed the same ox ahal reading. He pointed out to us the entries in the Cordemex dictionary of the Yucatec language (Barrera Vasquez 1980:3) that make some sense of these glyphic contexts. *Ah* is entered as "crear, despertar (to create, to wake up)." *Ahahbil* is "cosa clara y manifiesta (a clear and manifested thing)" and *ahal* is glossed as "despertar, recordar (to wake up, to remember, to call up, to evoke.")￼ *Ahal kab* is "ser el mundo creado (to be created the world)" and *ahi kab* is "desde el principio del mundo (since the beginning of the world)." Ahal also has the general meaning of "amanecer (to dawn, to appear)."[19]

All these meanings are variants of the concept of creation and to become visible and known, as in "waking up, evoking memory," or as in the appearing of the sun at dawn. It is in this sense that the ahal glyph may operate in the text of the Yaxchilán ballcourt scene. The first clause refers to u na ahal, "the first creation" of the event. The second clause records u cha ahal, "the second creation," and the third replication of the "axe" event results in the subject ending with the glyph ox ahal, "three (third) creation." As a location, this would be the place where the ensuing ballgame is played in the "black hole."

A case can also be made for the Ox Ahal glyph as a title carried by gods and people incarnating gods. In the Quiché Maya of the *Popol Vuh* (Edmonson 1971:61–62; Schultze-Jena 1972:210), ahal means "maker" or "creator" and appears as part of the names of several Lords of Xibalba—Ahal Puh or Pus Maker, Ahal Q'ana or Bile Maker, Ahal Tokob or Wound Maker, and Ahal Mez or Filth Maker. Ox Ahal as a title might thus read "Three Maker." The

word ox has other meanings than the number "three,"[20] so the title may have
been used to imply more than one meaning. In the "maker" names given in
the Quiché Maya *Popol Vuh*, that thing which is made follows the ahal term.
Schultze-Jena (1972:210) specifies that the term can refer both to the creator
of a thing and to the thing created. In GII's title from the Foliated Cross, ox
ahal k'ul may refer to GII as a creator—"a maker of holiness"—as well as a
created thing—"third created god."

   The supernatural mountain near where GII was born, and on which Chan-
Bahlum stands, is called the Yax Hal Witznal. In Yucatec (Barrera Vasquez
1980:174) the principal meaning of *hal* is given as "verdad, cierto, verdadero,
legitimo, necesario," rendering yax hal "first truth, certainly, true, legitimate,
necessity." This gives the reading "the first true mountain place." Nal (T86) is
a sign that reads in last position, although it may be written over the main sign
(Stuart pers. comm. 1987). As a root, nal means "maize" both in Yucatec (Barrera Vasquez 1980:557) and in Chorti (Wisdom n.d.:538), where *nar* has the
meaning of "maize (especially ear maize and on the stalk), ripe maize, tortilla
made of ripe maize." This particular suffix appears in locational nouns with
high frequency so its function here may simply be to reinforce the function of
the Yax Hal Witz glyph as a name. It should be noted, however, that maize
foliation emerges from the Yax Hal mountain. On Bonampak Stela 1, the king
stands upon a basal panel displaying a *witz* mountain image such as the one
Chan Bahlum stands upon the Foliated Cross Tablet, but here the maize is
replaced by a Young Maize Lord (Taube 1985). This image is repeated on Temple 22 at Copán (Schele 1986), which had the same Young Maize Lords all
around the entablature. The corners of this temple are stacks of witz monsters.
It was a Witznal in the sense of being a mountain sustaining maize.

   The association of maize with the mountain and the identification of the
location as the "First True Mountain Place" may be even more direct. The
story of the Fourth Creation in the *Popol Vuh* follows the third creation era
apotheosis of the Hero Twins subsequent to their success in Xibalba. This
story opens with the discovery of the great cleft, a mountain split open to
reveal abundant food (Edmonson 1971:146–148). The first food mentioned is
corn, yellow (*q'ana/kan*) and white (*zaqi/zac*) ears (hal).[21] The mountain upon
which Chan-Bahlum stands is clearly clefted in the Temple of the Foliated
Cross and corn plants are growing from the cleft.

   Thus Yax Hal may refer both to "first true" and to the "first maize ears" from
which humanity was created. In the *Popol Vuh* myth of the Fourth Creation
(Edmonson 1971:146), the original human beings were "formed and shaped"
out of corn with water (the blood of humanity, perhaps the sacrifice of First
Mother given in the Foliated Cross text) at this mountain. At Palenque, the
great Foliated Cross image is marked kan, "yellow," and carries the God C

images denoting *k'u*, "divinity," on its trunk. The ears of corn are, in fact, human heads in the creation story. The "First True (maize) Mountain" was not only the place where the gods were born, but it was where humanity was created.

The Ballgame and Corn Plant Mountain

In light of the contextual distribution of the Ox Ahal glyph, we have reason to search for a connection between the ballgame of the Otherworld and the corn plant mountain discussed above. Mary Miller (1986:84–88) has already analyzed this connection profitably in the murals of Bonampak. There is a group of six masked performers involved in a dance ritual in the lower register of Room 1. The event celebrated in this lower register is a house dedication ritual, in fact of the building containing the murals.[22] Five of these performers are wearing grotesque masks with large waterlilies attached to them (Figure 15.6). One of the beings is clearly a crustacean, another is probably a crocodile. They are not recognizable variants of known deities, but rather appear to represent creatures of the earth and water. One of these creatures holds

The Young Lord

Figure 15.6. The Underworld Dancers from Bonampak Room 1.

out an ear of corn, still in its green leaf wrapping, over the head of the only member of the group that is not masked. This individual does wear a large headdress decorated with a waterlily. This seated young lord was identified by Miller as the personification of young green corn.

Mary Miller (1986) notes the connection between the grotesque masks of these performers and masks worn by four ball-playing lords (Figures 15.7 and 15.8) depicted on the steps flanking Bird-Jaguar in front of Structure 33 at Yaxchilán. Miller further notes that some of the masked performers in the Bonampak pageant wear heavy belts of the kind worn by the ball players at Yaxchilán. The Yaxchilán ball players wear waterlilies like the Bonampak figures. In light of the distinctiveness of the masks, the resemblance is clear and significant.

The Yaxchilán ball-playing lords are flanking Bird-Jaguar's central performance, which we know to be in an Ox Ahal ballcourt-stairway. The occasion was probably the dedication of that ballcourt. Bird-Jaguar is part of the same pageant as the flanking lords, for he is sporting a massive backrack with a huge fish nibbling a waterlily and has put on ball-playing gear over his other costuming (Figure 14.6). At Bonampak, then, we have a corn ritual, which is also a dedication ritual; this corresponds to the sacrificial ball playing Ox Ahal event at Yaxchilán. Mary Miller (1986) notes the supplicant seated position of the young lord in the Bonampak scene and suggests that he might also be a sacrificial victim. Dedication events are known to have been accompanied by sacrifices among the Maya as among other Mesoamericans.

In the case of the Yaxchilán scene, we know that we are dealing with an Otherworld performance, for two of the steps (II, III) show women bringing forth the Vision Serpent (Figure 15.7). Furthermore, the woman on the second step is Bird-Jaguar's grandmother, who is long dead. She rides the Vision Serpent out of the "black hole" at the beginning of the game. A second woman, who was surely Bird-Jaguar's mother, Lady Ik-Skull, rides a second Vision Serpent on Step III. We further suggest that it is Bird-Jaguar's wife, Lady Zero-Skull, who tosses the ball out for play on Step I. It is perhaps significant that God K is the deity who emerges from the serpents held by the ancestral women. He is GII of the Palenque Triad, who is the Ox Ahal Ku on the Tablet of the Foliated Cross.

The grotesque masks worn by the outer ball players on the left and right of the main scene at Bonampak Room 1 (Figure 15.6) suggest that these are humans, some of them important cahalob, who impersonate Otherworld beings as they play. These scenes too are performed in the Otherworld. The particular creatures identifiable—crocodile, crustacean, and fish—are those associated with water. The surface of the Otherworld, where it meets the world of the living, was termed *nab* by the Classic Maya, or "still water" of the kind that would be found in lakes and canals. Nab is also the word for

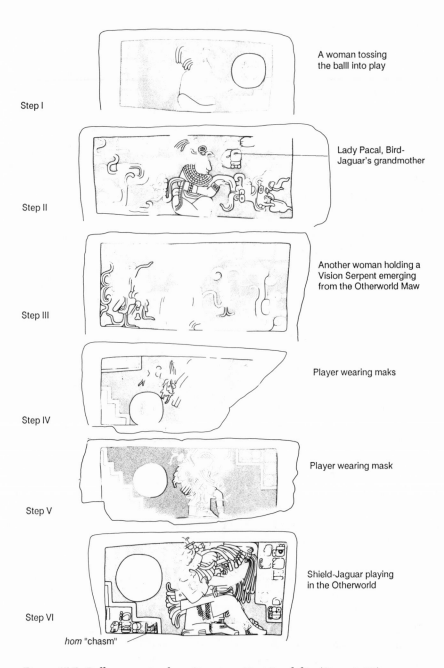

A woman tossing
the balll into play

Step I

Lady Pacal, Bird-
Jaguar's grandmother

Step II

Another woman holding a
Vision Serpent emerging
from the Otherworld Maw

Step III

Player wearing maks

Step IV

Player wearing mask

Step V

Shield-Jaguar playing
in the Otherworld

Step VI

hom "chasm"

Figure 15.7. Ballgame series from Structure 33 at Yaxchilán (Steps I–VI).

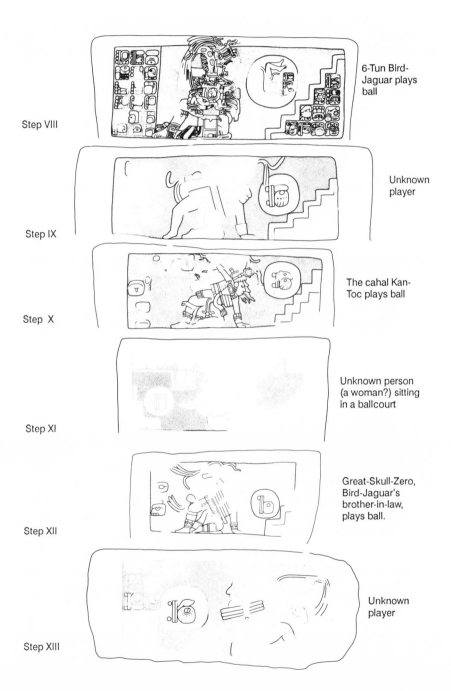

Step VIII — 6-Tun Bird-Jaguar plays ball

Step IX — Unknown player

Step X — The cahal Kan-Toc plays ball

Step XI — Unknown person (a woman?) sitting in a ballcourt

Step XII — Great-Skull-Zero, Bird-Jaguar's brother-in-law, plays ball.

Step XIII — Unknown player

Figure 15.8. Ballgame series from Structure 33 at Yaxchilán (Steps VIII–XIII).

waterlily (Schele 1988:301). The name of the cleft which held the corn in the *Popol Vuh* story of the Fourth Creation is Bitter Water (Edmonson 1971:146). As Karl Taube (1985:179) has pointed out, the famous paddler scenes on the carved bones from Tikal Burial 116 depict a maize god in a canoe on such still waters flanked by four supernatural beings. We suggest, then, that what the Bonampak and Yaxchilán scenes may share through the performers in grotesque masks is an allusion to that watery place in the heart of the mountain, a "black hole" surface of the Underworld, a portal to the Otherworld, where corn was first discovered and shaped into human beings and the place from which all agricultural abundance subsequently flows.

Yet if this cleft is the birthplace of humanity, it is also a place of the Dance of Death between Chac-Xib-Chac, Death Lords, and the Baby Jaguar on the painted vases of the Classic Maya. This is not only a death sacrifice scene, but also a rebirth scene (Robiscek and Hales 1988). We know from the *Popol Vuh* that the dance occurs in the ballcourt of Xibalba, but it is depicted as occurring on a clefted stone and earth marked head which is named witz, "mountain." Real masonry ballcourts are literally clefted mountains, so the analogy with the mythical clefted mountain is apparent. Grand stairways are more cliffs than clefts, and harken better to the path to Xibalba taken by the Ancestral Heroes in their journey to the ballcourt of the Lords of Death. Nevertheless, like the great cleft, the grand stairways are threshold places. The death and rebirth of the heroes following their ballgames in Xibalba are directly made analogous to the tasseling, withering, and tasseling again of a magical corn plant sustained by their grandmother in the center of the court above, *ox ahal*, thrice manifested. For human beings made of corn, the same cycle of birthing, dying and rebirthing is their lot and destiny.

There may be even more to the Ox Ahal ballcourts, for we must go back now to the name of the Naranjo and Copán Ballcourts. At Naranjo, we know that this ballgame was associated with a series of confrontations in which Naranjo lost a war with Caracol. The stairway recording the ballgame in question celebrated that victory and was very probably the site of exactly the kind of sacrifice shown in the Yaxchilán scene. We have no such direct evidence for the ballcourt at Copán and its adjacent hieroglyphic stairway, but all three sets of ballcourt markers that were mounted down its center alley show the confrontation of Hun Ahau with the Lord of Death. The markers from Courts IIa and IIb show the Lord of Death as the God of Zero. The markers of Court III are too badly eroded to make out the imagery, but it is still possible to confirm that the scenes in all three sets of ballcourt markers were surrounded by a quadrafoil shape. This shape is the cartouche in which the Classic Maya portrayed their ancestors, and it has an ancient history in Mesoamerica going back to the Olmec as the representation of the portal into the Otherworld.

The floor of the ballcourt at Copán was like a glass bottomed boat with windows that let one see into the watery Underworld.

The proper names of both the Naranjo and Copán courts were the Ox Ahal Em (Figure 15.1i, k). In Yucatec (Barrera Vasquez 1980:153), *emel* is "descender" and "bajarse." In proto-Cholan (Kaufman and Norman 1984:119) *ehm* is "go/come down." These two ballcourts are "thrice-made descents." And what were the three descents? We cannot know for sure without finding some written record of what they meant, but again the *Popol Vuh* gives a very good hint. The first descent was of Hun Hunahpu and Vuqub Hunahpu and in the Yaxchilán text the person named in the decapitation event is the severed head of the maize god. The second descent was of the Hero Twins, who were the offspring of the first twins and eventual victors over death. Who would fall in the third descent? There are two possibilities. At Yaxchilán, Bird-Jaguar's father plays a game in the hom (the chasm). On the other side of the Ox Ahal game, Bird-Jaguar's grandfather plays a game. The third descent may then be the soul of the king as the avatar of the Hero Twins. But it may also be the unfortunate character who tumbles down the stairway as the ball. The third descent may be the sending of the sacrificial victim to the Otherworld.

So what is the goal of ballgame sacrifice? It is the manifestation of death, the necessary prelude to life. It is the contesting of the Lords of Death in a lethal game in which the king, like the Ancestral Hero Twins, will truimph. The reward for the twins is apotheosis, celestial being; the reward for the king is to bring forth abundance and prosperity through the cleft, from the Land of Death, into his realm. Perhaps ox ahal is the ballcourt of the Third Creation in Xibalba, and, as the cleft, the portal to the Fourth Creation, the world of human beings. Perhaps it is a title meaning Three-Maker, the thrice manifested, the thrice created. GII is the third born of the Triad Gods. In the myth at Yaxchilán, it is the title taken by the one incarnated through the third sacrifice (as is the king, for indeed Bird-Jaguar's sacrifice is flanked by one of his father's and grandfather's at Yaxchilán who are carrying out the same ballgame ritual). At Copán and Naranjo, it was the "third manifestation of the fall or the descent" into the Otherworld to confront death. This, above all others, is the descent the king must make.

We suspect that both title and location are promising directions for further inquiry. Both lead down the Black Road, through the Cleft in the Milky Way (Tedlock 1985:38), from the ballcourts of the Maya to the Court of Creation in the Land of Death. For, in the last analysis, it is clear that the ballcourt, real or metaphorical, is a portal to the Otherworld.

The Classic Maya ballgame, played in elegant masonry courts or mimicked in lethal ritual on grand stairways, in all likelihood conveyed a heroic amplification of childhood games and communal sport played by people of modest

means on open fields, farmers reinforcing through competition the cooperation and solidarity necessary for their long-term survival. It was correlative to
the deadly game of war, which pitted noble against noble in a struggle to
capture, harvest, and plant human souls so that they might sprout as suste-
nance and abundance in their kingdoms. In such wars and rituals, kings as-
serted boundaries on their realms of farming constituencies and established
alliances of equal importance. The Maya king was a farmer of people, as his
people were farmers of corn. He returned, in ecstatic trance, to the divine
spirit of Hun Hunahpu, the skull hung on the tree at the Place of Ballgame
Sacrifice, source not only of people but also of corn and hence of life.

The reasons that the Maya nobility sustained a farmer's sport at the level of
passion play are not difficult to fathom: the audience for their rites was composed of these farmers, either directly or by hearsay, and the ultimate function of the noble game was to reinforce the mediating role of the royal players
in the perpetuation of social life and nature.

Notes

1. This location in Xibalba has been handled in various ways, with the note to the
Recinos translation, the best summary of the problem:

> *Ta x-e puz cut, x-e muc cit chi Pucbal-Chah u bi.* Ximénes (*Historia de la Pro-
> vincia de San Vicente de Chiapas y Guatemala*) translates this name as "the
> place where the ashes are dumped." Brasseur de Bourbourg translates it "the
> ashpan." It seems evident that there is an error in transcriptions here and that
> the name of this place must have been Puzbal-Chah; that is, the place of sac-
> rifice of the ballgame. *Puzbal* is "place of sacrifice," according to Besseta, and
> *chah* is the game of ball. Raynaud also gives this interpretation. (Recinos
> 1915:118)

Edmonson (1971:74) follows Ximénes, even altering the spelling of the original to
Puqubal Chaah. Tedlock (1985:112–113, 273) accepts the deductions of Recinos and
uses a similar translation. We believe the Recinos–Tedlock alternative is the most
likely in the context both of the Quichean original and the information discussed in
this paper.

2. These names from the Classic period are based on the Headband Twins and the
glyphic names that accompany them. The one who has large black spots on his face
and limbs is named Hun Ahau; his twin, who is marked by jaguar pelt on his jaw and
limbs, is named with the head variant of the number 9 and the glyph *yax*. Substitution
patterns in the *tz'ib* glyph in the Primary Standard Sequence on pottery support a
reading of *bal* for the jaguar-pelted human head and for the jaguar head that sometimes replaces it. Combining this head with the yax prefix gives Yax Bal or Yax Balam
as the name. However, the Hero Twins can also be identified with GI and GIII of the

Palenque Triad. GII and Hun Ahau can be associated with Venus. For example, the Hun Ahau deity appears in the Dresden Venus pages as the Morningstar and GI as Chac-Xib-Chac appears as the Eveningstar on the Cosmic Pot (Schele and Miller 1986:310–312). GIII has been identified as Ahau K'in by Lounsbury (1985:47–51). Another of his names—a decapitated jaguar following the glyph *kin-tan*—occurs as the name of a fully zoomorphic jaguar who carries a giant kin sign on his belly. (Schele and Miller 1986:50–51). We also believe he is the cruller-eyed, jaguar-eared anthropomorph who is often paired with GI or Chac-Xib-Chac. Although the Hero Twins have many avatars in the Classic period system, the association of one with Venus in its many aspects and the other with the sun in its various guises seems secure.

3. The chronology of the first half of this panel is extremely problematic. The first date is 13 Manik 5 Pax, but there is no way to place it in the Long Count with the information given. A Distance Number of 5.14.0.17 was supposed to lead from the first date to the second, but the arithmetic yields 9 Kan 12 Zec, instead of the 9 Kan 12 Xul that is written. We could accept this as an error of one month, except that the Distance Number between this date and the third one is also in error. It fits neither between the Calendar Round they wrote nor the one they apparently intended. The arithmetic requires 3.8.1.11.16 between 9 Kan 12 Xul and 1 Ahau 13 Xul and 3.9.14.2.16 between 9 Kan 12 Zec and 1 Ahau 13 Xul. They wrote the Distance Number 3.8.10.14.11, and unfortunately neither their intention nor the source of their error is apparent.

4. Although this date superficially looks like a Distance Number because of the glyph that ends the left texts, it is in fact an elaborate Long Count date. As it is written, the date has eight cycles higher than the baktun, all set at 13. However, if these cycles are simply ignored, the remaining cycles and their numbers 9.15.13.6.9 match the Calendar Round, 3 Muluc 17 Mac, that is recorded. The explanation of this notation is found on three monuments at Cobá which record the era date 4 Ahau 8 Cumku with twenty cycles above the katun, all set at 13. This date at Yaxchilán is simply an extended Long Count which registers that the higher cycles were still set on 13 when the event occurred. In actuality, all of them are still today set on 13, for the next cycle above the baktun—the 8000-tun pictun—will not change from 13 to 1 until October 15, 4772. The presence of the "kin-akbal" form of the Distance Number Introductory Glyph (DNIG) functions to warn that a change in temporal framework has occurred, but DNIGs can precede Long Count dates as well as Distance Numbers. For example, a DNIG precedes an Initial Series Introductory Glyph and Long Count dates on Copán Stela 4.

5. All transcriptions of Maya glyphs are given in the system published by J.E.S. Thompson (1962).

6. The association of this "axe" event with some astronomical event was noted by D. H. Kelley (1976:158). Kelley (1962) also first noted its association with a conflict between Copán and Quiriguá, an association that was consistent throughout the Classic period (cf. Schele 1982:Charts 14, 75, 107 for a summary of the contexts). Decapitation sacrifice is inferred from its constant war and sacrifice context in texts and

its logographic properties which tie iconographically with the action of decapitation. Donald Hales (Robiscek and Hales 1981:45 and Vessel 40) first noted this verb directly associated with scenes of decapitation on pottery. Nikolai Grube (pers. comm. 1989) and Jorge Orejel (1988) have both suggested a reading of *ch'ak* "to decapitate" for the verb. Since the axe carries T25 as a phonetic complement, this suggestion is one that should be tested in future research.

7. Mathews (1975) first identified this glyph as a sign for "successor" or "replacement" on the Early Classic lintel series at Yaxchilán. The same glyph also occurs in the Tablets of the Group of the Cross (Schele 1977, 1978a) as a record of "days or changeovers" elapsed between one event and another. The sense of the glyph, however, is less the idea of one thing replacing the other, as of nodes in a sequence or something like knots on a string. One follows the other in a count as taken in "succession."

In all these examples, the T676 compound is preceded by an ordinal number (formed in the Mayan languages by possessing a cardinal number as in *u ca* "second" from *ca* "two." Schele (1978b, 1980) first demonstrated the use of *u na* (T1.4) as the ordinal construction for "first" in the Cholan languages and in the east panel of the Temple of Inscriptions at Palenque. In this Yaxchilán text, the ordinals u na and u ca ("first" and "second") and the cardinal number "three" are used with the T676 compound.

8. This particular snake head appears as the proper name of Altar GI of Copán, which is the representation of a Vision Serpent, fleshed on its eastern side and skeletal on its western end.

9. This head is the sign that often appears in the north glyph and in Chac-Xib-Chac's name on the Cosmic Plate. In both these contexts, *xib* is an appropriate value. In fact, Lounsbury (pers. comm. 1975) has long identified the zoomorphic variant of this glyph as xib or *xim* in the Dresden Codex. Here the head is surrounded by a beaded border which normally signals the value *mo*. Combining the two signs may very well spell xim, a term recorded in Yucatec (Barrera Vasquez 1980:994) as "mazorca de maíz que guardan para semilla (the ear of maize that is kept for seed)." Preceded by *yax* "first" and followed by "earth ahau," this glyphic name seems to record a metaphor for "seed corn of the earth." If the first sacrifice is the young ear called *nal* and this one is Yax Xim, the ear kept for seed, then the second sacrifice may refer to another point in the cycle of maize. The metaphor of sacrifice clearly seems to be one drawn from the life cycle of maize.

10. David Stuart (pers. comm. 1988) has discovered the name of the Vision Serpent on Yaxchilán Lintel 14 (E3-D4) which also occurs on Copán Stela 10 and 13. It occurs to us that the Yaxol Hun Uinic Na-Chan phrase is also a name for one of the other Vision Serpents. This is supported by the occurrence in pottery scenes of the name Chih-Chan with a deer-antlered Vision Serpent—a creature who is still extant in Chorti mythology today. The Yucatec day name Chicchan is apparently borrowed from this Cholan name, but the Chol name for the same day is Na-Chan (Campbell 1988:375). Thus we have one name for the Vision Serpent Chihchan substituting for the other Na-chan.

11. It is our understanding that Stephen Houston, David Stuart, and Nikolai Grube have all noticed this same substitution and are testing or have accepted a *hv* value for the knot-skull glyph. Barbara MacLeod (pers. comm. 1989) has also suggested that the knot-skull may read logographically as *hil* in some of the "death" contexts. This alternative would explain the optional use of the *li* sign in this context.

12. Macri (n.d.) first took the helmet glyph to refer directly to a helmet worn as a direct reference to the Triad god. She also took the collocation *tup* to refer to earflares and she found the Tzeltal entries identifying *pixom* as a kind of headgear. In the 1989 Advanced Seminar on Maya Hieroglyph Writing at the University of Texas, Martha Macri, Janis Indrikis, Floyd Lounsbury, Peter Mathews, and Linda Schele debated and worked on these passages. It was during this interaction that the *uh* reading was discovered. In these discussions, we also concluded that the pixom, which means "a thing that is wrapped around," corresponds to the cloth that holds down the hair, as in Chan-Bahlum's portraits in the Group of the Cross. The headband is the ubiquitous Jester God headband, which is spelled phonetically in the first two passages and logographically in the last one. The kind of collar is specified for each god, as is the kind of helmet.

13. Ringle (1988), Carlson (1988), Stuart (1988) and others simultaneously realized that the "water group" prefix and its head variant simply read *ku*, "god," and with a *-vl* suffix, *kul* or "holy." Barthel (1952:92) suggested this *ku* value for the "water" group many years earlier. Schele (1989) has further suggested that these signs retained the phonetic value *ku* even in areas where Cholan languages were spoken, such as at Palenque and Copán.

14. Barbara MacLeod (pers. comm. 1987) has proposed that the event reads lok'ah yok tu witzil, "he came out, his feet (or steps) from the mountain." Nikolai Grube (in press) prefers to read the upright muluc with the ticks in its contour as *te* rather than *lo*. He reads the phrase tek'ah yoch tu witzil, "He stepped on the entrance to the mountain," using *tek'* in proto-Cholan meaning "to step on." Both readings impart approximately the same information—the youngster "came out on the feet" or "stepped on the entrance" to the mountain, which refers perhaps to the pyramid mountain in which his ancestor Kan Xul was entombed. Such sacred mountains held the portals to the Otherworld (Schele and Freidel in press). The idea is that the child put himself in the place of his ancestor by coming out of the mountain portal to the Otherworld, which he had entered presumably through the ecstatic ritual of the vision quest.

15. Bricker (1986:158) makes a strong argument that the *nawah* verb is based on the Cholti root *naual* "to adorn" or "to beautify" and is a reference to the dressing and painting of bodies in preparation for rituals of various sorts. She makes a cogent argument that the examples of this event from Piedras Negras refer to the dressing of a young girl in the marriage ritual that bound her to the male who would become ruler. She further argues that at Aguateca and elsewhere the "adorning" of a captive is associated with a color more appropriate to their status as captive. Since sacrificial victims are also known to have been painted in preparation for torture rituals, we find Bricker's

arguments very strong. In my original proposals for this glyph (Schele 1984), I was not aware of this Cholti entry. I now find the argument convincing.

16. Ringle (1985:154) first provided evidence for this value in its use with the *chum* seating glyph. Stuart (pers. comm. 1985) also found a spelling of Muan at Quiriguá which uses the same sign as *mu*.

17. The first glyph of this pair combines the *k'an* sign with T23 *na*, T21 *ab* (Grube pers. comm. 1986), and T501 *ba*. Together these read k'an-na-ab-ba, which can be parsed either as k'an aba or k'a-nab. I suspect this is a version of k'ak najb, the proto-Cholan term for "ocean" reconstructed by Kaufman and Norman (1984:123).

18. I first identified this tree with the na te kan glyph in the 1984 Workshop on Maya Hieroglyphic Writing at the University of Texas. *Na*, like *yak*, occurs in the Cholan languages as "first" (Schele 1978a).

19. We have been unable to find this root in any of the Cholan or Greater Tzotzilan languages, but it does seem to exist in some eastern Mayan languages. Schultze-Jena (1972:210) translates the Quiché word ahal as "Der Hervorbringer (procreator, giver of birth, causer, begetter, and in general anything made or worked, something created." In the same *Popol Vuh* context, Recinos (1950:110) translated Ahalpuh as "he who makes pus" and Ahalmez as "he who makes filth." Wirsing's (1930) Kekchi dictionary lists *aj* as "*wach, wachen, erwachen* (waking, wake up, be awake)." *Ajal* is listed as "*aufwachen, wachwerden* (awake, wake up)." Because this root exists in both eastern and western Maya languages, we presume it existed in the Cholan languages of the Classic period and thus was meaningful at Palenque.

20. It is a fact, however, that the Maya used numbers to convey not only their literal numerical value, but also to express their homophones. For example, the number six, *wac*, not only stands for that numerical value, but also stands for the concept of "to hoist up, to establish" as in *wac ah chan*, the name of the World Tree in the Temple of the Cross at Palenque (Schele 1987b). In the same way, ox has other meanings that should be considered in an interpretation of ox ahal phrase. Among the meanings listed for ox in the Cordemex dictionary (Barrera Vasquez 1980:611) is "*aire, aliente* (air, wind, breath)." There is a prospect that ox ahal means maker of "air" or "breath." GII of the Palenque Triad is the ox ahal k'ul. This might be read "third created divinity" because he is the third born of the Triad gods, but it might also read "Holy-air-maker" where breath has the connotation of spirit. Another meaning of ox in Yucatec is "scab" or the skin that heals a wound. Edmonson (1971:146) notes that the name of the Aztec hero who split open the mountain in which corn was hidden is Nanahuatl, "the sore covered." GII, who holds the Ox Ahal title, is clearly associated with a clefted corn mountain on the Tablet of the Foliated Cross. Because the construction is deliberately cardinal, alternative readings of ox should be left open to consideration.

21. Hal is the eastern Mayan cognate of the Yucatecan nal, "mazorca" or "maize ear."

22. Stuart and Schele have worked in detail on these dedication events mainly through recent studies of the Copán inscriptions. (See Schele [1982:350] for a listing of this verb and Schele [in press] and Freidel and Schele [1989] for a description of the event at Palenque.)

CHAPTER 16

Ballgames and Boundaries

Susan D. Gillespie

Rubber-ball games were played by many Native American societies over a wide geographical range and a span of time of perhaps two millennia. Despite the great variation in the procedures and symbolism of the ballgame among all the peoples who played it, there is an underlying unity. All of these games are related in their sharing of certain principles dealing with the purposes for which they were played. They have a unifying function which extends not only to rubber-ball games in North, Middle, and South America, but also to many of the other New World games, including shinny, hoop and pole, and lacrosse. The Mesoamerican rubber-ball game is not an isolate but is a manifestation of an ideology that is at least pan–New World.

The symbolism of the Mesoamerican game is explored here from this perspective by an examination of its mythology and iconography. The discussion begins with a summary of the current interpretations of ballgame iconography, in particular, solar movement and agricultural fertility themes and the assumption that these themes are associated with human sacrifice, especially by decapitation. The decapitation scenes that pervade the symbolism of the Mesoamerican game lead to an investigation of "Rolling Head" myths which are found in many New World societies and are intimately related to games. I argue that decapitation is a metonym for dismemberment, and that dismemberment—the separating of the body into its constituent parts—is metaphorically linked to the separation of time into agricultural seasons which are marked by the periodic movements of celestial bodies. All of these phenomena are associated with games because games involve a similar separation of society into groupings. I conclude with a discussion of the ballgame as a mechanism for establishing and maintaining the boundaries that mark the divisions within a variety of phenomena—temporal, spatial, and especially sociopolitical.

Current Interpretations of Mesoamerican Ballgame Symbolism

Many scholars of the Mesoamerican ballgame are more interested in the game as a ritual rather than as a sport because of its cult importance over a wide area of Mesoamerica, particularly during the Classic period but continuing into the Postclassic. The ritual significance of the game is reflected in the expenditure of effort in the building of ballcourts, many in ceremonial precincts, and in the artwork devoted to the game. Examining this evidence has provided much of the information on the symbolic themes that motivated the playing of the game. Many categories of artwork reveal aspects of the ballgame: carved panels, benches, and tenoned heads and rings on some ballcourts; presumed ballgame paraphernalia preserved as carved stone objects (yokes, *palmas*, *hachas*, handstones); stelae and other bas-relief carvings thought to represent the ballgame or ball players; depictions on ceramic vessels; and figurines and other portable artifacts. Additional information comes from Aztec and Mixtec painted codices showing the ballcourt, the game in action, and ball players.

Besides these iconographic representations, there are post-conquest written descriptions of the Aztec and Maya ballgames. The most influential account has been the *Popol Vuh* (Tedlock 1985), a cosmogonical narrative from Highland Guatemala which reveals a number of the mythical underpinnings of the game. Information about the game is also gained from the study of contemporary ballgames, especially in west Mexico (Anonymous 1986; Kelly 1980a [1943]; Leyenaar 1978).

Other sources of data for understanding the ballgame exist but are utilized less frequently because they come from outside of Mesoamerica. For instance, there are many versions of a rubber-ball game played in South America (Stern 1949). Attempts are rarely made to link the rubber-ball game with other kinds of games in the Americas (except in a historical way; see Krickeberg 1966 [1948]; Stern 1949), and with the exception of the *Popol Vuh*, myths about ballgames in Mesoamerica and neighboring areas are infrequently consulted (but see Krickeberg 1966; Pasztory 1976:207). This neglect is unfortunate since there is a rich corpus of information revealing the sharing of basic themes which structured the symbolic and ritual significance of many New World games.

Figure 16.1. The Lords of Day and Night play ball against each other on an I-shaped ballcourt divided into four quarters (Codex Colombino:Pl. 11).

Interest in the symbolism of the Mesoamerican ballgame seems to have begun at the turn of the century with Eduard Seler. Seler perceived a relationship between the path of the ball during play and the movements of the sun, an idea which reflects the solar symbolism popular during his time (Pasztory 1972:445; Stern 1949:68–69). Walter Krickeberg (1966) developed this notion further, seeing the ballgame as a symbolic reenactment of the struggle between day and night, between light and darkness. It therefore symbolized the daily and seasonal journey of the sun and other celestial bodies, their cyclical descent through the Underworld and ascent into the sky. Evidence for this interpretation is drawn, for example, from an illustration of a ballgame played between the Lords of the Day and the Lords of the Night (Figure 16.1) (*Codex Colombino* 1966:Pl. XI), from the orientation of some ballcourts which would suggest an association with astronomical movements, and from the *Popol Vuh* especially, which tells of a ballgame played by the sun and moon against Underworld forces.

A second major symbolic theme proposed for the ballgame is agricultural fertility (Pasztory 1972, 1976, 1978a; Stern 1949:71). It is evidenced by the flowering and fruiting plants on ballgame reliefs at El Tajín, Bilbao, and Chichén Itzá (Pasztory 1972:444) and the iconography of the ballcourt markers at Copán (Baudez 1984). Lee Parsons (1969:103) suggested that vegetal fertility was "perhaps the ultimate significance of ballgame sacrifice." This idea was also promoted by S. Jeffrey K. Wilkerson (1984; this volume) in his analysis of the Tajín South Ballcourt reliefs, which he interpreted as showing the sacrificial death of a ball player in order to gain *pulque*, the fermented sap of the maguey plant associated with agricultural fertility.

The fertility theme is not distinct from the solar symbolism but instead is inextricably linked to it (see also Brundage 1982:219). Agricultural fertility is a seasonal phenomenon, and seasonality is marked by the periodic movements of heavenly bodies such as the sun, moon, and constellations. Thus the ballgame cult is said to have "functioned to assure the continuation of the cosmic cycles of the sun, moon, and planets and the alternation of the dry and rainy seasons. . . . [Its aim was] the furthering of agricultural and natural fertility—a general preoccupation in Mesoamerica" (Pasztory 1978a:131).

The association between seasonal change and the ballgame, as suggested by Esther Pasztory, relies on the transforming mechanism of sacrificial death and rebirth:

> The essence of the ballgame seems to be a contest between opposing forces, which may be represented by male twins or a couple, a contest which often involves a cyclically recurring pattern of death, rebirth, and revenge. In each case, one contestant is devoured or beheaded (an act ritually recalled by the practice of human sacrifice), as a result of which great benefits inure to society, especially in the form of agricultural fertility. Because of the ambiguities inherent in the mythology, it is impossible and in fact unrewarding to try to decide in favor of the stellar or fertility interpretations of the ballgame. (Pasztory 1976:209–210)

A principal metaphor of this transformation is the movement of the sun. The ballgame is seen as reenacting the death and descent of the sun into the Underworld, an event which subsumes both diurnal and annual cycles (Pasztory 1978a:131, 138; see also Pasztory 1972:446). The death of the sun is presumably indicated by the descending sun god depicted on some ballgame reliefs (e.g., from Bilbao [Parsons 1969:Pl. 32–33]), skeletal deities, decapitation, and trophy heads. The rebirth of fertility is shown by water and plant representations, including plants emerging from the necks of decapitated players (Pasztory 1978a:138).

A slightly different idea was presented by Lothar Knauth (1961:197). He accepted the interpretation of sacrifice in a context of the cycles of heavenly bodies, but stated that it is the moon, symbol of fertility, and not the sun, which must be sacrificed. Another alternative (Moser 1973:48) is that the severed heads in ballgame iconography represent stars.

Marvin Cohodas has shown that all of these ideas are interrelated, forming part of a more complex ideology:

> The ball game, a game of action and motion, appears to have taken on the con-
> notations of the motion of the sun at the meeting points of the upperworld
> and underworld, for it represents these points of transition when the sun en-
> ters into and exits from the underworld. At the height of its popularity as a
> cult, the ballgame was probably played on the equinoxes to represent the bat-
> tle of celestial and infernal forces. The sacrifices which culminated the game
> were employed as sympathetic magic to bring about the two crucial events in
> the yearly cycle of the sun and of agricultural activity. (Cohodas 1975:110)

According to this interpretation, in the game played at the vernal equinox, forces of darkness defeat the forces of light and the sun descends into the underworld. The player on the losing side who is sacrificed at the end of the game represents the sun, an event which by sympathetic magic causes the descent of the sun. During the summer solstice, the sun mates with the moon to conceive the maize deity, who is the sun reborn. At the autumnal equinox the sacrificed player represents the moon goddess, indicating the victory of the forces of light over the forces of darkness since the death of the moon is coincident with the ascent of the sun (Cohodas 1975:108–110).

The current interpretations of ballgame symbolism can thus be summarized as follows: The ballgame is associated with the movements of celestial bodies, especially the sun and moon, which are related to seasonal agricultural fertil-ity. The ritual game concluded with a sacrifice of a player symbolizing the death (and eventual rebirth) of the sun or moon which was necessary for the cyclically recurring astral movements to proceed in their usual manner.

Decapitation and Sacrifice

Paramount in these interpretations is the notion that the sacrifice of a player was necessary to bring about the desired benefits which the game was thought to produce. "The ball game cult of the Middle Classic period was essentially a sacrificial cult" (Pasztory 1978a:138). The sun (or moon) was sac-rificed, as represented or caused by the sacrifice of a player, in order that it die so that it could then be reborn, continue its cyclical movement, and rejuvenate seasonal agricultural fertility (Pasztory 1972:444).

The evidence for ballgame-related sacrifice is overwhelming (e.g., Bor-hegyi 1969:507, 509; 1980; Knauth 1961), and only a few examples of this evi-dence can be listed here. At the Aztec annual Panquetzaliztli ceremony dedi-cated to the rebirth of Huitzilopochtli, an avatar of the sun, victims were sacrificed in the ballcourt (Sahagún 1950–1982:Bk. 2, Ch. 34). There is a sac-rificial scene (probably decapitation) on a bas-relief panel at El Tajín's South Ballcourt (Kampen 1972:Fig. 23). Depictions of the act of decapitation and disembodied heads or skulls are found on ballcourt reliefs at Chichén Itzá

*Figure 16.2. Divided ballcourt with two rings at midcourt, a central skull, and a rubber ball from which water flows, next to a decapitated man (*Codex Borbonicus:*Pl. 19).*

(Great Ballcourt [Tozzer 1957:Fig. 474] and Monjas Ballcourt [Bolles 1977:226]); with ballcourt representations in codices (e.g., *Codex Borbonicus* 1981:Pl. 19; *Codex Borgia* 1963:Pl. 21; *Codex Magliabechiano* 1983:Pl. 80; *Codex Nuttall* 1975:4) (Figure 16.2); on a gold pendant from Tomb 7 at Monte Albán with a skull depicted in the center of a ballcourt (Krickeberg 1966:Fig. 30); on Maya vases with ballgame scenes (e.g., Hellmuth 1985); and on ball-game-related objects, such as the Aparicio stela of a decapitated ball player (Moser 1973:Fig. 13), a *palma* with a decapitation scene (Moser 1973:Fig. 14) (Figure 16.3), and the Bilbao stelae which portray ball players with disembodied heads (Parsons 1969:Pl. 32a, 34a). There are stone *hachas*, worn at the waist of ball players, in the shape of heads and skulls (Parsons 1969:Pl. 21). The Mixtec "decapitated goddess" is shown in the codices with a ballcourt among her insignia (Furst 1978:167–168). There is also an architectural construction known as the *tzompantli* (skull rack), on which human skulls were displayed, located immediately adjacent to ballcourts at some sites (e.g., Chichén Itzá, Late Postclassic Tula, Tenochtitlán). Actual skulls have also been found associated with ballcourts as the result of archaeological investigations at various Mesoamerican sites (e.g., Norman Hammond pers. comm.; Weigand this volume).

Mythical evidence of ballgame-related sacrifice is said to be found in the *Popol Vuh*, in which the "father" and "son" twin pairs were killed by their ballgame opponents and one twin of each pair was decapitated (see Borhegyi

Figure 16.3. Relief on a Late Classic palma *from Coatepec, Veracruz, shows a man with a knife in one hand and a severed head in the other (after Moser 1973:Fig. 14).*

1969:501). A similar story of decapitation occurs in an Aztec myth in which the goddess Coyolxauhqui was beheaded by Huitzilopochtli. Although this act was not a ballgame sacrifice, it did occur in a ballcourt, at its center, the *itzompan*—"place of the skull" (Tezozomoc 1980:228–229; Stern 1949:54).

Almost all of the evidence for ballgame sacrifice concerns decapitation. Either the act itself is depicted or else the disembodied heads or skulls are shown. Thus it is widely supposed that ballgame-related decapitation as sacrifice was a major aspect of the ritual game (see especially Castro-Leal Espino 1972; Knauth 1961). There is some support for this view from mythology outside of Mesoamerica associated with other games. In a Pawnee myth (Dorsey 1906:236–239), Spider Woman played the twin-ball game and hung the heads of her losing opponents on her wall. A related Caddo myth (Weltfish 1937: 172–177) has "evil beings" who played the hoop and spear game and who also hung the losers' heads on the wall. Stephan F. de Borhegyi (1980:24) remarked on a possible symbolic association between the hanging of the losers' heads on the wall and the head-shaped *hachas* worn by players as well as the tenoned stone heads set into ballcourt walls.

Although the iconography of severed heads and disembodied skulls is indisputable, the presumption of actual sacrificial death of a player by decapitation following a loss in a ballgame is less certainly supported by this evidence.

Mesoamerican societies of the Classic and Postclassic periods used several methods of sacrificial execution, but decapitation was not principal among them (see, e.g., Boone 1984; Durán 1971). The fact that decapitation or its result is frequently depicted in connection with ballgame iconography therefore requires further investigation as to why this action predominates. More importantly, the notion that decapitation is actually an act of sacrifice must be confirmed, not just assumed.

The critical link between the act of decapitation and sacrificial death in association with the ballgame is the *Popol Vuh* (Brundage 1982:222). Within this epic, there are clear indications of sacrificial deaths of ball players, as well as acts of decapitation of ball players. Careful reading of the *Popol Vuh*, however, reveals that decapitation was not the cause of the players' sacrificial deaths. The acts of sacrifice were separated from the acts of decapitation. Of the two decapitated ball players in the story, one was already dead when decapitated, and the other did not die when decapitated. In the first instance of ball player decapitation, the victim was one of the "father" twins, One Hunahpu and Seven Hunahpu. Both of these heroes were sacrificed by their opponents, the Underworld Lords, before they even played the ballgame, but how they were killed is not mentioned. After he was dead, One Hunahpu was decapitated, and his head was hung in a tree (similar to the fate of the heads in the myths mentioned above). Thus the sacrifice itself was not by decapitation: "And then they were sacrificed and buried. They were buried at the Place of Ball Game Sacrifice, as it is called. The head of One Hunahpu was cut off; only his body was buried with his younger brother" (Tedlock 1985:113).

As for the "son" twins, the head of one of them, Hunahpu, was severed from his body, but this was done prior to the final ballgame. This decapitation was not explicitly an act of mortal sacrifice because Hunahpu did not die. His brother, Xbalanque, placed a pumpkin on his brother's neck which was transformed into Hunahpu's head (Tedlock 1985: 145; thus a pumpkin became a head, whereas with his father, One Hunahpu, his head was put into a tree and became a gourd). Furthermore, the eventual sacrificial deaths of the younger twins, which took place after Hunahpu's decapitation, did not result from their defeat in the ballgame because they won the contest. Afterwards, the younger twins allowed themselves to be killed by their enemies and were executed by being burned to death in a large stone oven, not by decapitation (Tedlock 1985:148–149).

When the boys revived a few days later, they sacrificed themselves in a plot to defeat their adversaries, the Underworld Lords: "And this is the sacrifice of Hunahpu by Xbalanque. One by one his legs, his arms were spread wide. His head came off, rolled far away outside. His heart, dug out, was smothered in a leaf . . ." (Tedlock 1985:153). Here the sacrifice is not an act of simple decapitation but head and heart removal, with a scattering of these body parts. Significantly, this was also the fate suffered by Coyolxauhqui, sacrificed in a ballcourt in the Aztec myth mentioned above; her head and heart were removed (Tezozomoc 1980:229). In another version of this myth (Sahagún 1950–1982:Bk. 3, Chap. 1), Coyolxauhqui was actually dismembered by Huitzilopochtli, and this more complete dispersal of body parts is a clue to the meaning of decapitation, as will be elaborated below.

The actors in the *Popol Vuh* ballgame and in this Aztec myth all have astronomical connotations. Coyolxauhqui is associated with the moon, while her brother deity, Huitzilopochtli, is an avatar of the sun. In the *Popol Vuh*, the older twins may be Venus in its Morning and Evening Star aspects (Coe 1975: 90), while the younger twins are explicitly named as the sun and the moon. Therefore, a relationship between ballgame/ballcourt sacrifice and celestial bodies has not been dismissed by these arguments, but the method of sacrifice was not simple decapitation.

While both decapitation and sacrifice are related to the ballgame, decapitation must refer to more than the method of sacrificial execution, especially considering the additional heart sacrifice in the myths. Heart sacrifice was common in Mesoamerica, and Hunahpu, in the excerpt above, was laid out in the correct position for heart removal. If the purpose of the act was merely to kill, there is no need to add decapitation to heart removal.

Thus, to understand the meaning of ballgame decapitation, one must go beyond the notion of sacrifice, and indeed, sacrificial death is not the only necessary outcome of decapitation. Simply put, decapitation is the removal of the head from the body, resulting in a headless body and a bodiless head. The *Popol Vuh* and other New World myths show that for symbolic purposes, a loss of life does not necessarily follow. Either the head alone may continue to live, or both head and body remain alive after their separation. Freeing decapitation from the concept of sacrificial death, which is proposed here, does not mean that currently accepted themes of periodic astral movements and agricultural fertility are incorrectly attributed to the ballgame. On the contrary, these themes are further supported and interrelated in a systematic way by a reanalysis of decapitation.

Rolling Heads

Christopher Moser (1973) has devoted an entire monograph to decapitation in Mesoamerica; here I wish to pursue only one aspect of this act—the bodiless head. The heads or skulls represented in ballgame iconography have not been given much attention apart from the idea that they are the outcome of mortal sacrifice. They are usually relegated to a "trophy head" cult (Borhegyi

1969:502; Henderson 1947; Parsons 1969:167; Pasztory 1972, 1978a:128). However, some data indicate that the head may be symbolically equivalent to the rubber ball; if so, this would be of great significance. The identity between the game ball and a human head is not confined to Mesoamerica but has been found elsewhere, including the Old World (Henderson 1947:17; Massingham 1929:224–226).

A famous Mesoamerican example of this equivalence is again found in the *Popol Vuh*, when the Underworld Lords substituted the severed head of Hunahpu for the rubber ball in the final game. Iconographic support for the ball as a head or skull is found in ballcourt reliefs at El Tajín (Figure 16.4) (Kampen 1972:Fig. 19a) and Chichén Itzá (Bolles 1977:226–227; Tozzer 1957:Fig. 474), which show a ball with a skull on it placed between opposing players. The skull between the players on the Monte Albán Tomb 7 pendant has also been interpreted as a ball (Clune 1963:70). There are depictions in the painted codices of ballcourts with balls which appear to have faces on them (e.g., *Codex Borgia* 1963:Pl. 35, 42), and a Veracruz carved ceramic vessel shows ball players with disembodied heads which may represent balls (Hellmuth 1978:Fig. 10). Thus, one way decapitation is related to the ballgame is that the ball, a necessary instrument of the game, is equated with a bodiless head, and it must be procured by removing someone's head, either symbolically or literally.

An important aspect of the ballgame was to keep the ball in constant motion in the air (Durán 1971:313). This was possible due to the elastic qualities of rubber. The rubber ball bounced back when struck and seemed to have its own internal source of motion, as seen in the fact that the Nahuatl word for the rubber ball (*olli*) has as its root the word for movement (*ollin*) (noted by Blom 1932:495; Wilkerson this volume). Given the symbolic equivalence of the ball in motion and the human head, then the head in this context would also have been considered animated, capable of its own movement. Decapitation would therefore bring about not a lifeless head, but a head that, once freed from the body, could jump, roll, and fly.

This hypothetical connection between a "living" head and a ball is actually found throughout the New World among peoples who played many types of games, not just those with rubber balls, so its meaning goes beyond the noted elasticity of rubber. The animate severed head is a defining motif in myths known collectively as "Rolling Head" or "Rolling Skull" stories. The occurrence of this motif ranges from the Arctic Circle to Tierra del Fuego (Lévi-Strauss 1979:55; see Waterman [1914] and Swanton [1929] for partial distributions of this myth in North America). Significantly, these myths about disembodied living heads are related to ballgames. They also deal with the changing seasons, the movements of the sun and moon, and agricultural

Figure 16.4. Pyramid of the Niches, Sculpture 7, from El Tajín, Veracruz, shows players in a ballcourt, one holding a knife, with a skull on the ball between them (after Kampen 1972:Fig. 19a).

fertility—all of the symbolic themes that have been suggested as underlying the Mesoamerican ballgame. They indicate a strong connection between these themes, games, and decapitation in a context other than simple sacrifice. While the myths cannot be analyzed here in detail, the linkage to the ballgame and its symbolic themes can be explored.

Rolling Heads Used as Balls

Borhegyi (1969:503) once suggested that the Mesoamerican ball players may have played with actual human heads. Mythical examples of the animated "Rolling Head" being used in ballgames are found outside of Mesoamerica as well, in societies lacking both rubber balls and ritual decapitation practices or trophy head cults. In a Seneca myth (Curtin and Hewitt 1918:285–296), a cannibal killed a woman and ate all but her head, breasts, and the boy twins she was pregnant with, which he placed in a hollow tree. The boys survived on the milk in the breasts and were later discovered by their father, who made them ball clubs and a ball to play with. The mother's skull was still alive, and in fear of it the boys and their father fled. The father, helped by his invisible brother, was chased by his wife's flying skull until it was finally killed. After the skull was dead, it was used as a ball in a game.

In this myth, not only is an animated head used as a ball in a ballgame, but there are other details of interest to Mesoamericanist scholars: the twins play ball with equipment given them by their father, a man who also has a "twin" (as in the *Popol Vuh*). Playing ball with a skull is not limited to human skulls, however. The Eskimo of Baffin Land (Boas 1901:146) and the Chukchee (Bogoras 1904–1909:324) believed that the Northern Lights were the souls of the dead who play ball with a live and roaring walrus head.

In South America, the Apinayé, who played rubber-ball games only at the boys' initiation ritual, told a myth about the origin of the rubber ball which again shows that the ball was once a rolling head. In this story (Nimuendajú 1939:175–177), a man who attacked people at night with his sharpened leg-bone was beaten to death by villagers, who cut off his head. His head jumped away, and returned in the daytime to attack the people, but they tricked it into falling into a hole and covered it with dirt. Later, youths going through their initiation came past the spot and noticed a rubber tree growing out of the head's grave. Using the sap from the tree they made the first rubber balls for the rubber-ball game. This myth has explicit connotations of the mutilated leg associated with nighttime and the severed head associated with daytime, indicating a division between day and night which is correlated with a division between upper and lower body parts (see below).

Rolling Head as Sun and Moon

In many interpretations of the Mesoamerican ballgame, the rubber ball is thought to be a symbol of the sun or moon. There are Rolling Head myths in which the head (a substitute for a ball) becomes the sun or moon. This equivalence is made in a number of ways. The Pawnee (Dorsey 1906:31–38) told the story of a girl chased by a noisy Rolling Skull. She was rescued by a man who struck the skull with an axe, breaking it into two parts. One part of the skull became the moon, and the other became the sun.

A different relationship between the Rolling Head and the sun and moon is found in a Blackfoot myth (Grinnell 1893:44–47). It begins with a woman whose foot and head were cut off by her husband when he discovered that she had a snake for a lover. The one-footed body of the woman chased after her husband, while her rolling head pursued her two sons. The head was eventually stopped by the boys, after which they separated, one to create white people and the other to create the Blackfeet. But the headless body, which became the moon, continues to chase her husband, who is the sun. If she can catch the sun, it will always be night, but as long as she does not catch him, day and night will continue to alternate.

The relationship between the sun and moon and the severed head appears as well in South America, where seasonal, monthly, and daily movements of these astral bodies are distinguished by different classes of Rolling Head myths (Lévi-Strauss 1979:107). There are several examples of the Rolling Head rising into the sky to become the moon (e.g., Kuniba and Cashinawa: Lévi-Strauss 1979:94–97). In the Cashinawa myth, a man invited a member of an enemy tribe to his home. The stranger's head was cut off and stuck up on a post. Some friends saw his head, which was still alive, and tried to help it, but the head demanded they give it ripe fruit to eat. Eventually it decided to become the moon, thereby making women menstruate. In this myth, the Rolling Head as the moon is associated with lunar periodicity and the female biological cycle.

Other myths of a severed head in this part of Amazonia differ in that the head, instead of rolling around, clings to a person and becomes an example of the "Clinging Woman" motif (Lévi-Strauss 1979:107). Her counterpart in North America is "Burr Woman" (e.g., Assiniboine [Lowie 1909:180–181], Wichita [Dorsey 1904:187–191]). The Clinging Woman is the upper half of a woman whose body has been cut in two (another indication of a division of the human body into upper and lower parts). She clings to other people, and is often metonymically represented by a head which attaches itself to its victims. In a Uitoto example (Lévi-Strauss 1979:54–55), the Rolling Head attached itself to her husband's shoulder, a nocturnal hunter, and eventually the man changed them both into a bird which sings at night while the moon shines. Preuss (1921[1]:110) explained this myth in terms of the phases of the moon.

Rolling Heads and Constellations

There are also Rolling Head stories about the origin of constellations, especially those whose cyclical movements were associated with the change in seasonal subsistence activities. One example is an Assiniboine myth (Lowie 1909:177–178) on the origin of the Big Dipper. As in the Blackfoot tale, a man discovered that his wife had a snake for a lover. While the woman was out, her husband told their six sons and one daughter to flee the house. When his wife returned and stuck her head in the door, the man cut it off. Her head rolled after the children, who escaped by forming a circle and throwing a ball to one another. While playing they rose into the sky and became the Big Dipper.

In this myth, the severed head is the motive for playing a ballgame which causes the seven siblings to leave the earth and enter the sky as a constellation. The Pawnee explained the origin of the Pleiades (Dorsey 1906:119–122) in a very similar way. A girl and six men were being chased by a Rolling Head.

The girl took a ball and kicked it in the air seven times. Each time she kicked it, one of them rose into the sky, where together they became the seven stars of the Pleiades. In a similar Gros Ventre tale (Kroeber 1907:105–108) in which the girl and her six brothers form the Big Dipper, the constellation itself is called Cut-Off-Head. A Wichita version (Dorsey 1904:63–69) has the girl escaping from a cannibal (here substituting for the rolling head; see below for the Southeastern myths), and using the ball she and six men became the Little Dipper.

Games and Periodicity

The Rolling Head has been shown to be equated with the ballgame ball and also to be associated with the basic Mesoamerican ballgame theme, the periodicity of celestial bodies. Periodicity is found as well in other myths which are related to the Rolling Head myths but do not explicitly deal with a Rolling Head. In an Arapaho tale (Dorsey and Kroeber 1903:153–159), the seven who became the Pleiades were chased not by a Rolling Head but by a round rock. The stone is clearly analogous to the severed head (Lévi-Strauss 1979:99), and the substitution of a rock for the head is fairly frequent (e.g., two almost identical Pawnee myths, Coyote and the Rolling Skull, and Coyote and the Rolling Stone [Dorsey 1906:447–448, 446–447]). This substitution takes on added interest in myths from the Southeastern United States, for here the stone that chases the people is the chunkee stone used in the chunkee game (e.g., Koasati [Swanton 1929:182–183], Alabama [Swanton 1929:131–132], Yuchi [Wagner 1931:89–96, 224–228]). Thus the part played by a Rolling Head in other myths, a head which is sometimes used as a ball in the ballgame, is here played by a game object equivalent to a ball.

The Alabama myth (Swanton 1929:131–132) illustrates this point. A cannibal kidnapped a girl and demanded that she cut up her body for him to eat. The girl managed to escape, and when the cannibal realized she was gone, he took out his chunkee stone and rolled it on the ground. The stone followed the girl's trail, with the cannibal close behind, but the girl's brothers struck the cannibal in the ankle and head with a cooking paddle, and killed both him and his chunkee stone.

In a Yuchi version (Wagner 1931:89–96), only the chunkee stone followed the girl, making a thunderous noise as it approached her. In several of the myths given above, the Rolling Head is also said to be very noisy (see also Pawnee [Dorsey 1906:31–38], Yana [Sapir 1910:123–128], Tembe [Lévi-Strauss 1979:92]). The Yuchi myth states that the noise is specifically that of thunder, and in an Arapaho myth (Dorsey and Kroeber 1903:278–282) the Rolling Head also makes a thundering noise. The connection between the head or playing stone and thunder is revealing since thunder is frequently associated with ballgames, giving a symbolic relationship among animated heads, thunder, and games. The Kavina of South America believe that thunder is caused by a small boy throwing a rubber ball (Métraux 1942:43). The North American Menomini associated the game of lacrosse with thunder (Skinner 1913:78, 55). In a Menomini myth very reminiscent of the *Popol Vuh* story, the Thunderers played ball against "Underground Beings" (Hoffman 1896:131–135). The same event takes place in a modern Sierra Totonac (Veracruz) myth in which the young maize god plays ball against the Thunderers (Ichon 1973:73–81), causing rain and establishing the agricultural seasons. In a Natchez Rolling Head myth (Swanton 1929:215–218) which relates all three of these concepts, a woman who had been pursued by a Rolling Head was helped to victory in a ballgame by her son, Thunder.

What these myths and beliefs indicate is an association between games and climatic events tied in with the cyclical movements of astral phenomena, revealing that the Mesoamerican rubber-ball game is only one example of a much more general relationship. Michael A. Salter's (1980, 1983) examination of the games of Eastern North America determined that many of them were part of calendric fertility rituals or rituals designed to cause climatic change. These games include hoop and pole, chunkee, lacrosse, football, shinny, whip-top, ring and pin, pole-ball, handball, and the straw, bowl, and hand-dice games (Salter 1980:73, 77; see Culin [1975] for descriptions of these games). An example is the lacrosse game played by the Indians of the Six Nations (Salter 1983), part of the Thunder ceremony performed to bring rain for the crops. It was played by seven old men, representing the Seven Thunderers, against seven young men of the opposing moiety. Similarly, in the Seneca hoop and pole game the two teams represented the sun and the moon (1983:215), and in the Arkansas shinny game they represented the earth and the sky (1983:216). The Delaware straw game and ring and pin game could be played only during the winter, and it was believed that playing the game resulted in a blizzard. Salter (1983:217–218) suggested that the Delaware played the game in order to keep such bad weather within the winter season and not allow it to occur during the growing season when crops would be damaged; that is, to keep the balance between the seasons, so that winter would not overtake summer (see below).

In Western North America, string games and cup and ball games were played by peoples from the Arctic Circle to California in order to affect the length of the summer and winter seasons (Lévi-Strauss 1979:173). Some Southwestern Indian games are similarly associated with seasonal change. The Tewa ritual relay race was performed at the summer solstice to strengthen the sun for its journey to its winter home (Ortiz 1969:108). Certain

Tewa games, such as marbles and jacks, are considered cold-producing and are played only during the winter, whereas shinny is played during the summer to strengthen the sun (1969:114).

What is it about games that relates them to seasonal changes associated with climatic events and the movements of celestial bodies? To answer this question one must first examine the phenomenon of seasonal change. Over the course of the year days and nights are of unequal length, shorter on one side and longer on the other; hence they "limp" (Lévi-Strauss 1973:463). If the process does not reverse itself, and the shortening winter days do not begin to lengthen, then one is faced with the prospect of eternal winter, eternal night. This is the fate predicted in the Blackfoot myth given above, and it is to prevent this fate that many rituals, including games, are performed: to ensure an alternation, and hence a balance, between the oppositions which make up the daily and seasonal cycles.

Limping is part of many seasonal rituals around the world (Lévi-Strauss 1973:460–462). The limping gait (as opposed to the normal gait in which the left and right legs are of equal length) represents the imbalance of night and day or of the seasons (1973:464). Similarly, games are "lame" if the purpose in playing them is to "shorten on one side and lengthen on the other" in imitation of the seasons (Lévi-Strauss 1979:174). They "limp" by introducing an inequality among the participants, serving to separate them into teams, or into winners and losers. "Games thus appear to have a *disjunctive* effect: they end in the establishment of a difference between individual players or teams where originally there was no indication of inequality" (Lévi-Strauss 1966:32).

In the same way, the daily, monthly, and seasonal cycles introduce an unequal separation of the cosmos. In all of the games that are thought to affect seasonal movements or climatic change, the result is obtained by playing the game itself, which repeats the disjunctive character of periodic cycles, and not by any "sacrificial death" as is usually suggested for the Mesoamerican game. Such sacrifices are merely redundant, for North American mythology indicates that "to win a game is symbolically to 'kill' one's opponent" (Lévi-Strauss 1966:32).

The concept of disjunction helps to explain why games are played during times of separation; for example, ritual games played on solstices (when inequality between day and night or between the seasons is greatest), on the first day of the planting season, or at the start of the rainy or dry season. This concept also extends to playing games at times of social separation as well, such as during the initiation of Apinayé youths when they are neither children nor adults. In many societies the game is a contest between the two major social divisions, the moieties of the Apinayé (Nimuendajú 1939:66), the Menomini, as noted above, and many of the other North American tribes (Krickeberg 1966:295).

Periodicity and Dismemberment

Games are associated with periodicity because they introduce or emphasize a disjunction within the society, while the periodic movements of astral bodies introduce a disjunction in time and space, separating the cosmos into night and day, summer and winter, rainy and dry season. Decapitation and the Rolling Heads symbolize exactly the same phenomenon—the introduction of a disjunction—in the division of the body into its parts. This is why dismemberment, rather than mortal sacrifice, may better explain the references to decapitation in Mesoamerican ballgame imagery. Dismemberment of the human body into its discrete parts represents *par excellence* the introduction of discontinuity into what was once a unified whole, for the human body is a symbol of the cosmos, a "microcosm of the universe" (Turner 1960). The belief in the equivalence of the body and the cosmos was exemplified in Mesoamerica in a number of ways, such as the linking of the five directions with the four limbs and body center (Klein [1976:13–14] citing Nuttall), relating the 20 day signs—a complete cycle—to the different parts of the body (e.g., *Codex Ríos* 1964:Pl. 73; *Codex Borgia* 1963:Pl. 53; see also Klein 1976:13–14), and the Yucatec Maya use of the same word for "man" and "20," the complete cycle associated with both time and space (Edmonson 1984:98). Cutting up the body thereby symbolizes the division of the cosmos into its constituent parts, both spatial (geographical) and temporal (cyclical).

The sacrifice involved in the Mesoamerican ballgame is not merely the loss of life but the loss of the unity of the body. The unity of the body represents the primordial unity of all phenomena prior to the creation of culture, for the invention of culture requires the separation of all things into meaningful categories. Since decapitation is really an aspect of the separation of body parts and the resulting loss of unity, which leads to the establishment of culturally constituted categories, it is not surprising that the South American Rolling Head myths (Lévi-Strauss 1979) are really dismemberment myths or myths dealing with mutilation of various parts of the body. This generalization applies to other Rolling Head myths as well. The California Yana Rolling Head myth is explicit in this regard (Sapir 1910:123–128, 202–203); for a similar Maidu myth see Dixon [1912:189–193]; see also a South American Kavina myth (Lévi-Strauss 1979:98). In the Yana tale, a man became a Rolling Head while up in a tree harvesting pine nuts. He took his body apart and threw the pieces down from the tree instead of the nuts, leaving only his moving head up in the tree.

Furthermore, dismemberment, and not just decapitation, is tied to the origin and movements of celestial phenomena. As we have seen, severed heads become the sun and moon or bring about the origin of constellations with seasonal significance. But it is not the heads alone which are so transformed or transforming. In both North and South America, several constellations are believed by different societies to have been formed from various body parts of legendary individuals (Lévi-Strauss 1969:222–225). Certain Amazonian myths correlate Orion and the Pleiades with lower-body mutilation, Berenice's Hair and the sun with middle-body mutilation, and the moon and unnamed stars with upper-body mutilation (Lévi-Strauss 1979:107).

Agricultural fertility is also an aspect of total body dismemberment. The Yana Rolling Head (dismemberment) myth given above takes place during the time of the pine-nut harvest. Other Rolling Head myths also involve ripened fruit (Natchez [Swanton 1929:215–218], Alabama [Swanton 1929:131–132], Cashinawa [Lévi-Strauss 1979:95–96]). And going back to the *Popol Vuh*, when the head of One Hunahpu was placed in the tree, the tree miraculously bore fruit (Tedlock 1985:113). In fact, the Mesoamerican world view shared in the nearly universal theme of dismemberment as a source of primordial creation and fertility (see, e.g., Baal [1966:222] for a famous Old World example). This belief is best shown in an Aztec document, the *Histoyre du Mechique* (1905:29). In this account of the formation of the world, two gods divided the earth deity into two halves. The upper part of her body formed the earth and the lower part the sky. Afterwards, various plants arose from specific parts of her upper body.

Dismemberment is an all-encompassing concept which connotes the same basic themes as the rubber-ball game: celestial periodicity and agricultural fertility. There is also some iconographic support for the broader concept of dismemberment (as opposed to simple decapitation) in association with Mesoamerican ballgame symbolism. Monument 1 at Bilbao, Guatemala, is a Classic period stela often cited for its representation of ballgame decapitation (Figure 16.5) (Parsons 1969:Pl. 34a). It depicts a large central figure and four smaller figures, one in each corner. The central personage is recognized by his accoutrements to be a ball player. He holds a severed head and a knife in his hands, while the four other figures also hold severed heads. However, the main personage is standing on a human torso, a torso lacking arms and legs as well as a head, and there are hollows carved on the torso to indicate sockets where the limbs were removed (noted by Parsons 1969:104). Thus, the stela depicts dismemberment. Other carvings from this site, some associated with the ballgame, also portray cut up human body parts (1969:Pl. 44; Parsons this volume; see also Borhegyi 1980).

Body Symbolism and the Ballgame

Because so much ballgame iconography deals with the cutting up of the body, it is useful to explore further the symbolism associated with the separation of

*Figure 16.5. Monument 1, Bilbao, Guatemala, depicts a ball player (with yoke)
standing on a dismembered human torso. He holds a knife and a severed head. The
four personages in the corners also hold severed heads (after Moser 1973:Fig. 16;
Parsons 1969:Pl. 34a).*

body parts. A clue to the significance of the act of dismemberment comes
from a ballgame device, a *palma* from Veracruz (Figure 16.6) (Parsons 1969:Pl.
61b, c), which depicts human body parts on both sides. On one side are the
legs and pelvis (lower body) and on the other are the arms and head (upper
body). This *palma* thereby incorporates the division of the body into upper
and lower parts which has already been noted in several myths.

The assignment of meaning to these body divisions is also revealed by the
playing of the ballgame itself, because there were strict rules as to which

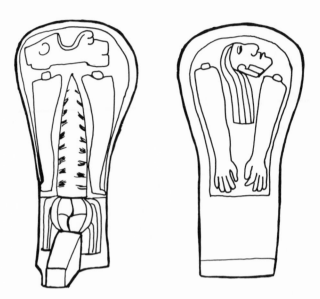

Figure 16.6. A Veracruz palma *shows dismembered human body parts on both sides* (*after Parsons 1969:Pl. 61b, c*).

areas of the body could be used to strike the ball (e.g., Métraux 1942; Stern 1949). For most of the Mesoamerican games, only the middle part of the body, usually the hips and buttocks, could touch the ball during play (Stern 1949:Map 3). This means the ball could touch a player only at the boundary between the upper and lower body, further reiterating the conceptual division of the body noted above for the Veracruz *palma*, an object which was worn at the player's waist, at the conceptual boundary.

A similar division into halves with a dividing line in between can be found on the ballcourt. Many representations of ballcourts in the codices show it as separated into two or four parts (see examples in Krickeberg 1966). Descriptions of the game by chroniclers (e.g., Durán 1971:315) and modern ethnographers (e.g., Kelly 1980a:166) mention a central dividing line separating the two teams. The line is often referred to by its Aztec name, *tlecotl* (Krickeberg 1966:195); in the Nayarit game it is called *analco*, meaning "from the other side, on the other shore of a river" (Kelly 1980a:166). What is significant about this division is that it parallels the division of the human body into halves or quarters as represented by the two limbs of the upper body and two limbs of the lower body. Furthermore, whereas the ballcourt has been thought to represent the earth and its four quarters (Stern 1949:69), the human body is also a representation of the earth or the cosmos. Therefore, the ballcourt is the same as the human body, divided in half or in quarters, as a symbolic representation of the same phenomenon.

Iconographic support for the supposition that the ballcourt represents the human body is found in the *Codex Borgia* (1963:Pl. 35) (Figure 16.7), where the splayed body of the anthropomorphized crocodilian earth is positioned on a ballcourt. The splayed or hocker position of the deity is related to the earth as earthmother since it is the birthing position (Klein 1976:15; Nicholson 1967:82). In the *Codex Borgia* picture, the four limbs of the deity's body are positioned in the four corners of the court, and the exaggerated circular midbody is at the center. Interestingly the head of the earth deity is not on any part of the ballcourt. This is because the ballcourt, as a four-part structure representing the four divisions of the human body, is headless. The ball, which moves back and forth from one end of the court to the other, is the

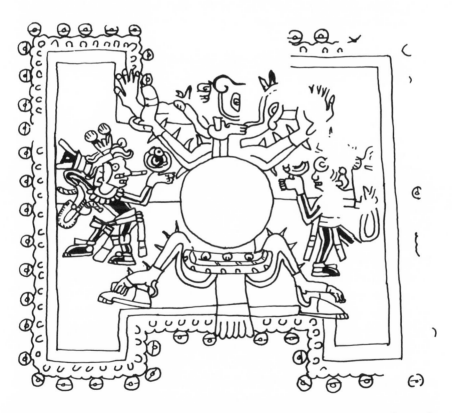

Figure 16.7. An anthropomorphic earth deity wearing a crocodilian skin is depicted in the splayed or hocker position with one limb on each quarter of a ballcourt, while two deities on either side hold balls with faces on them (Codex Borgia:Pl. 35).

severed head of the ballcourt, further emphasizing the separation of body parts and the symbolic significance of the head.

Another important part of the human body is its center, where the four divisions are joined. On the *Codex Borgia* deity, the center of the body is coincident with the center of the ballcourt. Ballcourts are often shown in the codices with centers marked by a circle (e.g., *Codex Colombino* 1966:Pl. 2; *Codex Bodley* No. 2858 [Krickeberg 1966:Fig. 19]), a *chalchihuitl* (jade jewel) symbol (*Codex Nuttall* 1975:74), or a skull (*Codex Nuttall* 1975:4; *Codex Borbonicus* 1981:Pl. 19). Many of the Aztec depictions of earth deities in the splayed or birthing position have the same or similar symbols marking the center of the body: a *chalchihuitl*; a quincunx (repeating the five-part directional symbolism of the body); a heart (Nicholson 1967:82); an *ollin* (movement) symbol, itself analogous with the four-quartered ballcourt (Krickeberg 1966:252); the sun symbol; and, very frequently, a skull. Personages in a similar splayed position with a central circle were also depicted on ballcourt markers at Tenam Rosario, Chiapas (Agrinier 1983). The ballcourt is thereby further linked to the body and to the earth by having its four quarters arrayed like the four limbs of the splayed earth deity, and by the sharing of the same symbols in its center, its "navel."

The "navel" of the earth is the entrance to the Underworld, as we know from myths of especially the Aztecs, and similarly, the ballcourt is an entrance to the Underworld (see, e.g., Brundage 1979:10; 1982:215; Cohodas 1975:110), specifically its center. The idea that the Underworld entrance is associated with the midbody is repeated in other aspects of the ballgame. For a certain distribution of the game (Hellmuth's [1975a] Toltec-Veracruz-Cotzumalhuapa-Tiquisate game), this part of the body is where another important piece of ballgame equipment was worn: the yoke. The iconography of many of these yokes depicts toads as zoomorphic representations of the earth (Nicholson 1967:83), or other individuals in the splayed position (see Proskouriakoff 1954) (Figure 16.8).

What is interesting about the use of this iconography on the stone yoke is that where one would expect to find the abdominal marker, the navel of the earth-deity, there is the opening of the yoke itself. When the yoke is worn, the ball player is positioned in this opening, in the navel, so that he is halfway in and halfway out of the Underworld (see also Wilkerson 1984:116). Because he wears the yoke at midbody, his lower body is in one realm, and his conceptually separate upper body is in another, so that his entire body is positioned at the threshold or boundary between the two realms. Being halfway in and out of the Underworld emphasizes the separation of the body into two parts, upper and lower, and the symbolic importance of the midbody, the only part allowed to touch the ball.

Figure 16.8. Relief carving of a toad in the hocker position decorates a Veracruz stone yoke. The opening of the yoke is located at the center of the toad's body (after Proskouriakoff 1954:Fig. 2).

Other scholars, as early as Preuss's work at the beginning of this century (cited in Krickeberg 1966:220), have observed that the yoke was probably conceived as an entrance to the Underworld, as were the vertical rings (see also Brundage 1979:10; 1982:215–216; Cohodas 1975:110) which were positioned on the ballcourt walls, notably at midcourt. The yoke, rings, and the idea of a central hole (whether or not real ballcourts actually had one [see Tozzer 1957:127]) reinforced the imagery of the ballcourt as an entrance to the Underworld, as did the fact that the court itself was often either partially sunken or had the appearance of being sunken into the ground (Brundage 1979:10), its inward sloping benches giving it the appearance of a V-shaped cleft (independently noted by Schele and Freidel this volume).

To be at the boundary between these two realms and thus have access to both is to be in a position of extraordinary power. As seen in other examples of Mesoamerican art, rulers had themselves depicted in the mouths of earth-monsters or niches representing entrances to the Underworld, demonstrating their singular ability to belong to both worlds. The ballcourt was therefore an extremely powerful place. As such, it was used for many other ritual activities besides the ballgame. The game itself can be viewed as equivalent to the "labyrinth," the difficult journey or test which must be overcome before one can gain entrance to the source of sacred power.[1]

Ballgames and Boundaries

In the symbolic separation of the body, in the separation of the space between the world of men and the world of gods, and in the separation of time into periods marked by celestial movements and the change of seasons, ballcourts and ballgames are associated with boundaries. Such boundaries marked the division of a unity into its discrete components. It was this principle which generated the surface symbolism seen in the iconography and mythology of game-playing peoples throughout the New World. Exactly how these ideas were expressed obviously differed in space and time, as various societies used the game to emphasize disparate kinds of boundaries, separating a variety of categories.

In keeping with its disjunctive quality, the ballgame also and most especially marked the separation of society into its component groupings, just as ballcourts were the loci where this separation was made manifest, and ballgame paraphernalia and costuming were the implements for symbolizing or accomplishing this separation. As noted above, there are examples from both North and South America of moieties playing one another in the game. In the Apinayé game, for example, the Kolti moiety (associated with the sun) played against the Kolre moiety (associated with the moon). It was only on this occasion that individuals addressed one another by their moiety name instead of their personal name (Nimuendajú 1939:67), further demonstrating that social separation was a crucial motive for the game. Furthermore, the rubber-ball game was played by the Apinayé only during the time of the boys' initiation, when they were in a liminal state, on the boundary between being children and adults.

The Classic Maya also associated ballgame imagery with a change in personal status, in this case, the accession of a king (Schele and Freidel this volume). There is iconographic evidence that the king dressed in ball player regalia, although it is uncertain if he actually played a game, in order to draw on the connotations of disjunction, as well as to demonstrate his personal link to cyclical cosmic forces. For example, Step VII of Yaxchilán Structure 33's Hieroglyphic Stairs depicts in bas-relief a ruler in ballgame regalia in position to strike a descending "ball," on which is carved a bound prisoner (Figure 14.6). These sacrificial victims, who were probably war captives and were identified with the ball, indicate the symbolic linking of the ballgame, interpolity warfare, and certain celestial events, particularly Venus events (Schele and Miller 1986:250). The game was thus a boundary maintenance mechanism between polities, with the sacrificial victim representing a "social decapitation," the removal of a member of the society (sometimes its ruler, its political "head") from the "body politic."

Other sacred histories relate that even a change in entire political hegemonies was accomplished via a ballgame, which served as the dynamic threshold between succeeding empires. In an Aztec myth (Mendieta 1945: 88), a ballgame defeat by the Toltec king Quetzalcóatl caused him to abandon his capital city, thus marking the end of the Toltec empire. Another story (*Leyenda de los Soles* 1975:126) also has the Toltec empire falling into ruin because of a ballgame, this time due to a victory by a Toltec king. This king, Huémac, played ball with the rain gods (similar to the North American "Thunderers" who played ball), but his failure to accept the winnings he was offered brought Toltec hegemony to an end and paved the way for the rise of the Aztecs. In a later historical episode, the ruler of Azcapotzalco essentially brought the Tepanec empire to an end, allowing the Mexica of Tenochtitlán to take its place, by his loss in a ballgame (Chimalpahin 1965:96, 194).

Just as the game connoted a temporal and sociopolitical boundary marker, the ballcourt itself marked a spatial division. Metaphorically, it lay at the boundary between the earth's surface world and the Underworld, as we have seen. Building a ballcourt was an act of territorial possession in which the natural landscape was transformed into cultural space (Leyenaar 1978:13), at the threshold between nature and culture. According to an Aztec document (Tezozomoc 1975:31) which tells the story of the Mexica migration to Tenochtitlán, their patron deity, Huitzilopochtli, built a ballcourt with its adjacent *tzompantli* (skull rack) as the first act in their settlement of Coatepec. Destruction of this same ballcourt, after Huitzilopochtli killed and decapitated Coyolxauhqui there, forced the people to leave that place (Tezozomoc 1980: 229; see Gillespie 1989).

The location of ballcourts in those societies which built these special structures also indicates their use as marking a variety of boundaries. Where a motive was to emphasize the distinction between diverse, probably competitive ethnic groups, ballcourts would be located at the edges of their respective territories, where their geographical boundaries coincided. Ritual ball playing here would have served as a boundary-maintenance mechanism, to keep the balance in the established "distances" (in all senses of the word) between the two groups. This seems to have been the case in Postclassic Highland Guatemala where the ballgame was played between the Quiché and other ethnic groups on the frontier (Fox 1981:342, this volume). Similarly, in the Valley of Oaxaca during the Monte Albán II period, a time of decentralization when ethnic/political/territorial distinctions may have been emphasized, there is evidence for ball playing particularly on the outer perimeter of the valley, on its frontier (Kowalewski et al. 1983:51; Kowalewski et al. this volume).

In contrast to these examples, there are also ballcourts at the centers of sites. Here an internal boundary was indicated, relating to divisions within the society. At Utatlán in Highland Guatemala, there is also a central ballcourt which bisected a line dividing moietal residential areas (Fox this volume). At Classic period Copán, Honduras, the Main Group is located between two roadways running east and west and leading to certain household types. "Not coincidentally, this central point in the Main Group coincides almost exactly with the location of the main ballcourt" (Fash 1983:283). In many of the west Mexican sites, ballcourts separate different circular residential complexes (Weigand this volume).

The boundary created by the ballcourt also marked cosmological divisions

associated with rulership and the separation of the ruling lineage from its sub-
jects. At Classic period Quiriguá, Guatemala, a ballcourt lies on the boundary
between the northern/sacred/ritual area of the Great Plaza Acropolis and the
southern/profane/worldly area (Ashmore 1983:9). At Preclassic Cerros in
Belize, there is also a "mediating ballcourt" between a tall northern structure
and a low southern structure which compose the Str. 50 Group (Ashmore
1983:11; see Ashmore 1989 and Scarborough [this volume] for further examples of mediating ballcourts in Maya settlement patterning).

Aztec Tenochtitlán's sacred precinct also has a pronounced north–south division most emphasized by the Templo Mayor itself (see map in León-Portilla
1978:App. II). An imaginary east–west line running through the precinct,
separating the Tlaloc and Huitzilopochtli temples on top of the main pyramid,
would cut the ballcourt in half. The two halves of the ballcourt may therefore
have been invested with the same oppositional meaning as the pairing of the
temples of Tlaloc (on the north, associated with rain and earth) and Huitzilopochtli (on the south, associated with sun and sky), notably in the annual
north–south movement of the sun corresponding to the alternation of rainy
and dry seasons and their related ceremonies.[2] This ballcourt is also situated
at the entrance to the ceremonial precinct itself, at the threshold between
sacred and profane.

Periodicity as Metaphor for Sociopolitical Divisions

The ballgame was an event that manifested the separation of a unity into its
parts—symbolized by the two teams, each on its own side of the playing
field—but which simultaneously provided for an ongoing relationship connecting these parts to one another in a structured way, by the movement of
the ball back and forth between the two sides. The nature of the game further
provided that in this relationship, a correct distance be maintained between
the divided parts so that one side did not consistently overtake the other (one
team did not take possession of the entire court). Although one team would
temporarily have an advantage in the winning of the game (and thus the game
would "limp"), such imbalance would be evened out over time as future
games were played.

The themes of the Mesoamerican ballgame revealed in the iconography
and mythology—astronomical periodicity and agricultural seasonality, related to dualism and the involvement of twins—have all been reiterated in
the interpretation presented here. However, these themes should be understood as specific examples, even metaphoric representations, of a more general principle: The ballgame introduces a disjunction and further serves to
maintain the boundary between the opposing categories that make up that

disjunction. While much of the Mesoamerican iconographic and textual imagery of the ballgame is explicitly related to seasonal fertility and celestial phenomena, I doubt that this was the major concern of the game. Instead, the dynamic cyclicity associated with the movement of heavenly bodies—though important to an agricultural society—*was itself a symbol* of the segmentation of, and the maintenance of the "correct" distance between, sociopolitical categories.

The concern for marking social boundaries would obviously be great in societies at a state level of organizational complexity, but even much smaller groups played the game for identical reasons. The ballgame of the Sherente of South America (Nimuendajú 1942:19–22) perhaps most clearly reveals how the game serves as a balancing act for social divisions, while at the same time takes on symbolic connotations of periodicity. The Sherente are divided into moieties affiliated with the sun and the moon. From knowledge of the symbolism of the Mesoamerican game, one would expect that each moiety fielded its own team so that the sun and moon could "struggle" with each other to symbolize the duality of day and night. In this case, however, the game is played only by the "foreign" clans which are not part of the moiety organization, in order to emphasize the recognized role these clans have in mediating between the two autochthonous moieties. By playing the game, and by their nature as outsiders, the foreign clans maintain the boundary (the correct "distance") between the sun and the moon, and more obviously, between the social categories represented by the moiety divisions.

The notion that the boundaries being marked and the distances maintained were not simply tied to seasonal periodicity is supported by other evidence, such as the Mixtec codices, which indicate the intercommunity and intracommunity mediating functions served by the ballcourts (Molloy 1985), and the Rolling Head myths. Although many of the myths from Amazonia are about the origin of the moon (the Rolling Head introducing monthly periodicity), in fact they really deal with marriage alliances (Lévi-Strauss 1979:73). They are concerned with maintaining the proper social distances among persons, and thus they examine both incest (where the relationship is too close) and marriage with animals (a relationship that is too distant).

Indeed, many of the myths about the sun and moon deal with social relationships (Lévi-Strauss 1979:91–92, 157). In these myths the sun and moon are placed in their proper locations in the heavens, at their proper distances from the earth and from one another. Therefore, each will have its turn during the day and nighttime, and the cyclical system will remain balanced. Nevertheless, the spatial axis between sky and earth, in which the sun is kept at a certain correct distance—not too far (= eternal night, cold) or too near (= eternal day, drought)—is related to the ideal distance between two potential spouses in the marriage alliance system (Lévi-Strauss 1979:174).

In North America, the Rolling Head myths are concerned with the more fundamental separation between humans and animals (Lévi-Strauss 1979:74) rather than the separation of people into marriage categories. In the Blackfoot myth and others, the wife has an animal for a lover, thereby failing to distinguish animals from humans. Her decapitation, the introduction of disjunction in her body, is the pretext for emphasizing the separation of humans and animals. (The Blackfoot Rolling Head myth introduced a further ethnic separation, between whites and Indians; see above.)

In the Southeastern United States, the Rolling Head was replaced by a chunkee stone which was owned by a cannibal. Cannibals eat people, and confuse people with food (animals). In some versions the cannibal even ate his own wife; he eats what he should have sex with. He is an inversion of the Plains woman who has sex with what she should eat. In all these examples, one must look beyond the obvious references to astronomical, agricultural, calendrical, or other overt symbols to determine the more fundamental categorical separations that are being examined.

Conclusions

The unity of the rubber-ball game in its many manifestations, and its link to similar New World games, are based on the premise that by its nature a game marks a disjunction, a separation into opposing categories, while maintaining a balanced relationship between those categories. The balance may be attained by the action of the ball itself as it alternates between the teams, or in the alternation of winners and losers in successive games. The complicated scoring procedures of the surviving west Mexican rubber-ball games, in which points can be both gained and lost in various ways (Kelly 1980a:169; Leyenaar 1985), reveals how difficult it was for either side to overtake quickly the other. This underlines the notion that what was desired was a recognition of the separation of phenomena into categories with a simultaneous balance between them.

The diversity of the ballgames, seen in the playing rules, the configuration of the courts (or their absence), the equipment and costuming, and the iconography of related artworks, results in part from the diversity of boundaries that were of concern to the New World peoples who played the games. The more abstract conceptions frequently were not made explicit but were couched in the easily grasped metaphoric representations of the separation of the cosmos into seasons or day and night by the cyclical movements of astral phenomena, separations which were already meaningful to the people. These ideas were further symbolized by the ritual act of decapitation, separating the head from the body. In Mesoamerica in particular, the headless body represented the ballcourt itself, its four quarters the symbol of the divisions of the cosmos, and the animated head represented the ball which conjoined those divisions by its movement between them.

Notes

1. The link with the Underworld—source of supernatural power—also helps to explain the prognostication or divinatory aspects sometimes associated with the game.

2. The sun at equinox appears to rise precisely between the two temples on top of the Templo Mayor pyramid, an event said to account for an early map of Tenochtitlán in which the "sun" is represented by a head peering between the two temples (Aveni 1980:246–248). Also appearing in this map is a headless body placed in front of the Templo Mayor—right where the ballcourt was located. Continuing this argument to its logical conclusion, during the year the sun will move north and south of this equinoctial line. In the summer it will move into Tlaloc's "court" in the north, with great danger that the sun-ball will become "dead"—it will cease moving—when it reaches the end of that "court" at the solstice. This may be why points were lost in the game when the ball became dead at the end of the court (according to Durán 1971:314), when it ceased to move at its farthest extreme, when the seasons seemed to "limp" the most. In that case there would be permanent summer, and seasonal balance would be lost. What was needed to avoid this imbalance was for the sun-ball to be returned to Huitzilopochtli's side of the "court," which it entered at the autumnal equinox on its southern journey. During the winter, the dry season, "when the sun was weak . . . Huitzilopochtli was feasted and celebrated . . . to coax him, as sun fire, to retrace his journey in the ecliptic and recreate a balance with the earth" (Hunt 1977:126–127).

Bibliography

Acosta, Jorge R., and Hugo Moedano Köer. 1946. Los Juegos de Pelota. In *México Prehispánico: Culturas, Deidades, Monumentos*, ed. J. A. Vivó, pp. 365–384. Antología de Esta Semana, México, D.F.

Adams, Richard E.W. 1981. Settlement Patterns of the Central Yucatán and Southern Campeche Regions. In *Lowland Maya Settlement Patterns*, ed. Wendy Ashmore, pp. 211–257. University of New Mexico Press, Albuquerque.

Adams, Richard E.W., ed. 1984. *Río Azul Project Report*, 1. Center for Archaeological Research. The University of Texas, San Antonio.

Adams, Richard E.W., and Woodruff D. Smith. 1981. Feudal Models for Classic Maya Civilization. In *Lowland Maya Settlement Patterns*, ed. Wendy Ashmore, pp. 335–349. University of New Mexico Press, Albuquerque.

Adams, Richard N. 1975. *Energy and Structure: A Theory of Social Power*. University of Texas Press, Austin.

Adams, Robert McC. 1970. Patrones de Cambio de la Organización Territorial. In *Ensayos de Antropología en la Zona Central de Chiapas*, pp. 43–76. Instituto Nacional Indigenista, Mexico.

Agrinier, Pierre. 1969a. Reconocimiento del Sitio Varejonal, Municipio de Jiquipilas, Chiapas. In *Anales, 1969–1968*, Séptima Época, Tomo I, pp. 69–93. Instituto Nacional de Antropología e Historia, Mexico.

———. 1969b. Dos Tumbas Tardías y Otro Descubrimientos en Chinkultic. *Boletín INAH*, no. 36. Instituto Nacional de Antropología e Historia, Mexico.

———. 1972. Summary Report of Archaeological Investigation at Mound 1. New World Archaeological Foundation, San Cristobal de las Casas.

———. 1975. The Classic Period in Central Chiapas and Teotihuacan. Paper presented at the Brigham Young University Centennial Social Science Symposium No. 1, "Uncovering Mesoamerican Civilization," October 28–29. Provo.

347

————. 1976. Newly Discovered Classic Maya Sculptures at Tenam Rosario, Chiapas. Paper presented in the Second Cambridge Symposium on Recent Research in Mesoamerican Archaeology, Cambridge.

————. 1983. Tenam Rosario: Una Posible Relocalización del Clásico Tardío Terminal Maya Desde el Usumacinta. In *Antropología e Historia de los Mixe-Zoques y Mayas: Homenaje a Frans Blom*, ed. Lorenzo Ochoa and Thomas A. Lee, Jr., pp. 241–254. Universidad Nacional Antónoma de México, Mexico City.

Alegria, Ricardo E. 1983. *Ball Courts and Ceremonial Plazas in the West Indies*. Yale University Publications in Anthropology, no. 79. Department of Anthropology, Yale University, New Haven.

Andrews, Anthony P. 1983. *Maya Salt Production and Trade*. The University of Arizona Press, Tucson.

Andrews, Anthony P., and Fernando Robles C. 1985. Chichén Itzá and Coba: An Itza-Maya Standoff in Early Postclassic Yucatán. In *The Lowland Maya Postclassic*, ed. Arlen F. Chase and Prudence M. Rice, pp. 62–72. University of Texas Press, Austin.

Andrews, E. Wyllys, V. 1976. *The Archaeology of Quelepa, El Salvador*. Middle American Research Institute, pub. 42. Tulane University, New Orleans.

————. 1981. Dzibilchaltún. In *Supplement to the Handbook of Middle American Indians, Volume 1, Archaeology*, ed. Jeremy A. Sabloff, pp. 313–341. University of Texas Press, Austin.

Andrews, George F. 1975. *Maya Cities: Placemaking and Urbanization*. University of Oklahoma Press, Norman.

————. 1984. *Edzna, Campeche, Mexico: Settlement Patterns and Monumental Architecture* (rev. ed.). Foundation for Latin American Anthropological Research, Culver City, Calif.

Anonymous. 1986. *El Juego de Pelota: Una Tradición Prehispánica Viva*. Instituto Nacional de Antropología e Historia, México, D.F.

Anton, Ferdinand, 1970. *Art of the Maya*. G.P. Putnam's Sons, New York.

Anyon, Roger. 1984. Mogollon Settlement Patterns and Communal Architecture. Master's thesis, Department of Anthropology, University of New Mexico, Albuquerque.

Anyon, Roger, and Steven A. LeBlanc. 1984. *The Galaz Ruin, a Prehistoric Mimbres Village in Southwestern New Mexico*. Maxwell Museum of Anthropology and the University of New Mexico Press, Albuquerque.

Ashmore, Wendy. 1983. Ideological Structure in Ancient Maya Settlement Patterns. Paper presented at the 82nd Annual Meeting of the American Anthropological Association, Chicago.

————. 1989. Construction and Cosmology: Politics and Ideology in Lowland Maya Settlement Patterns. In *Word and Image in Maya Culture*, ed. William F. Hanks and Don S. Rice, pp. 272–286. University of Utah Press, Salt Lake City.

Auguet, Roland. 1972. *Cruelty and Civilization: The Roman Games*. George Allen and Unwin Ltd., London.

Aulie, H. Wilbur, and Evelyn W. de Aulie. 1978. Diccionario Ch'ol-Español-Ch'ol. *Serie de Vocabulario y Diccionarios Indigenas "Mariano Silva y Aceves"* 21. Instituto Lingüistico de Verano, México.

Aveleyra A., Luis. 1963. An Extraordinary Composite Stela from Teotihuacán. *American Antiquity* 29:235–237.

Aveni, Anthony F. 1980. *Skywatchers of Ancient Mexico*. University of Texas Press, Austin.

Aveni, Anthony F., Horst Hartung, and J. Charles Kelley. 1982. Alta Vista (Chalchihuites): Astronomical Implications of a Mesoamerican Ceremonial Outpost at the Tropic of Cancer. *American Antiquity* 47:316–335.

Baal, Jan van. 1966. *Dema. Description and Analysis of Marind-Amin Culture (South New Guinea)*. Koninklijki Institut voor Taal-, Land- en Volkenkunde, The Hague.

Ball, Joseph W. 1978. Archaeological Pottery of the Yucatán-Campeche Coast. In *Studies in Archaeology of Coastal Yucatán and Campeche, Mexico*, Middle American Research Institute, pub. 46, pp. 69–146. Tulane University, New Orleans.

———. 1979. Ceramics, Culture History, and the Puuc Tradition: Some Alternative Possibilities. In *The Puuc: New Perspectives*, ed. L. Mills, pp. 18–35. Central College Press, Pella.

———. 1983. Teotihuacán, the Maya, and Ceramic Interchange: A Contextual Perspective. In *Highland–Lowland Interaction in Mesoamerica: Interdisciplinary Approaches*, ed. A. Miller, pp. 125–145. Dumbarton Oaks, Washington, D.C.

Bardsley, Sandra. 1987. *Inaugural Art of Bird Jaguar IV: Rewriting History at Yaxchilán*. Ms. thesis, Department of Fine Arts, University of British Columbia.

Barrera Vasquez, Alfredo. 1980. *Diccionario Maya Cordemex*. Ediciones Cordemex, Merida, Yucatán, Mexico.

Barthel, Thomas. 1952. Der Morgensternkult in den Darstellungen der Desdener Mayahandschrift. *Ethnos* 17:73–112.

Batres, Leopoldo. 1903. *Visita a los Monumentos Arqueologicos de "La Quemada," Zacatecas*. Mexico. (Reprinted without illustrations as "Visit to the Archaeological Remains of La Quemada, Zacatecas" in *The North Mexican Frontier*, ed. Basil C. Hedrick, J. Charles Kelley, and Carroll L. Riley, pp. 1–20, 1971. Southern Illinois University, Carbondale.)

Baudez, Claude F. 1984. Le Roi, la Balle et la Maïs. Images du Jeu de Balle Maya. *Journal de la Société des Américanistes de Paris* 70:139–152.

Baudez, Claude F., and Peter Mathews. 1979. Capture and Sacrifice at Palenque. In *Tercera Mesa Redonda de Palenque*, ed. Merle Greene Robertson and Donnan Call Jeffers, pp. 31–40. Pre-Columbian Art Research Center, Palenque and Herald Printers, Monterey.

Beals, Ralph L. 1933. *The Acaxee, A Mountain Tribe of Durango and Sinaloa. Ibero-Americana*. 6. University of California Press, Berkeley.

Becker, Marshall J. 1979. Priests, Peasants, and Ceremonial Centers: The Intellectual History of a Model. In *Maya Archaeology and Ethnohistory*, ed. Norman Hammond and Gordon R. Willey, pp. 3–20. University of Texas Press, Austin.

Becquelin, Pierre, and Claude F. Baudez. 1979–82. *Tonina. Une Cité Maya du Chiapas*. Coll. *Études Mésoaméricaines*, Tome 1, MAEFM tomes 2 and 3, ADPF. Editions Recherches sur les Civilisations, Mexico and Paris.

———. 1982. Tonina, Une Cité Maya du Chiapas. *Études Mésoaméricaines* IV. Mission Archéologique Francaise au Mexique. Editions Recherche sur les Civilisations, Paris.

Bedoian, William H. 1973. *Oro y Maiz: The Economic Structure of the Mexican Empire and its Effects on Social Stratification and Political Power*. Ms. thesis, Department of Anthropology, Pennsylvania State University, University Park.

Beetz, C. P., and L. Satterthwaite. 1981. *The Monuments and Inscriptions of Caracol, Belize*. *University Museum* Monograph 45. University of Pennsylvania, Philadelphia.

Benavides Castillo, Antonio. 1976. Cobá, Reporte de Actividades. In *Cobá: Un Sitio Maya en Quintana Roo*, pp. 1–104. *Quadernos de los Centros*, Numero 26. Instituto Nacional de Antropología e Historia, México, D.F.

Benson, Elizabeth P. 1967. *The Maya World*. Thomas Y. Crowell, New York.

Berdan, Frances. 1982. *The Aztecs of Central Mexico: An Imperial Society*. Holt, Rinehart, and Winston, New York.

Beristáin Bravo, Francisco. 1983. Análisis Arquitectónico del Juego de Pelota en el Área Central de México. *Revista Maya de Estudios Antropológicos* 29(1):211–242.

Berlin, Heinrich. 1963. The Palenque Triad. *Journal de la Société des Américanistes*, N.S., 52:91–99.

Berlo, Janet C. 1983. The Warrior and the Butterfly: Central Mexican Ideologies of Sacred Warfare and Teotihuacan Iconography. In *Text and Image in Pre-Columbian Art*, ed. Janet C. Berlo, pp. 79–117. British Archaeological Reports, International Series, Oxford.

———. 1984. *Teotihuacan Art Abroad: A Study of Metropolitan Style and Provincial Transformations in Incensario Workshops*. British Archaeological Reports, International Series, Oxford.

Bernal, Ignacio. 1965. Archaeological Synthesis of Oaxaca. In *Handbook of Middle American Indians*, vol. 3. *Archaeology of Southern Mesoamerica*, Pt. 2, ed. Gordon R. Willey, pp. 788–813. University of Texas Press, Austin.

———. 1968. The Ball Players of Dainzu. *Archaeology* 21:246–251.

———. 1969a. El Juego de Pelota Mas Antiguo de Mexico. *Artes de Mexico* 119:28–33.

———. 1969b. *The Olmec World*. University of California Press, Berkeley.

———. 1973. Stone Reliefs in the Dainzu Area. In *The Iconography of Middle American Sculpture*, ed. Gordon R. Willey, pp. 13–23. Metropolitan Museum of Art, New York City.

Bernal, Ignacio, and Lorenzo Gamio. 1974. *Yagul: El Palacio de los Seis Patios*. Universidad Nacional Autónoma de México, México, D.F.

Beutelspacher, Ludwig. 1982. El Magueyal, Chiapas: Un Asentamiento Postclásico del Valle de Osumacinta. Thesis to obtain the title of Archaeologist, Instituto Nacional de Antropología e Historia, México, D.F.

Beyer, Herman. 1933. Shell Ornament Sets from the Huasteca, Mexico. *Middle American Research Series*, pub. 5, pp. 161–213. Tulane University, New Orleans.

Blanton, Richard E. 1972. Prehispanic Settlement Patterns of the Ixtapalapa Region, Mexico. *Occasional Papers in Anthropology* 6. Department of Anthropology, Pennsylvania State University, University Park.

———. 1975. Texcoco Region Archaeology. *American Antiquity* 40:227–230.

———. 1976. Anthropological Studies of Cities. *Annual Review of Anthropology* 5:249–264.

————. 1978. *Monte Albán: Settlement Patterns at the Ancient Zapotec Capital*. Academic Press, New York.

Blanton, Richard E., and Gary Feinman. 1984. The Mesoamerican World System. *American Anthropologist* 86:673–683.

Blanton, Richard E., Stephan A. Kowalewski, Gary Feinman, and Jill Appel. 1981. *Ancient Mesoamerica: A Comparison of Change in Three Regions*. Cambridge University Press, Cambridge.

————. 1982. *Monte Albán's Hinterland*, Pt. 1: *The Prehispanic Settlement Patterns of the Central and Southern Parts of the Valley of Oaxaca, Mexico*. *Memoirs of the Museum of Anthropology* 15. University of Michigan, Ann Arbor.

Blom, Frans. 1930. Preliminary Notes on Two Important Finds. *Proceedings of the 23rd International Congress of Americanists* pp. 165–171. New York, 1928.

————. 1932. The Maya Ball-Game "*Pok-ta-pok*," called *Tlachtli* by the Aztecs. *Middle American Research Series Publication* 4, pp. 485–530. Tulane University, New Orleans.

————. Archives, Na Bolom. San Cristobal de Las Casas.

Blom, Frans, and Gertrude Duby. 1957. *La Selva Lacandona*, vol. 2. Editorial Cultura T.G., S.A., Mexico.

Blom, Frans, and Oliver La Farge. 1926. *Tribes and Temples* vol. 2. *Middle American Research Institute*, Pub. 1. Tulane University, New Orleans.

Boas, Franz. 1901. *The Eskimo of Baffin Land and Hudson Bay. Bulletin of the American Museum of Natural History* 15, pt. 1. New York.

Bogoras, Waldemar. 1904–1909. *The Chukchee. Publications of the Jesup North Pacific Expedition*, vol. 7. *Memoirs of the American Museum of Natural History*, vol. 11. New York.

Bolles, John S. 1977. *Las Monjas: A Major Pre-Mexican Architectural Complex at Chichén Itzá*. University of Oklahoma Press, Norman.

Bolz-Augenstein, Ingborg. 1975. *Meisterwerke Altindianischer Kunst: Die Sammlung Ludwig im Rautenstrauch-Joest-Museum Köhn*. A. Bongers, Recklinghausen.

Boone, Elizabeth H., ed. 1984. *Ritual Human Sacrifice in Mesoamerica*. Dumbarton Oaks, Washington, D.C.

Borhegyi, Stephan F. de. 1959. Underwater Archaeology in the Maya Highlands. *Scientific American* 200(3):100–113.

————. 1960. America's Ballgame. *Natural History* 69:48–59.

————. 1961. Ball-game Handstone and Ball-game Gloves. In *Essays in Precolumbian Art and Archaeology*, ed. Samuel Lothrop et al., pp. 126–151. Harvard University Press, Cambridge.

————. 1963. The Rubber Ball Game of Ancient America. *Lore* 13(2):44–53.

————. 1969. The Precolumbian Ball-game: A Pan-mesoamerican Tradition. *Proceedings of the 38th International Congress of Americanists*, 1968, Munich, 1:499–515.

————. 1980. *The Pre-Columbian Ballgames: A Pan-Mesoamerican Tradition. Contributions in Anthropology and History* no. 1. Milwaukee Public Museum, Milwaukee.

Bourne, Frank C. 1966. *A History of the Romans*. D.C. Heath, Boston.

Brady, James E. 1989. Man-Made Caves: An Unrecognized Architectural Form in the Maya Highlands. Paper presented at the Tercer Simposio de Arqueología Guatemalteca. Guatemala City.

Brand, Donald D. 1939. Notes on the Geography and Archaeology of Zape, Durango. In *So Live the Words of Men*, ed. Donald D. Brand and Fred E. Harvey, pp. 75–106. University of New Mexico Press, Albuquerque.

Bricker, Victoria. 1986. A Grammar of Mayan Hieroglyphs. *Middle American Research Institute* Pub. 56. Middle American Research Institute, Tulane University, New Orleans.

Brown, Kenneth L. 1973. The B-III-5 Mound Group: Early and Middle Classic Civic Architecture. In *The Pennsylvania State University Kaminaljuyú Project: 1969, 1970 Seasons*. Pt. 1: *Mound Excavations*, ed. Joseph W. Michels and William T. Sanders, pp. 391–463. *Occasional Papers in Anthropology* 9. Pennsylvania State University, University Park.

———. 1977. The Valley of Guatemala: A Highland Port of Trade. In *Teotihuacán and Kaminaljuyú: A Study in Prehistoric Culture Contact*, ed. William T. Sanders and Joseph W. Michels, pp. 205–396. Pennsylvania State University Press Monograph Series on Kaminaljuyú, University Park.

———. 1983. Archaeology, Ethnohistory and Quiché Maya: A Study of Social Organization. Paper presented at the 82nd Annual Meeting of the American Anthropological Association, Chicago.

———. 1984. Settlement Systems, Ceramic Designs, and the Political Organization of the Late Postclassic Quiche Maya Empire. Paper presented at the 83rd Annual Meeting of the American Anthropological Association, Denver.

———. 1985. Postclassic Relationships between the Highland and Lowland Maya. In *The Lowland Maya Postclassic*, ed. Arlen F. Chase and Prudence M. Rice, pp. 270–281. University of Texas Press, Austin.

Brumfiel, Elizabeth M. 1980. Specialization, Market Exchange, and the Aztec State: A View from Huexotla. *Current Anthropology* 21:459–478.

Brundage, Burr Cartwright. 1979. *The Fifth Sun: Aztec Gods, Aztec World*. University of Texas Press, Austin.

———. 1982. *The Phoenix of the Western World. Quetzalcoatl and the Sky Religion*. University of Oklahoma Press, Norman.

Bryant, Douglas. 1982. The Early Classic Maya Occupation at Ojo de Agua, Chiapas, Mexico. Unpublished manuscript on file. New World Archaeological Foundation. San Cristobal de las Casas.

Bullard, William R., Jr. 1960. Maya Settlement Pattern in Northeastern Petén, Guatemala. *American Antiquity* 25:355–372.

Bullard, William R., Jr., and Mary R. Bullard. 1965. *Late Classic Finds at Baking Pot, British Honduras. Royal Ontario Museum Art and Archaeology Occasional Papers*, no. 8. Toronto.

Bushnell, Geoffrey H.S. 1965. *Ancient Art of the Americas*. F.A. Praeger, London.

Cable, John S., and David E. Doyel. 1985. The Pueblo Patricio Sequence: Its Implications for the Study of Hohokam Origins, Pioneer Period Site Structure and the Processes of Sedentism. In *City of Phoenix, Archaeology of the Original Townsite, Block 24-East*, ed. John S. Cable, Kathleen S. Hoffman, David E. Doyel, and Frank Ritz, pp. 211–272. *Soil Systems Publications in Archaeology* 8, Phoenix.

Calnek, Edward E. 1972. Settlement Pattern and Chinampa Agriculture at Tenochtitlán. *American Antiquity* 37:104–115.

————. 1976. The Internal Structure of Tenochtitlán. In *The Valley of Mexico: Studies of Pre-Hispanic Ecology and Society,* ed. Eric R. Wolf, pp. 287–302. University of New Mexico Press, Albuquerque.

Campbell, Lyle. 1988. The Linguistics of Southeast Chiapas, Mexico. *Papers of the New World Archaeological Foundation* 50. Brigham Young University, Provo.

Canouts, Valetta, assembler. 1975. *An Archaeological Survey of the Orme Reservoir.* Arizona State Museum Archaeological Series 92. Arizona State Museum, University of Arizona, Tucson.

Carlson, John. 1981. A Geomantic Model for the Interpretation of Mesoamerican Sites: An Essay in Cross-Cultural Comparison. In *Mesoamerican Sites and World-Views,* ed. Elizabeth P. Benson, pp. 143–211. Dumbarton Oaks, Washington, D.C.

————. 1988. The Divine Lord: The Maya God C as the Personification of *k'u,* Divinity, Spirit, and the Soul. Paper presented at the 46th International Congress of Americanists, Amsterdam.

Carmack, Robert M. 1981. *The Quiché Mayas of Utatlán.* University of Oklahoma Press, Norman.

Carr, Robert F., and James E. Hazard. 1961. *Map of the Ruins of Tikal, El Petén, Guatemala. Tikal Report* no. 11, University. Museum Monographs, University of Pennsylvania, Philadelphia.

Carrasco, Pedro. 1978. La Economia del Mexico Prehispánico. In *Economia Política e Ideología en el México Prehispánico,* ed. Pedro Carrasco and Johanna Broda, pp. 15–76. Editorial Nueva Imagen, México D.F., Mexico.

————. 1981. Comment. *Current Anthropology* 22(1):50.

————. 1982. The Political Economy of the Aztec and Inca States. In *The Inca and Aztec States, 1400–1800,* ed. George A. Collier, Renato I. Rosaldo, and John D. Wirth, pp. 23–39. Academic Press, New York.

Case, Henry A. 1911. *Views on and of Yucatán.* Henry Case, Mérida, Yucatán.

Caso, Alfonso. 1942. El Paraíso Terrenal de Teotihuacán. *Cuadernos Americanos* I, no. 6, pp. 127–136. Mexico.

Castro-Leal Espino, Marcia. 1972. La Decapitación y el Juego de Pelota. In *Religión en Mesoamérica,* ed. Jaime Litvak King and Noemí Castillo Tejero, pp. 457–462. Sociedad Mexicana de Antropología, México, D.F.

Cepeda Cardenas, Gerardo. 1972. Dos Construcciones Rituales del Juego de Pelota Mesoamericano. In *Religión en Mesoamerica.* XII Mesa Redonda, pp. 127–134. Sociedad Mexicana de Antropología, México, D.F.

Cervantes Salazar, F. 1936. *Cronica de Nueva Espana.* México, D.F.

Chard, Chester S. 1940. Distribution and Significance of Ball Courts in the Southwest. *Papers of the Excavators Club* 1(2):7–18.

Charlton, Thomas H. 1978. Teotihuacán, Tepeapulco, and Obsidian Exploitation. *Science* 200:1227–1236.

Charnay, Desire. 1888. *Ancient Cities of the New World.* Chapman and Hall, London.

Chase, Arlen F., and Diane Z. Chase. 1987. *Investigations at the Classic Maya City of Caracol, Belize: 1985–1987. Pre-Columbian Art Research Institute* Monograph 3. San Francisco, California.

Cheek, Charles D. 1977. Excavations at the Palangana and the Acropolis, Kaminaljuyú. In *Teotihuacán and Kaminaljuyú: A Study in Prehistoric Culture Contact,* ed. William T. Sanders and Joseph W. Michels, pp. 1–204.

Pennsylvania State University Press Monograph Series on Kaminaljuyú, University Park.

Chimalpahin Cuauhtlehuanitzin, Francisco de San Antón Muñón. 1965. *Relaciones Originales de Chalco Amaquemecan*, trans. Sylvia Rendón. Fondo de Cultura Económica, México, D.F.

Chontal Text, The. 1968 [1567–1603]. The Chontal Text, App. A. *The Maya Chontal Indians of Acalan-Tischel*, by France V. Scholes and Ralph L. Roys, pp. 359–405. University of Oklahoma Press, Norman.

Claessen, Henri J., and Peter Skalnik, eds. 1978. *The Early State*. Mouton, The Hague.

Clancy, Flora S., Clemency C. Coggins, and T. Patrick Culbert. 1985. Exhibition Catalogue. In *Maya: Treasures of an Ancient Civilization*, ed. Clancy et al., pp. 97–231. Abrams, New York.

Clarke, David. 1978. *Analytical Archaeology*, 2nd ed. Columbia University Press, New York.

Clune, Francis J. 1963. *A Functional and Historical Analysis of the Ball Game in Mesoamerica*. Ph.D. diss., Department of Anthropology, University of California, Los Angeles.

———. 1976. The Ballcourt at Amapa. In *The Archaeology of Amapa, Nayarit*, ed. Clement W. Meighan, pp. 275–298. Institute of Archaeology, University of California, Los Angeles.

Codex Borbonicus. 1981. Siglo Veintiuno, México, D.F.

Codex Borgia. 1963. Fondo de Cultura Económica, México, D.F.

Codex Colombino. 1966. Sociedad Mexicana de Antropología, México, D.F.

Codex Dresden. 1880. *Die Maya-Handschrift der Königlichen Bibliothek zu Dresden*, ed. E. Förstemann. Röder, Leipzig.

Codex Magliabechiano. 1983. University of California Press, Berkeley.

Codex Mendoza. 1938. Waterlow and Sons, London.

Codex Nuttall. 1975. Dover Publications, New York.

Codex Ríos. 1964. *Antigüedades de México Basadas en la Recopilacíon de Lord Kingsborough*, ed. José Corona Núñez, vol. 3. Secretaría de Hacienda y Crédito Público, México, D.F.

Coe, Michael D. 1965a. Archaeological Synthesis of Southern Veracruz and Tabasco. In *Handbook of Middle American Indians*, vol. 3, ed. Robert Wauchope; *Archaeology of Southern Mesoamerica*, pt. 2, ed. Gordon R. Willey, pp. 679–715. University of Texas Press, Austin.

———. 1965b. *The Jaguar's Children: Pre-Classic Central Mexico*. The Museum of Primitive Art, New York.

———. 1973. *The Maya Scribe and His World*. The Grolier Club, New York.

———. 1975. Death and the Ancient Maya. In *Death and the Afterlife in Pre-Columbian America*, ed. Elizabeth P. Benson, pp. 87–104. Dumbarton Oaks, Washington, D.C.

———. 1977. Olmec and Maya: A Study in Relationships. In *The Origins of Maya Civilization*, ed. R.E.W. Adams, pp. 183–196. University of New Mexico Press, Albuquerque.

———. 1978. *Lords of the Underworld, Masterpieces of Classic Maya Ceramics*. The Art Museum, Princeton University, Princeton.

———. 1981. San Lorenzo Tenochtitlán. In *Supplement to the Handbook of Middle*

American Indians, vol. 1, ed. Jeremy A. Sabloff, pp. 117–146. University of
Texas Press, Austin.

———. 1982. *Old Gods and Young Heroes*. Israel Museum, Jerusalem.

Coe, Michael D., and Richard A. Diehl. 1980. *In the Land of the Olmec. The
Archaeology of San Lorenzo Tenochtitlán*, vol. 1. University of Texas Press,
Austin.

Coe, William R. 1962. A Summary of Excavation and Research at Tikal, Guatemala:
1956–1961. *American Antiquity* 27:479–507.

———. 1967. *Tikal: A Handbook of the Ancient Maya Ruins*. University Museum,
University of Pennsylvania, Philadelphia.

Coggins, Clemency. 1980. The Shape of Time: Some Political Implications of a
Four-Part Figure. *American Antiquity* 45:727–739.

Cohen, Abner. 1976. *Two-Dimensional Man*. University of California Press,
Berkeley.

Cohodas, Marvin. 1974. The Iconography of the Panels of the Sun, Cross, and
Foliated Cross at Palenque, pt. II. In *Primera Mesa Redonda de Palenque*, ed.
M. Greene, pp. 96–107. Robert Louis Stevenson School, Pebble Beach, Calif.

———. 1975. The Symbolism and Ritual Function of the Middle Classic Ballgame
in Mesoamerica. *American Indian Quarterly* 2(2):99–130.

———. 1978a. Diverse Architectural Styles and the Ball Game Cult: The Late
Middle Classic Period in Yucatán. In *Middle Classic Mesoamerica A.D. 400–700*,
ed. Esther Pasztory, pp. 86–107. Columbia University Press, New York.

———. 1978b. *The Great Ball Court at Chichén Itzá, Yucatán, Mexico*. Garland
Press, New York.

———. 1980. Radial Pyramids and Radial-associated Assemblages of the Central
Maya Area. *Journal of the Society of Architectural Historians* 39(3):208–223.

———. 1982. The Bicephalic Monster in Classic Maya Sculpture. *Anthropologica*
24:105–146.

———. 1985. Public Architecture of the Maya Lowlands. *Cuadernos de
Arquitectura Mesoamericana* 6:51–58.

———. 1989a. Transformations: Relationships Between Image and Text in the
Ceramic Paintings of the Metropolitan Master. In *Word and Image in Maya
Culture*, ed. William F. Hanks and Don S. Rice, pp. 198–231. University of Utah
Press, Salt Lake City.

———. 1989b. The Epiclassic Problem: A Review and Alternative Model. In
Mesoamerica After the Decline of Teotihuacán: A.D. 700–900, ed. Richard A.
Diehl and Janet C. Berlo, pp. 219–240. Dumbarton Oaks, Washington, D.C.

Con Uribe, María José. 1981. Laguna Francesa. *Colección Científica (Arqueología)
100*. Instituto Nacional de Antropología e Historia, Mexico.

Cook, Scott. 1982. *Zapotec Stoneworkers: The Dynamics of Rural Simple
Commodity Production in Modern Mexican Capitalsim*. University Press of
America, Washington, D.C.

Corbett, John M. 1939. Ball Courts and Ball Games of the Ancient American
Indians. Master's thesis, Department of Anthropology, University of Southern
California, Los Angeles.

Cordell, Linda S. 1984. *Prehistory of the Southwest*. Academic Press, New York.

Corona Nuñez, José. 1946. Cuitzeo. Estudio Antropogeográfico. *Acta Antropologica*
II:1. Mexico.

Corson, Christopher. 1975. Stylistic Evolution of Jaina Figurines. *The Master Key* 49(4):130–138.

Coulborn, Rushton. 1956. *Feudalism in History.* Princeton University Press, Princeton.

C'oyoi. 1973 [ca. 1550–1570]. Titulo C'oyoi. In *Quichean Civilization*, by Robert M. Carmack, pp. 265–345. University of California Press, Berkeley.

Culbert, T. Patrick. 1965. *The Ceramic History of the Central Highlands of Chiapas, Mexico.* Papers of the New World Archaeological Foundation, no. 19, Provo, Utah.

———. 1988. The Collapse of Classic Maya Civilization. In *The Collapse of Ancient States and Civilizations*, ed. Norman Yoffee and George L. Cowgill, pp. 69–101. University of Arizona Press, Tucson.

Culebro, C. Alberto. 1939. Chiapas Prehistórico, su Arqueología. *Folleto* no. 1. Huixtla, Chiapas.

Culin, Stewart. 1975 [1907]. *Games of the North American Indians.* Dover Publications, New York.

Curtin, Jeremiah, and J.N.B. Hewitt. 1918. *Seneca Fiction, Legends, and Myths.* 32nd Annual Report of the Bureau of American Ethnology, 1910–1911, Washington, D.C.

Cushing, Frank H. 1893. The Hemenway Southwestern Archeological Expedition, Part 2. Manuscript on file, Southwest Museum, Los Angeles.

Dalton, George. 1977. Aboriginal Economies in Stateless Societies. In *Exchange Systems in Prehistory*, ed. Timothy K. Earle and Jonathan E. Ericson, pp. 191–212. Academic Press, New York.

Davies, Nigel. 1973. *The Aztecs: A History.* MacMillan, New York.

———. 1977. *The Toltecs: Until the Fall of Tula.* University of Oklahoma Press, Norman.

———. 1980. *The Toltec Heritage: From the Fall of Tula to the Rise of Tenochtitlán.* University of Oklahoma Press, Norman.

Delgado, Agustín. 1965. Excavation at Santa Rosa, Chiapas, Mexico. In *Archaeological Research at Santa Rosa, Chiapas and in the Region of Tehuantepec.* Papers of the New World Archaeological Foundation, no. 17 (in Pub. no. 13). Brigham Young University, Provo.

De Montmollin, Olivier. 1985. *Classic Maya Settlement and Politics in the Rosario Valley, Chiapas, Mexico.* Department of Anthropology, University of Michigan, Ann Arbor.

Diaz, Clara. 1980. Chingu: Un Sitio Clásico del Area de Tula, Hgo. *Colección Científica* 90, Instituto Nacional de Antropología e Historia, México, D.F.

Diehl, Richard A. 1981. Tula. In *Supplement to the Handbook of Middle American Indians*, vol. 1, *Archaeology*, ed. Jeremy A. Sabloff, pp. 277–295. University of New Mexico Press, Albuquerque.

———. 1983. *Tula: The Toltec Capital of Ancient Mexico.* Thames and Hudson, New York.

Di Peso, Charles C. 1974. *Casas Grandes: A Fallen Trading Center of the Gran Chichimeca*, vols. 1–3. Amerind Foundation 9, Dragoon, Arizona.

Di Peso, Charles C., John B. Rinaldo, and Gloria Fenner. 1974. *Casas Grandes: A Fallen Trading Center of the Gran Chichimeca*, vols. 4–8. Amerind Foundation 9, Dragoon, Arizona.

Dixon, Roland B. 1912. Maidu Texts. *Publications of the American Ethnological Society*, vol. 4. AMS Press, New York.

Dockstader, Frederick J. 1968. Miniature Ball-Game Objects from Mesoamerica. *American Antiquity* 33:251–253.

Doelle, William H. 1988. Preclassic Community Patterns in the Tucson Basin. In *Recent Research on Tucson Basin Prehistory: Proceedings of the Second Tucson Basin Conference*, ed. William H. Doelle and Paul R. Fish, pp. 277–312. Institute for American Research Anthropological Papers 10. Tucson.

Dorsey, George A. 1904. *The Mythology of the Wichita*. Carnegie Institution of Washington Publication no. 21, Washington, D.C.

———. 1906. *The Pawnee. Mythology*. Carnegie Institution of Washington Publication no. 59, Washington, D.C.

Dorsey, George A., and Alfred L. Kroeber. 1903. *Traditions of the Arapaho*. Field Columbian Museum Pub. 81. Anthropological Series, vol. 5. Chicago.

Doyel, David E. 1980. Hohokam Social Organization and the Sedentary to Classic Transition. In *Current Issues in Hohokam Prehistory, Proceedings of a Symposium*, ed. David Doyel and Fred Plog, pp. 23–40. *Arizona State University Anthropological Research Papers* 23.

———. 1984. From Foraging to Farming: An Overview of the Preclassic in the Tucson Basin. *The Kiva* 49(3–4):147–166.

Drennan, Robert D. 1976. *Fabrica San Jose and Middle Formative Society in the Valley of Oaxaca*. Memoirs of the Museum of Anthropology 8, The University of Michigan, Ann Arbor.

Drennan, Robert D., ed. 1979. *Prehistoric Social, Political, and Economic Development in the Area of the Tehuacán Valley: Some Results of the Palo Blanco Project*. Museum of Anthropology, University of Michigan, Technical Reports 11. Ann Arbor.

Drennan, Robert D., and J. A. Nowack. 1984. Exchange and Sociopolitical Development in the Tehuacán Valley. In *Trade and Exchange in Early Mesoamerica*, ed. Kenneth G. Hirth, pp. 147–156. University of New Mexico Press, Albuquerque.

Drennan, Robert D., and Rafael Vásquez Cruz. 1975. Reconocimiento Arqueologico al Norte del Valle de Oaxaca. Manuscript in files of author.

Drucker, Phillip. 1943. Ceramic Sequences at Tres Zapotes, Veracruz, Mexico. *Bureau of American Ethnology Bulletin* 140. United States Government Printing Office, Washington, D.C.

Durán, Fray Diego. 1967. *Historia de las Indias de Nueva Espana e Islas de la Tierra Firme*. Editorial Porrua, México D.F.

———. 1971. *Book of The Gods and Rites and The Ancient Calendar*, trans. Fernando Horcasitas and Doris Heyden. University of Oklahoma Press, Norman.

Durkheim, Emile. 1954. *The Elementary Forms of Religious Life*. The Free Press, Glencoe.

Eaton, Jack D., and Barton Kunstler. 1980. Excavations at Operation 2009: A Maya Ballcourt. In *The Colhá Project: Second Season, 1980 Interim Report*, ed. T.R. Hester, J.D. Eaton, and H.J. Shafer, pp. 121–132. Center for Archaeological Research, University of Texas at San Antonio, and Centro Studi e Ricerche Ligabue, Venezia. San Antonio.

Edmonson, Munro S., trans. 1971. *The Book of Counsel: The Popol Vuh of the*

Quiché Maya of Guatemala. Middle American Research Institute Pub. 35.
Tulane University, New Orleans.

——. 1982. *The Ancient Future of the Itzá, the Book of Chilam Balam of Tizimin*.
University of Texas Press, Austin.

——. 1984. Human Sacrifice in the Books of Chilam Balam of Tizimin and
Chumayel. In *Ritual Human Sacrifice in Mesoamerica*, ed. Elizabeth H. Boone,
pp. 91–99. Dumbarton Oaks, Washington, D.C.

Effland, Richard W., Jr. 1985. The Middle Gila Basin Revisited: An Examination of
Settlement-Subsistence Patterns and Change. In *Proceedings of the 1983
Hohokam Symposium*, pt. I, ed. Alfred E. Dittert, Jr. and Donald E. Dove, pp.
353–372. Phoenix Chapter, Arizona Archaeological Society, Phoenix.

Ekholm, Gordon F. 1946. The Probable Use of Mexican Stone Yokes. *American
Anthropologist* n.s., 48(4):593–606.

——. 1949. Palmate Stones and Thin Stone Heads: Suggestions on Their Possible
Use. *American Antiquity* 15:1–9.

——. 1961. Puerto Rican Stone "Collars" as Ballgame Belts. In *Essays in
Precolumbian Art and Archaeology*, ed. Samuel Lothrop et al., pp. 356–371.
Harvard University Press, Cambridge.

Ekholm, Susanna M. 1973. *The Olmec Rock Carving at Xoc, Chiapas, Mexico*.
Papers of the New World Archaeological Foundation no. 32, Provo, Utah.

——. 1976. Investigations at Lagartero, Chiapas. In Lowe 1975–1976, pp. 42–48.
Unpub. ms., New World Archaeological Foundation, San Cristobal de las Casas.

Eliade, Mircea. 1951. *Shamanism, Archaic Techniques of Ecstasy*, trans. Willard R.
Trask. Princeton University Press (Bollingen Series), Princeton.

Elson, Mark D., and William H. Doelle. 1987. Archaeological Survey in Catalina
State Park with a Focus on the Romero Ruin. *Institute for American Research
Technical Report* 87-4. Tucson.

English, Paul W. 1966. *City and Village in Iran: Settlement and Economy in the
Kirman Basin*. The University of Wisconsin Press, Madison.

Ester, Michael R. 1976. The Spatial Allocation of Activities at Teotihuacán, Mexico.
Ph.D. diss., Brandeis University.

Etzioni, Amatai. 1961. *A Comparative Analysis of Complex Organizations: On
Power, Involvement, and Their Correlates*. The Free Press, New York.

Evans, John, and Harry F. Hillman. 1981. Casa Grande, An Ancient Astronomical
Observatory. *Arizona Highways* 57(10):32.

Evans, Susan. 1980. Spatial Analysis of Basin of Mexico Settlement: Problems with
the Use of the Central Place Model. *American Antiquity* 45:866–875.

Fash, William L., Jr. 1983. Deducing Social Organization from Classic Maya
Settlement Patterns: A Case Study from the Copán Valley. In *Civilization in the
Ancient Americas: Essays in Honor of Gordon R. Willey*, ed. Richard M.
Leventhal and Alan L. Kolata, pp. 261–288. University of New Mexico Press and
Peabody Museum of Archaeology and Ethnology, Cambridge.

——. 1988. Maya Statecraft from Copán, Honduras. *Antiquity* 62(234):157–169.

Federico, Teresa. 1972. Algunos Aspectos del Desarrollo Histórico Mesoamericano
y el Juego de Pelota. In *XII Mesa Redonda: Religion en Mesoamerica*, pp. 435–
439. Sociedad Mexicana de Antropología, México, D.F.

——. 1973. Simbolismo del Juego de Pelota en el Popol Vuh. *Estudios de Cultura
Maya* 9:127–134.

Feinman, Gary. 1985. *Etla Valley Settlement Pattern Project Progress Report: 1984–1985*. Department of Anthropology, University of Wisconsin.

Ferdon, Edwin N., Jr. 1955. A Trail Survey of Mexican-Southwestern Architectural Parallels. *School of American Research, Museum of New Mexico Monographs* 21. Santa Fe.

————. 1967. The Hohokam "Ball Court": An Alternative View of Its Function. *The Kiva* 33(1):1–14.

Ferg, Alan. 1984. Site Descriptions, AZ EE:25:105—the Ballcourt Site. In *Hohokam Habitation Sites in the Northern Santa Rita Mountains*, by Alan Ferg et al., pp. 94–119. Arizona State Museum Archaeological Series 147, vol. 2, pt. 1. University of Arizona, Tucson.

Fernandez Valbuena, José Antonio. 1990. Elites Celestres: Simbología y Cosmología de los Nima-Quiché de Gumarcaah. Ph.D. diss., Facultad de Geografia e Historia, Universidad Complutense de Madrid, Spain.

Fewkes, J. Walter, Aleš Hrdlička, William D. Dall, James W. Gidley, Austin H. Clark, William H. Holmes, Alice C. Fletcher, Walter Hough, Stansbury Hagar, Paul Bartsch, Alexander F. Chamberlain, and Roland B. Dixon. 1912. The Problems of the Unity or Plurality and the Probable Place of Origin of the American Aborigines. *American Anthropologist*, n.s., 14(1):1–59.

Firth, R. 1930. A Dart Match in Tikopia: A Study in the Sociology of Primitive Sport. *Oceania* 1(1):64–96.

Flannery, Kent V. 1968. Archaeological Systems Theory and Early Mesoamerica. In *Anthropological Archaeology in the Americas*, ed. B. J. Meggers, pp. 67–87. The Anthropological Society of Washington, Washington, D.C.

————. 1972. The Cultural Evolution of Civilizations. *Annual Review of Ecology and Systematics* 3:399–426.

Flannery, Kent V., ed. 1976. *The Early Mesoamerican Village*. Academic Press, New York.

Flannery, Kent V., and Joyce Marcus. 1976. Evolution of the Public Building in Formative Oaxaca. In *Cultural Change and Continuity: Essays in Honor of James Bennett Griffin*, ed. Charles Cleland, pp. 205–221. Academic Press, New York.

Flannery, Kent V., and Joyce Marcus, eds. 1983. *The Cloud People: Divergent Evolution of the Zapotec and Mixtec Civilizations*. Academic Press, New York.

Flannery, Kent V., Joyce Marcus, and Stephen A. Kowalewski. 1981. The Preceramic and Formative of the Valley of Oaxaca. In *Supplement to the Handbook of Middle American Indians*, vol. 1, *Archaeology*, ed. Jeremy A. Sabloff, pp. 48–93. University of New Mexico Press, Albuquerque.

Folan, William J. 1980. Chichén Itzá, el Cenote Sagrado y Xibalba: Una Nueva Visión. *Boletín de la Escuela de Ciencias Antropológicas de la Universidad de Yucatán* 44:70–76.

Folan, William J., ed. 1985. *Contribution to the Archaeology and Ethnohistory of Greater Mesoamerica*. Southern Illinois University Press, Carbondale.

Folan, William J., Ellen R. Kintz, and Loraine A. Fletcher. 1983. *Coba: A Classic Maya Metropolis*. Academic Press, New York.

Fondo Editorial de la Plástica Mexicana. 1964. *Flor y Canto de Arte Prehispánico de México*. México. D.F.

Foster, Michael S. 1985. The Loma San Gabriel Occupation of Zacatecas and

Durango, Mexico. In *The Archaeology of West and Northwest Mesoamerica*, ed.
Michael S. Foster and Phil C. Weigand, pp. 327–351. Westview Press, Boulder.

Fox, John W. 1978. *Quiché Conquest.* University of New Mexico Press,
Albuquerque.

———. 1980. Lowland to Highland Mexicanization Processes in Southern
Mesoamerica. *American Antiquity* 45(1):43–54.

———. 1981. The Late Postclassic Eastern Frontier of Mesoamerica: Cultural
Innovation Along the Periphery. *Current Anthropology* 22:321–346.

———. 1987. *Maya Postclassic State Formation.* Cambridge University Press,
Cambridge and London.

———. 1989. On the Rise and Fall of Tulans and Maya Segmentary States.
American Anthropologist 91(3):656–681.

Fox, John W., Dwight T. Wallace, and Kenneth L. Brown. In press. Venus and the
Emergent Quiche Elite: The Putun-Palenque Connection. In *Mesoamerican
Elites, An Archaeological Perspective.* eds. Arlen and Diane Chase. University of
Oklahoma Press, Norman.

Freidel, David A. 1981a. The Political Economics of Residential Dispersion among
the Lowland Maya. In *Lowland Maya Settlement Patterns*, ed. Wendy Ashmore,
pp. 371–382. University of New Mexico Press, Albuquerque.

———. 1981b. Civilization as a State of Mind: The Cultural Evolution of the
Lowland Maya. In *The Transition to Statehood in the New World*, ed. G. Jones
and R. Kautz, pp. 188–227. Cambridge University Press, Cambridge.

———. 1986. Maya Warfare: An Example of Peer Polity Interaction. In *Peer Polity
Interaction and the Development of Sociopolitical Complexity*, ed. Colin Renfrew
and John F. Cherry, pp. 93–108. Cambridge University Press, Cambridge.

Freidel, David, and Linda Schele. 1989. Dead Kings and Living Temples:
Dedication and Termination Rituals among the Ancient Maya. In *Word and
Image in Maya Culture*, ed. William F. Hanks and Don S. Rice. University of
Utah Press, Salt Lake City.

Furst, Jill Leslie. 1978. *Codex Vindobonensis Mexicanus I: A Commentary.* Institute
for Mesoamerican Studies, State University of New York at Albany, pub. no. 4.
Albany.

García Cook, Angel. 1974. Transición del Clásico al Post-Clásico en Tlaxcala: Fase
Tenanyecac. *Revista Cultura y Sociedad* 1:83–98.

———. 1978. Tlaxcala: Poblamiento Prehispánico. *Comunicaciones Puebla-Tlaxcala*
15:173–187.

———. 1981. The Historical Importance of Tlaxcala in the Cultural Development
of the Central Highlands. In *Supplement to the Handbook of Middle American
Indians*, vol. 1, *Archaeology*, ed. Jeremy A. Sabloff, pp. 244–276. University of
New Mexico Press, Albuquerque.

García Cook, Angel, and E.C. Trejo. 1977. Lo Teotihuacano en Tlaxcala.
Comunicaciones Puebla-Tlaxcala 14:57–78.

García Moll, Roberto. 1977. Los Escalones Labrados del Edificio 33, Yaxchilan,
Chiapas. *Revista Mexicana de Estudios Antropológicos*, 23(3):395–424.

García Payón, José. 1971. Archaeology of Central Veracruz. In *Archaeology of
Northern Mesoamerica*, pt. II, ed. Gordon F. Ekholm and Ignacio Bernal, pp.
505–542. *Handbook of Middle American Indians*, vol. 11, ed. Robert Wauchope.
University of Texas Press, Austin.

———. 1973. Chacmol en la Apoteosis del Pulque. In *Los Enigmas de El Tajín,*

Colección Científica 3. Instituto Nacional de Antropología e Historia, México, D.F.

Garza, Silvia, and Edward B. Kurkack. 1980. Atlas Arqueológica del Estado de Yucatán, Dos Tomosa. Instituto Nacional de Antropología e Historia, México, D.F.

Geertz, Clifford. 1972. Deep Play: Notes on the Balinese Cockfight. *Daedalus* 101:1–37.

Gendrop, Paul. 1970. *Arte Prehispánico en Mesoamérica*. Editorial Trillas. Mexico.

Gillespie, Susan D. 1989. *The Aztec Kings: The Construction of Rulership in Mexica History.* University of Arizona Press, Tucson.

Gillmeister, Heiner. 1987. Os Métodos de Investigaçao e o Desporto Medieval: Resultados Recientes e Perspectivas. *Desporto e Sociedade*, no. 39. Ministerio da Educaçao e Cultura. Lisbon.

Girard, Raphael. 1979. *Esotericism of the Popol Vuh*. Trans. Blair A. Moffett, Theosophical University Press, Pasadena.

Gladwin, Harold S. 1930. An Outline of Southwestern Pre-History. *Arizona Historical Review* 3(1):71–87.

———. 1931. Gila Pueblo Conference. Simmons Collection, Arizona State Museum Library, University of Arizona, Tucson.

———. 1938. Excavations at Snaketown II: Comparisons and Theories. *Medallion Papers* 26. Globe, Arizona.

Gladwin, Harold S., Emil W. Haury, E.B. Sayles, and Nora Gladwin. 1937. Excavations at Snaketown I: Material Culture. *Medallion Papers* 25. Gila Pueblo, Globe.

Gladwin, Winifred, and Harold S. Gladwin. 1935. *The Eastern Range of the Red-on-Buff Culture*. Medallion Papers 16. Gila Pueblo, Globe.

Gluckman, Max, and Mary Gluckman. 1983. On Drama, and Games and Athletic Contests. In *Play, Games, and Sport in Cultural Contexts*, ed. Janet C. Harris and Roberta J. Park, pp. 191–209. Human Kinetics Publishers, Inc., Champaign, Ill.

Gomara, Francisco Lopez de. 1826. *Historia de las Conquistas de Hernando Cortes*. Imprenta de la Testimentaria de Ontiveros, México, D.F.

Graham, Ian. 1980. *Corpus of Maya Hieroglyphic Inscriptions* 2(3), *Ixkun, Ucanal, Ixtutz, Naranjo*. Peabody Museum of Archaeology and Ethnology, Harvard University, Cambridge.

———. 1982. *Corpus of Maya Hieroglyphic Inscriptions* (3), *Yaxchilán*. Peabody Museum of Archaeology and Ethnology, Harvard University, Cambridge.

Graulich, Michael. 1981. The Metaphor of the Day in Ancient Mexican Myth and Ritual. *Current Anthropology* 22(1):45–60.

Greenberg, Joseph H. 1987. *Language in the Americas*. Stanford University Press, Stanford.

Greenberg, Joseph H., Christy H. Turner, and Steven Zegurz. 1986. The Settlement of the Americas. *Current Anthropology* 27:477–497.

Greene Robertson, Merle. 1972. The Ritual Bundles of Yaxchilán. Paper presented at the Tulane Symposium on the Art of Latin America, 1972. New Orleans.

Gregory, David A., and Thomas R. McGuire. 1982. *Las Colinas Testing: Research Design*. Arizona State Museum Archaeological Series 157, University of Arizona, Tucson.

Griffin, Gillett G. 1972. Xochipala, the Earliest Great Art Style in Mexico. *American*

Philosophical Society Proceedings 116:301–309.

Grinnell, George Bird. 1893. A Blackfoot Sun and Moon Myth. *Journal of American Folk-lore* 6:44–47.

Grove, David C. 1981. The Formative Period and the Evolution of Complex Culture. In *Archaeology, Supplement to the Handbook of Middle American Indians*, ed. Jeremy A. Sabloff, 1:373–391.

———. 1984. *Chalcatzingo: Excavations on the Olmec Frontier*. Thames and Hudson, New York.

Grove, David C., and H.B. Nicholson. 1965. Excavación de un Juego de Pelota en Ixtapaluca Viejo, Valle de México. *Boletín de INAH* 22, Instituto Nacional de Antropología e Historia, México, D.F.

Grube, Nikolai. In press. An Investigation of the Primary Standard Sequence on Classic Maya Ceramics. *The Sixth Round Table of Palenque*. University of Oklahoma Press, Norman.

Guevara López, Germán. 1981. *Reporte de la Zona Arquelógica de Chacalilla, Municipio de San Blás, Nayarit*. Cuadernos de los Centros Regionales, Centro Regional de Antropología e Historia de Occidente. Instituto Nacional de Antropología e Historia, México, D.F.

Guillemin, Jorge F. 1967. The Ancient Cakchiquel Capital of Iximche. *Expedition* 9:33–35.

———. 1977. Urbanism and Hierarchy at Iximche. In *Social Process in Maya Prehistory*, ed. Norman Hammond, pp. 227–264. Academic Press, London.

Gussinyer, Jordi. 1972a. Rescate Arqueologico en la Presa de la Angostura (Primera Temporada). Boletín Instituto Nacional de Antropología e Historia, no. 1, Epoca 11/Abril–Junio 1972, pp. 3–14. México, D.F.

———. 1972b. Segunda Temporada de Salvamento Arqueológico en la Presa de "La Angostura," Chiapas. *ICACH*, Segunda Epoca, nos. 5–6 (23–24), pp. 41–56. Instituto de Ciencis y Artes de Chiapas, Tuxtla Gutiérrez.

Hallowell, A. Irving. 1960. The Beginnings of Anthropology in America. In *Selected Papers from the American Anthropologist, 1899–1920*, ed. Fredrica de Laguna, pp. 1–90. Row and Peterson, Evanston, Ill.

Hammond, Norman. 1975a. *Lubaantún: A Classic Maya Realm*. Peabody Museum Monograph, no. 2. Harvard University, Cambridge.

———. 1981. Settlement Patterns in Belize. In *Lowland Maya Settlement Patterns*, ed. W. Ashmore, pp. 157–186. University of New Mexico Press, Albuquerque.

Hammond, Norman, ed. 1973. *British Museum-Cambridge Project, 1973 Interim Report*. Cambridge University, Cambridge.

———. 1975b. *British Museum-Cambridge Project, 1974–75 Interim Report*. Cambridge University, Cambridge.

Hammond, Norman, Sara Donaghey, Colleen Gleason, J.C. Stanero, Dirk Van Tuerenhout, and Laura J. Kosakowsky. 1987. Excavations at Nohmul, Belize, 1985. *Journal of Field Archaeology* 14(3):257–282.

Harris, Janet C., and Roberta J. Park. 1983. Introduction to the Sociological Study of Play, Games, and Sports. In *Play, Games, and Sports in Cultural Contexts*, ed. Janet C. Harris and Robert J. Park, pp. 1–36. Human Kinetics Publishers, Champaign.

Harris, Janet C., and Roberta J. Park, eds. 1983. *Play, Games, and Sports in Cultural Contexts*. Human Kinetics Publishers, Inc., Champaign.

Harrison, Peter D. 1979. The Lobil Postclassic Phase in the Southern Interior of the Yucatán Peninsula. In *Maya Archaeology and Ethnohistory*, ed. Norman Hammond and Gordon R. Willey, pp. 189–207. University of Texas Press, Austin.

Hassig, Ross. 1985. *The Sixteenth-Century Political Economy of the Valley of Mexico*. University of Oklahoma Press, Norman.

Haury, Emil W. 1937. A Pre-Spanish Rubber Ball from Arizona. *American Antiquity* 2:282–288.

———. 1945. The Problem of Contacts Between the Southwestern United States and Mexico. *Southwestern Journal of Anthropology* 1:55–74.

———. 1976. *The Hohokam: Desert Farmers and Craftsmen*. University of Arizona Press, Tucson.

Haviland, William A. 1967. Stature at Tikal: Implications for Ancient Maya Demography and Social Organization. *American Antiquity* 32:316–325.

———. 1970. Tikal, Guatemala and Mesoamerican Urbanism. *World Archaeology* 2:186–198.

Hay, Clarence L., Ralph L. Linton, Samuel K. Lothrop, Harry L. Shapiro, and George C. Vaillant, eds. 1940. *The Maya and Their Neighbors*. D. Appleton-Century, New York.

Healan, Dan M., Janet M. Kerley, and George J. Bey III. 1983. Excavation and Preliminary Analysis of an Obsidian Workshop in Tula, Hidalgo, Mexico. *Journal of Field Archaeology* 10:127–145.

Hedrick, Basil C., J. Charles Kelley, and Carroll L. Riley, eds. 1971. *The North Mexican Frontier: Readings in Archaeology, Ethnology, and Ethnography*. Southern Illinois University Press, Carbondale.

Hellmuth, Nicholas M. 1975a. *Pre-Columbian Ball Game: Archaeology and Architecture*. Foundation for Latin American Anthropological Research Progress Report, vol. 1, no. 1. Guatemala and Los Angeles.

———. 1975b. *The Escuintla Hoards: Teotihuacán Art in Guatemala*. Foundation for Latin American Anthropological Research Progress Report, vol. 1, no. 2. Guatemala and Los Angeles.

———. 1976. *Maya Archaeology: Travel Guide*. Foundation for Latin American Anthropological Research, Guatemala City.

———. 1978. Teotihuacan Art in the Escuintla, Guatemala Region. In *Middle Classic Mesoamerica: A.D. 400–700*, ed. Esther Pasztory, pp. 71–85. Columbia University Press, New York.

———. 1985. Unresolved Problems of Chronology and Iconography in the Regionally Distinct Ballgames of 6th-8th Century Guatemala: Escuintla versus Petén. Paper presented at the International Symposium on the Mesoamerican Ballgame, Tucson. Arizona State Museum Library, University of Arizona, Tucson.

Henderson, Robert W. 1947. *Ball, Bat, and Bishop: The Origin of Ball Games*. Rockport Press, New York.

Hernandez, Fray. 1946. *Antiquedades de la Nueva Espana*. Mexico City, Mexico.

Hester, Thomas R., Jack D. Eaton, and Harry J. Shafer, eds. 1980. *The Colhá Project: Second Season, 1980 Interim Report*. Center for Archaeological Research, University of Texas at San Antonio, and Centro Studi e Ricerche Ligabue, Venezia. San Antonio.

———. 1982. *Archaeology at Colhá, Belize: The 1981 Interim Report*. Center for

Archaeological Research, University of Texas at San Antonio, and Centro Studi e Ricerche Ligabue, Venezia. San Antonio.

Historia de México (vols. 1 and 2). 1974. Salvat Editores de México, México, D.F.

"Histoyre du Mechique." 1905. *Journal de la Société des Américanistes de Paris*, n.s. 2:1–41.

Hoffman, Walter James. 1896. *The Menomini Indians*. 14th Annual Report of the Bureau of American Ethnology, 1892–1893, pp. 3–328, Washington, D.C.

Houston, Stephen D. 1983. Ballgame Glyphs in Classic Maya Texts. In *Contributions to Maya Hieroglyphic Decipherment, I*, ed. Stephen Houston, pp. 26–30. Human Relations Area Files, New Haven, Connecticut.

Huckell, Bruce B. 1984. *The Archaic Occupation of the Rosemont Area, Northern Santa Rita Mountains, Southeastern Arizona*. Arizona State Museum Archaeological Series 147(1). University of Arizona, Tucson.

——. 1988. Late Archaic Archaeology of the Tucson Basin: A Status Report. In *Recent Research on Tucson Basin Prehistory: Proceedings of the Second Tucson Basin Conference*, ed. William H. Doelle and Paul R. Fish, pp. 57–80. Institute for American Research, Anthropological Papers 10. Tucson.

Hunt, Eva. 1977. *The Transformation of the Hummingbird: Cultural Roots in a Zinacantan Mythical Poem*. Cornell University Press, Ithaca.

Ichon, Alain. 1973. *La Religión de los Totonacas de la Sierra*. Instituto Nacional Indigenista, Mexico, D.F.

Ichon, Alain, M. F. Fauvet-Berthelot, C. Plocieniak, R. Hill II, R. Gonzalez Lauck, and M.A. Bailey. 1980. *Archéologie de Sauvetage dans la Vallee du Rio Chixoy, Cawinal*, no. 2. Institut d'Ethnologie, Paris.

Ichon, Alain, Nicole Percheron, Michele Bertrand, and Alain Breton. 1982. *Rabinal et la Vallee Moyenne du Rio Chixoy, Baja Verapaz-Guatemala*. Cahiers de la R.C.P. 500. Centre Nacional de la Recherche. Institut d'Ethnologie, Paris.

Ingram, John M. 1971. Time and Space in Ancient Mexico: The Symbolic Dimensions of Clanship. *Man*, n.s., 6(4):615–629.

Isaac, Barry L. 1983. The Aztec "Flowery" War: A Geopolitical Explanation. *Journal of Anthropological Research* 39:415–432.

Ixtlilxochitl, Fernando de Alva. 1952. *Obras Historicas*. Editora Nacional, México, D.F.

Jewell, Brian. 1977. *Sports and Games: History and Origins*. Midas Books, Tunbridge Wells, U.K.

Johnson, Captain A. R. 1848. Notes of a Military Reconnaissance from Fort Leavenworth, in Missouri, to San Diego, in California, including part of the Arkansas, Del Norte, and Gila Rivers. 30th Congress, 1st Session (House), Ex. Doc. 41. Washington, D.C.

Johnson, Gregory A. 1978. Information Sources and the Development of Decision-Making Organizations. In *Social Archaeology: Beyond Subsistence and Dating*, ed. Charles L. Redman et al., pp. 87–112. Academic Press, New York.

Jones, Christopher, and Robert J. Sharer. 1986. Archaeological Investigations in the Site Core of Quirigua, Guatemala. In *The Southeast Maya Periphery*, ed. Patricia A. Urban and Edward M. Schortman, pp. 27–34. University of Texas Press, Austin.

Josserand, Kathryn, and Nicholas Hopkins. 1988. Chol (Mayan) Dictionary Database: pt. II. Sources. The Final Performance Report for the National Endowment for the Humanities Grant RT-20643-86.

Joyce, Thomas A. 1933. The Pottery Whistle Figures of Lubaantún. *Journal of the Royal Anthropological Institute of Great Britain and Ireland* 63:15–25.

Kampen, Michael E. 1972. *The Sculptures of El Tajín, Veracruz, Mexico.* University of Florida Press, Gainesville.

Kaufman, Terrence S., and William M. Norman. 1984. An Outline of Proto-Cholan Phonology, Morphology, and Vocabulary. In *Phoneticism in Mayan Hieroglyphic Writing*, ed. Lyle Campbell and John S. Justeson, pp. 77–167. Center for Mesoamerican Studies, Albany.

Kelley, David H. 1962. Glyphic Evidence for a Dynastic Sequence at Quiriguá, Guatemala. *American Antiquity* 27:323–335.

———. 1965. The Birth of the Gods at Palenque. In *Estudios de Cultura Maya* 5, pp. 93–134. Universidad Nacional Autónoma de México, México.

———. 1976. *Deciphering the Maya Script.* University of Texas Press, Austin.

———. 1982. Notes on Puuc Inscriptions and History. In *The Puuc: New Perspectives*. Central College, Pella, Iowa.

Kelley, Ellen Abbott. 1976. Gualterio Abajo: An Early Mesoamerican Settlement on the Northwestern Frontier. In *Las Fronteras de Mesoamerica, XIV Mesa Redonda*, ed. Jaime Litvak King and Paul Schmidt, pp. 41–50. Sociedad Mexicana de Antropología, Tegucigalpa, Honduras, 1975. Tomo I. Mexico.

Kelley, J. Charles. 1956. Settlement Patterns in North-Central Mexico. In *Prehistoric Settlement Patterns in the New World*, ed. Gordon R. Willey, pp. 128–139. Wenner-Gren Foundation for Anthropological Research, Inc., New York.

———. 1971. Archeology of the Northern Frontier: Zacatecas and Durango. In *Archaeology of Northern Mesoamerica*, ed. Gordon F. Ekholm. *Handbook of Middle American Indians* 11(2):768–804.

———. 1983. "Hypothetical Functioning of the Major Postclassic Trade System of West and Northwest Mexico." Paper delivered at the XVIII Mesa Redonda de la Sociedad Mexicana de Antropología, El Occidente de Mexico. Taxco, Mexico.

———. 1985. The Chronology of the Chalchihuites Culture. In *The Archaeology of West and Northwest Mesoamerica*, ed. Michael S. Foster and Phil C. Weigand, pp. 269–287. Westview Press, Boulder.

Kelley, J. Charles, and Ellen Abbott Kelley. 1975. An Alternative Hypothesis for the Explanation of Anasazi Culture History. In *Collected Papers in Honor of Florence Hawley Ellis*, ed. Theodore R. Frisbie, pp. 178–223. Papers of the Archaeological Society of New Mexico 2, Albuquerque.

Kelley, Klara B. 1976. Dendritic Central-Place Systems and the Regional Organization of Navaho Trading Posts. In *Regional Analysis*, vol. 1: *Economic Systems*, ed. Carol A. Smith, pp. 219–254. Academic Press, New York.

Kelly, Isabel. 1980a [1943]. Notes on a West Coast Survival of the Ancient Mexican Ball Game. *Notes on Middle American Archaeology and Ethnology* 1(26):163–175. Carnegie Institution of Washington.

———. 1980b. *Ceramic Sequence in Colima: Capacha, An Early Phase*, University of Arizona Anthropological Papers 37, Tucson.

Kelly, Roger E. 1963. The Socio-Religious Roles of Ball Courts and Great Kivas in the Prehistoric Southwest. Ms. thesis, Department of Anthropology, University of Arizona, Tucson.

Kemrer, Meade F., Jr. 1968. A Re-Examination of Ballgame in Pre-Columbian Mesoamerica. *Ceramica de Cultura Maya* 5:1–25.

Kidder, Alfred V. 1924. *An Introduction to the Study of Southwestern Archaeology.*

Department of Archaeology, Phillips Academy, Andover, Massachusetts.

Kidder, Alfred V., Jesse D. Jennings, and Edwin M. Shook. 1946. *Excavations at Kaminaljuyu, Guatemala*. Carnegie Institution Pub. 561. Carnegie Institution, Washington, D.C.

Kirchhoff, Paul. 1943. Mesoamérica, sus Límites Geográficos, Composición Etnica y Carácteres Culturales. *Acta Americana* 1:92–107.

Kitto, Humphrey D. F. 1951. *The Greeks*. Penguin Books, Baltimore.

Klein, Cecilia F. 1975. Post-Classic Death Imagery as a Sign of Cyclic Completion. In *Death and the Afterlife in Pre-Columbian America*, ed. Elizabeth P. Benson, pp. 69–86, Dumbarton Oaks, Washington, D.C.

———. 1976. *The Face of the Earth: Frontality in Two-Dimensional Mesoamerican Art*. Garland Publications, New York.

Knauth, Lothar. 1961. El Juego de Pelota y el Rito de la Decapitación. *Estudios de Cultura Maya* 1:183–198.

Kowalewski, Stephen A., Richard E. Blanton, Gary Feinman, and Laura Finsten. 1983. Boundaries, Scale, and Internal Organization. *Journal of Anthropological Archaeology* 2:32–56.

Kowalewski, Stephen A., Gary Feinman, Laura Finsten, Richard E. Blanton, and Linda Nicholas. 1989. *Monte Albán's Hinterland*, pt. II: *Prehispanic Settlement Patterns in Tlacolula, Etla, and Ocotlán, The Valley of Oaxaca, Mexico*. Museum of Anthropology, University of Michigan Technical Reports, Ann Arbor.

Kowalski, Jeff K. 1985. Who Am I Among the Itza? Paper presented at the 84th Annual Meeting of the American Anthropological Association, Washington, D.C.

Krader, Lawrence. 1968. *Formation of the State*. Prentice-Hall, Englewood Cliffs, N.J.

Krickeberg, Walter. 1966. El Juego de Pelota Mesoamericano y su Simbolismo Religioso. Originally published in *Paideuma Mitteilungen zur Kulturkunde* 3(3–5), 1948. In *Traducciones Mesoamericanistas*, trans. Juan Brom O., vol. I, pp. 191–313. Sociedad Mexicana de Antropología, México, D.F.

Krochock, Ruth. In press. Dedication Ceremonies at Chichén Itzá: the Glyphic Evidence. In *The Sixth Mesa Redonda de Palenque*. University of Oklahoma Press, Norman.

Kroeber, Alfred L. 1907. Gros Ventre Myths and Tales. *Anthropological Papers of the American Museum of Natural History* 1:55–139.

Kubler, George. 1962. *The Art and Architecture of Ancient America: The Mexican, Maya, and Andean Peoples*. Penguin, Baltimore.

———. 1974. Mythological Ancestries in Classic Maya Inscriptions. In *Primera Mesa Redonda de Palenque*, ed. Merle G. Robertson, vol. II, pp. 23–43. Robert Louis Stevenson School, Pebble Beach, California.

———. 1975. *The Art and Architecture of Ancient America*. Penguin Books, Harmondsworth, England.

Kunst der Maya: Aus Staats- und Privatbesitz der Republik Guatemala der USA und Europas. 1967. Linden-Museum für Völkerkunde zu Stuttgart, Stuttgart.

Kurjack, Edward B. 1974. *Prehistoric Lowland Maya Community and Social Organization: A Case Study at Dzibilchaltún*. Middle American Research Institute Pub. 38, Tulane University, New Orleans.

Landa, Diego de. 1941 [1566]. *Landa's Relación de las Cosas de Yucatán*. A translation edited with notes by Alfred M. Tozzer. *Papers Peabody Museum*, vol. 18. Peabody Museum, Harvard University, Cambridge.

LeBlanc, Steven A. 1982. Temporal Change in Mogollon Ceramics. In *Southwestern Ceramics: A Comparative Review*, ed. Albert H. Schroeder, pp. 107–128. *The Arizona Archaeologist* 15. Arizona Archaeological Society, Phoenix.

———. 1983. *The Mimbres People*. Thames and Hudson, London.

Lee, Thomas A., Jr. 1975. Activities and Field Investigations: Coxoh Maya Project, Jan.-May 1975. Unpublished report. New World Archaeological Foundation, San Cristobal de las Casas.

Lee, Thomas A., Jr., and Michael Blake. An Archaeological Reconnaissance of the Upper Grijalva River Tributaries Region, Chiapas, Mexico. Papers of the New World Archaeological Foundation.

Lee, Thomas A., Jr., and John E. Clark. 1980. Archaeological Investigations in the Cancum-Guanajaste Region, Chiapas. Preliminary Report of the Field Season, January–April 1980. New World Archaeological Foundation, San Cristobal de las Casas.

Lee, Thomas A., Jr., and Carlos Navarrete. An Archaeological Reconnaissance of the Middle Grijalva, Mal Paso Dam Basin. Papers of the New World Archaeological Foundation.

Lehmann, Henri. 1968. *Mixco Viejo: Guia de las Ruinas de la Plaza Pocomam*. Tipografia Nacional, Guatemala.

Lekson, Stephen H. 1987. Chacoan Settlement Patterns. Paper prepared for Advanced Seminar on Cultural Complexity in the Arid Southwest: The Hohokam and Chacoan Regional Systems. School of American Research, Santa Fe, October 25–31, 1987.

León-Portilla, Miguel. 1978. *México-Tenochtitlán: Su Espacio y Tiempo Sagrados*. Instituto Nacional de Antropología e Historia, México, D.F.

Lerup, Lars. 1977. *Building the Unfinished: Architecture and Human Action*. Sage Publications, Beverly Hills.

Lévi-Strauss, Claude. 1966. *The Savage Mind*. University of Chicago Press, Chicago.

———. 1969. *The Raw and the Cooked*. Harper and Row, New York.

———. 1973. *From Honey to Ashes*. Harper and Row, New York.

———. 1979. *The Origin of Table Manners*. Harper and Row, New York.

Leyenaar, Ted J. J. 1978. *Ulama, the Perpetuation in Mexico of the Pre-Spanish Ball Game Ullamaliztli*, trans. Inez Seeger. Brill, Leiden.

———. 1985. Ulama, the Survival of the Mesoamerican Ballgame. Paper presented at the 1985 International Symposium on the Mesoamerican Ballgame. Tucson. On file, Arizona State Museum Library, University of Arizona, Tucson.

Leyenaar, Ted J. J., and Lee A. Parsons. 1988. *Ulama: The Ballgame of the Mayas and Aztecs*. Spruyt, Van Mantgem and De Does bv, Leiden.

Leyenda de los Soles. 1975. In *Códice Chimalpopoca*, trans. Primo Feliciano Velázquez. Universidad Nacional Autónoma de México, México, D.F.

Lincoln, Charles E. 1985. *Chichén Itzá: Informe, Primera Temporada*. Harvard University, Cambridge.

———. 1986. The Chronology at Chichén Itzá: A Review of the Literature. In *Late Lowland Maya Civilization: Classic to Postclassic*, ed. J. Sabloff and E.W. Andrews V, pp. 141–196. School of American Research, University of New Mexico Press, Albuquerque.

Lothrop, Samuel K. 1923. Stone Yokes from Mexico and Central America. *Man* 23:97–98.

Lounsbury, Floyd G. 1974. The Inscription of the Sarcophagus Lid at Palenque.

Primera Mesa Redonda de Palenque, pt. II, ed. Merle Greene Robertson, pp. 5–20. Robert Louis Stevenson School, Pebble Beach.

———. 1982. Astronomical Knowledge and its Uses at Bonampak, Mexico. In *Archaeo-astronomy in the New World*, ed. Anthony F. Aveni, pp. 143–168. Cambridge University Press, England.

———. 1985. The Identities of the Mythological Figures in the 'Cross Group' of Inscriptions at Palenque. In *Fourth Round Tablet of Palenque, 1980*, vol. 6, general ed., Merle Greene Robertson; volume ed., Elizabeth Benson, pp. 45–58. Pre-Columbian Art Research Institute, San Francisco.

Lowe, Gareth W. 1959. Archaeological Exploration of the Upper Grijalva River, Chiapas, Mexico. In *Research in Chiapas, Mexico. Papers of the New World Archaeological Foundation* no. 2. Brigham Young University, Provo.

———. 1977a. The Upper Grijalva Basin Project. Reports on Field Work of 1966–76. New World Archaeological Foundation, College of Social Sciences, Brigham Young University, Provo.

———. 1977b. The Mixe-Zoque as Competing Neighbors of the Early Lowland Maya. In *The Origin of Maya Civilization*, ed. Richard E. W. Adams, pp. 197–248. University of New Mexico Press, Albuquerque.

Lowe, Gareth W., Thomas A. Lee, Jr., and Eduardo Martínez Espinosa. 1982. *Izapa: An Introduction to the Ruins and Monuments*. Papers of the New World Archaeological Foundation, no. 31. Brigham Young University, Provo.

Lowe, John W. G. 1985. *The Dynamics of Apocalypse*. University of New Mexico Press, Albuquerque.

Lowie, Robert H. 1909. *The Assiniboine*. Anthropological Papers of the American Museum of Natural History, vol. 4., pt 1. New York.

MacNeish, Richard S. 1964. Ancient Mesoamerican Civilization. *Science* 143:531–537.

———. 1972. Summary of the Cultural Sequence and its Implications. In *The Prehistory of the Tehuacan Valley*, vol. 5: *Excavations and Reconnaissance*, by Richard S. MacNeish et al., pp. 496–504. University of Texas Press, Austin.

MacNeish, Richard S., Melvin L. Fowler, Angel García Cook, Frederick A. Peterson, Antoinette Nelken-Terner, and James A. Neely. 1972. *The Prehistory of the Tehuacán Valley*, vol. 5: *Excavations and Reconnaissance*. University of Texas Press, Austin.

MacNeish, Richard S., Frederick A. Peterson, and James A. Neely. 1972. The Archaeological Reconnaissance. In *The Prehistory of the Tehuacán Valley*, vol. 5: *Excavations and Reconnaissance*, by Richard S. MacNeish et al., pp. 341–495. University of Texas Press, Austin.

Macri, Martha. A Descriptive Grammar of 9.10 Palenque Maya. An early draft of a dissertation presented to the Department of Anthropology, University of California at Berkeley. Copy provided by author, 1988.

Majewski, Teresita, and Kenneth L. Brown. 1983. Of Toltecs, Documents, and Nontesting Dogmatic Thought: The Prehistoric Quiché Maya. Paper presented at the 82nd Annual Meeting of the American Anthropological Association, Chicago.

———. 1985. A Conjunctive Approach to Quiche Mayan Prehistory. In *Demographic and Ethnohistoric Research in the Colonial Americas*, ed. Teresita Majewski, *Bibliotheca Americana* (manuscript copy).

Maldonado Cardenas, Rubén. 1979. Intervención de Restauración en el Juego de Pelota de Uxmal, Yucatán. *Instituto Nacional de Antropología e Historia, Centro*

Regional del Sureste, Memoria del Congreso Interno, 1979, pp. 233–243. Instituto Nacional de Antropología e Historia, México, D.F.

Malmstrom, Vincent H. 1981. Architecture, Astronomy, and Calendrics in Pre-Columbian Mesoamerica. In *Archaeoastronomy in the Americas,* ed. Ray A. Williamson, pp. 249–262. Ballena Press, Los Altos, California.

Marcus, Joyce. 1976. *Emblem and State in the Classic Maya Lowlands.* Dumbarton Oaks, Washington, D.C.

———. 1980. Zapotec Writing. *Scientific American* 242:50–64.

Markman, Charles W. 1981. *Prehispanic Settlement Dynamics in Central Oaxaca, Mexico: A View from the Miahuatlan Valley.* Vanderbilt University Publications in Anthropology no. 26. Nashville.

Marquina, Ignacio. 1951. *Arquitectura Prehispanica.* Instituto Nacional de Antropología e Historia. México, D.F.

Martin, Paul S., and Fred Plog. 1973. *Archaeology of Arizona.* Natural History Press, Doubleday, New York.

Mason, J. Alden. 1937. Late Archaeological Sites in Durango, Mexico, from Chalchihuites to Zape. In *Twenty-fifth Anniversary Studies.* Publications of the Philadelphia Anthropological Society 1:117–126. Also republished without illustrations in *The North Mexican Frontier,* ed. Basil C. Hedrick, J. Charles Kelley, and Carroll L. Riley. Southern Illinois University Press, Carbondale.

Massingham, Harold J. 1929. Origins of Ball Games. In *The Heritage of Man,* pp. 208–227. J. Cape Publishing, London.

Mastache, Guadalupe, and Ana Maria Crespo. 1974. La Ocupación Prehispánica en el Area de Tula, Hgo. In *Proyecto Tula,* ed. Eduardo Matos Mo., pp. 71–103. *Collección Científica* 15, Instituto Nacional de Antropología e Historia, México, D.F.

Mathews, Peter. 1975. The Lintels of Structure 12, Yaxchilán, Chiapas. A paper presented at the Annual Conference of the Northeastern Anthropological Association, Wesleyan University, October 1975.

———. 1977. The Inscription on the Back of Stela 8, Dos Pilas, Guatemala. Paper presented at the International Symposium on Maya Art, Architecture, Archaeology and Hieroglyphic Writing, Guatemala City. On file, Department of Archaeology, University of Texas, Austin.

Mathien, Frances Joan, and Randell H. McGuire, eds. 1986. *Ripples in the Chichimec Sea: New Consideration of Southwestern-Mesoamerican Interactions.* Southern Illinois University Press, Carbondale.

Matos Moctezuma, Eduardo. 1966. Un Juego de Pelota Doble en San Isidro, Chiapas. *Boletín de Instituto Nacional de Antropología e Historia* no. 25, México, D.F.

———. 1968. Piezas de Saqueo Procedentes de Jerécuaro, Gto. *Boletín de Instituto Nacional de Antropología e Historia* 33:30–35, México, D.F.

Mayer, Karl Herbert. 1978. *Maya Monuments: Sculptures of Unknown Provenance in Europe,* trans. Sandra Brizee. Acoma Books, Ramona, California.

———. 1980. *Maya Monuments: Sculptures of Unknown Provenance in the United States,* trans. Sandra Brizee. Acoma Books, Ramona, California.

———. 1984. *Maya Monuments: Sculptures of Unknown Provenance in Middle America,* trans. Sally Robinson and K.H. Mayer. Verlag Karl-Friedrich von Flemming, Berlin.

McGregor, John C. 1965. *Southwestern Archaeology.* University of Illinois Press, Urbana.

McGuire, Randall H. 1980. The Mesoamerican Connection in the Southwest. *The Kiva* 46(1–2):3–38.

Meighan, Clement W., ed. 1976. *The Archaeology of Amapa, Nayarit. Monumenta Archaeologica*: 2. The Institute of Archaeology, The University of California, Los Angeles.

Meighan, Clement W., and H.B. Nicholson. 1970. The Ceramic Mortuary Offerings of Prehistoric West Mexico. In *Sculpture of Ancient West Mexico: Nayarit, Jalisco, Colima*, pp. 17–110. Los Angeles County Museum of Art, Los Angeles.

Mendieta, Fr. Gerónimo de. 1945. *Historia Eclesiástica Indiana*. Editorial Salvador Chavez Hayhoe, México, D.F.

Métraux, Alfred. 1942. *The Native Tribes of Eastern Bolivia and Western Mato Grosso*. Bureau of American Ethnology, Bulletin no. 134, Washington, D.C.

Michels, J.W. 1979. The Kaminaljuyu Chiefdom. In *Pennsylvania State University Monograph Series on Kaminaljuyu*, ed. J.W. Michels and W.T. Sanders, pp. 229–232. University Park.

Miller, Arthur G. 1986. From the Maya Margins: Images of Postclassic Politics. In *Late Lowland Maya Civilization: Classic to Postclassic*, ed. Jeremy A. Sabloff and E. Wyllys Andrews V, pp. 199–222. University of New Mexico Press, Albuquerque.

Miller, Donald E. 1976. La Libertad: A Major Middle and Late Preclassic Ceremonial Center in Chiapas, Mexico. A Preliminary Report. New World Archaeological Foundation, San Cristobal de Las Casas.

Miller, Donald E., and Gareth W. Lowe. 1977. Test Excavations at the Sites on and near the La Libertad. Entre Rios Peninsula. Report to the Instituto de Nacional Antropología y Historia, México, D.F.

Miller, Mary E. 1986. *The Murals of Bonampak*. Princeton University Press, Princeton.

Miller, Mary E., and Stephen D. Houston. 1987. Stairways and Ballcourt Glyphs: New Perspectives on the Classic Maya Ballgame. *RES* 14:47–66.

Millon, Rene. 1973. *Urbanization at Teotihuacán*, vol. 1, *The Teotihuacán Map*. University of Texas Press, Austin.

———. 1976. Social Relations in Ancient Teotihuacán. In *The Valley of Mexico: Studies in Pre-Hispanic Ecology and Society*, ed. Eric R. Wolf, pp. 205–248. University of New Mexico Press, Albuquerque.

———. 1981. Teotihuacán: City, State, and Civilization. In *Supplement to the Handbook of Middle American Indians*, vol. 1, *Archaeology*, ed. J.A. Sabloff, pp. 198–243. University of Texas Press, Austin.

Molloy, John. 1969. The Casa Grande Archaeological Zone: Pre-Columbian Astronomical Observation. Manuscript, Western Archeological Center, National Park Service, Tucson.

Molloy, John. 1985. Ball Courts and the Oaxaca Codices. Paper presented at the International Symposium on the Mesoamerican Ballgame, Tucson. On file, Arizona State Museum Library, University of Arizona, Tucson.

Mora, Jesús. 1971. Proyecto Angostura. Field notes on file, New World Archaeological Foundation, San Cristobal de las Casas.

Morley, Sylvanus G. 1913. Archaeological Research at the Ruins of Chichén Itzá, Yucatán. In *Reports upon the Present and Future Needs of the Science of Anthropology*. Carnegie Institution of Washington, Washington, D.C.

————. 1935. *Guide Book to the Ruins of Quiriguá*. Carnegie Institute of Washington Supplemental Pub. 16. Washington, D.C.

————. 1938. *The Inscriptions of Petén*. Carnegie Institute of Washington Pub. 437. Washington, D.C.

————. 1941. Annual Report. *Yearbook 40*, pp. 295–297. Carnegie Institution of Washington, Washington, D.C.

Morley, Sylvanus G., and George W. Brainerd. 1983. *The Ancient Maya*, revised by Robert J. Sharer. Stanford University Press, Stanford.

Moser, Christopher L. 1973. *Human Decapitation in Ancient Mesoamerica*. Dumbarton Oaks Studies in Pre-Columbian Art and Archaeology no. 11, Washington, D.C.

Motolinia, Fray Toribio de Benavente. 1970. *Memoriales e Historia de los Indios de la Nueva Espana: Estudio Preliminar por Fidel de Lejarza*. Ediciones Atlas, Madrid.

Mountjoy, Joseph B., and David A. Peterson. 1973. *Man and Land in Prehispanic Cholula*. Vanderbilt University Publication in Anthropology 4, Vanderbilt University, Nashville.

Muñoz Camargo, D. 1892. *Historia de Tlaxcala*. México D.F., Mexico.

Navarrete, Carlos. 1960. *Archaeological Exploration in the Region of the Frailesca, Chiapas, Mexico*. Papers of the New World Archaeological Foundation no. 7 (Pub. no. 6). Orinda.

————. 1966. *The Chiapenec, History and Culture*. Papers of the New World Archaeological Foundation no. 21 (Pub. no. 16). Brigham Young University, Provo.

————. 1969. Reconocimiento Arqueológico de la Costa de Chiapas. Unpublished manuscript on file. New World Archaeological Foundation, San Cristobal de Casas.

————. 1974. Tradiciones Esculturales en la Costa Pacífica de Chiapas. Paper presented at the 41st International Congress of Americanists, Mexico City.

————. 1984. *Guia para el Estudio de los Monumentos Esculpidos de Chinkultic, Chiapas*. Universidad Nacional Autónoma de México, México, D.F.

————. 1986. *The Sculptural Complex at Cerro Bernal on the Coast of Chiapas*. Notes of the New World Archaeological Foundation no. 1. Brigham Young University, Provo.

Navarrete, Carlos, María José Con Uribe, and Alejandro Martínez Muriel. 1979. *Observaciones Arqueógicas en Cobá, Quintana Roo*. Universidad Nacional Autónoma de México, México, D.F.

Naylor, Thomas N. 1985. Casas Grandes Outlier Ball Courts in Northwest Chihuahua. In International Symposium on the Mesoamerican Ballgame, assembled by David R. Wilcox and Vernon L. Scarborough, pp. 536–553. On file, Arizona State Museum Library, University of Arizona, Tucson.

Needham, Rodney. 1975. Polythetic Classification: Convergence and Consequences. *Man* 10(3):349–369.

Nelson, Richard S. 1986. Pochtecas and Prestige: Mesoamerican Artifacts in Hohokam Sites. In *Ripples in the Chichimec Sea*, ed. Frances Joan Mathien and Randall H. McGuire, pp. 154–182. Southern Illinois University Press, Carbondale.

Nicholson, Henry B. 1967. A Fragment of an Aztec Relief Carving of the Earth

Monster. *Journal de la Société des Américanistes* 56:81–94.

Nimuendajú, Curt. 1939. *The Apinayé*, trans. Robert H. Lowie. Catholic University of America Anthropological Series no. 8. Washington, D.C.

———. 1942. *The Sherente*, trans. Robert H. Lowie. The Southwest Museum, Los Angeles.

Noguera, Eduardo. 1960. *La Quemada, Chalchihuites. Guia Oficial.* Instituto Nacional de Antropología e Historia, México.

Norton, Thomas E. 1984. *One Hundred Years of Collecting in America: The Story by Sotheby Parke Bernet.* H.N. Abrams, New York.

Offner, Jerome A. 1983. *Law and Politics in Aztec Texcoco.* Cambridge University Press, New York.

Oliveros, J. Arturo. 1972. Sobrevivencia del Juego de Pelota Prehispanico. In *XII Mesa Redonda: Religion en Mesoamerica*, pp. 463– 468. Sociedad Mexicana Oliveros, Arturode Antropología, México, D.F.

———. 1974. Nuevas Exploraciones en El Opeño, Michoacan. In *The Archaeology of West Mexico*, ed. Betty Bell, pp. 120–131. West Mexican Society for Advanced Study, Ajijic.

Olson, Ronald. 1933. Clan and Moiety in Native America. *University of California Publications in American Archaeology and Ethnology* 33(4). Berkeley.

Orejel, Jorge. 1988. An Analysis of the Inscriptions of the Petex Batun. A paper prepared for a graduate seminar on Maya Hieroglyphic Writing, University of Texas at Austin.

Ortiz, Alfonso. 1969. The Tewa World. University of Chicago Press, Chicago.

Pacheco, Romano, Carlos Navarrete, and Victor Segovia. 1981. *Kohunlich, Una Ciudad Maya del Clásico Temprano.* Ediciones San Angel, México, D.F.

Pailes, Richard A. 1980. The Upper Rio Sonora Valley in Prehistoric Trade. In *New Frontiers in the Archaeology and Ethnohistory of the Greater Southwest*, ed. Carroll L. Riley and Basil C. Hedrick. *Transactions of the Illinois State Academy of Science* 72(4):20–39.

Pailles, Maricruz H. 1988. *Cuevas de las Region Zoque de Ocozocoautla y el Río La Venta.* El Diario de Campo, 1945 de Matthew W. Stirling con Notas Arqueologicas. Notes of the New World Archaeological Foundation, no. 6, Provo.

Palacios, Enrique. 1939. *Los yugos y su simbolismo.* 25th International Congress of Americanists, Tomo 1, pp. 549–565. Mexico.

Parsons, Jeffrey R. 1971. *Prehistoric Settlement Patterns in the Texcoco Region, Mexico.* Memoirs of the Museum of Anthropology 3, University of Michigan, Ann Arbor.

———. 1976. The Role of Chinampa Agriculture in the Food Supply of Aztec Tenochtitlan. In *Cultural Change and Continuity: Essays in Honor of James Bennett Griffin*, ed. Charles E. Cleland, pp. 233–257. Academic Press, New York.

Parsons, Lee Allen. 1964. The Middle American Co-Tradition. Ph.D. diss., Department of Anthropology, Harvard University.

———. 1967. *Bilbao, Guatemala: An Archaeological Study of the Pacific Coast Cotzumalhuapa Region*, vol. 1. Publications in Anthropology, vols. 11 and 12, Milwaukee Public Museum, Milwaukee.

———. 1969. *Bilbao, Guatemala: An Archaeological Study of the Pacific Coast Cotzumalhuapa Region*, vol. 2. Publications in Anthropology 12, Milwaukee Public Museum, Milwaukee.

————. 1974. *Pre-Columbian America: The Art and Archaeology of South, Central, and Middle America*. Publications in Anthropology and History no. 2. Milwaukee Public Museum, Milwaukee.

————. 1978. The Peripheral Coastal Lowlands and the Middle Classic Period. In *Middle Classic Mesoamerica: A.D. 400–700*, ed. Esther Pasztory, pp. 25–34. Columbia University Press, New York.

————. 1980. *Pre-Columbian Art: The Morton D. May and the Saint Louis Art Museum Collections*. Harper and Row, New York.

————. 1986. *The Origins of Maya Art: Monumental Stone Sculpture of Kaminaljuyú, Guatemala, and the Southern Pacific Coast*. Studies in Pre-Columbian Art and Archaeology 28. Dumbarton Oaks, Washington, D.C.

Parsons, Lee A., and Barbara J. Price. 1971. Mesoamerican Trade and its Role in the Emergence of Civilization. *Contributions of the University of California Archaeological Research Facility* 11:169–195.

Pasztory, Esther. 1972. The Historical and Religious Significance of the Middle Classic Ball Game. In *Religión en Mesoamérica*, ed. Jaime Litvak King and Noemí Castillo Tejero, pp. 441–455. Sociedad Mexicana de Antropología, México, D.F.

————. 1976. *The Murals of Tepantitla, Teotihuacán*. Garland Press, New York.

————. 1978a. Artistic Traditions of the Middle Classic Period. In *Middle Classic Mesoamerica: A.D. 400–700*, ed. E. Pasztory, pp. 108–142. Columbia University Press, New York.

Pasztory, Esther, ed. 1978b. *Middle Classic Mesoamerica: A.D. 400–700*. Columbia University Press, New York.

Pendergast, D.M. 1969. *Altun Ha: A Guidebook to the Ancient Maya Ruins*. University of Toronto Press, Toronto.

————. 1979. *Excavations at Altun Ha, Belize 1964–1970*, vol. 1. Royal Ontario Museum Publications in Archaeology, Toronto.

————. 1981. Lamanai, Belize: Summary of Excavation Results, 1974–1980. *Journal of Field Archaeology* 8(1):29–53.

Pennington, Campbell W. 1969. *The Tepehuan of Chihuahua*. University of Utah Press, Salt Lake.

Perez, Chronicle. 1949 [1557]. *The Maya Chronicles*, trans. and ed. Alfredo Barrera Vasquez and Sylvanus G. Morley. Contributions to American Anthropology and History, Pub. 585. Carnegie Institution of Washington, Washington, D.C.

Peterson, Fredrick A. Some Notes on the Cave Survey of 1957–1958. New World Archaeological Foundation, San Cristobal de Las Casas.

Piña Chan, Román. 1955. *Las Culturas Preclasicas de la Cuenca de Mexico*. Fondo de Cultura Economica, México, D.F.

————. 1967. Atlas Arqueológico de la República Mexicana: Chiapas. Instituto Nacional de Antropología e Historia, México, D.F.

————. 1968. *Jaina*. Instituto Nacional de Antropología e Historia, México, D.F.

————. 1969. *Games and Sport in Old Mexico*, Edition Leipzig, Leipzig, German Democratic Republic.

————. 1975. *Teotenango: El Antiguo Lugar de la Muralla*. Dirección de Turismo, Gobierno del Estado de México, México.

————. 1982. *Exploraciones Arqueológicas en Tingambato, Michoacan*. Instituto Nacional de Antropología e Historia, México.

Piña Chan, Román, Amalia Cardós, and Noemí Castillo Tejero. 1976. La Cultura Maya. In *Los Pueblos y Señoríos Teocráticos: El Periodo de Las Ciudades*

Urbanas, Segunda Parte, pp. 165–245. Instituto Nacional de Antropología e Historia, México, D.F.

Piña Chan, Román, and Carlos Navarrete. 1967. *Archaeological Researches in the Lower Grijalva Region, Tabasco, Chiapas*. Papers of the New World Archaeological Foundation, no. 22. Brigham Young University, Provo.

Pinkley, Frank. 1981 [1918]. Seventeen Years Ago. Published in 1981. In *Hohokam Ballcourts and Their Interpretation* by David R. Wilcox and Charles Sternberg, pp. 16–26. Arizona State Museum Archaeological Series 155, University of Arizona, Tucson.

Pires-Ferreira, Jane W. 1975. *Formative Mesoamerican Exchange Networks with Special Reference to the Valley of Oaxaca*. Memoirs of the Museum of Anthropology 7, University of Michigan, Ann Arbor.

Plog, Fred, Steadman Upham, and Phil C. Weigand. 1982. A Perspective on Mogollon-Mesoamerican Interaction. In *Mogollon Archaeology, Proceedings of the 1980 Mogollon Conference*, ed. Patrick H. Beckett and Kim Silverbird, pp. 227–238. Acoma Books, Ramona, California.

Pollock, H.E. 1970. Architectural Notes on Some Chenes Ruins. In *Monographs and Papers in Maya Archaeology*, ed. William R. Bullard, Jr., pp. 1–88. Papers of the Peabody Museum of Archaeology and Ethnology, vol. 61. Harvard University, Cambridge.

————. 1980. *The Puuc: An Architectural Survey of the Hill Country of Yucatan and Northern Campeche, Mexico*. Peabody Museum of Archaeology and Ethnology, Harvard University, Cambridge.

Porter, Muriel N. 1953. *Tlatilco and the Pre-Classic Cultures of the New World*. Viking Fund Publications in Anthropology no. 19. Wenner-Gren Foundation for Anthropological Research, New York.

Preuss, Konrad Theodor. 1921. *Religion und Mythologie der Uitoto*. 2 vols. Vandenhoeck and Ruprecht, Gottingen.

Proskouriakoff, Tatiana. 1954. *Varieties of Classic Central Veracruz Sculpture*. Carnegie Institution Publication 606, Carnegie Institution, Washington, D.C.

————. 1964. Historical Data in the Inscriptions of Yaxchilán, pt. II. *Estudios de Cultura Maya 4*, pp. 177–201. Universidad Nacional Autónoma de México, México.

Putnam, Fredrick Ward. 1895. A Problem in American Anthropology. *Annual Report of the Smithsonian Institution*, 1895, pp. 478–486.

Quirarte, Jacinto. 1977. The Ballcourt in Mesoamerica: Its Architectural Development. In *Pre-Columbian Art History*, ed. A. Cordy-Collins and J. Stern, pp. 191–212. Peek Publications, Palo Alto.

Rabinal Achi. 1955. *Teatro Indigena Prehispanico: Rabinal Achi*, ed. F. Monterde. Biblioteca del Estudiante Universitario no. 71. Universidad Nacional Autónoma, México, D.F.

Rands, Robert L. 1977. The Rise of Classic Maya Civilization in the Northwestern Zone: Isolation and Integration. In *The Origins of Maya Civilization*, ed. R.E.W. Adams, pp. 159–180. University of New Mexico Press, Albuquerque.

Rands, Robert L., and Barbara C. Rands. 1965. Pottery Figurines of the Maya Lowlands. *Handbook of Middle American Indians*, vol. 2, ed. Robert Wauchope; *Archaeology of Southern Mesoamerica*, pt. 2, ed. Gordon R. Willey, pp. 535–560. University of Texas Press, Austin.

Rathje, William L. 1970. Socio-political Implications of Lowland Maya Burials:

Methodology and Tentative Hypotheses. *World Archaeology* 1:359–374.

Recinos, Adrian. 1950. *Popol Vuh, the Sacred Book of the Ancient Quiché Maya,* trans. Delia Goetz and S.G. Morley, University of Oklahoma Press, Norman.

Rediscovered Masterpieces of Mesoamerica: Mexico–Guatemala–Honduras. 1985. Editions Arts, Boulogne, France.

Redmond, Elsa Marion. 1981. A Fuego y Sangre: Early Zapotec Imperialism in the Cuicatlán Cañada, Oaxaca. Ph.D. diss., Yale University, New Haven.

Reents, Doris. 1985. *The Late Classic Maya Holmul Style Polychrome Pottery.* Ph.D. diss., University of Texas, Austin.

Reff, Daniel T. 1987. Old World Diseases and the Dynamics of Indian and Jesuit Relations in Northwestern New Spain, 1520–1660. In *Ejidos and Regions of Refuge in Northwestern Mexico,* ed. N. Ross Crumrine and Phil C. Weigand, pp. 85–94. Anthropological Papers of the University of Arizona, 46, Tucson.

Relaciones de Yucatán. 1898 [1579]. *Relaciones Histórico-Geográficas de las Provincias de Yucatán, Tabasco.* vol. I, Tomo Num. 11. Colleción de Documentos Inéditos. La Real Académica de la Histórica, Madrid.

Renfrew, Colin, and John F. Cherry, eds. 1986. *Peer Polity Interaction and Socio-Political Change.* Cambridge University Press, Cambridge.

Rice, D.S., and D.E. Puleston. 1981. Ancient Maya Settlement Patterns in the Petén, Guatemala. In *Lowland Maya Settlement Patterns,* ed. W. Ashmore, pp. 121–156. University of New Mexico Press, Albuquerque.

Riley, Carroll L. 1982. *The Frontier People: The Greater Southwest in the Protohistoric Period.* Southern Illinois University at Carbondale, Center for Archaeological Investigations Occasional Papers 1.

Riley, Carroll L., and Howard D. Winters. 1963. The Prehistoric Tepehuan of Northern Mexico. *Southwestern Journal of Anthropology* 19(2):177–185.

Ringle, William. 1985. Notes of Two Tablets of Unknown Provenance. *Fifth Palenque Round Table, 1983,* vol. VII, general ed., Merle Greene Robertson, volume ed., Virginia M. Fields, pp. 151–158. The Pre-Columbian Art Research Institute, San Francisco.

———. 1988. *Of Mice and Monkeys: The Value and Meaning of T1016, the God C Heiroglyph.* Research Reports on Ancient Maya Writing 18. Center for Maya Research, Washington, D.C.

Rivero, T. Sonia. 1979. Field Notes. Reconnaissance of the Comitán Region. Unpublished manuscript on file. New World Archaeological Foundation, San Cristobal de Casas.

———. 1983. Late Classic Rural Settlement Patterns in the San Gregorio Region, Chiapas, Mexico, vols. I and II. Ph.D. diss., Faculty of Archaeology, Cambridge University.

Robiscek, Francis, and Donald M. Hales. 1981. *The Maya Book of the Dead, The Ceramic Codex.* University of Virginia Art Museum, Charlottesville, and University of Oklahoma Press, Norman.

———. 1988. A Ceramic Codex Fragment: The Sacrifice of Xbalanque. In *Maya Iconography,* ed. Elizabeth P. Benson and Gillet G. Griffin, pp. 260–276. Princeton University Press, Princeton.

Roys, Lawrence, and Edwin M. Shook. 1966. *Preliminary Report on the Ruins of Ake, Yucatán.* Memoirs of the Society for American Archaeology no. 20. Salt Lake City.

Ruppert, Karl J. 1952. *Chichén Itzá: Architectural Notes and Plans.* Carnegie

Institution of Washington Pub. 595. Carnegie Institution, Washington, D.C.

Ruppert, Karl, and John H. Denison. 1943. *Archaeological Reconnaissance in Campeche, Quintana Roo, and Petén*. Carnegie Institution of Washington, Pub. 543. Washington, D.C.

Ruz Lhuillier, Alberto. 1948. El Juego de Pelota de Uxmal. Report on file, Instituto Nacional de Antropología e Historia, México, D.F.

———. 1958. El Juego de Pelota de Uxmal. In *Miscellanea Paul Rivet*, vol. 1, pp. 635–677. Universidad Nacional Autónoma de México, México, D.F.

———. 1961. Exploraciones Arqueológicas en Palenque, 1957. *Anales del Instituto Nacional de Antropología e Historia*, 14(43):35–90.

Sabloff, Jeremy A., and William L. Rathje. 1975. The Rise of a Maya Merchant Class. *Scientific American* 233(4):72–82.

Sacapulas. 1968 [1551]. *Título de los señores de Sacapulas*, trans. Rene Acuna. Latin American Center, University of California at Los Angeles.

Sahagún, Bernardino de. 1950–82. *The Florentine Codex. General History of the Things of New Spain*. 13 vols., trans. Arthur J.O. Anderson and C.E. Dibble. University of Utah Press, Salt Lake City.

———. 1956. *Historia General de las Cosas de Nueva España*, ed. Angel Ma. Garibay K., 4 vols. Biblioteca Porrúa 8–11, México.

Sahlins, Marshall D. 1961. The Segmentary Lineage: An Organization of Predatory Expansion. *American Anthropologist* 63:322–345.

Salter, Michael A. 1980. Play in Ritual: An Ethnohistorical Overview of Native North America. In *Play and Culture: 1978 Proceedings of the Association for the Anthropological Study of Play*, ed. Helen B. Schwartzman, pp. 70–82. Leisure Press, West Point.

———. 1983. Meteorological Play-Forms of the Eastern Woodlands. In *Play, Games and Sports in Cultural Contexts*, ed. Janet C. Harris and Roberta J. Park, pp. 211–223. Human Kinetics Publishers, Champaign.

Sanders, William T. 1968. Hydraulic Agriculture, Economic Symbiosis, and the Evolution of States in Central Mexico. In *Anthropological Archaeology in the Americas*, ed. Betty J. Meggers, pp. 88–107. Anthropological Society of Washington, Washington, D.C.

———. 1977. Ethnographic Analogy and the Teotihuacán Horizon Style. In *Teotihuacán and Kaminaljuyú: A Study in Prehistoric Culture Contact*, ed. William T. Sanders and Joseph W. Michels, pp. 397–410. Pennsylvania State University Press, University Park.

———. 1981. Classic Maya Settlement Patterns and Ethnographic Analogy. In *Lowland Maya Settlement Patterns*, ed. Wendy Ashmore, pp. 351–369. University of New Mexico Press, Albuquerque.

Sanders, William T., and Joseph W. Michels, eds. 1977. *Teotihuacán and Kaminaljuyú: A Study in Prehistoric Culture Contact*. Pennsylvania State University Press, University Park.

Sanders, William T., Deborah Nichols, Rebecca Storey, and Randolph Widmer. 1982. A Reconstruction of a Classic Period Landscape in the Teotihuacán Valley. Final Report to the National Science Foundation, Department of Anthropology, Pennsylvania State University, University Park.

Sanders, William T., Jeffrey R. Parsons, and Robert S. Santley. 1979. *The Basin of Mexico: Ecological Processes in the Evolution of a Civilization*. Academic Press, New York.

Sanders, William T., and Robert S. Santley. 1978. Review of "Monte Albán: Settlement Patterns at the Ancient Zapotec Capital," by Richard E. Blanton. *Science* 202:303–304.

————. 1983. A Tale of Three Cities: Energetics and Urbanization in Prehistoric Central Mexico. In *Prehistoric Settlement Patterns, Essays in Honor of Gordon R. Willey,* ed. Evon Vogt and Richard Leventhal, pp. 243–291. University of New Mexico Press, Albuquerque.

Santley, Robert S. 1979. Toltec Settlement Patterns in the Basin of Mexico. Paper presented at the conference entitled "Simposio sobre Tula," Pachuca, Hidalgo, Mexico.

————. 1980. Dissembedded Capitals Reconsidered. *American Antiquity* 45:132–145.

————. 1983a. Obsidian Trade and Teotihuacán Influence in Mesoamerica. In *Highland-Lowland Interaction in Mesoamerica: Interdisciplinary Approaches,* ed. Arthur Miller, pp. 69–124. Dumbarton Oaks, Washington, D.C.

————. 1983b. Ancient Population at Monte Albán: A Reconsideration of Methodology and Culture History. *Haliksa'a: University of New Mexico Contributions to Anthropology* 2:64–84.

————. 1983c. Review Article: Monte Albán's Hinterland, pt. I, by Richard Blanton, Stephen Kowalewski, Gary Feinman, and Jill Appel, *Journal of Anthropological Research* 39:96–111.

————. 1984. Obsidian Exchange, Economic Stratification, and the Evolution of Complex Society in the Basin of Mexico. In *Trade and Exchange in Early Mesoamerica,* ed. Kenneth Hirth, pp. 43–86. University of New Mexico Press, Albuquerque.

————. 1985. Review Article: The Political Economy of the Aztec Empire. *Journal of Anthropological Research* 41:327–337.

————. 1986. Prehispanic Roadways, Transport Network Geometry, and Aztec Politico-Economic Organization in the Basin of Mexico. In *Economic Aspects of Prehispanic Highland Mexico,* ed. Barry L. Isaac, pp. 223–244. Research in Economic Anthropology, Suppl. 2. J.A.I. Press, Greenwich.

————. In press a. The Structure of the Aztec Transport Network. In *Transportation Networks in the New World,* ed. Charles Trombold. Stanford University Press, Palo Alto.

————. In press b. The Evolution of Dendritic Politico-Economies. In *New Models for the Political Economies of Precolumbian Polities,* ed. Patricia Netherly and David Freidel, Cambridge University Press.

————. The Politico-Economic Organization of Ancient Teotihuacan. In *Pattern and Process in Ancient Mesoamerica,* ed. Robert S. Santley, Jeffrey R. Parsons, and Richard A. Diehl.

Santley, Robert S., and Philip J. Arnold. 1984. Review Article: Obscured by Clouds. *Journal of Anthropological Research* 40:211–230.

Santley, Robert S., Janet M. Kerley, and Ronald R. Kneebone. 1986. Obsidian Working, Long-Distance Exchange, and the Politico-Economic Organization of Early States in Central Mexico. In *Economic Aspects of Prehispanic Highland Mexico,* ed. Barry L. Isaac, pp. 101–132, Research in Economic Anthropology, Suppl. 2. J.A.I. Press, Greenwich.

Santley, Robert S., Thomas W. Killion, and Mark T. Lycett. 1986. On the Maya Collapse. *Journal of Anthropological Research* 42:123–159.

Santley, Robert S., Ronald R. Kneebone, and Janet M. Kerley. 1985. Rates of Obsidian Utilization in Central Mexico and on the South Gulf Coast. *Lithic Technology* 14:107–119.

Santley, Robert S., Ponciano Ortiz, Thomas W. Killion, Philip J. Arnold, and Janet M. Kerley. 1984. Final Field Report of the Matacapan Archaeological Project: The 1982 Season. Research Papers Series 15. Latin American Institute, University of New Mexico, Albuquerque.

Santley, Robert S., Clare Yarborough, and Barbara A. Hall. 1987. Enclaves, Ethnicity, and the Archaeological Record at Matacapan. In *Ethnicity and Culture*, ed. Reginald Auger, Margaret F. Glass, Scott MacEachern, and Peter H. McCartney, pp. 85–100. Archaeological Association, University of Calgary, Calgary.

Sapir, Edward. 1910. *Yana Texts*. University of California Publications in American Archaeology and Ethnology, volume 9, no. 1.

Satterthwaite, Linton, Jr. 1933. *The South Group Ballcourt, with a Preliminary Note on the West Group Ballcourt*. University of Pennsylvania Museum. PNPP No. 11. Philadelphia.

———. 1944. *Piedras Negras Archaeology: Architecture*, pt. IV, no. 1, *Ball Courts*. University Museum, University of Pennsylvania, Philadelphia.

Sauer, Carl. 1932. *The Road to Cibola. Ibero-Americana*: 3. University of California Press, Berkeley.

Saul, Frank P. 1973. Disease in the Maya Area: The Pre-Columbian Evidence. In *The Classic Maya Collapse*, ed. T. Patrick Culbert, pp. 301–324. University of New Mexico Press, Albuquerque.

Scarborough, Vernon. 1985. Courting the Southern Maya Lowlands. Paper presented at the International Symposium of the Mesoamerican Ballgame, Tucson, Arizona State Museum Library, University of Arizona, Tucson.

Scarborough, Vernon, Beverely Mitchum, Sorraya Carr, and David Freidel. 1982. Two Late Preclassic Ballcourts at the Lowland Maya Center of Cerros, Northern Belize. *Journal of Field Archaeology* 9:21–34.

Scarborough, Vernon L., and Robin A. Robertson. 1986. Civic and Residential Settlement in a Late Preclassic Maya Center. *Journal of Field Archaeology* 13:155–175.

Schaafsma, Polly. 1980. *Indian Folk Art of the Southwest*. School of American Research and University of New Mexico Press, Albuquerque.

Schele, Linda. 1976. Accession Iconography of Chan-Bahlum in the Group of the Cross at Palenque. In *The Art, Iconography, and Dynastic History of Palenque, Part III. Proceedings of the Segunda Mesa Redonda de Palenque*, ed. Merle Greene Robertson, pp. 9–34. Pebble Beach, California: Robert Louis Stevenson School.

———. 1977. An Analysis of the Tablets of the Group of the Cross. A preliminary study in preparation for a publication of the Miniconferences held at Dumbarton Oaks between 1974 and 1976.

———. 1978a. A Preliminary Commentary on the Tablets of the Temple of Inscriptions at Palenque, Chiapas. A preliminary study in preparation for a publication of the Miniconferences held at Dumbarton Oaks between 1974 and 1976.

———. 1978b. *Notebook for the Maya Hieroglyphic Writing Workshop at Texas* (with commentaries on the tablets of the Group of the Cross). Institute of Latin American Studies, University of Texas, Austin.

————. 1979. Genealogical Documentation in the Tri-figure Panels at Palenque. In *Tercera Mesa Redonda de Palenque*, vol. IV, ed. Merle Greene Robertson, pp. 41–70. Pre-Columbian Art Research, Palenque and Herald Printers, Monterey.

————. 1980. *Notebook for the Maya Hieroglyphic Writing Workshop at Texas* (with commentaries on the panels of the Temple of the Inscriptions at Palenque). Institute of Latin American Studies, University of Texas, Austin.

————. 1981. *Notebook for the Maya Hieroglyphic Writing Workshop at Texas* (with commentaries on tablets from the Cross, the Foliated Cross, and the Sun). Institute of Latin American Studies, University of Texas, Austin.

————. 1982. *Maya Glyphs: The Verbs*. University of Texas Press, Austin.

————. 1984. Human Sacrifice Among the Classic Maya. In *Ritual Human Sacrifice in Mesoamerica*, ed. Elizabeth P. Benson, pp. 7–48. Dumbarton Oaks Research Library and Collection, Washington, D.C.

————. 1986. Interim Report on the Iconography of the Architectural Sculpture of Temple 22 (from the 1986 season). *Copán Mosaic Project Copán Note 19*. Department of Art, University of Texas, Austin.

————. 1987a. The Reviewing Stand of Temple 11. *Copán Note 32*. Copán Mosaics Project and the Instituto Hondureño de Antropología e Historia. Copán, Honduras.

————. 1987b. *Notebook for the Maya Hieroglyphic Writing Workshop at Texas* (with commentaries on the tablets of the Group of the Cross). Art Department, University of Texas, Austin.

————. 1988. The Xibalba Shuffle: A Dance after Death. In *Maya Iconography*, ed. Elizabeth Benson and Gillet Griffin, pp. 294–317. Princeton University Press, Princeton.

————. 1989. *Notebook for the Maya Hieroglyphic Writing Workshop at Texas* (with commentaries on the inscriptions of Copán). Art Department, University of Texas, Austin.

————. In press. House Names and Dedication Rituals at Palenque. In *Visions and Revisions*, ed. Flora Clancy. University of New Mexico Press, Albuquerque.

Schele, Linda, and David Freidel. In press. *A Forest of Kings. Royal Histories of the Ancient Maya*. William Morrow and Co., New York.

Schele, Linda, and Nikolai Grube. 1990. "Six-Staired Ballcourts," note 83 in *Copan Mosaics Project, Copan Notes* (Copán, Honduras).

Schele, Linda, and Jeffrey Miller. 1983. *The Mirror, the Rabbit, and the Bundle: 'Accession' Expressions from the Classic Maya Inscriptions*. Studies in Precolumbian Art and Archaeology no. 25. Dumbarton Oaks Research Library and Collection, Washington, D.C.

Schele, Linda, and Mary Ellen Miller. 1986. *The Blood of Kings: Dynasty and Ritual in Maya Art*. Kimbell Art Museum, Fort Worth and Braziller, New York.

Schortman, Edward M. 1986. Interaction Between the Maya and Non-Maya along the Late Classic Southeast Maya Periphery. The View from the Lower Motagua Valley, Guatemala. In *The Southeast Maya Periphery*, ed. Patricia A. Urban and Edward M. Schortman, pp. 115–137. University of Texas Press, Austin.

Schroeder, Albert H. 1940. A Stratigraphic Survey of Pre-Spanish Trash Mounds of the Salt River Valley, Arizona. Unpublished Master's thesis, Department of Anthropology, University of Arizona, Tucson.

————. 1949. Cultural Implications of the Ball Courts in Arizona. *Southwestern Journal of Anthropology* 5(1):28–36.

Schultze-Jena, Leonard. 1972. Popol Vuh, das heilige Buch der Quiche-Indianer von Guatemala. *Quellenwerke sur alten Geschichte amerikas, Aufgezeichnet in den Sprachen der Eingeborenen.* Verlag W. Kohlhammer, Stuttgart.

Seler, Eduard. 1963. *Comentarios al Codice Borgia.* 3 vols. Trans. Mariana Frenk. Fondo de Cultura Economica, Mexico.

Sharer, Robert J. 1978. Archaeology and History at Quiriguá. *Journal of Field Archaeology* 5:51–70.

Sharer, Robert J., Christopher Jones, Wendy Ashmore, and Edward M. Schortman. 1979. The Quiriguá Project: 1976 Season. *Quiriguá Reports,* vol. 1, Paper no. 5. Museum Monograph 37, University Museum, University of Pennsylvania, Philadelphia.

Shook, Edwin M. 1956. An Archaeological Reconnaissance in Chiapas, Mexico. *New World Archaeological Foundation Publication* no. 1, pp. 20–37. Orinda.

————. 1965. Archaeological Survey of the Pacific Coast of Guatemala. In *Handbook of Middle American Indians,* ed. Robert Wauchope and Gordon R. Willey, vol. 2, pp. 180–194. University of Texas Press, Austin.

Sidrys, Raymond V. 1983. *Archaeological Excavations in Northern Belize, Central America.* Institute of Archaeology Monograph 17, University of California, Los Angeles.

Skinner, Alanson. 1913. Social Life and Ceremonial Bundles of the Menomini Indians. *Anthropological Papers of the American Museum of Natural History,* vol. 13, pt. 1. New York.

Smith, A. Ledyard. 1950. *Uaxactún, Guatemala, Excavations of 1931–37.* Carnegie Institution of Washington Pub. 588. Washington, D.C.

————. 1955. *Archaeological Reconnaissance in Central Guatemala.* Carnegie Institution of Washington Pub. 608. Carnegie Institution of Washington, Washington, D.C.

————. 1961. Types of Ball Courts in the Highlands of Guatemala. In *Essays in Precolumbian Art and Archaeology,* ed. Samuel K. Lothrop et al., pp. 100–125. Harvard University Press, Cambridge.

————. 1972. *Excavations at Altar de Sacrificios. Architecture, Settlements, Burials and Caches.* Papers of the Peabody Museum of Archaeology and Ethnology, vol. 62, no. 2, Harvard University, Cambridge.

————. 1982. *Excavations at Seibal: Major Architecture and Caches.* Memoirs of the Peabody Museum of Archaeology and Ethnology, vol. 15, no. 1. Cambridge.

Smith, Carol A. 1976. Exchange Systems and the Spatial Distribution of Elites: The Organization of Stratification in Agrarian Societies. In *Regional Analysis,* vol. 2, *Social Systems,* ed. Carol A. Smith, pp. 390–474. Academic Press, New York.

Smith, Michael E. 1979. The Aztec Marketing System and Settlement Pattern in the Valley of Mexico: A Central Place Analysis. *American Antiquity* 44:110–125.

————. 1980. The Role of the Marketing System in Aztec Society and Economy: Reply to Evans. *American Antiquity* 45:876–883.

Smith, Robert E. 1971. *The Pottery of Mayapán.* Papers of the Peabody Museum of Archaeology and Ethnology, Peabody Museum, Harvard University, vol. 66, no. 1. Cambridge.

Sorenson, John L. 1956. An Archaeological Reconnaissance of West-Central

Chiapas, Mexico. *New World Archaeological Foundation*, Publication no. 1, pp. 7–19. Orinda.

Spence, Michael W. 1981. Obsidian Production and the State in Teotihuacán. *American Antiquity* 46:769–788.

———. 1984. Craft Production and Polity in Early Teotihuacán. In *Trade and Exchange in Early Mesoamerica*, ed. Kenneth G. Hirth, pp. 87–114. University of New Mexico Press, Albuquerque.

Spencer, Charles S. 1979. Irrigation, Administration, and Society in Formative Tehuacán. In *Prehistoric Social, Political, and Economic Development in the Area of the Tehuacán Valley: Some Results of the Palo Blanco Project*, ed. Robert D. Drennan, pp. 13–75. Technical Reports of the Museum of Anthropology 11, University of Michigan, Ann Arbor.

———. 1982. *The Cuicatlán Cañada and Monte Albán: A Study of Primary State Formation*. Academic Press, New York.

Stephens, John L. 1843. *Incidents of Travel in Yucatán*. 2 vols. Harper and Brothers, New York.

Stern, Theodore. 1949. *The Rubber-Ball Game of the Americas*. Monographs of the American Ethnological Society no. 17. J.J. Augustin, New York.

Stone, Andrea. 1987. Disconnection, Foreign Insignia, and Political Expansion: Teotihuacán and the Warrior Stelae of Piedras Negras. In *Mesoamerica After the Decline of Teotihuacán: A.D. 700–900*, ed. Richard Diehl and Janet Berlo. Dumbarton Oaks, Washington, D.C.

Strebel, Hermann. 1890. Studien über Steinjoche aus Mexiko und Mittel-Amerika. *International Archiv für Ethnographie* 3:16–28, 49–61.

———. 1893. Nachtrag zu Studien über Steinjoche. *International Archiv für Ethnographie* 6:44–48.

Stroessner, Robert J. 1973. Free Standing Portable Sculpture Related to Teotihuacán during the Early Classic Period. Manuscript. The Denver Art Museum.

Stromsvik, Gustav. 1952. *The Ball Courts at Copán, with Notes on Courts at La Union, Quiriguá, San Pedro Pinula and Asuncion Mita*. Carnegie Institution of Washington Pub. 596, Contribution 55. Washington, D.C.

Stuart, David. 1987. Ten Phonetic Syllables. *Research Reports on Ancient Maya Writing* 14. Center for Maya Research, Washington, D.C.

———. 1988. A letter to Linda Schele relating proposed readings of T1016 and the Glyph B elbow. Dated April 1988.

Stuart, David, and Stephen Houston. Classic Maya Place Names. *Research Reports on Ancient Maya Writing*. Center for Maya Research, Washington, D.C.

Stuart, David, and Linda Schele. 1986. Interim Report on the Hieroglyphic Stair of Structure 26. *Copán Note* 17. Copán Mosaics Project and the Instituto Hondureño de Antropología e Historia. Copán, Honduras.

Stuart, George E. 1981. Maya Art Treasures Discovered in Cave. *National Geographic* 160:2.

Stuart, George E., and Gene S. Stuart. 1977. *The Mysterious Maya*. National Geographic Society, Washington, D.C.

Swanton, John R. 1929. *Myths and Tales of the Southeastern Indians*. Bureau of American Ethnology Bulletin no. 88. Washington, D.C.

Sweezey, William R. 1972. La Pelota Mixteca. In *Religión en Mesoamerica*, XII Mesa Redonda, pp. 471–478. Sociedad Mexicana de Antropología, México, D.F.

Taladoire, Eric. 1976. Analyse Préliminaire de Quelques Panneaux Mayas Classiques. Université de Paris I, pp. 62–73. Paris.

———. 1979. La Pelota Mixteca. Un Juego Contemporáneo, con Origenes Complejos. *XV Mesa Redonda* 1:431–439. Sociedad Mexicana de Antropología, México.

———. 1981. *Les Terrains de Jeu de Balle (Mesoamérique et Sud-Ouest des Etats Unis)*. *Etudes Mesoaméricaines*, Series II, no. 4. Mission Archéologique et Ethnologique Française au Mexique, México.

Tate, Carolyn E. 1985. The Carved Ceramics Called Chochola. In *Fifth Palenque Round Table, 1983*, vol. 7, ed. Merle G. Robertson and Virginia Fields, pp. 123–133. Pre-Columbian Art Research Institute, San Francisco, California.

———. 1986. The Language of Symbols in the Ritual Environment of Yaxchilán, Chiapas, Mexico. Ph.D. diss., University of Texas at Austin.

Taube, Karl. 1985. The Classic Maya Maize God: A Reappraisal. In *Fifth Palenque Round Table, 1983*, vol. 7, ed. Merle G. Robertson, volume ed. Virginia M. Fields, pp. 171–181. Pre-Columbian Art Research Institute, San Francisco.

Taylor, Dicey. 1979. The Cauac Monster. In *Tercera Mesa Redonda de Palenque*, vol. 4, ed. Merle G. Robertson and Donnan Jeffers, pp. 79–89. Pre-Columbian Art Research Center, Palenque, México.

Tedlock, Barbara. 1982. *Time and the Highland Maya*. University of New Mexico Press, Albuquerque.

Tedlock, Dennis. 1985. *Popol Vuh: The Definitive Edition of the Mayan Book of the Dawn of Life and the Glories of Gods and Kings* (translation). Simon and Schuster, New York.

———. 1989. Copán as Tulan. Paper presented at the 13th Maya Hieroglyphic Writing Conference, Texas Symposium, Austin, Texas.

Tezozomoc, Hernando Alvarado. 1975. *Crónica Mexicayotl*, trans. Adrian Leon. Universidad Nacional Autonoma de México, México, D.F.

———. 1980. *Crónica Mexicana*. Editorial Porrúa, México, D.F.

Thompson, J. Eric S. 1931. *Archaeological Investigations in the Southern Cayo District, British Honduras*. Field Museum of National History Anthropological Series, vol. 17, no. 3. Chicago.

———. 1939. *Excavations at San Jose, British Honduras*. Carnegie Institution of Washington Pub. 506. Washington, D.C.

———. 1941. Yokes or Ball Game Belts? *American Antiquity* 6:320–326.

———. 1948. *An Archaeological Reconnaissance in the Cotzumalhuapa Region, Escuintla, Guatemala*. Contributions to American Anthropology and History 44. Carnegie Institution of Washington, Pub. 574. Washington, D.C.

———. 1962. *A Catalog of Maya Hieroglyphics*. University of Oklahoma Press, Norman.

———. 1966a. *Maya Hieroglyphic Writing*. University of Oklahoma Press, Norman.

———. 1966b. *The Rise and Fall of Maya Civilization*, 2nd ed. University of Oklahoma Press, Norman.

———. 1970. *Maya History and Religion*. University of Oklahoma Press, Norman.

Thompson, J.E.S., Harry E.D. Pollock, and Jean Charlot. 1932. *A Preliminary Study of the Ruins of Coba, Quintana Roo, Mexico*. Carnegie Institution of Washington, Pub. 424. Washington, D.C.

Tichy, Franz. 1981. Order and Relationship of Space in Mesoamerica: Myth or

Reality? In *Mesoamerican Sites and World Views*, ed. Elizabeth P. Benson, pp. 217–245. Dumbarton Oaks Research Library and Collection, Washington, D.C.

Tizimin and Mani, Books of Chilam Balam. 1949. *The Prophecies for the Maya Tuns or Years in the Books of Chilam Balam of Tizimin and Mani*, ed. Ralph L. Roys, pp. 156–186, Contributions to American Anthropology and History 51, Pub. 585. Carnegie Institution of Washington, Washington, D.C.

Torquemada, Juan de. 1943–44. *Monarquía Indiana*. 3 vols. Editorial Chávez Hayhoe, México.

Toscano, Salvador. 1945. Informe sobre la Existencia de Jugadores de Pelota Mayas en la Ceramica Escultorica de Jaina. *Notes on Middle American Archaeology and Ethnology* 2(54):182–183. Carnegie Institution of Washington, Cambridge.

Totonicapan. 1953. *Title of the Lords of Totonicapan*, trans. Delia Goetz and Dionision Jose Chonay. University of Oklahoma Press, Norman.

Tourtellot III, Gair, Norman Hammond, and Richard M. Rose. 1978. A Brief Reconnaissance of Itzan. *Peabody Museum of Archaeology and Ethnology* 14(3):241–250.

Tourtellot III, Gair, Jeremy A. Sabloff, and Robert Sharik. 1978. A Reconnaissance of Cancuen. In *Excavations at Seibal, Department of Petén, Guatemala*. Peabody Museum of Archaeology and Ethnology. Memoirs vol. 14, no. 2, pp. 191–240. Harvard University, Cambridge.

Townsend, Richard F. 1979. *State and Cosmos in the Art of Tenochtitlán*. Studies in Pre-Columbian Art and Archaeology no. 20. Dumbarton Oaks, Washington, D.C.

Tozzer, Alfred M. 1930. Maya and Toltec Figures at Chichén Itzá. *Proceedings of the 23rd International Congress of Americanists* (New York, 1928), pp. 155–164.

———. 1941. *Landa's Relacion de las Cosas de Yucatán, A Translation*. Peabody Museum Papers XVIII. Cambridge.

———. 1957. *Chichén Itzá and its Cenote of Sacrifice: A Comparative Study of Contemporaneous Maya and Toltec*. Memoirs of the Peabody Museum of Archaeology and Ethnology, vols. 11–12. Cambridge.

Trinkhaus, Kathryn M., ed. 1987. *Polities and Partitions: Human Boundaries and the Growth of Complex Societies*. Arizona State University Anthropological Research Papers, no. 37. Tempe.

Turner, Ellen Sue, Norman I. Turner, and R.E.W. Adams. 1981. Volumetric Assessment, Rank Ordering, and Maya Civic Centers. In *Lowland Maya Settlement Patterns*, ed. Wendy Ashmore, pp. 71–88. University of New Mexico Press, Albuquerque.

Turner, Victor W. 1960. Betwixt and Between: The Liminal Period. In *Rites of Passage*, trans. M.B. Vizedom and G.L. Caffee. University of Chicago Press, Chicago.

Underhill, Ruth M. 1948. Ceremonial Patterns in the Greater Southwest. *Monographs of the American Ethnological Society* 13. University of Washington, Seattle.

Upham, Steadman. 1982. *Polities and Power*. Academic Press, New York.

Vance, James E. 1970. *The Merchant's World*. Prentice-Hall, Englewood Cliffs.

Villacorta, Jorge A., trans. 1962. *Popol Vuh*. Ministerio de Educación Publica, Guatemala.

Vivian, R. Gwinn. 1970. An Apache Site on Ranch Creek, Southeastern Arizona. *The Kiva* 35:125–130.

von Euw, Eric. 1977. *Corpus of Maya Hieroglyphic Inscriptions* vol. 4, pt. 1, *Etzimte, Pixoy, Tzum.* Peabody Museum of Archaeology and Ethnology, Cambridge.

von Winning, Hasso. 1965. Relief-Decorated Pottery from Central Veracruz, Mexico. *Ethnos* 30:105–135.

von Winning, Hasso, and Olga Hammer. 1972. *Anecdotal Sculpture of Ancient West Mexico.* Ethnic Arts Council of Los Angeles, California.

Wagner, Günter. 1931. *Yuchi Tales.* Publications of the American Ethnological Society, vol. 13. New York.

Wallace, Dwight T. 1977. An Intra-Site Locational Analysis of Utatlán: The Structure of an Urban Site. In *Archaeology and Ethnohistory of the Central Quiché*, ed. Dwight T. Wallace and Robert M. Carmack, pp. 20–54. Institute for Mesoamerican Studies, SUNY Albany.

Wallace, Henry D. 1987. Regional Context of the Prehistoric Rancho Vistoso Sites: Settlement Patterns and Socioeconomic Structure. In *Prehistoric Settlement in the Cañada del Oro Valley, Arizona: The Rancho Vistoso Survey Project* by Douglas B. Craig and Henry D. Wallace, pp. 117–166. Institute for American Research Anthropological Papers 8. Tucson.

Wallace, Henry D., and Douglas B. Craig. 1988. A Reconsideration of the Tucson Basin Hohokam Chronology. In *Recent Research on Tucson Basin Prehistory: Proceedings of the Second Tucson Basin Conference*, ed. William H. Doelle and Paul R. Fish pp. 9-30. Institute for American Research Anthropological Papers 10. Tucson.

Wallace, Henry D., and James P. Holmlund. 1986. Petroglyphs of the Picacho Mountains, South Central Arizona. Institute for American Research Anthropological Papers 6. Tucson.

Warren, Claude N. 1984. The Desert Region. In *California Archeology* by Michael J. Moratto, pp. 339–430. Academic Press, New York.

Wasley, William W. 1960. A Hohokam Platform Mound at the Gatlin Site, Gila Bend, Arizona. *American Antiquity* 26(2):244–262.

Wasley, William W., and Alfred E. Johnson. 1965. *Salvage Archaeology in Painted Rocks Reservoir, Western Arizona.* Anthropological Papers of the University of Arizona 9. Tucson.

Waterman, T. T. 1914. The Explanatory Element in the Folk-tales of the North American Indians. *Journal of American Folklore* 27:1–54.

Waters, Michael R. 1987. Holocene Alluvial Geology and Geoarchaeology of AZ BB:13:14 and the San Xavier Reach of the Santa Cruz River, Arizona. In *The Archaeology of the San Xavier Bridge Site (AZ BB:13:14) Tucson Basin, Southern Arizona*, ed. John C. Ravesloot, pt I, pp. 39–60. Arizona State Museum Archaeological Series 171. University of Arizona, Tucson.

Weaver, Muriel Porter. 1981. *The Aztecs, Maya, and Their Predecessors: Archaeology of Mesoamerica.* 2nd ed. Academic Press, New York.

Webster, David L. 1977. Warfare and the Evolution of Maya Civilization. In *The Origins of Maya Civilization*, ed. Richard E.W. Adams, pp. 335–372. University of New Mexico Press, Albuquerque.

Webster, David, and Elliot M. Abrams. 1983. An Elite Compound at Copán, Honduras. *Journal of Field Archaeology* 10:285–296.

Weeks, John M. 1983. *Chisalin: A Late Postclassic Maya Settlement in Highland Guatemala.* British Archaeological Reports, International Series 169. Oxford.

Weigand, Phil C. 1978. The Prehistory of the State of Zacatecas: An Interpretation (pt. 1). *Anthropology* 2(1):67–87.

———. 1979a. The Prehistory of the State of Zacatecas: An Interpretation (pt. 2). *Anthropology* 2(2):22–41.

———. 1979b. The Formative-Classic and Classic-Postclassic Transitions in the Teuchitlán-Etzatlán Zone of Jalisco. In *Los Procesos de Cambio*, XV Mesa Redonda de la Sociedad Mexicana de Antropología, Tomo I, pp. 413–423.

———. 1985. Evidence for Complex Societies during the Western Mesoamerican Classic Period. In *The Archaeology of Western and Northwestern Mesoamerica*, ed. Michael S. Foster and Phil C. Weigand, pp. 47–91. Westview Press, Boulder.

Weigand, Phil C., Garman Harbottle, and Edward V. Sayre. 1977. Turquoise Sources and Source Analysis: Mesoamerica and the Southwestern U.S.A. In *Exchange Systems in Prehistory*, ed. Timothy K. Earle and Jonathan E. Ericson, pp. 15–34. Academic Press, New York.

Weltfish, Gene. 1937. *Caddoan Texts. Pawnee, South Band Dialect.* Publications of the American Ethnological Society, vol. 17.

Whalen, Michael. 1981. *Excavations at Santo Domingo Tomaltepec: Evolution of a Formative Community in the Valley of Oaxaca, Mexico.* Memoirs of the Museum of Anthropology 12, University of Michigan, Ann Arbor.

White, Willett E. 1975. The Ecological Potential of North-Central Veracruz in Ancient Mesoamerica. Thesis, University of the Americas, Cholula.

Wicke, Charles. 1957. The Ball Court at Yagul, Oaxaca: A Comparative Study. *Mesoamerican Notes* 5:37–76.

Wilcox, David R. 1976. How the Pueblos Came to Be as They Are: The Problem Today. Preliminary Exam Paper, on file at Arizona State Museum Library, University of Arizona, Tucson.

———. 1979a. The Hohokam Regional System. In *An Archaeological Test of Sites in the Gila Butte-Santan Region, South-Central Arizona*, by Glen Rice et al., pp. 77–116. Arizona State University Anthropological Research Papers 18. Tempe.

———. 1979b. Warfare Implications of Dry-Laid Masonry Walls on Tumamoc Hill. *The Kiva* 45(1–2):15–38.

———. 1980. The Current Status of the Hohokam Concept. In "Current Issues in Hohokam Prehistory, Proceedings of a Symposium," ed. David Doyel and Fred Plog. Arizona State University Anthropological Research Papers 23:236–242.

———. 1984. One Hundred Years of Archaeology at Pueblo Grande. Manuscript, Pueblo Grande Museum, Phoenix.

———. 1985. Preliminary Report on New Data on Hohokam Ballcourts. In *Proceedings of the 1983 Hohokam Symposium*, pt. II, ed. Alfred E. Dittert, Jr. and Donald E. Dove, pp. 641–654. Arizona Archaeological Society Occasional Paper 2. Phoenix.

———. 1986a. A History of Research on the Question of Mesoamerican-Southwestern Connections. In *Ripples in the Chichimec Sea*, ed. Frances Joan Mathien and Randall H. McGuire, pp. 9–44. Southern Illinois University Press, Carbondale.

———. 1986b. The Tepiman Connection: A Model of Mesoamerican-Southwestern Interaction. In *Ripples in the Chichimec Sea*, ed. Frances Joan Mathien and Randall H. McGuire, pp. 135–153. Southern Illinois University Press, Carbondale.

———. 1986c. Excavations of Three Sites on Bottomless Pits Mesa, Flagstaff,

Arizona. Interim Report submitted to the Coconino National Forest. Flagstaff.

———. 1987a. The Evolution of Hohokam Ceremonial Systems. In *Astronomy and Ceremony in the Prehistoric Southwest*, ed. John Carlson and W. James Judge, pp. 149–168. Papers of the Maxwell Museum of Anthropology 2, Albuquerque.

———. 1987b. *Frank Midvale's Investigation of the Site of La Ciudad.* Arizona State University Anthropological Field Studies 19, Tempe.

———. 1988. The Regional Context of the Brady Wash and Picacho Area Sites. In *Hohokam Settlement Along the Slopes of the Picacho Mountains, Synthesis and Conclusions, Tucson Aqueduct Project*, ed. Richard Ciolek-Torrello and David R. Wilcox, pp. 244–267. Museum of Northern Arizona Research Paper 35, Vol. 6. Flagstaff.

———. 1989. Hohokam Warfare. In *Cultures in Conflict: Current Archaeological Perspectives*, ed. Diana Claire Tkaczuk and Brian C. Vivian, pp. 163–172. Proceedings of the Twentieth Annual Chacmool Conference. University of Calgary, Calgary.

———. 1991. Changing Contexts of Pueblo Adaptations, A.D. 1250–1600. In *Farmers, Hunters, and Colonists: Interactions Between the Southwest and the Southern Plains*, ed. Katherine A. Spielmann, pp. 128–154. University of Arizona Press, Tucson.

———. n.d. A Processual Model of Charles C. Di Peso's Babocomari Site and Related Systems. Manuscript on file, Museum of Northern Arizona, Flagstaff.

Wilcox, David R., Thomas R. McGuire, and Charles Sternberg. 1981. *Snaketown Revisited.* Arizona State Museum Archaeological Series 155. University of Arizona, Tucson.

Wilcox, David R., and Lynette O. Shenk. 1977. *The Architecture of the Casa Grande and Its Interpretation.* Arizona State Museum Archaeological Series 115. University of Arizona, Tucson.

Wilcox, David R., and Charles Sternberg. 1983. *Hohokam Ballcourts and Their Interpretation.* Arizona State Museum Archaeological Series 160. Arizona State Museum, University of Arizona, Tucson.

Wilkerson, S. Jeffrey K. 1968. Prehistoric Cult Dynamics, Figurine Cults of Central Veracruz. Ms. in possession of author.

———. 1971. Un yugo 'en situ' de la region del Tajín. In *Boletín del Instituto Nacional de Antropología e Historia*, pp. 41–45. 41 Sep. 1970, México.

———. 1972. *Ethnogenesis of the Huastecs and Totonacs.* University Microfilms, Ann Arbor.

———. 1974. Sub-Culture Areas of Eastern Mesoamerica. In *Primera Mesa Redonda de Palenque*, pt. II, pp. 89–102. Robert Louis Stevenson School, Pebble Beach (paper presented 1973).

———. 1976. *El Tajín.* University Gallery, University of Florida.

———. 1980. Man's Eighty Centuries in Veracruz. *National Geographic* 158(2):202–231.

———. 1984. In Search of the Mountain of Foam: Human Sacrifice in Eastern Mesoamerica. In *Ritual Human Sacrifice in Mesoamerica*, ed. Elizabeth H. Boone, pp. 101–132. Dumbarton Oaks, Washington, D.C.

Willey, Gordon R. 1979. The Concept of the "Disembedded Capital" in Comparative Perspective. *Journal of Anthropological Research* 35:123–137.

Willey, Gordon R., and A. Ledyard Smith. 1970. *The Ruins of Altar de Sacrificios,*

Department of Petén, Guatemala. Papers of the Peabody Museum of Archaeology and Ethnology vol. 62, pt. 1. Harvard University, Cambridge.

Willey, Gordon R., A. Ledyard Smith, Gair Tourtellot III, and Ian Graham. 1975. *Excavations at Seibal: Introduction, the Site and its Setting.* Peabody Museum of Archaeology and Ethnology Memoirs, vol. 13, no. 1. Cambridge.

Wirsing, Paul. 1930. Q'uec Chi. Kekchi-German Dictionary in manuscript form. Copy of the handwritten manuscript in the author's possession.

Wisdom, Charles. Materials on the Chorti Languages. Collection of Manuscripts from the Middle American Cultural Anthropology, Fifth Series, no. 20. Microfilm, University of Chicago.

Wittfogel, Karl. 1957. *Oriental Despotism.* Yale University Press, New Haven.

Wolf, Eric R. 1966. *Peasants.* Prentice-Hall, Englewood Cliffs.

Wolf, Eric R., ed. 1976. *The Valley of Mexico: Studies in Pre-Hispanic Ecology and Society.* University of New Mexico Press, Albuquerque.

Woodbury, Richard B., and James A. Neely. 1972. Water Control Systems of the Tehuacán Valley. In *The Prehistory of the Tehuacán Valley*, vol. 4: *Chronology and Irrigation*, ed. Frederick Johnson, pp. 81–153. University of Texas Press, Austin.

Woodbury, Richard B., and Aubrey S. Trik. 1953. *The Ruins of Zaculeu, Guatemala.* 2 vols. United Fruit Co., New York.

Woodward, Arthur. 1931. *The Grewe Site. Occasional Papers of the Los Angeles Museum of History, Science, and Art* 1.

———. 1941. Hohokam Mosaic Mirrors. *Los Angeles County Museum Quarterly* 1(4):6–11.

Wyshak, Lillian Worthing, Rainer Berger, John A. Graham, and Robert F. Heizer. 1971. A Possible Ball Court at La Venta, Mexico. *Nature* 232:650–651.

Xajil. 1953 [1493–1600]. *Annals of the Cakchiquels,* trans. Adrian Recinos and Delia Goetz. University of Oklahoma Press, Norman.

Yadeun A., Juan. 1974. Analisis Espacial de la Zona Arqueologica de Tula, Hgo. In *Proyecto Tula*, ed. Eduardo Matos M., pp. 53–59. *Colección Científica* 15, Instituto Nacional de Antropología e Historia, México, D.F.

Index